Regional Security in South Asia and the Gulf

As we move towards a world without superpowers, the dynamics within and between regions are of growing significance. Against this backdrop, this book explores the links between South Asia and the Gulf, which have existed for centuries but are undergoing important shifts in the transition to multipolarity. With a special focus on India, Pakistan, Iran, Bangladesh, Saudi Arabia, the United Arab Emirates, Sri Lanka and Oman, this volume brings together scholars from across these regions to investigate what the decentring world order means for the relationship between South Asia and the Gulf. It employs Regional Security Complex Theory to examine the changing global patterns of power and their impact on the inter-regional patterns of amity and enmity between states in South Asia and the Gulf. It employs both constructivist and realist approaches, seeking to understand how power and social processes influence the political and security linkages between these regions.

Umer Karim is a doctoral researcher in the Department of Political Science and International Studies at the University of Birmingham. His academic research focuses on Saudi foreign policy and broader geopolitics of the Middle East. Karim also works on Pakistan's foreign policy outlook and its engagement with the Middle East. He is an Associate Fellow at the King Faisal Center for Research and Islamic Studies and a Fellow of the SEPAD Project at Lancaster University's Richardson Institute.

Saloni Kapur is an Assistant Professor of International Studies in the Department of Social Sciences at FLAME University. Her research interests include critical security studies, decoloniality and South and West Asia. Saloni holds a PhD in International Relations from Lancaster University. She is the author of *Pakistan after Trump: Great Power Responsibility in a Multi-Polar World* (Cambridge Scholars Publishing, 2021) and the co-editor of *Securitisation in the Non-West* (Routledge, 2019).

Changing Dynamics in Asia-Middle East Relations
Series editor: Jonathan Fulton

A number of political and economic initiatives in recent years underscore the surge in relations across Eurasia and the Indian Ocean region. The USA's Indo-Pacific strategy, China's Belt and Road Initiative, India's Look East and Look West strategies and several less formal but no less important state-to-state relationships all indicate that ties across Eurasia are growing. Economic relations between Persian Gulf states and various Asian energy markets have diversified to the point that trade, investment and finance are complemented with diplomatic and security cooperation. Soft power initiatives are building relations across non-elite levels, creating familiarity in language, culture and religion. At the same time, increased interactions present potential for tensions as competition between Asian states plays out in the Middle East, and Middle Eastern rivalries affect the trajectory of Asian states' regional involvement.

This series publishes monographs and edited collections on the political, economic, strategic and diplomatic interactions between Middle East and Asian states. Contributions from a diverse range of perspectives and all regions are welcome on International Relations, International Political Economy, Foreign Policy and issue-specific topics such as security cooperation, politics of sport, politics of religion, energy politics, Belt and Road Initiative and Eurasian development.

South Korea's Middle Power Diplomacy in the Middle East
Development, Political and Diplomatic Trajectories
Hae Won Jeong

Asian Perceptions of Gulf Security
Li-Chen Sim and Jonathan Fulton

Regional Security in South Asia and the Gulf
Umer Karim and Saloni Kapur

For more information, please visit the series webpage:
https://www.routledge.com/Changing-Dynamics-in-Asia-Middle-East-Relations/book-series/CDAMER

Regional Security in South Asia and the Gulf

Edited by
Umer Karim and Saloni Kapur

LONDON AND NEW YORK

First published 2023
by Routledge
4 Park Square, Milton Park, Abingdon, Oxon OX14 4RN

and by Routledge
605 Third Avenue, New York, NY 10158

*Routledge is an imprint of the Taylor & Francis Group,
an informa business*

© 2023 selection and editorial matter, Umer Karim and Saloni Kapur;
individual chapters, the contributors

The right of Umer Karim and Saloni Kapur to be identified as
the authors of the editorial material, and of the authors for their
individual chapters, has been asserted in accordance with sections 77
and 78 of the Copyright, Designs and Patents Act 1988.

All rights reserved. No part of this book may be reprinted or
reproduced or utilised in any form or by any electronic, mechanical,
or other means, now known or hereafter invented, including
photocopying and recording, or in any information storage or retrieval
system, without permission in writing from the publishers.

Trademark notice: Product or corporate names may be trademarks
or registered trademarks, and are used only for identification and
explanation without intent to infringe.

British Library Cataloguing-in-Publication Data
A catalogue record for this book is available from the British Library

Library of Congress Cataloging-in-Publication Data
Names: Karim, Umer, editor. | Kapur, Saloni, editor.
Title: Regional security in South Asia and the Gulf / edited by Umer
    Karim, and Saloni Kapur.
Description: Abingdon, Oxon ; New York, NY : Routledge, 2022. |
    Series: Changing dynamics in Asia-Middle East relations | Includes
    bibliographical references and index.
Identifiers: LCCN 2022042731 (print) | LCCN 2022042732 (ebook) |
    ISBN 9781032254142 (hardback) | ISBN 9781032254180
    (paperback) | ISBN 9781003283058 (ebook)
Subjects: LCSH: South Asia--Relations--Persian Gulf Region. |
    Persian Gulf Region--Relations--South Asia. | Security,
    International--South Asia. Security, International--Persian Gulf
    Region.
Classification: LCC DS341 .R444 2022 (print) | LCC DS341 (ebook) |
    DDC 953/.053--dc23/eng/20221101
LC record available at https://lccn.loc.gov/2022042731
LC ebook record available at https://lccn.loc.gov/2022042732

ISBN: 978-1-032-25414-2 (hbk)
ISBN: 978-1-032-25418-0 (pbk)
ISBN: 978-1-003-28305-8 (ebk)

DOI: 10.4324/9781003283058

Typeset in Times New Roman
by KnowledgeWorks Global Ltd.

Contents

List of Tables		vii
List of Contributors		viii

Introduction 1
UMER KARIM AND SALONI KAPUR

1 **India, the Persian Gulf and the Emergence of a Supercomplex** 16
SALONI KAPUR

2 **Pakistan and the Gulf** 39
ZAHID SHAHAB AHMED AND KHURRAM ABBAS

3 **The Estranged Partners: Iran's Complicated Relations with India and Pakistan** 62
MOHAMMAD SOLTANINEJAD

4 **Complex Interdependence and Security Architecture: Charting Bangladesh-Gulf Ties and Political Engagements** 82
LAILUFAR YASMIN

5 **Sri Lanka and the Gulf States** 105
SHAKTHI DE SILVA AND ROBIN VOCHELET

6 **Oman's Relations with Pakistan and India** 130
MEHMET RAKIPOĞLU AND GÖKHAN ERELI

7 **Pakistan and Saudi Ties: An Overview of Political, Strategic, Economic and Defence Linkages** 152
UMER KARIM

vi *Contents*

**8 India and the United Arab Emirates: Upgrading the Strategic
Partnership**   180

RHEA ABRAHAM

Index   205

Tables

1.1	India's official discourse on relations with the Persian Gulf	24
4.1	The timeline of Bangladesh receiving diplomatic recognition from the gulf countries	89
4.2	The remittances Bangladesh receives from different parts of the world	94
5.1	Sri Lanka's trade relations with the GII	109
5.2	The main export products of Sri Lanka to the GII	110
5.3	Breakdown of the main Sri Lankan export product to each GII country	111
5.4	Sri Lanka's labour migration to countries of the GII	112
5.5	Remittances received by Sri Lanka	112
5.6	Country and climate change agreements signed	123

Contributors

Khurram Abbas is a Non-Resident Fellow at the Research Centre for Asian Studies (RCAS), China, as well as Research Fellow at the Islamabad Policy Research Institute, Pakistan. He earned his PhD in Peace and Conflict Studies (PCS) from the Centre for International Peace and Stability (CIPS), NUST, Islamabad. His areas of interest include the geopolitics of the Persian Gulf and Arabian Peninsula, the foreign policy of Iran, civil resistance and the foreign policies of China, India and Pakistan towards the GCC and Iran.

Rhea Abraham is MENA Analyst for a private security consultancy firm. She previously worked as Research Volunteer for various UN organisations and an Associate Fellow for the Center for Air Power Studies, New Delhi. She has a doctorate in Gulf Studies from the India-Arab Culture Centre, Jamia Millia Islamia, New Delhi. Her research interests include the Middle East with a focus on India-Gulf relations and migration.

Zahid Shahab Ahmed is a Research Fellow at Alfred Deakin Institute for Citizenship and Globalization, Deakin University. He is also a Non-Resident Research Fellow at the University of Singapore's Institute of South Asian Studies. During 2017–2019, he was a Non-Resident Research Fellow with the University of Southern California's Center on Public Diplomacy. He is the author of *Regionalism and Regional Security in South Asia: The Role of SAARC* (Routledge, 2013).

Shakthi De Silva teaches International Relations as a Visiting Lecturer at the Bandaranaike Centre for International Studies and the Bandaranaike International Diplomatic Training Institute (affiliated with Sri Lanka's Ministry of Foreign Affairs). His research has been published in the *Journal of the Indian Ocean Region, South Asian Survey* and the *University of Colombo Review.*

Gökhan Ereli is a PhD Candidate in International Relations at Middle East Technical University (METU). At the same time, Ereli works as the Gulf Studies Coordinator at the Center for Middle Eastern Studies (ORSAM) and is interested in the Gulf (Saudi Arabia, the United Arab Emirates and Qatar) and American foreign policy. His academic interests are the Middle East in World Politics, identity politics and post-positivist International Relations Theories.

Saloni Kapur is an Assistant Professor of International Studies in the Department of Social Sciences at FLAME University. Her research interests include critical security studies, decoloniality and South and West Asia. Saloni holds a PhD in International Relations from Lancaster University. She is the author of *Pakistan after Trump: Great Power Responsibility in a Multi-Polar World* (Cambridge Scholars Publishing, 2021) and the co-editor of *Securitisation in the Non-West* (Routledge, 2019).

Umer Karim is a doctoral researcher in the Department of Political Science and International Studies at the University of Birmingham. His academic research focuses on Saudi foreign policy, broader geopolitics of the Middle East and Pakistan's engagement with the Middle East. He is an Associate Fellow at the King Faisal Center for Research and Islamic Studies and a Fellow of the SEPAD Project at Lancaster University's Richardson Institute.

Mehmet Rakipoğlu is currently a PhD candidate at Sakarya University Middle East Institute. His doctoral thesis topic is Saudi Arabian foreign policy. Rakipoglu was a non-resident fellow at ORSAM from 2020 to 2021. His research areas include the hedging theory, the foreign policy in the Gulf, Turkey's policies towards the Gulf region and political Islam. He is the editor of the book named *Global Muslim Brotherhood: The Relationship of the Muslim Brotherhood with the Regimes and Its Transnational Character* published in Turkish (Ketebe, 2022).

Mohammad Soltaninejad is an Assistant Professor at the Faculty of World Studies-University of Tehran. He teaches courses on Iran's foreign policy and the Middle East and North Africa security. His main research interests are Iran's foreign relations with a special focus on Iran-Arab World and Iran-South Asia relations.

Robin Vochelet is a journalist and researcher currently pursuing a master's degree in International Affairs at the Lee Kuan Yew School of Public Policy, National University of Singapore. His work covers youth culture, social movements and queer identities across Southeast Asia. He has also been published in The Diplomat, East Asia Forum, Southeast Asia Globe and more.

Lailufar Yasmin is a Professor at the Department of International Relations, University of Dhaka, Bangladesh. She has been a recipient of the US Fulbright, the British Chevening and the Australian International Post-Graduate Research Scholarship (IPRS). Her latest publications are on the Rohingya issue (London) and the development of International Relations in South Asia (Oxford Encyclopedia).

Introduction

Umer Karim and Saloni Kapur

At the time of this writing in June 2022, India was facing a backlash from all eight Gulf countries and the Gulf Cooperation Council (GCC) over derogatory comments about the Prophet Muhammad (PBUH) made by two spokespersons of India's ruling Bharatiya Janata Party (BJP) (*Scroll.in*, 2022). In addition to official protests by these states, a campaign to boycott Indian goods in the Gulf marked an anomaly in a history of four to five millennia of commercial, cultural, religious and intellectual ties between the Persian Gulf region and India (Ahmad, 2015, 2020; Ghodvaidya, 2022).

Trade links between the Persian Gulf and South Asia are believed to have existed since the Harappan civilisation of 3,300 to 1,300 BCE. Two thousand years before the advent of Islam in 610 CE, there is thought to have been migration between the Gulf and South Asia, and residents of the two regions seem to have been familiar with one another's religious practices, cultures and societal norms and values (Ahmad, 2020).

In this introduction, we draw on the rich work of scholars including Eaton (2019), Onley (2007), Ahmad (2015, 2020) and Mahajan (2015) to offer an overview of the historical ties between the Gulf region and pre-Independence India (including present-day Pakistan and Bangladesh). We focus on pre-Independence India due to the intensity of interaction between this part of South Asia and the Gulf before decolonisation and the emergence of the modern state system. This historical backdrop is intended to provide the context for the theoretical and empirical analyses of contemporary ties between South Asia and the Gulf that follow in the remainder of this introduction and book.

Historical connections between South Asia and the Persian Gulf

After the revelation of Islam, the military invasion of Sindh in 718–800 CE marked the first significant interaction between the Islamic world and India/Pakistan. During the 12th and 13th centuries CE, the teachings of Hindu Vaishnava sages including Vishnuswami, Ramanuja, Nimbarka and Madhava appear to have been influenced by Sufism. In the 14th century,

DOI: 10.4324/9781003283058-1

Moroccan traveller Ibn Batuta reported seeing Persians and Yemenis living along the south Indian coast, which was frequented by Arab merchants and travellers (Ahmad, 2020).

In the 1380s and 1390s, the Central Asian warlord Timur conquered parts of Iran and Iraq in the Persian Gulf, before capturing areas in Russia, Georgia, Syria and Turkey. In 1398, he entered India, defeating the Tughluq army in Panipat and sacking Delhi. Although he returned to Samarqand with his booty in 1399, Timur launched what is known as India's "long 15th century," which began with his invasion and ended with the commencement of Mughal rule in 1526 (Eaton, 2019).

In Punjab, Khizr Khan became Timur's chieftain governor of Multan, Lahore and Dipalpur. He gained control of Delhi in 1414, thus commencing the rule of the Saiyid dynasty. However, he ruled as viceroy of Shah Rukh, the son and successor of Timur. Further north, in Kashmir, Sultan Sikandar went to Timur and pledged his loyalty. Elsewhere in India, the impact of the Timurid Empire was seen in the spread of Timurid architecture thanks to the movement of artisans, diplomats, intellectuals, pilgrims, traders and travellers (Eaton, 2019).

In the Deccan Plateau, the Deccani Sultan Firuz Bahmani sent gifts and envoys to Timur after he captured Delhi. Timur offered him "sovereignty over Gujarat and Malwa." Firuz worked to Persianise his court, sending ships to Iran to recruit administrators, soldiers, artisans and scholars. He employed Timurid architecture in his palace city of Firuzabad, located south of Gulbarga (Eaton, 2019).

Firuz's brother, Sultan Ahmad Bahmani, succeeded him in 1422. Sultan Ahmad shifted the capital to Bidar, which was located at the crossroads of the Kannada-, Telugu- and Marathi-speaking areas of the Deccan Plateau. Like his brother, Ahmad emulated Timur's architectural style when constructing his new capital. The madrasa in Bidar was frequented by Mahmud Gawan, a merchant from Iran. Sultan Ahmad II Bahmani, who took over in 1436, made Gawan an amir and gave him a 1,000 cavalrymen. In 1458, Gawan became the chief minister of the kingdom, acquiring the title of *malik al-tujjar* (prince of merchants). In 1466, he became the regent, ruling in place of two successive child kings (Eaton, 2019).

Large numbers of *gharbian* (Westerners) had started migrating from West Asia to the Deccan Plateau after a revolt against the Tughluqs by the Bahmanis in 1347. After severing their connection with the Tughluq dynasty in Delhi, the Bahmani rulers sought war horses and administrative talent from West Asia. Most of the people they recruited were Turks and Persians. However, a rift between these *gharbian* and the native Deccani Muslims adversely affected the stability of the Bahmani state, which found itself caught between its desire to be part of the Timurid world, and the need to appease local people (Eaton, 2019).

Late in the 15th century, Yusuf 'Adil Khan, the governor of Bijapur, declared independence from the Bahmani sultanate. An immigrant from

Introduction   3

Anatolia, Yusuf established Shi'ism as the state religion of Bijapur in 1503, shortly following its establishment as the state religion of Iran under the Safavid dynasty in 1501. Bijapur's military engineers, who were based in Goa, obtained arms technology from Mamluk, Ottoman and European sources. Yusuf's son and successor, Isma'il, who was brought up by his Iranian aunt, banished native Deccani Muslims from his court, preferring *gharbian* from West Asia. From 1519 onwards, Bijapur offered Friday prayers for Iran's Safavid family and its army adopted the Safavid scarlet caps that had twelve points to represent the twelve imams of Ithna 'Ashari Shi'ism. Isma'il's grandson, 'Ali 'Adil Shah, who succeeded the throne in 1558, was the author of *Nujum al-'Ulum* (Stars of the Sciences). The book was written in Farsi, but it contained many Dakani words and called on Indic, Turkic, Islamic and Greek traditions of knowledge, thus demonstrating the pluralistic consciousness of the medieval Deccan court. The illustrations in the book combined the Sanskrit and Persianate styles of illustration, revealing the cultural cosmopolitanism of 'Ali and the medieval Deccan Plateau (Eaton, 2019).

In the eastern part of the Deccan, Sultan Quli declared independence in 1497 and founded the Qutb Shahi dynasty with its capital in Golconda. Quli was an immigrant from Iran who had become the governor of Telangana under the Bahmanis in 1496, acquiring the title of Qutb al-Mulk. Under the Qutb Shahi dynasty's rule in the 16th century, a Telugu poet composed the *Yayati Caritramu*, which adapted a section of the *Mahabharata* but also tried to purge Telugu of words borrowed from Sanskrit. The poet was inspired by Firdausi, whose *Shah-Nama* tried to rid Farsi of words taken from Arabic (Eaton, 2019). This points to the intellectual ties linking South Asia and the Gulf at the time.

Further south, the kingdom of Vijayanagara had started to absorb elements of Persianate culture even before Timur's invasion. In 1442, the kingdom made its first direct contact with the Timurid court through a visit by an envoy of Shah Rukh to India. When the ambassador, 'Abd al-Razzaq, landed in Calicut, King Deva Raya II summoned him to his court. In his report, 'Abd al-Razzaq noted that the king wore a Persian tunic and headgear, and had adopted the Persian title of sultan. The capital of Vijayanagara was designed similarly to the other Persianate courts in India and Iran. Vijayanagara was dependent on war horses from the Gulf and on maritime trade with the region. In 1535, King Rama Raya recruited 3,000 Western soldiers who had been dismissed by Bijapur's Sultan Ibrahim 'Adil Shah I. Most of them were from Iran, further highlighting the military links between India and the Gulf at this time. In addition, the extent to which Deccan rulers had absorbed cultural influences from the Gulf is demonstrated by friezes of Vijayanagara's King Krishna Raya. While some of the friezes depict him in scenes from the *Ramayana*, others show him wearing the tall conical headgear known as *kulah* in Farsi and *kullayi* in Telugu (Eaton, 2019).

In Kashmir, Shaikh 'Ali Hamadani and his son, Shaikh Saiyid Muhammad Hamadani were Sufi saints who had immigrated from Iran. The Kashmiri

4   *Umer Karim and Saloni Kapur*

king, Zain al-'Abidin, encouraged the interaction of the Sanskrit and Farsi literary cultures, including the translation of classics between the two languages. He made Farsi the official language of Kashmir. Brahmins serving the king transitioned from using Sanskrit to Farsi. They studied the Farsi classics at *maktabs* that were often run by Brahmins. During this period, many Sufi shrines of saints from Iran and Central Asia appeared in the valley too (Eaton, 2019). Thus, we can observe the intense cultural, intellectual, military and economic impact of the Persian Gulf on both north and south India during the medieval period.

Although the influence of regional languages started to grow from the 15th century, Farsi continued to flourish. In the 17th century, courtiers in the *nayaka* states of the Deccan continued to don Persian-style garments. Trade along the Malabar coast was monopolised by foreigners, especially Arabs due to caste restrictions among Hindus. Arabs had played a major role in Malabar trade since the 9th century, and Arab merchants started to settle down along the Malabar coast. They were referred to as *pardesis* (foreigners). As locals began to convert to Islam and the *pardesis* started to intermarry with local people, a new community known as the Mappilas emerged. The Mappilas practised a culture that combined elements of Malayali and Arab culture. While most of the *pardesis* departed upon the arrival of the Portuguese, the Mappalis took over control of trade along the coast (Eaton, 2019).

However, European colonialism by no means marked an end to the potent interactions between South Asia and the Persian Gulf. In the 18th century, the British East India Company instituted a residency system in parts of Asia and Africa. Originally commercial, the system evolved into a form of political control as many of the states surrounding India gradually ceded control of their external affairs and defence to the East India Company and, thereafter, the British Government of India (Onley, 2007).

The British resident in the Gulf took orders from the governor of Bombay Province until 1873. Subsequently, he reported to the Government of India and the Indian Foreign Department in Calcutta (Onley, 2007). Onley (2007) describes "the Gulf Residency and the Fars Consulate-General as [...] part informal empire and part sphere of influence." He claims "that the Indian Empire was, in reality, much larger than is generally believed," with Arabia left off maps of the Indian Empire despite Bahrain, the United Arab Emirates (UAE—then known as the Trucial States), Kuwait and Qatar becoming British-protected states—just like the Indian princely states— during the late 19th and early 20th centuries. He also explains that Oman had informally been under British protection since the beginning of the 19th century. He suggests that maps of India left out the Arabian protected states/protectorates "for diplomatic and pragmatic reasons." While British India's official maps showed the British Indian provinces in pink and the British protected states and protectorates in yellow, they only depicted the Indian princely states consistently in the yellow zone. Nepal and Bhutan were only shown as yellow for ten years, while Arabia was not included in

Introduction 5

the maps at all. This leads Onley to posit that the popular perception of the British Indian Empire falls short of its true size. He lists Nepal, Afghanistan, Kuwait, Bahrain, the Trucial States (UAE), Aden and British Somaliland as protected states/protectorates that were left off official maps of British India. In addition to the Arabian protectorates/protected states listed above by Onley, Mahajan (2015) points to a subsidy that the Government of India paid to the Sultan of Muscat until Indian independence in 1947. Furthermore, the East India Company in 1616 opened a Persia Agency in the Iranian port of Jask. The Persia Agency managed the company's economic interests in the Gulf. From 1862 onwards, the British India Steam Navigation Company commenced maritime trade between Bombay and the Gulf ports of Basrah, Muscat, Manamah, Qatif, Kuwait, Dubai and Sharjah (Onley, 2007).

The strategic importance of West Asia to the British was the need to control routes to the Indian Empire and ward off possible challengers to British colonial rule over India, such as the Ottoman Empire, France, Russia and Germany (Ahmad, 2015; Mahajan, 2015). Control over Bahrain and Oman was important for safeguarding Britain's shipping routes connecting Iran, Iraq, Oman and India. From 1797 to 1819, Arab "pirates" from the UAE (then the Trucial Coast) threatened British maritime trading. The Lower Gulf Agency was established in 1820 and succeeded by the Gulf Residency in 1822–1823 to "stabilise" the Gulf states to secure British shipping routes. Both were located in Iran—the Lower Gulf Agency was situated on Qishm Island, while the Gulf Residency was set up in Bushire. However, their purpose was to manage ties with the political leadership in Eastern Arabia and Southern Persia to further and protect British interests in the Gulf. The Bushire Residency had existed since 1763; the responsibilities of the Lower Gulf Agency were transferred to the Bushire Residency in 1822–1823 due to "the unhealthy climate" in Qishm. The British treated Iran and Muscat as buffer states after the former formed a military alliance with France in 1807–1809; British envoys travelled from India to Persia and Muscat and managed to get the rulers of both states to sign anti-French treaties, in return for which the British offered them protection (Onley, 2007; The National Archives, no date).

In 1871–1872, after the Ottomans annexed Qatar and Hasa, the risk of so-called piracy to British ships rose and the British became apprehensive that the Ottomans would seek to annex other parts of Eastern Arabia that were what Onley (2007) refers to as "a *de facto* part of the British Indian Empire." In the 1880s and 1890s, the British Government of India concluded Exclusive Agreements with Bahrain, Dubai, Sharjah, Abu Dhabi, Umm al-Qaiwain, 'Ajman, Ras al-Khaimah and Kuwait. It concluded a narrower Exclusive Agreement with Muscat/Oman that forbade the sultan "from ceding, selling, or leasing his domains to any foreign government or person, except the British Government." Nevertheless, from the 1900s, the British controlled Oman's external affairs, with the permission of the

6 *Umer Karim and Saloni Kapur*

sultan, except for its relations with the United States and France. Another Exclusive Agreement was signed with Qatar in 1916.

Through these agreements, the rulers of these kingdoms granted control over their foreign affairs to the British Government of India. For Onley (2007), "this was the final step in the Gulf shaikhdoms' formal incorporation into the Indian Empire," although the British worked to maintain the illusion that these states remained semi-autonomous.

Thus, the India-Pakistan-Bangladesh subregion's strong link to the Persian Gulf continued into the colonial period, with some states in the Gulf turning into undeclared parts of Britain's Indian Empire. This history of political, economic, security, cultural and religious interlinkages forms the backdrop to our investigation into the contemporary South Asian RSC and Gulf sub-complex. In particular, we are concerned with the question of whether we are witnessing the emergence of a South Asia-Gulf supercomplex, or a relatively more embedded security interaction, as the next section will explain.

Regional security complex theory

Regional security dynamics and their interplay on a global scale have been explained comprehensively by Buzan and Waever (2003). They have come up with a theoretical framework that illuminates the security linkages both on a global and a regional level and explains how states behave in response to threats emanating on these different levels and the nature and level of threats that eventually sensitise states to adopt their core patterns of securitisation. Buzan and Waever build upon Walt's notion of states prioritising threats emanating from their immediate neighbours rather than those from geographically distant actors (Walt, 1990). They argue that these patterns of enmity or amity between neighbouring states push them to make alliances with other regional actors in order to maintain a favourable balance of power. This results in a sub-systemic and geographically coherent pattern of security interdependence among states in a particular region as compared to the security linkages between the states inside such a regional complex and those outside of it. Although Buzan and Waever have relatively diluted their state-centric approach and have gradually adopted a rather multi-dimensional approach that encapsulates non-state actors and transnational social, political and cultural movements but their regional security complexes (RSCs) remain largely state centric. Eventually, they define a RSC as "a set of units whose major processes of securitisation, desecuritisation, or both are so interlinked that their security problems cannot reasonably be analysed or resolved apart from one another" (Buzan & Waever, 2003, pp. 40–44).

The regional level or sub-systemic security dimension is important as it focuses on the security interdependence of the states in a rather regional sphere while combining both their national and global level threat perceptions at a relatively intense and appropriate security junction. This also puts into perspective how medium sized powers develop strategies to dominate

Introduction 7

their regional political sphere and address the political and security threats faced by them. Although, the authors simultaneously argue that once a regional power attains status of a great power, it develops the ability to penetrate several adject RSCs (Buzan & Waever, 2003, p. 46). This does not mean necessarily a resolution of the securitised environment in its home regional complex. India and Turkey are two interesting examples in this regard as they have penetrated multiple RSCs.

Buzan and Waever have argued that an international system bearing anarchic characteristics will likely have RSCs as its constituent substructures. These RSCs in turn will have impact upon the functionality of international system and great power competition. This clearly makes this theoretical premise workable alongside the realist and liberalist traditions. However, as the origin and function of the RSCs remained tied to the patterns of amity and enmity within regional states, the basic units of an RSC. The tendency in this theoretical construct to accord privilege to the agency of the actors and their respective strategies and actions rather than simply translating the systemic balance of power dynamics makes its appeal dialectical. However, this makes the epistemological relevance of RSCs inadvertently dependent upon the security approaches of individual actors as they are not a discursive construction. In case of a comprehensive change in the character of a regional actor, as there has been in case of Iraq post-American invasion, the patterns of security interaction based on enmity or amity vis-à-vis a regional rival will change subsequently changing the nature of that specific RSC (Buzan & Waever, 2003, p. 48).

The question of South Asia and Gulf security linkages

In the Buzan and Waever RSC theoretical model South Asia holds a prominent spot. South Asia remains a durable and relatively objective RSC exhibiting visible patterns of security interdependence between its constituent states mainly India and Pakistan based on a clear pattern of bilateral enmity. Lack of functional and strong regional institutions or trust-building regimes between the principal regional protagonists have made South Asia's security environment prone to conflict formation. The notion of security interdependencies in South Asia and the region constituting an exclusive security infrastructure was first floated by Buzan and Rizvi in their edited volume in 1986 (Buzan & Rizvi, 1986). Afterwards in the above-discussed work Regions and Powers by Buzan and Waever, South Asia was presented as a comprehensive RSC revolving around the bilateral confrontation between India and Pakistan. Other smaller South Asian states in particular Bangladesh, Sri Lanka and Nepal had remained part of the South Asian complex owing to their economic and cultural linkages with India. However, they have not played a significant role with regards to the regional security infrastructure. There has been no attempt by these smaller states to enter any sort of security partnership with Pakistan to balance

8 Umer Karim and Saloni Kapur

against India, neither have they attempted to bandwagon alongside India. Except for Bhutan, all other South Asian states have maintained a semblance of political and military autonomy vis-à-vis the other two larger and nuclear-armed states. It has also been argued that this RSC remains well insulated from adjacent security complexes in the west and east thanks to the states of Afghanistan and Myanmar which act as security insulators. The interaction and penetration of global superpowers with this complex have largely been governed by the conflict between India and Pakistan and thereby the regional actors have been able to mediate the global balance of power dynamics in accordance with their own security needs (Buzan & Waever, 2003, pp. 100–104).

This scholarship concluded that the South Asian complex is undergoing internal and external transformations. The internal transformation was a direct consequence of the reduction in Pakistan's political and economic capital with regards to India which owing to its economic liberalisation in the 1990s was emerging as a new Asian economic powerhouse and thereby reaching the status of a great power. The external transformation highlighted the meteoric rise of China as a global superpower and its burgeoning conflict with India and the potential impact of this Indo-Chinese rivalry on regional security calculus. Buzan and Waever also touched upon Pakistan's attempts to forge partnerships with extra-regional players in the Arabian Peninsula particularly Saudi Arabia through the prism of anti-Soviet Jihad in Afghanistan and by sending troops to help with the internal security. This engagement was meant to garner leverage against India. Similarly, the relationship between India and Israel also had a Pakistan variable. Yet these engagements were not able to overcome the regional security divides in any comprehensive manner (Buzan & Waever, 2003, p. 105). In an updated version of this scholarship on the nature of South Asian Security Complex, Buzan adheres to his previous argumentation and has suggested that the internal particulars of the South Asian RSC remain the same. On the external front he has argued that the nature of security interaction with the Arabian Gulf region has remained same while that with East Asia has been increasing owing to the rise of China (Buzan, 2011).

As this study also explores security and political linkages between South Asia and the Wider Gulf region involving its both coasts, the assertions of Buzan and Waever regarding South Asia-Gulf linkages remain relevant. The notion that Pakistan has tried to cultivate ties with Gulf States in order to increase its political capital in South Asia and to balance against India does indeed makes sense. Gulf States and in particular Saudi Arabia have historically maintained a pro-Pakistan stance on the core issue of Kashmir. Saudi Arabia has also remained a key financial support base for Pakistan both in terms of direct government aid and through the remittances sent by Pakistani expatriates in the kingdom. Pakistan and Saudi Arabia worked together on the Afghan file (Weinbaum & Khurram, 2014), and it has also been alleged that Saudi Arabia provided Pakistan with much-needed

Introduction 9

financial assistance to develop its nuclear program, Pakistan's key defence deterrent against India (Dyke & Yetiv, 2011).

This study departs from the assertion Buzan and Waever on two accounts both of which remain interconnected. Firstly, in the last decade, the strategic, economic and security linkages between South Asian actors have increased manifold with actors within the Arabian Peninsula and with Iran something that has been dealt extensively in this volume. This changing security environment necessitates a reinterpretation of the assertion that inter-regional security interaction has not been able to overcome or establish formidable linkages with the security infrastructure of the South Asian RSC. From Indian investment in the port of Chahbahar (Pant & Mehta, 2018) to the exponential increase in India's strategic ties with Gulf States, the security environment in the broader Gulf region is becoming increasingly connected with that of South Asia. The increased coordination between Oman and India in the maritime domain has a direct bearing on the maritime security of Pakistan's west coast, where the port of Gwadar, the epicentre of China Pakistan Economic Corridor (CPEC) is also located. Pakistan's increased financial dependency on the Gulf States has further increased the leverage enjoyed by the Gulf vis-à-vis Pakistan. As this has happened alongside a change in Gulf-India relationship, the political positionality of the Gulf States with regards to the Indo-Pak rivalry has further changed which has direct relevance for regional security in South Asia (Quamar, 2018).

Secondly, Buzan and Waever's argument regarding the separation of the Gulf and South Asian regional complexes rests upon the presence of an insulator in the form of Afghanistan. It can be argued that the inter-regional involvement in Afghanistan didn't result into a greater degree of integration between the two regions' security sensitivities and infrastructure as Saudi Arabia revised its policy to remain actively engaged within Afghanistan. However, same cannot be said about Saudi arch-rival Iran which has maintained political and religious linkages with different groups in Afghanistan (Milani, 2006).

During the 1990s, this inter-regional competition was at the top as Iran backed Shi'ite Hazara groups alongside other Persian-speaking non-Pushtun elements. These groups also received support from India and Russia. On the other hand, they were fighting against mostly Pushtun groups backed by Pakistan and Saudi Arabia (Harpviken, 2010). After the American invasion of Afghanistan, the Indian involvement increased even further. This was in the backdrop of a new Afghan government that had an uneasy relationship with Pakistan. This rang alarm bells in Pakistan that had traditionally seen Afghanistan as a potential zone of strategic depth. Thereby Afghanistan at least with reference to the South Asian RSC remained a virtual battlefront between India and Pakistan (Grare, 2003). The withdrawal of the United States, subsequent collapse of the Afghan Republican Government of President Ashraf Ghani and the country's takeover again by the Taliban again has implications for regional security. These developments have also

10 *Umer Karim and Saloni Kapur*

pushed inter-regional coordination as well as some degree of contestation for the newly created political space in Afghanistan. This pushes us to view Afghanistan not as an insulator but rather as a bridgehead between the two regions. The country emerges as a unique geography where inter-regional rivalries and alignments crisscross and instead of insulating South Asian and Gulf security environs from each other, it becomes an intersectional point of inter-regional security. Moreover, Indian attempts to forge commercial and economic connectivity with Central Asia can only be successful by circumventing Pakistan and relying upon Iran and Afghanistan. Barring an India-Pakistan rapprochement which in any case will transform the regional security pattern within South Asia, this inter-regional political and economic linkage will increase and impact upon the inter-regional security dynamics.

This study, therefore, suggests that the South Asian RSC and its engagement with the Gulf sub-RSC have been undergoing a significant transformation. Even though both regions retain distinct patterns of enmity driving their respective securitisations, the inter-regional security integration has moved ahead with new levels of security interactions emerging. This has partially been owing to the internal transformation within the South Asian RSC that has seen a further weakening of Pakistan and its increased dependence upon the Gulf States for economic assistance. As this dependence is likely to increase and as India emerges further as an economic and security partner, the relevance of Gulf States in the South Asian security picture will also increase. These new trends in inter-regional security dynamics will bond the two regions further together and although both regional complexes will maintain their distinct securitisation characteristics, this inter-regional engagement will gradually become relatively more embedded as has been the case between the Gulf's subregional security complex and that of Horn of Africa (Karim, 2022).

The organisation of the book

The chapters that follow focus on individual states within South Asia and the Persian Gulf to throw light on specific aspects of the interlinkages between the two (sub)regions. In Chapter 1, Kapur applies the method of content analysis to the online archives of the Indian Ministry of External Affairs and argues that India's pivot away from Iran and towards the Arab Gulf states took place under Prime Minister Manmohan Singh. Thus, she challenges the common perception that this shift in India's approach to the Gulf occurred under Prime Minister Narendra Modi. She further suggests that India has employed a discourse of being a rising power since the premiership of Atal Bihari Vajpayee in 1998–2004 and has consistently couched its statements on the Persian Gulf region in this discourse. This points to India's active effort to project its power into the Gulf through its growing economic and security engagement with the sub-region. This, she posits, fits within the framework of regional security complex theory (RSCT) and its ideas about the emergence of a supercomplex. For Kapur, India's policy towards the Gulf is less about a pivot away from Iran and more about an active thrust towards the Gulf in its entirety. She underlines the positive tone of India's official narrative on Iran even when the Singh government sought to emphasise ties with the Arab Gulf states. She links this effort to US pressure on India to curtail relations with Iran in the context of the imposition of international sanctions on Iran and the US-India nuclear deal. Hence, she suggests that any revival of the Iranian nuclear deal would probably reinvigorate Indo-Iranian ties simultaneously with India's continuing engagement of the Arab Gulf states.

In Chapter 2, Ahmed and Abbas provide a comprehensive and nuanced overview of Pakistan's relations with the GCC states. They offer detailed analyses of Pakistan's bilateral ties with each of the six GCC states: Saudi Arabia, the UAE, Bahrain, Qatar, Kuwait and Oman. They go on to outline the major irritants in Pakistan's equations with the GCC countries, namely, Pakistan's effort to maintain ties with Saudi rival Iran, and the GCC states' strong relations with Pakistani rival India. Finally, Ahmed and Abbas explain three recent challenges that have emerged in the Pakistan-Gulf relationship. These include Pakistan's initial decision not to participate in the Saudi-led Islamic Military Alliance to Fight Terrorism (IMAFT) and get involved in the Yemen War, its refusal to succumb to Saudi pressure to take sides in the Qatar/Gulf crisis, and its unwillingness to recognise Israel in the context of the 2020 signing of the Abraham Peace Accords by Bahrain and the UAE. Ahmed and Abbas employ the framework of RSCT to argue that both Pakistan and the Gulf states view their security in RSC-centric terms. Thus, while Pakistan's security concerns are India-centric, the Gulf states' security perception is focused on West Asian dynamics.

Chapter 3 focuses on Iran's ties to Pakistan and India. Soltaninejad traces the trajectory of the India-Iran relationship and outlines the pressures on the relationship from both internal and external factors. He goes on to explore the equally complicated Iran-Pakistan equation, and concludes the chapter with a section on the role that Saudi Arabia has played in curtailing both India and Pakistan's ties to Iran. For Soltaninejad, Iran's relations with both India and Pakistan are a story of unfulfilled potential, inhibited by the India/Pakistan, Iran/Saudi Arabia and Iran/US conflicts. He emphasises the interests that Iran shares with Pakistan as well as India and the tremendous potential for greater economic and strategic cooperation. The chapter contributes to the broader theoretical framing of this book by pointing to the intertwining security logics of India, Pakistan, Saudi Arabia and Iran. Soltaninejad highlights the crucial role played by Saudi Arabia in "the security interconnectedness between Iran and South Asia" and "the balancing acts between Tehran, Delhi and Islamabad." Thus, his chapter points to a possible merging of the security dynamics in the South Asian RSC and the Gulf subcomplex. Additionally, he underlines India's quest for great-power status as a driving factor in India's thrust towards the Persian Gulf and its

12   *Umer Karim and Saloni Kapur*

growing relationship with Saudi Arabia, thus playing into Kapur's argument in Chapter 1 about the emergence of a South Asia-Gulf supercomplex. Furthermore, Soltaninejad's chapter is distinctive for its articulation of Iran's vision of "developing regionally integrated mechanisms of trade that include India, Pakistan and China" and its hope of establishing Chabahar as a regional hub through which it might strengthen commercial ties not only with India but also with China and Pakistan.

In Chapter 4, Yasmin places Bangladesh's ties to the Persian Gulf in the broader context of the complex interdependence of the globalised 21st century and the global transition to multipolarity. She explores the intertwined security and economic links between Bangladesh and the Gulf states. She emphasises Bangladesh's remarkable socio-economic development and its growing relevance for the Gulf countries. Additionally, Yasmin studies Bangladesh's bilateral economic ties with Saudi Arabia, the UAE, Qatar, Kuwait, Bahrain and Oman—the six GCC countries. Finally, Yasmin points to the Rohingya refugee crisis and the Gulf countries' support for Bangladesh as a country of refuge for the Rohingyas. Her chapter argues that security and economics can no longer be clearly distinguished in an age of complex interdependence. She uses the case of Bangladesh-Gulf relations to illustrate this point. She demonstrates how multiple factors, including Bangladesh's remarkable economic success, the Gulf states and Bangladesh's dependence on migrant worker flows, religious ties, the Rohingya humanitarian crisis and Bangladesh's defence ties with Saudi Arabia and Kuwait are intertwining factors that have fortified the web of interdependence between Bangladesh and the GCC states.

In Chapter 5, De Silva and Vochelet explore the linkages between the South Asian RSC and the Gulf subcomplex, drawing on insights from RSCT. This chapter analyses the degree of security interdependence and securitisation between the Gulf, Iran and Israel (GII) on the one hand and the South Asian Island of Sri Lanka. This attempt is made to trace commonalities in the securitisation strategies of South Asian and Middle Eastern nations in the interest of identifying a larger RSC. By examining the degree of security independence between the two—from a Sri Lankan standpoint—the authors conclude that Sri Lanka and the GII differ in their perceptions of threats and tend to politicise—more often than securitise—common threats. The chapter delves into several types of security threats ranging from global threats (climate change) to regional threats (terrorism within the region).

In Chapter 6, Rakipoğlu and Ereli have tried to explore Oman's special relationship with India and Pakistan within the concept of regional cooperation and rivalries. The chapter starts with a comprehensive overview of the historical nature of Oman's relationship with India. Being a seafaring nation, Omani state has held age-old ties with the Indian subcontinent. This part of the chapter delves into the nature of these rather localised political connections and how they evolved under the British rule in India. This is followed by an appraisal of the modern-day ties between the Indian republic

Introduction 13

and the Sultanate of Oman. Afterwards Oman's relationship with Pakistan is examined. The authors have argued that Oman has maintained a careful balance in its relationship between India and Pakistan.

The authors have mentioned that ethnic Balochis hailing from the Makran Coast of Pakistan's Balochistan province hold a special place In Oman's security infrastructure. This force remained critical during the Dhofar rebellion. In this manner, Oman's security and geographical linkages with Pakistan have exhibited a more active character. Yet this dynamic has not impacted upon the country's relationship with India. There is a specific focus on the expatriate communities of both India and Pakistan in Oman and how they have contributed towards strengthening the bilateral relationship of their respective home countries with the Sultanate. This chapter concludes by emphasising that Oman has established partnerships with India and Pakistan to ensure maritime security in the waterways of the Gulf, the Strait of Hormuz and the Arabian Sea. This cooperation with the two South Asian states remains a fulcrum of Oman's Foreign Policy and contributes towards regional endeavours to combat piracy, terrorism and to prevent non-state actors from creating instability in the seas.

In Chapter 7, Karim explores the evolution of Pakistan-Saudi Arabia relationship and its evolution through different phases. In order to map out this special relationship and understand the functionalities impinging on the trajectory of bilateral ties, this chapter first investigates the historical nature of these ties and the interpersonal linkages established between the leaderships of both sides. Afterwards, the focus is upon the extent of strategic congruence between the two sides particularly during the anti-Soviet resistance in Afghanistan and later during the First Gulf War.

Then the chapter analyses how external and internal developments within both countries have impacted the bilateral relationship and their strategic outlook. The debate centres around Pakistan's refusal to become part of the Saudi-led military intervention in Yemen and the country's reaction to Saudi-led quartet's boycott of Qatar. It is argued that these episodes considerably damaged the bilateral relationship but also showed the increasingly divergent political and strategic outlook of both states. Afterwards, the writer gives an account of the Iran and India variables in the relationship and how the security infrastructure of South Asia and the Gulf region are impacting upon the foreign and security policies of Saudi Arabia and Pakistan and subsequently their bilateral relationship. This is followed by a comprehensive overview of the Pak-Saudi defence and economic cooperation. Lastly, the current trends in the bilateral relationship are discussed and it is concluded that though the bilateral relationship remains cordial yet owing to divergent political and security outlooks of the two countries vis-à-vis India and Iran, the bilateral relationship can no longer be characterised as an informal strategic partnership.

In Chapter 8, Abraham offers a broad overview of India-UAE relations under the leadership of Prime Minister Narendra Modi and Sheikh

14 *Umer Karim and Saloni Kapur*

Mohammed Bin Zayed Al Nahyan—their historical origins, accomplishments, as well as prospects for a renewed and robust policy amidst the involvement of external heavyweight China and regional ally Pakistan—and concludes with the implications for the Indian-UAE rendezvous and recommendations for policymakers of the Middle East. The chapter aims to highlight the upgrading of India-UAE relations from bilateral relations to partners in multilateral, regional and global forums, grounded on security interdependency and geographical coherence. In doing so, the theory of regional security by Barry Buzan and Ole Weaver is applied to these strategic geopolitical trajectories in the Middle Eastern and South Asian regions. It attempts to understand the interaction of the RSCs mainly through the prism of interaction between the UAE and India, and whether a merged West Asian RSC is the way forward.

The chapter concludes with an estimate that the quest to advance India-UAE relations in bilateral and regional initiatives has a newfound level of strategic depth and contributes to the enormous potential for collaboration on multilateral forums. There is a mutual recognition between the two countries to use the theory of regional security and multilateralism to advance economic interests, add value to south-south cooperation, enhance international partnerships, contribute to the fulfilment of the United Nations Sustainable Development Goals and ultimately promote peace and security in the region. The foreign policies of Gulf States towards India are no longer linked with Pakistan as it has lost its status as a credible and dependable security player. This has inadvertently further helped India to cement its strategic importance in the broader Gulf region particularly in the security and economic domains.

References

Ahmad, T. (2015). The Gulf Region. In D.M. Malone, C.R. Mohan, & S. Raghavan (eds.), *The Oxford Handbook of Indian Foreign Policy* (pp. 539–555). Oxford: Oxford University Press.

Ahmad, T. (2020) "How Hindutva hatred is jeopardising India's Gulf ties," *The Wire*, 27 April. Available at: https://thewire.in/diplomacy/hindutva-india-gulf-ties (Accessed: 14 June 2022).

Buzan, B. (2011). The South Asian Security Complex in a Decentring World Order: Reconsidering Regions and Powers Ten Years On. *International Studies*, *48*(1), 1–19. doi:10.1177/002088171204800101

Buzan, B., & Rizvi, G. (1986). *South Asian Insecurity and the Great Powers*. New York: Palgrave Macmillan.

Buzan, B., & Waever, O. (2003). *Regions and Powers: The Structure of International Security*. Cambridge: Cambridge University Press.

Dyke, K.V., & Yetiv, S.A. (2011). Pakistan and Saudi Arabia: The Nuclear Nexus. *Journal of South Asian and Middle Eastern Studies*, *34*(4), 68–84. doi:10.1353/jsa.2011.0015

Eaton, R.M. (2019). *India in the Persianate Age: 1000–1765*. London: Allen Lane.

Ghodvaidya, A. (2022). "Calls grow to boycott Indian goods as Islam insult riles Mideast," *Bloomberg*, 8 June. Available at: https://www.bloomberg.com/news/articles/2022-06-08/calls-grow-to-boycott-indian-goods-as-islam-insult-riles-mideast#xj4y7vzkg (Accessed: 14 June 2022).

Grare, F. (2003). *Pakistan and the Afghan Conflict, 1979–1985: With an Afterword Covering Events from 1985–2001*. London: Oxford University Press.

Harpviken, K.B. (2010). *Afghanistan in a Neighbourhood Perspective: General Overview and Conceptualisation*. Oslo: Peace Research Institute Oslo.

Karim, U. (2022). Inter-Regional Embedded Security Model: Turkish and Emirati Engagement in the Horn of Africa. In R. Mason, & S. Mabon (eds.), *The Gulf States and the Horn of Africa: Interests, Influences and Instability (*pp. 151–170). Manchester: Manchester University Press.

Mahajan, S. (2015). The Foreign Policy of the Raj and Its Legacy. In D.M. Malone, C.R. Mohan, and S. Raghavan (eds.) *The Oxford Handbook of Indian Foreign Policy* (pp. 78–94). Oxford: Oxford University Press.

Milani, M.M. (2006). Iran's Policy Towards Afghanistan. *The Middle East Journal, 60*(2), 235–279. doi:https://doi.org/10.3751/60.2.12

Onley, J. (2007) *The Arabian Frontier of the British Raj: Merchants, Rulers, and the British in the Nineteenth-Century Gulf*. Oxford: Oxford University Press.

Pant, H.V., & Mehta, K. (2018). India in Chabahar. *Asian Survey, 58*(4), 660–678. https://doi.org/10.1525/AS.2018.58.4.660

Quamar, M.M. (2018). The Changing Nature of the Pakistan Factor in India-Gulf Relations: An Indian Perspective. *Asian Affairs, 49*(4), 625–644. https://doi.org/10.1080/03068374.2018.1521134

Scroll.in (2022). "More nations condemn remarks on Prophet Muhammad, opposition says BJP's bigotry has isolated India," 7 June. Available at: https://scroll.in/latest/1025627/more-nations-condemn-remarks-on-prophet-muhammad-opposition-says-bjps-bigotry-has-isolated-india (Accessed: 14 June 2022).

The National Archives (no date) *Residency Agency, Trucial Coast*. Available at: https://discovery.nationalarchives.gov.uk/details/r/861f2200-f694-4497-b2cd-d2cf023f284d (Accessed: 14 June 2022).

Walt, S. (1990). *The Origin of Alliances*. London: Cornell University Press.

Weinbaum, M.G., & Khurram, A.B. (2014). Pakistan and Saudi Arabia: Deference, Dependence and Deterrence. *Middle East Journal, 68*(2), 211–28. doi:10.3751/68.2.12.

1 India, the Persian Gulf and the Emergence of a Supercomplex

Saloni Kapur[1]

Introduction

This chapter will explore whether the patterns of amity and enmity linking India to the Persian Gulf have shifted since Narendra Modi took over as Indian Prime Minister in 2014. Empirically, this has been a significant period for India-Gulf relations. Former US President Donald Trump withdrew from the Joint Comprehensive Plan of Action (JCPOA) and reimposed sanctions on Iran in 2018. US President Joe Biden has been unable to reinstate the JCPOA after coming to power in January 2021. Meanwhile, Iran and China signed a 25-year cooperation agreement in March 2021 (Landler, 2018; Marcus, 2018; Afterman, 2021; Davison, 2021; Motamedi, 2021; Robinson, 2021; Sharifi, 2021; *The Hindu*, 2021b). Finally, India-Gulf relations suffered a setback in June 2022 as Gulf states reacted to disparaging remarks about the Prophet Muhammad made by two politicians from Modi's Bharatiya Janata Party (BJP) (Roche, 2022). Theoretically, this area of inquiry is grounded in Regional Security Complex Theory (RSCT) and its ideas about the emergence of a supercomplex when a great power projects its "power into adjacent regions." If interregional dynamics supersede dynamics within a Regional Security Complex (RSC), this would mean that the two adjacent RSCs are merging to form a single RSC (Buzan and Wæver, 2003).

This chapter will employ the theoretical framework provided by RSCT to seek to understand whether any such thinning of the boundary between the South and West Asian RSCs has taken place due to India's rise to great-power status and the projection of its power into the Gulf subcomplex (Buzan, 2002; 2011a; Buzan and Wæver, 2003; Pardesi, 2015). It will contribute to the empirical understanding of the shifting alliance structure linking South Asia to the Gulf, focusing on India's ties to the Gulf states.

The chapter will address the following research question: Has India undergone a paradigm shift in its relations with the Gulf under Modi? Given the descriptive nature of this question, I will adopt an interpretive approach focused on "the world of meanings inhabited by the actor," in this case, the Indian state, as evidenced by the official discourse of representatives of the government on relations with the Gulf (Halperin and Heath, 2012).

DOI: 10.4324/9781003283058-2

Empirical and theoretical reflections on India's evolving foreign policy

Numerous scholars and foreign-policy analysts have noted India's growing proximity to the Arab Gulf under Modi. For instance, Ahmad (2020) writes, "In his six years as prime minister, Narendra Modi has expended more time, effort and commitment to cultivating ties with the Gulf region than any of his predecessors." In parallel, proponents of RSCT have suggested that an Asian supercomplex is emerging as the international order moves towards a state of *decentred globalism* in which there are no superpowers and several great powers (Buzan, 2011a). Meanwhile, scholars within and outside RSCT have debated whether they should count India as a great power amid this global power shift (Buzan, 2002; 2011a; Buzan and Wæver, 2003; Pardesi, 2015; Pröbsting, 2020). In this section, I critically analyse these three themes within the existing literature to provide the foundation for a theoretically grounded and evidence-based explanation for India's apparent pivot towards the Arab Gulf states and away from Iran under Modi.

India's purported pivot towards the Arab Gulf

Several scholars have analysed the impact of US sanctions on India's relationship with Iran.

Authors such as Hafeez (2019), Wani, Mir and Shah (2019), Siyech and K.R. Singh (2018), Johny (2017) and Saran (2020) have noted the detrimental impact of US pressure on India on India-Iran trade and strategic cooperation. This includes a reduction in Indian oil imports from Iran, greater Indian reliance on oil imports from the Arab Gulf states, and Iran's perception that India has pivoted towards its adversaries in the Arab Gulf and the United States. These scholars and analysts argue that this jeopardises Indian investments in Iran's Chabahar port, as well as its strategic autonomy.

Other authors, including Ahmad (2015), Burton (2019), Chaudhuri (2017a; 2017b), Hussain (2017), Siyech (2017), Mohan (2020) and Pradhan (2020), have emphasised India's deepening ties with the Arab states of the Gulf region, particularly Saudi Arabia and the United Arab Emirates (UAE). Chaudhuri (2017a) attributes the shift to the Gulf monarchies' frustration with Pakistan, their apprehensions about the possibility of a US-Iran breakthrough, their recognition of India's rising power and growing proximity to the United States, and India's desire to "isolate" Pakistan and attract investment. Chaudhuri (2017b) also claims that Iran has fallen down the list of Indian priorities under its new, Modi-fied foreign policy because of "India's push for renewable energy, its desire to diversify energy supplies away from the Persian Gulf, and the lack of a sizable Indian diaspora in Iran." In addition to commenting on Iran's equivocation on giving India equity in its Farzad B gas field and Indian companies' reluctance to trade

18 *Saloni Kapur*

with Iran due to US sanctions, Chaudhuri (2017b) also claims that India no longer sees the Arab Gulf as merely a source of oil and gas but rather "a source of strategically-driven, long-term investments."

Hussain (2017) emphasises the deepening India-Saudi Arabia relationship since Manmohan Singh's term in office and the Riyadh Declaration of 2010, which elevated the connection to a strategic partnership. Indian private-sector investment in Saudi Arabia and Saudi Arabian investment in India have expanded, India is training Saudi personnel, and the two countries are cooperating in defence manufacturing. Hussain points to a Strategic Energy Partnership, intelligence sharing, extradition treaties, counterterrorism cooperation and opportunities for students to receive higher education and conduct research in one another's countries. He suggests that "India and Saudi Arabia seem to have reached the point where, unlike in the past, they are both determined not to permit the further development of ties between them to be bracketed by their relations with third countries (e.g., Iran or Pakistan)."

Similarly, Siyech (2017) focuses on the India-UAE strategic partnership, noting the UAE's tilt towards India and away from Pakistan, evident in its statement on a terrorist attack in India-administered Jammu and Kashmir (J&K) in October 2016. Mohan (2020) suggests that under Modi, India has undergone a paradigm shift away from viewing the Gulf monarchies "as a collection of extractive petro-states run by conservative feudatories" and as sources "of extremist religious ideology that destabilised the Subcontinent." Pradhan (2020) recalls the UAE's bestowal of the Order of Zayed upon Modi and his receipt of the Abdulaziz Sash Award from Saudi Arabia and the King Hamad Order of the Renaissance from Bahrain. He also points to cooperation between India and the Gulf states, particularly Kuwait and the UAE, to deal with the coronavirus crisis.

Tempering these gushing accounts, Ganguly and Blarel (2020) and Ahmad (2020) underline the negative impact of Hindutva ideology and Islamophobic discourse in India on ties with the Arab Gulf states. Both articles point to the rhetoric against Muslims in India during the coronavirus crisis as jeopardising the Arab Gulf countries' support for India that was in evidence when India revoked Article 370 of its constitution on J&K and during religious riots in Delhi in 2020. Similarly, in the aftermath of the diplomatic crisis over two BJP spokespersons' pejorative comments about the Prophet Muhammad, several op-ed articles speculated on how the incident would affect India's relations with the Gulf subregion in particular, and the West Asian region more broadly (*Al Jazeera*, 2022; Gopal, 2022; Malhotra, 2022; Roche, 2022).

RSCT

RSCT categorises powerful states into superpowers, great powers and regional powers (Buzan and Wæver, 2003). Buzan and Wæver (2003) suggest that a 1+4

India, the Persian Gulf and the Emergence of a Supercomplex   19

system containing one superpower (the United States) and four great powers (the European Union (EU), Japan, China and Russia) characterised the Cold War era. During this period, India consistently claimed to be a great power. However, it did not meet the requirements to qualify as one since it did not have the requisite material capability or recognition from other states. Furthermore, it did not form part of the strategic calculations of other states in such a way as to suggest that it was a great power.

Buzan and Wæver (2003) understand RSCs to be "regions as seen through the lens of security." They define an RSC as *"a set of units whose major processes of securitisation, desecuritisation, or both are so interlinked that their security problems cannot reasonably be analysed or resolved apart from one another."* Within the West Asian RSC, the Persian Gulf is seen as a subcomplex that has its own "distinctive patterns of security interdependence that are nonetheless caught up in a wider pattern that defines the RSC as a whole."

Furthermore, Buzan and Wæver (2003) point to the potential for the external transformation of an RSC through the shifting of its outer boundary. They suggest that one way in which this might happen would be if two RSCs were to merge. However, they also lay out the potential for the emergence of a supercomplex when a great power in one RSC projects its power into an adjacent region, thus creating a strong and sustained interregional security dynamic. This interregional dynamic will not override regional dynamics, so the original RSCs will remain intact. They perceive the emergence of a supercomplex linking East and South Asia due to the rise of China and the projection of its power into South Asia.

In terms of the connection between the South and West Asian RSCs, Buzan and Wæver (2003) recognise the potential for a merger of these two adjacent RSCs due to Pakistan's close ties first with Iran and subsequently with Saudi Arabia, including military relations with the latter, as well as Israel and India's shared concern about Pakistan's nuclear bomb. However, they do not consider these developments strong enough to suggest the unification of the South and West Asian RSCs and see Afghanistan as an effective insulator separating these two RSCs. They explain, "Between South Asian and Middle Eastern regional security dynamics, Afghanistan was always an insulator that faced simultaneously north, east, and west, engaging its neighbours on all fronts, but keeping them apart much more than pulling them together" (Buzan and Wæver, 2003).

Finally, Buzan and Wæver (2003) present the possibility of India transcending "its region by rising to the status of a third Asian great power." They see evidence to suggest that this is happening, with India "steadily transcending its longstanding confinement to South Asia, and beginning to carve out a wider role as an Asian great power." However, they find "continuity in the patterns between South Asia and the Middle East." They argue that "the boundaries between the South Asian complex and its neighbours were *not* breaking down and forming new configurations of amity/enmity and polarity." Rather, Buzan and Wæver posit that while the boundaries

20 *Saloni Kapur*

separating RSCs remain stable, India is starting to increasingly operate at the interregional level as a great power.

In a subsequent article, Buzan (2011a) proposes that the international order is moving towards a state of decentred globalism in which there are "great and regional powers, but no superpowers." He further argues that "India's claim for great power status is now plausible," given that it is increasingly recognised as one. Thus, he claims that "India is arguably now a great power at the global level and therefore also within Asia."

India as a great power

There are various perspectives in the non-RSCT literature on India's status as a great power. For instance, Pardesi (2015) argues that India *has* attained great-power status because of its successful projection of its power into Southeast Asia and its transcendence of its home region of South Asia. He points to the Indian Ocean Region (including the Persian Gulf) as another potential region where India operates or will soon operate as a great power.

In contrast, Pröbsting (2020) casts doubt on this argument by pointing to India's low per-capita income, high levels of poverty and inequality, major social divisions, rise in indebtedness and severe economic crisis under the Modi regime. He further highlights the claim by Arvind Subramanian, India's former chief economic advisor under Modi, that previous governments' official figures on the growth of the gross domestic product were grossly exaggerated. Pröbsting underscores the high levels of "bad loans" accumulated by Indian banks and the phenomenon of capital flight from India. Based on these factors, he contends that India is nowhere close to being a great power. He also discusses India's influence abroad, insisting that "its influence is almost entirely limited to South Asia," where Pakistan and China regularly challenge it.

Focusing on the impact of the coronavirus pandemic on India's power, S. Singh (2021) warns that India's inadequate response to the health crisis has severely damaged its soft power. Arguing that India's reputation as a liberal democracy was already undermined under the Modi regime, S. Singh contends that the damage to India's soft power by its poor response to the coronavirus crisis is significant in terms of India's claim to great-power status since "it was soft power that allowed New Delhi to assert itself for a seat at the global high table to begin with." He emphasises India's acceptance of foreign aid, its inability to deliver on Quad plans to supply vaccines to countries in the Indo-Pacific, and its weakened negotiating position vis-à-vis China and Pakistan as indicators of the impact of the pandemic on India's power. He further highlights India's failure to meet commitments to supply vaccines to Asian and African states, and China's success in stepping in to support other South Asian states in battling the virus, thus leaving India behind in the race "to be an attractive and reliable partner in South Asia."

Conclusion

Much has already been written about India's ties with the Gulf. However, the existing empirical literature on India and the Gulf fails to employ any theoretical framework that might help scholars apply insights from studies conducted in other parts of the world to understand interregional dynamics between South and West Asia, specifically India and the Gulf. This chapter applies the framework offered by RSCT to the relations between India and the Persian Gulf, to offer insights that might not be accessible through a purely empirical study.

Furthermore, the existing literature on India's status as a great power has tended to focus on either material or reputational factors. Although Buzan (2011a) and Pardesi (2015) claim to incorporate both aspects of power into their definitions, both rely on India's growing reputation as a great power as evidence of its acquisition of this status. Similarly, S. Singh's (2021) empirical assessment highlights India's waning soft power, indicating a fall in global reputation. Conversely, Pröbsting (2020) focuses almost exclusively on material factors while neglecting the question of how other states perceive India.

In this chapter, I take as a given RSCT's three-fold criteria for categorising a state as a great power. My understanding of great power is based on Buzan and Wæver's (2003) classification of states as great powers based on (1) their material capabilities; (2) their recognition by other states as great powers; and (3) other states' practical response to the state as if it were a great power, based on system-level calculations. Thus, great-power status depends on a state's actual material capabilities *and* how other states perceive it. While acknowledging the varying scholarly perspectives on whether India is indeed a great power, I take as the foundation for my analysis Buzan's (2002; 2011a) RSCT-based assessment that India is beginning to operate as an Asian great power. I build on his argument by considering whether it is doing so not only in Southeast Asia as Buzan and Pardesi argue, but also in the Persian Gulf.

While the literature on RSCT has emphasised the breakdown of the boundary between South and East Asia due to China's rise but maintained that the South and West Asian RSCs remain separated by Afghanistan as an insulator, this chapter explores whether this is still the case. As Pardesi (2015) notes from a non-RSCT perspective, there is a possibility that India is already operating as a great power within the Indian Ocean Region. This is a development that RSCT has thus far failed to consider. This chapter fills that gap in the theoretical literature on RSCT.

India's perceived paradigm shift

As noted above, empirical scholars and political analysts have pointed out a shift in India's relations with the Persian Gulf, proposing that India has distanced itself from Iran while moving closer to the Arab Gulf states. They have attributed this shift to various causes, including US and Israeli pressure, especially pressure by the Trump administration on the Modi government (Siyech and K.R. Singh, 2018; Hafeez, 2019; Saran, 2020). They have also pointed to the Modi administration's effort to bolster ties with Israel, the Arab Gulf and Iran under its Look West policy, and the obstacle posed by Israel and the Arab Gulf states' animosity towards Iran, along with US sanctions (Burton, 2019). In addition, they have laid out the incentives driving India's push towards the Arab Gulf, including wanting to attract investment and to "isolate" Pakistan (Chaudhuri, 2017a). They have described Iran's waning appeal in Indian eyes due to various factors, including the lack of a sizeable Indian diaspora in Iran—in contrast to the Arab Gulf; India's effort to diversify its sources of energy by looking beyond the Persian Gulf; and its quest for renewable energy sources (Chaudhuri, 2017b). Furthermore, they have pointed to Modi's personality and focus on international status and power as factors driving India's tilt towards the Arab Gulf. They have also noted that India's trade with the Arab Gulf monarchies is expanding well beyond hydrocarbons to incorporate diverse sectors, including infrastructure, arms, agriculture and the maritime industry (Siyech, 2017).

On the other hand, scholars have explained the Arab Gulf states' desire to enhance ties with India in terms of their "frustration" with Pakistan, their circumspection regarding the JCPOA, and their recognition of India's rise and its deepening relationship with the United States (Chaudhuri, 2017a). Furthermore, they have highlighted that as the United States reduces its dependence on foreign oil, the Gulf states have a growing need for stable alternative markets such as India (Siyech, 2017).

Mohan (2020) describes the change as "a paradigm shift" under Modi. At the same time, Siyech and K.R. Singh (2018) speculate that Iran must perceive India's increased oil purchases from the Arab Gulf amid US sanctions on "Iran as 'a strategic "tilt"'." Meanwhile, Hussain (2017) underlines the continuity in India's policy towards the Arab Gulf under Singh and Modi, highlighting the deepening of Indo-Saudi ties under both prime ministers.

Based on these empirical observations, this analysis begins with the hypothesis that India *has* undergone a paradigm shift in its relations with the Gulf, especially since the Modi administration came to power in 2014. However, based on the insights offered by RSCT, I propose that this paradigm shift is due to India's effort to carve out a role for itself as an Asian great power, with Modi's personality and emphasis on global status acting as an intervening variable. Thus, the dependent variable is India's paradigmatic shift and strategic tilt away from Iran and towards the Arab Gulf. The independent variable is India's desire to rise to the status of a great power, which already existed in the post-Cold War era but has received an impetus in the contemporary international order that is moving towards what Buzan refers to as decentred globalism (Buzan and Wæver, 2003; Buzan, 2011a; Halperin and Heath, 2012).

The implication is that whether or not the United States returns to the JCPOA under the Biden administration, India's current trajectory of moving closer to the Arab Gulf states will continue. This is because the US sanctions on Iran and the personalities of Modi and Trump are intervening variables that have influenced India's paradigm shift, but the independent variable that has caused India's strategic tilt is its longstanding quest for great power and the structural transition of the international system towards decentred globalism (Halperin and Heath, 2012).

Researching India's paradigm shift

I have employed a longitudinal design for this study to explore how Indian policymakers have viewed relations with the Persian Gulf under the administrations of prime ministers Atal Bihari Vajpayee (1998–2004), Singh (2004–2014) and Modi (2014–present) (Halperin and Heath, 2012). In 2004, Buzan (2011b) argued "that the most likely scenario for the coming decades was continuation of the US as the sole superpower accompanied by several great powers." His "second most likely scenario" was that the world would transition to an international order with no superpowers and only great powers. Subsequently, in 2011, he asserted that this second possibility was becoming increasingly likely and that the international system was "now palpably moving towards a world without superpowers in which the most likely scenario is what I call *decentred globalism*" (Buzan, 2011a). Hence, we can assume that this transition towards a decentred world order occurred during Singh's prime ministerial term. Therefore, if my hypothesis is to hold, this would suggest that India's push for recognition as an Asian great power gained momentum during this period. Its effort to play a more significant role in the Arab Gulf also started to manifest itself at this time.

As a longitudinal "cohort" study, this chapter studies the statements of Indian policymakers during the prime ministerial terms of Vajpayee, Singh and Modi to assess whether a paradigmatic shift in relations with the Gulf took place over these three terms. These cases are critical to understanding this shift because they will enable us to evaluate whether RSCT's propositions about great powers seeking to transcend their regions and project their power into adjacent regions hold in the case of India's rise to great-power status and its concurrent attitude towards West Asia (Halperin and Heath, 2012). If RSCT's propositions hold, this would be evident in a shift in discourse from the Vajpayee era to the Singh era. This would contradict the general perception in the empirical literature on India-Gulf ties, which perceives a shift under Modi rather than Singh.

India's official discourse on relations with the Gulf

I have employed the method of content analysis to interpret the statements made by Indian officials under the Vajpayee, Singh and Modi administrations vis-à-vis relations with the Gulf. I have referred to the Indian Ministry

24 *Saloni Kapur*

of External Affairs (MEA) archives posted on the ministry's official website. These include speeches and statements, press releases, bilateral/multilateral documents, responses to media queries, media briefings, interviews, parliamentary questions and answers and media reports. During my research, I focused mainly on relations with Iran, Saudi Arabia and the UAE. Among the Arab Gulf states, I chose to focus on Saudi Arabia and the UAE because of their significance in terms of the size of their territories, populations and economies and their importance to India as destinations for emigrants and trading partners. I referred to 2 documents from the Vajpayee era (1998–2004), 21 documents from the Singh era (2004–2014) and 130 documents from the Modi era (2014–present). The disparity in the number of records from each period is due to their correspondingly disparate availability in the MEA web archives.

Both the reports from the Vajpayee period contain positive statements towards Iran (see Table 1.1). For instance, in a speech by External Affairs Minister Yashwant Sinha in December 2003, he lauded the signing of the New Delhi Declaration during a visit by Iranian President Mohammad Khatami in January that year. He asserted that India and Iran were on the "road to strategic partnership" though their bilateral trade was "much below its potential." He referred to the North-South Corridor, the Chabahar-Milak-Zaranj-Delaram route, the Deranj-Delaram road, the Chabahar port project

Table 1.1 India's official discourse on relations with the Persian Gulf

The Vajpayee Era (1998–2004)		
Documents demonstrating a negative attitude towards Iran	0/2	0%
Documents demonstrating a neutral attitude towards Iran	0/2	0%
Documents demonstrating a positive attitude towards Iran	2/2	100%
Documents demonstrating a negative attitude towards the Arab Gulf	0/2	0%
Documents demonstrating a neutral attitude towards the Arab Gulf	0/2	0%
Documents demonstrating a positive attitude towards the Arab Gulf	0/2	0%
Documents highlighting India's quest for great-power status	1/2	50%
The Singh Era (2004–2014)		
Documents demonstrating a negative attitude towards Iran	4/21	19%
Documents demonstrating a neutral attitude towards Iran	3/21	14%
Documents demonstrating a positive attitude towards Iran	6/21	29%
Documents demonstrating a negative attitude towards the Arab Gulf	3/21	14%
Documents demonstrating a neutral attitude towards the Arab Gulf	2/21	10%
Documents demonstrating a positive attitude towards the Arab Gulf	19/21	90%
Documents highlighting India's quest for great-power status	8/21	38%
The Modi Era (2014–Present)[2]		
Documents demonstrating a negative attitude towards Iran	4/130	3%
Documents demonstrating a neutral attitude towards Iran	19/130	15%
Documents demonstrating a positive attitude towards Iran	53/130	41%
Documents demonstrating a negative attitude towards the Arab Gulf	6/130	5%
Documents demonstrating a neutral attitude towards the Arab Gulf	6/130	5%
Documents demonstrating a positive attitude towards the Arab Gulf	62/130	48%
Documents highlighting India's quest for great-power status	35/130	27%

India, the Persian Gulf and the Emergence of a Supercomplex 25

and the Chabahar-Fahraj-Bam railway line. Significantly, the speech places India and Iran's "growing strategic convergence" and "economic and commercial cooperation" in the context of globalisation and India's desire to build economic relationships "in its extended neighbourhood," as well as India's strong growth rate (at the time), the size of its economy in purchasing-power-parity terms, and its effort to "make [its] presence felt in the globalised economy participating as equal partners." Thus, India's "consolidated [...] relations" with Iran were already being framed in terms of India's quest for great-power status (Ministry of External Affairs, 2003a; 2003b). Notably, this push for stronger ties with Iran under Vajpayee came in the wake of sanctions on Iran imposed by the US in 1984 and 1996, but before the United Nations Security Council (UNSC) sanctions of 2006 (Davenport, 2021).

During the Singh era, 19 per cent of the documents studied contained statements that projected a negative attitude towards Iran, 14 per cent had comments showing a neutral attitude towards Iran and 29 per cent contained words demonstrating a positive attitude towards Iran. Fourteen per cent contained negative statements about the Arab Gulf, while 10 per cent contained neutral comments about the Arab Gulf. As many as 90 per cent had positive comments about the Arab Gulf (see Table 1.1). Some documents included more than one of these categories simultaneously, discussing India's ties to Iran and the Arab Gulf states simultaneously or presenting a nuanced position with sentences or paragraphs within a single report projecting different attitudes. For instance, in a speech by External Affairs Minister Salman Khurshid in February 2013, he describes Iran as "a friend of India" with "strong civilisational links." However, he then goes on to refer to the international condemnation of Iran's nuclear programme and to wonder whether India ought to "be cautious and remain aloof in this process or [...] engage actively in the dialogue that Iran has with the world in achieving a peaceful resolution of the issue." He also obliquely refers to India's votes against Iran at the International Atomic Energy Agency, acknowledging that "we have had to take positions that obviously not necessarily align themselves with the aspirations or at least perceived aspirations of Iran." Despite this, he insists that "we have remained friends with Iran" despite not "stand[ing] by them in critical moments" and that "we would want our engagement to continue growing." Crucially, Khurshid articulates India's effort to balance its relations with Iran and the United States, asserting that "we remain good friends with the United States of America; we are extremely good friends with Iran" (Ministry of External Affairs, 2013a).

Based on Khurshid's explicit articulation of India's conundrum vis-à-vis its friendship with Iran, the overwhelmingly positive attitude towards the Arab Gulf during the Singh years can be understood in terms of India's desire not to antagonise the United States in the wake of the India-US nuclear deal of 2005–2008, as well as sanctions imposed on Iran by the UNSC, the United States and the EU in 2006–2010 over its nuclear programme (Bajoria and Pan, 2010; Ministry of External Affairs, 2013a; Davenport, 2021). However, it is also pertinent to note that during this period, despite the UNSC sanctions and the India-US nuclear deal, Indian official statements vis-à-vis Iran were more often positive than negative. This underscores India's effort to maintain friendly ties with Iran, the Arab Gulf and the United States amid a decentring world order and a rising Asia. Not only does this hark back to the non-alignment of the Jawaharlal Nehru era, but it also speaks to India's growing focus on expanding its influence in Asia as it increasingly saw itself as a rising Asian great power.

Eight of the 21 documents (38 per cent) from this period allude to India's rise. For instance, in a speech delivered in Tehran in November 2008, External Affairs Minister Pranab Mukherjee described India as "poised at a stage when its creative strength derived from a rich civilisational history, has been unleashed." He referred to India as "instinctively multipolar." He thus hinted at the global power shift underway. He placed his comments on India and Iran's "fundamental complementarities" in the context of "the rise of Asia" and the "new" India's "place in the international matrix," citing the size of its economy, its growth rate and its democracy (Ministry of External Affairs, 2008). Thus, he pointed to both material and reputational factors in making a case for India as a great power.

Foreign secretary Nirupama Rao made similar comments during a talk on India and Iran in New Delhi in July 2010. She predicted, "The India-Iran relationship will become even more important with the inevitable rise of both India and Iran in this century, which has been dubbed by many as the Asian century." She described India's economy as "among the fastest growing in the world" and referred to India's "commitment to multi-polarity over uni-polarity" (Ministry of External Affairs, 2010). Subsequently, in his February 2013 speech on India's conundrum vis-à-vis Iran, Khurshid framed India's interest in the Chahbahar Port and the Iran-Pakistan-India and Turkmenistan-Afghanistan-Pakistan-India gas pipelines in terms of the growing needs of the Indian economy and India's interest in Afghanistan. The reference to Afghanistan underlines India's desire to assert its power within South Asia as a regional power. Still, its effort to do so via the Gulf and Central Asia points to a projection of this power beyond South Asia into West and Central Asia (Ministry of External Affairs, 2013a).

Simultaneously, while addressing an India-Saudi Arabia Youth Forum in March 2012, Minister of State for External Affairs E. Ahamed placed the signing of the Riyadh Declaration by India and Saudi Arabia in the context of "the new global realities and unfolding opportunities of the 21st century" (Ministry of External Affairs, 2012). In a May 2013 statement made in Jeddah, Khurshid argued that Indo-Saudi cooperation would "contribute significantly to the stability and security of the entire region and beyond" and defined "India and Saudi Arabia [as] two major countries in the region." He went on to assert that "in this century of Asia," Indo-Saudi cooperation would benefit "the entire region" (Ministry of External Affairs, 2013b). This

India, the Persian Gulf and the Emergence of a Supercomplex   27

is significant because he described India and Saudi Arabia as regional powers in a single region, implying the collapse of the boundary between the South and West Asian RSCs.

In an interview with _Arab News_ the same month, Khurshid reiterated his claim that Indo-Saudi cooperation would "contribute to regional stability" while clarifying that India would not be part of a Saudi military coalition against terrorism. He explained this in terms of India's capacity and philosophy—pointing to an effort to project power beyond South Asia without sending troops abroad. Interestingly, he went on to insist that "for us, the priority is, of course, our own region. Afghanistan is our priority. [...] Your immediate priority should be your immediate neighbourhood" (Ministry of External Affairs, 2013c). Thus, there is evidence at this point of ambiguity within Indian foreign policymaking as to whether to assert oneself as an Asian great power or remain content with acting as a South Asian regional power, and a reluctance to project military power beyond South Asia. Significantly, India has not interfered in the domestic politics of the Gulf states, which contrasts with its behaviour as a regional power within South Asia. Here, it has interfered in smaller states' internal politics on multiple occasions (e.g., during the 1971 Bangladesh war, the dispatch of Indian troops to Sri Lanka to fight Tamil separatists in 1987, and India's facilitation of an agreement between Nepal's Maoists and other political parties in 2004 (Babu, 1998; Ojha, 2015; Saran, 2018)). This points to a tension between India's desire to be recognised as a great power, and its Gandhian and Nehruvian legacy of anti-colonialism, non-violence, idealism and non-alignment (Kennedy, 2015).

Finally, during the ongoing Modi period, 3 per cent of documents contained statements portraying a negative attitude towards Iran, 15 per cent had comments revealing a neutral attitude towards Iran and 41 per cent contained words demonstrating a positive attitude towards Iran. Five per cent contained statements showing a negative attitude towards the Arab Gulf, another 5 per cent included comments suggesting a neutral attitude towards the Arab Gulf and 48 per cent contained statements indicating a positive attitude towards the Arab Gulf. Twenty-seven per cent had words revealing a quest for great-power status and expanding India's influence in the Gulf (see Table 1.1). These figures raise serious doubts about the hypothesis of a decisive tilt away from Iran and towards the Arab Gulf, which was based on the existing secondary literature on India's evolving relations with the Persian Gulf.

It is pertinent to note that for most of the Modi government's term so far, the United States was a signatory of the JCPOA. When the Modi administration came into power in May 2014, the ink was still fresh on the JCPOA, signed only seven months previously, in November 2013. This goes a significant way towards explaining why the Modi government's Link West policy can be seen to have encompassed both Iran and the Arab Gulf states. It was a full four years into the Modi government's term, in May 2018, that the

28   *Saloni Kapur*

United States withdrew from the JCPOA, and 11 months later, in April 2019, that it announced an end to a waiver it had granted to India for importing oil from Iran (Davenport, 2021).

Indeed, 31 out of 53 documents containing positive remarks about Iran, i.e., 58 per cent of the reports containing positive statements, were published by the Modi administration between May 2014 and May 2018, when the United States stepped out of the JCPOA. Another nine documents containing positive comments vis-à-vis Iran, i.e., 17 per cent of the records containing positive statements, were published between June 2018 and April 2019, when the United States announced the termination of the waiver to India for oil imports from Iran. Thus, 40 out of 53, or 75 per cent of the documents containing positive statements about Iran, were published before India's waiver officially ended in May 2019. However, the period from May 2014 to April 2019 also accounts for only 5 out of 7 years of the Modi government's rule up to 2021 (since I have collected data up to 2021), or about 71 per cent of its term up to 2021. This means that the positive statements about Iran continued at a similar rate even after April 2019.

Indeed, in response to a question posed in parliament in July 2019 vis-à-vis pressure on India to reduce oil imports from Iran, the government reiterated its oft-repeated stance that "India's bilateral relations with Iran stand on their own and are not influenced by India's relations with any third country" (Ministry of External Affairs, 2019a). In September 2019, during consultations between the foreign offices of the two countries, both sides "agreed to maintain the momentum" of cooperation and exchanges (Ministry of External Affairs, 2019b). The same month, at a meeting between Modi and Iranian President Hassan Rouhani on the sidelines of the United Nations General Assembly, "the two leaders positively assessed the progress in bilateral relations since their first meeting at Ufa in 2015" and "especially mentioned operationalisation of Chabahar Port" (Ministry of External Affairs, 2019c).

In September 2020, in response to a parliamentary question about the widely reported Iran-China deal, the government once again insisted that India's relations with Iran stood "on their own footing and are independent of its relations with third countries" (Ministry of External Affairs, 2020a). Responding to other questions about whether India was still involved in the Chabahar-Zahedan rail project and the construction of the Chabahar port, the government insisted that India remained engaged with both projects (Ministry of External Affairs, 2020b; 2020c; 2020d). Indeed, in 2021, the Indian media reported that India had resumed work on the Chabahar port project, though the Indian public-sector ONGC Videsh Ltd had lost the development rights for Iran's Farzad-B gas field, with Iranian sources reportedly telling the international media that Indian companies were unwilling to participate in the project due to US sanctions (MEED, 2021; K. Singh and Roy, 2021; *The Eurasian Times*, 2020; *The Hindu*, 2021a).

India, the Persian Gulf and the Emergence of a Supercomplex 29

In terms of relations with the Arab Gulf, the Modi government in its statements has highlighted India's "vital stakes" in the region: the sizeable Indian diaspora resident there, crude-oil imports from the Gulf, and the fact that the area is India's largest trading partner (Ministry of External Affairs, 2014). It has emphasised Modi's personal "commitment to further strengthening India's close relations with Saudi Arabia" (Ministry of External Affairs, 2015a). Similarly, it has highlighted Modi's initiative in visiting the UAE in 2015, the first visit by a sitting Indian prime minister in 34 years, as the basis for the forging of a strategic partnership between India and the UAE (Ministry of External Affairs, 2015b). However, the Modi administration has also acknowledged the success of the India-Saudi Arabia strategic partnership established by the previous Singh government through the Riyadh Declaration of 2010 (Ministry of External Affairs, 2016a).

It has described India's ties to Saudi Arabia as "special" and "extremely important" and underlined the growing defence cooperation between the two states. During a media briefing in March 2016, the Joint Secretary (Gulf), Mridul Kumar, underscored the vitality of Saudi Arabia to India's national interest in terms of being a key source of energy supplies, the host to a large Indian diaspora, and the destination for Haj pilgrims from India. He also highlighted Modi's commitment to bolstering political ties with the Gulf region, underlining security cooperation with Saudi Arabia (Ministry of External Affairs, 2016b; 2016c).

During a subsequent media briefing on the outcomes of Modi's 2016 visit to Saudi Arabia, the Secretary (Economic Relations) Amar Sinha offered a fascinating glimpse into Modi's attitude towards Saudi Arabia. He recounted how the Indian delegation was "surprised" to hear women employees of India's Tata Consultancy Services in Riyadh chanting "Modi, Modi." He shared that it had been Modi's first visit to Saudi Arabia and that "the experiences that he had, he had not expected." He said that Modi had "expressed [...] happiness" over the visit and that Saudi Arabia's conferral of the King Abdulaziz Special Sash on Modi was "a huge surprise" that "pleasantly surprised everybody." He further spoke of "the closeness between the two leaders"—Modi and King Salman (Ministry of External Affairs, 2016d; *The Economic Times*, 2021).

Five years later, in a joint statement issued by India and Saudi Arabia during a visit to India by Crown Prince Mohammed bin Salman, the two sides described Modi's 2016 trip as a "landmark visit" and celebrated the two countries' growing defence ties. They acknowledged the progress made during the Singh era through signing a memorandum of understanding on defence cooperation in February 2014 during a visit to India by King Salman and the Riyadh Declaration of February 2010 (Ministry of External Affairs, 2019d).

Similarly, during a media briefing on External Affairs Minister Sushma Swaraj's attendance at an Organisation of Islamic Cooperation (OIC)

30 *Saloni Kapur*

meeting in 2019, the Indian ambassador to the UAE, Navtej Suri, celebrated "the increasing depth" of the India-UAE relationship. Secretary (Economic Relations) T.S. Tirumurti attributed the cementing of India's ties to the UAE and the Gulf to visits by the Emirati and Saudi crown princes to India in 2017 and 2019, respectively, and to Modi's trip to the UAE in 2018. He ascribed India's invitation to attend the OIC meeting as the guest of honour to the "very deep and very close relations" between India and the UAE, as well as "India's standing in the comity of nations" (Ministry of External Affairs, 2019e).

Thus, in a continuation of the discourse of the Singh administration, the Modi government's rhetoric on ties to the Gulf has been focused not only on Modi's initiative and India's national interest in terms of trade and migrant flows but also on India's rise and the global power shift. For example, in a 2015 joint statement put out by India and the UAE, they claimed that bilateral economic cooperation would "advance progress in the region and help realise the vision of an Asian Century." The statement also described India "as one of the major world powers" and "one of the anchors of the global economy" (Ministry of External Affairs, 2015b). Similarly, in a joint statement issued by India and Saudi Arabia, the two countries referred to "their responsibility for promoting peace, stability and security in the region and the world," evoking the English School idea that the great powers have special duties and responsibilities towards securing the international society of states (Ministry of External Affairs, 2016e; Kapur, 2021).

Similarly, in response to a parliamentary question posed in July 2017, the government emphasised the utility of the Chabahar port in providing Afghanistan with access to regional markets. It thus demonstrated India's desire to act as a regional power vis-à-vis Afghanistan but in a way that transcends South Asia, projecting India's power into Iran to circumvent Pakistan (Ministry of External Affairs, 2017). This represents the behaviour of a state with the ability to transcend its region and project its power into a neighbouring region. Furthermore, in a joint statement by India and Iran, the two countries emphasised "the unique role of Iran and India in promoting multi-modal connectivity within and across the region," referring to the Chabahar port as "a new gateway to and from Afghanistan, Central Asia and beyond" (Ministry of External Affairs, 2018). This suggests an effort to project power into Central Asia via the Gulf, thus going beyond the confines of South Asia.

Finally, in a continuation of the diplomacy between India and the Arab Gulf states during the Vajpayee and Singh eras, which included statements of support by the Gulf states for India's permanent membership of the UNSC, multiple statements issued during the Modi era saw the Arab Gulf states, as well as Iran, express support for India's candidacy (Ministry of External Affairs, 2004; 2015b; 2015c; 2018; 2019d). This is another example of India's quest for recognition as a great power through its Link West policy.

Conclusion

At the beginning of this chapter, I proposed that, based on the existing empirical literature on India-Gulf ties, India had undergone a paradigmatic shift vis-à-vis its relations with the Gulf, especially under Modi. This paradigmatic shift was supposed to have involved a tilt away from Iran and towards the Arab Gulf. I further suggested that, based on the premises of RSCT, this tilt was caused by India's quest for recognition as a great power, which was propelled by the movement of the international order towards what Buzan calls decentred globalism (Buzan, 2011b).

The content analysis conducted above reveals that, indeed, during the prime ministerial terms of Vajpayee, Singh and Modi, the Indian official discourse on relations with the Gulf has consistently been couched in language that articulates India's desire to assert itself as a great power through greater engagement with the Gulf. This has been a consistent theme in statements about Iran and the Arab Gulf states. Statements about ties with the Arab Gulf have also emphasised the region's importance for India as the host to a large Indian diaspora and a crucial source of energy supplies.

However, the documents analysed do not suggest a paradigmatic shift away from Iran under Modi. Instead, the thrust towards the Arab Gulf and away from Iran appears to have taken place during the Singh years, when positive statements about the Arab Gulf states appeared in 90 per cent of the documents studied. This contrasted with only 29 per cent of the documents containing positive comments about Iran. This marked a significant change from the previous Vajpayee era, when the content studied was solely focused on relations with Iran and had an unambiguously positive tone.

Finally, during the Modi era, the attitude towards the Arab Gulf and Iran seems to be more balanced, with 41 per cent of the documents containing positive statements about Iran and 48 per cent having positive comments about the Arab Gulf. Furthermore, this shifting trend in the approach to the Persian Gulf under Vajpayee, Singh and Modi can be explained in terms of both international sanctions and India's quest for great power. While the Indian rhetoric during all three prime ministerial periods points to a desire to be recognised as a great power underpinning India's thrust towards the Persian Gulf, the ebb and flow of relations with Iran seems to have a relationship with the imposition and lifting of international sanctions. Although Iran was already under US sanctions as a "state sponsor of terror" during the Vajpayee era, the international sanctions over its nuclear programme were only imposed during Singh's term (Davenport, 2021). This, combined with Singh's landmark nuclear deal with the United States, offers an explanation for why India's relations with the Arab Gulf states seemed to take precedence over ties with Iran during this period.

Finally, during most of the Modi period studied (2014–2021), the United States was part of the JCPOA, or India enjoyed a waiver for oil imports

32   *Saloni Kapur*

from Iran. Furthermore, the Modi government was in a much more secure position vis-à-vis its alliance with the United States. Modi came into power almost a decade after the US-India nuclear deal was signed, with the United States' nuclear sanctions against India a distant memory (Bajoria and Pan, 2010).

While ties with Iran have ebbed and flowed in response to international sanctions, the broader trend of seeking to project power into an adjacent RSC has followed the pattern laid out by RSCT. As the international order has moved towards multi-polarity and decentred globalism, a rising India has sought to transcend the South Asian RSC and project its power into the adjacent West Asian RSC, particularly the Gulf subcomplex. In practical terms, this suggests that regardless of whether the Biden administration can return to the JCPOA, India's deepening of ties with the Arab Gulf is likely to continue in a sustained manner. On the other hand, the analysis does not reveal a shift in attitude towards Iran after the United States withdrew from the JCPOA. The existing empirical literature points to a reduction in oil imports from Iran. Media reports suggest that Indian companies have hesitated to move forward on major collaborative ventures such as the Chabahar-Zahedan rail link and the Farzad-B gas field (Haidar, 2020; *The Eurasian Times*, 2020; MEED, 2021). However, the content analysis above suggests that the tone of the Indian official discourse has mainly remained positive towards Iran. Hence, I understand India's approach towards the Gulf less as a pivot away from Iran and towards the Arab Gulf and more as an effort to project power into the Persian Gulf in its entirety. If international sanctions against Iran are lifted, India is likely to reinvigorate its efforts at economic and strategic cooperation with Iran while maintaining the positive momentum of ties with the Arab Gulf states.

In RSCT terms, this aligns with Buzan and Wæver's (2003) outline of the scenario where a great power projects its power into an adjacent RSC, causing the emergence of a supercomplex. Thus, based on my analysis of the discourses of India's policymakers over the past two decades, I put forth the argument that India is actively seeking to project its power into the Gulf subcomplex. This takes forward Buzan (2011a) and Pardesi's (2015) ideas about India possibly functioning as a great power in Asia, including the Gulf. I propose that a supercomplex of South and West Asia has emerged due to India's projection of its power into the Gulf. The original South and West Asian RSCs remain intact because their intra-regional dynamics remain significant. Nevertheless, India's primary emphasis on security, defence and economic cooperation with the Persian Gulf states on both sides of the Iran/Saudi Arabia rivalry fits the pattern outlined by Buzan and Wæver of the external transformation of an RSC through a great power projecting its influence into an adjacent RSC, leading to the emergence of a supercomplex.

The insufficient data from the Vajpayee era limit this research, and there is scope for further research to confirm the broad trend that has emerged

India, the Persian Gulf and the Emergence of a Supercomplex   33

from this analysis. Furthermore, while this chapter has focused on India and the Gulf, it would be revealing for further research to explore how other West and South Asian states are affected by the emergence of a supercomplex. In Chapter 2, Ahmed and Abbas begin to do so by exploring how the changing patterns of amity and enmity linking South Asia to the Gulf, and particularly India's warming ties to the Arab Gulf states, are causing shifts in Pakistan's structure of alliances within the Gulf subcomplex.

Notes

1 I am grateful to Jessica Northey of Coventry University and the two anonymous reviewers for their constructive feedback on this chapter.
2 Data was collected up to 2021.

References

Afterman, G. (2021) 'Why overhyped US$400 billion deal changes little for China, Iran or Middle East', *South China Morning Post*, 9 April. Available at: https://www.scmp.com/comment/opinion/article/3128725/why-overhyped-us400-billion-deal-changes-little-china-iran-or (Accessed: 16 September 2021).

Ahmad, T. (2015) 'The Gulf region', in Malone, D.M., Mohan, C.R. and Raghavan, S. (eds.) *The Oxford handbook of Indian foreign policy*. Oxford: Oxford University Press, pp. 539–555.

Ahmad, T. (2020) 'How Hindutva hatred is jeopardising India's Gulf ties', *The Wire*, 27 April. Available at: https://thewire.in/diplomacy/hindutva-india-gulf-ties (Accessed: 16 September 2021).

Al Jazeera (2022) 'How will the Prophet remarks row affect India-GCC ties?', 14 June. Available at: https://www.aljazeera.com/news/2022/6/14/how-will-the-prophet-row-affect-india-gcc-ties (Accessed: 17 June 2022).

Babu, B.R. (1998) 'Indian intervention in Sri Lanka: Anatomy of a failure', *World Affairs*, 2 (3), pp. 132–145. Available at: https://www.jstor.org/stable/45064546 (Accessed: 16 September 2021).

Bajoria, J. and Pan, E. (2010) *The U.S.-India nuclear deal*. Available at: https://www.cfr.org/backgrounder/us-india-nuclear-deal (Accessed: 16 September 2021).

Burton, G. (2019) *India's 'Look West' policy in the Middle East under Modi*. Available at: https://www.mei.edu/publications/indias-look-west-policy-middle-east-under-modi (Accessed: 9 June 2021).

Buzan, B. (2002) 'South Asia moving towards transformation: emergence of India as a great power', *International Studies*, 39 (1), pp. 1–24. doi: 10.1177/002088170203900101.

Buzan, B. (2011a) 'The South Asian security complex in a decentring world order: reconsidering *Regions and powers* ten years on', *International Studies*, 48 (1), pp. 1–19. doi: 10.1177/002088171204800101.

Buzan, B. (2011b) 'The inaugural Kenneth N. Waltz annual lecture: a world order without superpowers: decentred globalism', *International Relations*, 25 (1), pp. 3–25. doi: 10.1177/0047117810396999.

Buzan, B. and Wæver, O. (2003) *Regions and powers: the structure of international security*. Cambridge: Cambridge University Press.

34 *Saloni Kapur*

Chaudhuri, P.P. (2017a) *Think west to go west: origins and implications of India's West Asia policy under Modi (part I)*. Available at: https://www.mei.edu/publications/think-west-go-west-origins-and-implications-indias-west-asia-policy-under-modi-part-i (Accessed: 9 June 2021).

Chaudhuri, P.P. (2017b) *Think west to go west: origins and implications of India's West Asia policy under Modi (part II)*. Available at: https://www.mei.edu/publications/think-west-go-west-origins-and-implications-indias-west-asia-policy-under-modi-part-ii (Accessed: 9 June 2021).

Davenport, K. (2021) *Timeline of nuclear diplomacy with Iran*. Available at: https://www.armscontrol.org/factsheets/Timeline-of-Nuclear-Diplomacy-With-Iran (Accessed: 30 September 2021).

Davison, D. (2021) 'Joe Biden is killing the Iran nuclear deal', *Jacobin*, 29 March. Available at: https://www.jacobinmag.com/2021/03/iran-nuclear-deal-biden-administration-jcpoa (Accessed: 30 September 2021).

Ganguly, S. and Blarel, N. (2020) 'Why Gulf states are backtracking on India', *Foreign Policy*, 5 May. Available at: https://foreignpolicy.com/2020/05/05/gulf-states-backtracking-india/ (Accessed: 30 September 2021).

Gopal, N. (2022) 'Dangerous flames', *The Telegraph*, 15 June. Available at: https://www.telegraphindia.com/opinion/dangerous-flames-narendra-modis-west-asia-outreach-is-in-peril/cid/1870031 (Accessed: 17 June 2022).

Hafeez, M. (2019) 'India-Iran relations: challenges and opportunities', *Strategic Studies*, 39 (3), pp. 22–36. Available at: https://www.jstor.org/stable/48544308 (Accessed: 30 September 2021).

Haidar, S. (2020) 'Months after starting Chabahar rail project without India, Iran seeks equipment', *The Hindu*, 7 November. Available at: https://www.thehindu.com/news/national/months-after-starting-chabahar-rail-project-without-india-iran-requests-help-with-equipment/article33048813.ece (Accessed: 30 September 2021).

Halperin, S. and Heath, O. (2012) *Political research methods and practical skills*. 2nd edn. Oxford: Oxford University Press.

Hussain, Z. (2017) *India-Saudi Arabia relations: new bilateral dynamics*. Available at: https://www.mei.edu/publications/india-saudi-arabia-relations-new-bilateral-dynamics (Accessed: 9 June 2021).

Johny, S. (2017) *India's balancing act in the Gulf*. Available at: https://www.mei.edu/publications/indias-balancing-act-gulf (Accessed: 9 June 2021).

Kapur, S. (2021) *Pakistan after Trump: great power responsibility in a multi-polar world*. Newcastle upon Tyne: Cambridge Scholars Publishing.

Kennedy, A.B. (2015) 'Nehru's foreign policy: realism and idealism conjoined', in Malone, D.M., Mohan, C.R. and Raghavan, S. (eds.) *The Oxford handbook of Indian foreign policy*. Oxford: Oxford University Press, pp. 127–139.

Landler, M. (2018) 'Trump abandons Iran nuclear deal he long scorned', *The New York Times*, 8 May. Available at: nytimes.com/2018/05/08/world/middleeast/trump-iran-nuclear-deal.html (Accessed: 6 October 2021).

Malhotra, J. (2022) 'Modi moved heavens to mend ties with Arab world. But Nupur Sharma, Tejasvi Surya hurting it', *The Print*, 7 June. Available at: https://theprint.in/opinion/global-print/modi-moved-heavens-to-mend-ties-with-arab-world-but-nupur-sharma-tejasvi-surya-hurting-it/986533/ (Accessed: 17 June 2022).

Marcus, J. (2018) 'Trump re-imposes Iran sanctions: now what?', *BBC*, 3 November. Available at: https://www.bbc.com/news/world-middle-east-46075179 (Accessed: 6 October 2021).

India, the Persian Gulf and the Emergence of a Supercomplex   35

MEED (2021) *Iran awards $1.8bn Farzad B gas field contract*. Available at: https://www.offshore-technology.com/comment/iran-farzad-b-contract/ (Accessed: 7 June 2021).

Ministry of External Affairs (2003a) *EAM's speech at the 7th India-Iran Joint Business Council meeting, Tehran*. Available at: https://mea.gov.in/Speeches-Statements.htm?dtl/5647/eams+speech+at+the+7th+indiairan+joint+business+council+meeting+tehran (Accessed: 7 June 2021).

Ministry of External Affairs (2003b) *The Republic of India and the Islamic Republic of Iran 'the New Delhi Declaration'*. Available at: https://www.mea.gov.in/other.htm?dtl/20182/The+Republic+of+India+and+th&quantity=1 (Accessed: 7 June 2021).

Ministry of External Affairs (2004) *Address by Shri K. Natwar Singh, Minister of External Affairs, at the Indian Association for Central and West Asian Studies (IACWAS), Jamia Milia Islamia*. Available at: https://mea.gov.in/Speeches-Statements.htm?dtl/3873/address+by+shri+k+natwar+singh+minister+of+external+affairs+at+the+indian+association+for+central+and+west+asian+studies+iacwas+jamia+milia+islamia (Accessed: 8 June 2021).

Ministry of External Affairs (2008) *Address by H.E. Mr. Pranab Mukherjee, Minister of External Affairs at a seminar on 'India and Iran: ancient civilisations and modern nations' in Tehran*. Available at: https://mea.gov.in/Speeches-Statements.htm?dtl/1768/address+by+hemr+pranab+mukherjee+minister+of+external+affairs+at+a+seminar+on+india+and+iran++ancient+civilizations+and+modern+nations+in+tehran (Accessed: 7 June 2021).

Ministry of External Affairs (2010) *Speech by foreign secretary at IDSA-IPIS strategic dialogue on India and Iran: an enduring relationship*. Available at: https://mea.gov.in/Speeches-Statements.htm?dtl/706/speech+by+foreign+secretary+at+idsaipis+strategic+dialogue+on+india+and+iran+an+enduring+relationship (Accessed: 7 June 2021).

Ministry of External Affairs (2012) *Remarks by Minister of State Shri E. Ahamed at the India Saudi Arabia Youth Forum*. Available at: https://mea.gov.in/Speeches-Statements.htm?dtl/19171/remarks+by+minister+of+state+shri+e+ahamed+at+the+indiasaudi+arabia+youth+forum (Accessed: 7 June 2021).

Ministry of External Affairs (2013a) *External affairs minister's speech at Global India Foundation conference on 'Iran's Eurasian dynamic: mapping regional and extra-regional interests'*. Available at: https://mea.gov.in/Speeches-Statements.htm?dtl/21246/external+affairs+ministers+speech+at+global+india+foundation+conference+on+irans+eurasian+dynamic+mapping+regional+and+extraregional+interests (Accessed: 7 June 2021).

Ministry of External Affairs (2013b) *Opening statement by external affairs minister at joint press conference with foreign minister of Kingdom of Saudi Arabia, in Jeddah*. Available at: https://mea.gov.in/Speeches-Statements.htm?dtl/21748/opening+statement+by+external+affairs+minister+at+joint+press+conference+with+foreign+minister+of+kingdom+of+saudi+arabia+in+jeddah (Accessed: 7 June 2021).

Ministry of External Affairs (2013c) *External affairs minister's interview to Arab News, Saudi Arabia May 27, 2013*. Available at: https://mea.gov.in/interviews.htm?dtl/21752/external+affairs+ministers+interview+to+arab+news+saudi+arabia+may+27+2013 (Accessed: 7 June 2021).

Ministry of External Affairs (2014) *Official visit of external affairs minister to United Arab Emirates (10–12 November, 2014)*. Available at: https://mea.gov.in/press-releases.htm?dtl/24203/official+visit+of+external+affairs+minister+to+united+arab+emirates+1012+november+2014 (Accessed: 8 June 2021).

36 *Saloni Kapur*

Ministry of External Affairs (2015a) *Prime minister's telephonic conversation with King Salman bin Abdul Aziz al Saud of Saudi Arabia.* Available at: https://mea.gov.in/press-releases.htm?dtl/25030/prime+ministers+telephonic+conversation+with+king+salman+bin+abdul+aziz+al+saud+of+saudi+arabia (Accessed: 8 June 2021).

Ministry of External Affairs (2015b) *Joint statement between the United Arab Emirates and the Republic of India.* Available at: https://mea.gov.in/bilateral-documents.htm?dtl/25733/joint+statement+between+the+united+arab+emirates+and+the+republic+of+india (Accessed: 8 June 2021).

Ministry of External Affairs (2015c) *Transcript of media briefing by foreign secretary in Dubai on prime minister's ongoing visit to United Arab Emirates (August 17, 2015).* Available at: https://mea.gov.in/media-briefings.htm?dtl/25735/transcript+of+media+briefing+by+foreign+secretary+in+dubai+on+prime+ministers+ongoing+visit+to+united+arab+emirates+august+17+2015 (Accessed: 8 June 2021).

Ministry of External Affairs (2016a) *Official visit of foreign minister of Saudi Arabia to India (March 07–08, 2016).* Available at: https://mea.gov.in/press-releases.htm?dtl/26478/official+visit+of+foreign+minister+of+saudi+arabia+to+india+march+0708+2016 (Accessed: 8 June 2021).

Ministry of External Affairs (2016b) *Prime minister's statement prior to his departure to Belgium, USA and Saudi Arabia.* Available at: https://mea.gov.in/Speeches-Statements.htm?dtl/26570/prime+ministers+statement+prior+to+his+departure+to+belgium+usa+and+saudi+arabia (Accessed: 8 June 2021).

Ministry of External Affairs (2016c) *Transcript of media briefing on prime minister's visit to Belgium, US and Saudi Arabia (March 28, 2016).* Available at: https://mea.gov.in/media-briefings.htm?dtl/26569/transcript+of+media+briefing+on+prime+ministers+visit+to+belgium+us+and+saudi+arabia+march+28+2016 (Accessed: 8 June 2021).

Ministry of External Affairs (2016d) *Transcript of media briefing by secretary (ER) in Riyadh on prime minister's visit to Saudi Arabia (April 3, 2016).* Available at: https://mea.gov.in/media-briefings.htm?dtl/26598/transcript+of+media+briefing+by+secretaryer+in+riyadh+on+prime+ministers+visit+to+saudi+arabia+april+3+2016 (Accessed: 8 June 2021).

Ministry of External Affairs (2016e) *India-Saudi Arabia joint statement during the visit of prime minister to Saudi Arabia (April 03, 2016).* Available at: https://mea.gov.in/bilateral-documents.htm?dtl/26595/indiasaudi+arabia+joint+statement+during+the+visit+of+prime+minister+to+saudi+arabia+april+03+2016 (Accessed: 8 June 2021).

Ministry of External Affairs (2017) *Question no. 512 mediation by Iran.* Available at: https://mea.gov.in/lok-sabha.htm?dtl/28640/question+no512+mediation+by+iran (Accessed: 8 June 2021).

Ministry of External Affairs (2018) *India-Iran joint statement during visit of the president of Iran to India (February 17, 2018).* Available at: https://mea.gov.in/bilateral-documents.htm?dtl/29495/indiairan+joint+statement+during+visit+of+the+president+of+iran+to+india+february+17+2018 (Accessed: 8 June 2021).

Ministry of External Affairs (2019a) *Question no. 1932 trade agreement with Iran.* Available at: https://mea.gov.in/lok-sabha.htm?dtl/31536/question+no1932+trade+agreement+with+iran (Accessed: 7 June 2021).

Ministry of External Affairs (2019b) *Foreign Office consultations between India and Iran.* Available at: https://mea.gov.in/press-releases.htm?dtl/31828/foreign+office+consultations+between+india+and+iran (Accessed: 7 June 2021).

India, the Persian Gulf and the Emergence of a Supercomplex   37

Ministry of External Affairs (2019c) *Prime minister meets president of Iran.* Available at: https://mea.gov.in/press-releases.htm?dtl/31869/prime+minister+meets+president+of+iran (Accessed: 7 June 2021).

Ministry of External Affairs (2019d) *India-Saudi Arabia joint statement during the state visit of His Royal Highness the Crown Prince of Saudi Arabia to India.* Available at: https://mea.gov.in/bilateral-documents.htm?dtl/31072/indiasaudi+arabia+joint+statement+during+the+state+visit+of+his+royal+highness+the+crown+prince+of+saudi+arabia+to+india (Accessed: 8 June 2021).

Ministry of External Affairs (2019e) *Transcript of media briefing by secretary (ER) during visit of EAM to UAE for the OIC Foreign Minister's Council (March 01, 2019).* Available at: https://mea.gov.in/media-briefings.htm?dtl/31110/transcript+of+media+briefing+by+secretary+er+during+visit+of+eam+to+uae+for+the+oic+foreign+ministers+council+march+01+2019 (Accessed: 8 June 2021).

Ministry of External Affairs (2020a) *Question no. 517 Iran-China deal.* Available at: https://mea.gov.in/lok-sabha.htm?dtl/32980/question+no517+iranchina+deal (Accessed: 7 June 2021).

Ministry of External Affairs (2020b) *Question no. 1362 MoU with Iran on Chabahar port.* Available at: https://mea.gov.in/rajya-sabha.htm?dtl/33036/question+no1362+mou+with+iran+on+chabahar+port (Accessed: 7 June 2021).

Ministry of External Affairs (2020c) *Question no. 1675 Chabahar port.* Available at: https://mea.gov.in/lok-sabha.htm?dtl/33013/question+no1675+chabahar+port (Accessed: 7 June 2021).

Ministry of External Affairs (2020d) *Question no. 1783 Chabahar-Zahedan rail project.* Available at: https://mea.gov.in/lok-sabha.htm?dtl/33022/question+no1783+chabaharzahedan+rail+project (Accessed: 7 June 2021).

Mohan, C.R. (2020) 'India must seize the new strategic possibilities with the Gulf', *The Indian Express*, 24 November. Available at: https://indianexpress.com/article/opinion/columns/india-gulf-nations-relations-trade-crude-oil-jaishankar-visit-7062948/ (Accessed: 6 October 2021).

Motamedi, M. (2021) 'Iran and China sign 25-year cooperation agreement', *Al Jazeera*, 27 March. Available at: https://www.aljazeera.com/news/2021/3/27/iran-and-china-sign-25-year-cooperation-agreement-in-tehran (Accessed: 6 October 2021).

Ojha, H. (2015) 'The India-Nepal crisis', *The Diplomat*, 27 November. Available at: https://thediplomat.com/2015/11/the-india-nepal-crisis/ (Accessed: 6 October 2021).

Pardesi, M.S. (2015) 'Is India a great power? Understanding great power status in contemporary international relations', *Asian Security*, 11 (1), pp. 1–30. doi: 10.1080/14799855.2015.1005737.

Pradhan, D. (2020) 'View: how India-Gulf ties are undergoing a fundamental reset', *The Economic Times*, 7 December. Available at: https://economictimes.indiatimes.com/news/economy/foreign-trade/view-how-india-gulf-ties-are-undergoing-a-fundamental-reset/articleshow/79602451.cms (Accessed: 6 October 2021).

Pröbsting, M. (2020) 'Is India a new emerging great power?', *Critique*, 48 (1), pp. 31–49. doi: 10.1080/03017605.2019.1706783.

Robinson, K. (2021) *What is the Iran nuclear deal?* Available at: https://www.cfr.org/backgrounder/what-iran-nuclear-deal (Accessed: 6 October 2021).

Roche, E. (2022) 'Will Prophet remarks controversy shake India-Middle East trade?', *Al Jazeera*, 16 June. Available at: https://www.aljazeera.com/economy/2022/6/16/will-prophet-remarks-controversy-shake-india-middle-east-trade-ties (Accessed: 17 June 2022).

38 Saloni Kapur

Saran, S. (2018) *How India sees the world: Kautilya to the 21st century.* New Delhi: Juggernaut Books.

Saran, S. (2020) 'Tightrope walk in the Gulf', *The Tribune*, 2 December. Available at: https://www.tribuneindia.com/news/punjab/tightrope-walk-in-the-gulf-178704 (Accessed: 6 October 2021).

Sharifi, M. (2021) 'Iran-China deal: the pro-agreement and anti-agreement division returns', *TRT World*, 30 March. Available at: https://www.trtworld.com/magazine/iran-china-deal-the-pro-agreement-and-anti-agreement-division-returns-45454 (Accessed: 6 October 2021).

Singh, S. (2021) 'The end of Modi's global dreams', *Foreign Policy*, 3 May. Available at: https://foreignpolicy.com/2021/05/03/india-vishwaguru-modi-second-wave-soft-power-self-sufficiency/ (Accessed: 6 October 2021).

Singh, K. and Roy, S. (2021) 'OVL loses operating rights for Iran's Farzad-B gas field', *The Indian Express*, 19 May. Available at: https://indianexpress.com/article/business/ovl-loses-operating-rights-for-irans-farzad-b-gas-field-7320606/ (Accessed: 6 October 2021).

Siyech, M.S. (2017) *The India-U.A.E. strategic partnership in regional context: a zero-sum game?* Available at: https://www.mei.edu/publications/india-uae-strategic-partnership-regional-context-zero-sum-game (Accessed: 9 June 2021).

Siyech, M.S. and Singh, K.R. (2018) *India's Iran quandary.* Available at: https://www.mei.edu/publications/indias-iran-quandary (Accessed: 9 June 2021).

The Economic Times (2021) 'TCS completes acquisition of GE's stake in TCS Saudi Arabia', 27 May. Available at: https://economictimes.indiatimes.com/tech/information-tech/tcs-completes-acquisition-of-ges-stake-in-tcs-saudi-arabia/articleshow/83009603.cms (Accessed: 7 October 2021).

The Eurasian Times (2020) 'India was never serious on Farzad-B gas field, wanted the US sanctions off first—Top Iranian source', 21 October. Available at: https://eurasiantimes.com/india-was-never-serious-in-farzad-b-gas-field-wanted-the-sanctions-off-first-iran/ (Accessed: 30 September 2021).

The Hindu (2021a) 'India has accelerated work on Chabahar port, likely to be declared operational by May: CRS', 9 April. Available at: https://www.thehindu.com/news/international/india-has-accelerated-work-on-chabahar-port-likely-to-be-declared-operational-by-may-crs/article34277332.ece (Accessed: 30 September 2021).

The Hindu (2021b) 'Reviving the Iran deal: on Biden attempt to revive JCPOA', 3 March. Available at: https://www.thehindu.com/opinion/editorial/reviving-the-iran-deal-on-biden-attempt-to-revive-jcpoa/article33974350.ece (Accessed: 6 October 2021).

Wani, S.H., Mir, M.A. and Shah, I.A. (2019) 'India-Iran trade relations under the shadow of USA sanctions', *Foreign Trade Review*, 54 (4), pp. 399–407. doi: 10.1177/0015732519874222.

2 Pakistan and the Gulf

Zahid Shahab Ahmed and Khurram Abbas

Introduction

While for decades Pakistan enjoyed trouble-free cooperative relations with the Gulf states, its bilateral relations have been tested by a variety of factors during 2010–2020. Even though Pakistan provides millions of workers to and has close security cooperation with the member states of the Gulf Cooperation Council (GCC), it is economically dependent on aid and remittances from them. This dynamic has been exploited by stronger Gulf states like Saudi Arabia and this was reflected following the Pakistani Parliament's decision to not participate in the Saudi-led military coalition to fight the Yemeni Houthis (Ahmed, 2018). Alongside this has been the challenge of Pakistan's neutrality in the Qatar-Gulf crisis in which Islamabad chose to mediate instead of taking a side. Among other irritants in Pakistan's relations with the Gulf, there have been longstanding issues involving India's cooperation and Iran's conflictual relations with the GCC states. The Abraham Peace Accords signed in 2020 have created another challenge for Pakistan as its close allies in the Gulf, such as Bahrain and the United Arab Emirates (UAE), have normalised their relations with Israel. By analysing these changing geopolitical dynamics, this chapter examines the impact of multiple factors on Pakistan's relations with the Gulf. The theoretical concept of Regional Security Complexes (RSCs) will be applied to this analysis because here clearly a split in Pakistan's relations with the GCC states is based on their divergent security concerns. In terms of GCC states, Bahrain, Saudi Arabia and the UAE view their relations with Israel as crucial to their security problems involving Iran. They also want to enhance their economic cooperation with Pakistan's arch-rival India which has the bigger economic potential compared to that of Pakistan. Islamabad needs to understand the Gulf states' security concerns, which are regional, to avoid any further troubles involving its ties with the GCC states.

We use RSCT to understand the degree to which the regional security environment of the Gulf region influences Pakistan's relations with the Gulf monarchies. Though significant literature is available on Pakistan's relations with GCC states (Ahmed and Bhatnagar, 2010; Ahmed, 2018; Ahmed and

DOI: 10.4324/9781003283058-3

40   *Zahid Shahab Ahmed and Khurram Abbas*

Akbarzadeh, 2020), the erstwhile literature has not used RSCT to examine the divergences between Pakistan and some GCC states. We believe that Pakistan needs to broaden its understanding of the Gulf region's geopolitical realities to re-evaluate its options in terms of cooperation, especially in security matters, with the Gulf states. As the chosen theory argues, actors' security concerns are limited to their immediate neighbourhood, which in the case of the Gulf states would be the Middle East. This dynamic is particularly relevant because Pakistan has been consistently disappointed by the lack of support it has received from the Gulf states concerning its disputes with India, for example, on the Jammu and Kashmir issue. While Pakistan continues to enjoy security cooperation with all the Gulf states, it is becoming clear that regional security dynamics facing the Gulf states, for example, the Iranian threat, are moving them closer to Israel. As scholars have argued, "Simple physical adjacency tends to generate more security interaction among neighbours than among states located in different areas" (Buzan and Waever, 2003: 45). In their work on RSCT, Buzan and Waever (2003) even point to the Middle East as an ideal case study where the security dynamics have remained the same since the Cold War:

> Security features at the level of regions are durable. They are substantially self-contained not in the sense of being totally free-standing, but rather in possessing a security dynamic that would exist even if other actors did not impinge on it. This relative autonomy was revealed by the ending of the Cold War, when enmities such as that between Israel and Syria, and Iraq and the Gulf Arab States, easily survived the demise of a superpower rivalry that had supported, but not generated, them.
>
> (Buzan and Waever, 2003: 47)

While Pakistan enjoys multifaceted cooperation with Gulf monarchies, its relations with some have been challenged by various developments including the Saudi demand for Pakistani troops against Yemeni Houthis, the Qatar-Gulf crisis and the Abraham Peace Accords. Among other irritants are the Gulf States' relations with India and Iran. This chapter examines all these issues and factors through the lens of regional dynamics to present a holistic picture of Pakistan's relations with GCC member states. In terms of the organisation of the paper, the chapter begins with an overview of Pakistan's relations with GCC states. This is followed by an analysis of various factors that influence Pakistan's relations with the Gulf region.

Pakistan's relations with the Gulf States

Pakistan values its vital social, financial and security relations with the GCC states. Except for a few political hiccups following the choice of Pakistan's parliament to not join the Saudi-led military campaign in Yemen,

Pakistan-GCC relations remained consistently cordial with all the Gulf nations. The relations are reinforced through several economic and security agreements including the provision of Pakistan's security umbrella to Saudi Arabia, which makes Islamabad the second-largest security guarantor of the Kingdom after the US. Pakistan's workforce for the GCC has remained crucial during the developmental phase of the GCC countries after their independence in the 1970s. The overwhelming presence of the Pakistani workforce in the GCC is also a reliable source of remittances for Pakistan. In terms of remittances from the GCC region, Pakistan received the most amount from Saudi Arabia (US$4.52 billion), the UAE (US$3.47 billion) and Qatar (US$302 million) (Siddiqa, 2017). To understand Pakistan's relationship with the GCC countries, it is important to dwell upon countries one by one including Saudi Arabia, the UAE, Qatar and Bahrain. These four GCC countries not only have an economic influence on Pakistan but also both sides had pegged high expectations to each other for diplomatic and military support during the time of any conflict or crisis.

Saudi Arabia

Saudi Arabia due to its two holiest sites—Mecca and Medina—maintains a significant position in the Muslim world. Pakistan being an Islamic Republic considers Saudi Arabia to be the most sacred land. Since Pakistan's independence, Pakistan and Saudi Arabia have established a multifaceted relationship including political, economic and cultural aspects. As an Islamic Republic and the second-biggest Muslim country, thousands of Pakistanis visit Saudi Arabia every year for *Hajj* and *Umrah*. In 2017, Pakistan's *Hajj* quota was increased from 143,368 to 179,210 (Ali, 2017). In 2016, *Umrah* pilgrims from Pakistan were 761,330, the second largest after the Egyptians (*Al Arabiya*, 2016). Since King Faisal's era, Saudi Arabia has been financially supporting thousands of Pakistani religious seminaries. The visit of the Imam-e-Kaaba to Pakistan has been considered one of the most celebrated events at the political and social levels in the country. Dr Saleh Bin Humaid, the Imam-e-Kaaba, visited Islamabad in October 2017 and was invited to attend a cabinet session by Prime Minister Shahid Khaqan Abbasi (*The Nation*, 2017b). Both countries attach great importance to consistent official dialogues; therefore, leading Saudi monarchs have regularly visited Pakistan. From the first visit of King Saud bin Abdulaziz Al Saud in 1954, his successors travelled to Pakistan in 1966, 1974, 1976 and 1980. King Abdullah visited as the then-crown prince in 1984, 1988, 1997 and 2003, and King Salman as a crown prince in 2014, while Crown Prince Mohammed bin Salman (MBS) visited in 2019, signed over 20 billion dollars of bilateral economic agreements, and provided aid and a soft loan as a bailout package for Pakistan.

Due to its fragile economy, Pakistan has undertaken extensive internal and external debts (Chaudhury, 2021). Therefore, Pakistan is dependent upon its friendly countries, especially Saudi Arabia, for economic assistance. Saudi Arabia has rescued Pakistan multiple times during economic crises, such as in 1965 and 1971, as well as during the economic sanctions of 1998–2001 (Abbas, 2016). During the economic sanctions on Pakistan, Saudi Arabia provided oil support and labelled the donation "a gift in times of need" (Ahmad, 2016a). Saudi Arabia also granted Pakistan a loan of US$380 million at the Tokyo Donor Conference in 2009 and presented a gift of US$300 million to help abate the high oil prices in 2015 (Karam, 2009; Naviwala, 2015). During 2003–2012, Pakistan was also the top recipient of humanitarian aid from the GCC countries. Also, Saudi Arabia is hosting the largest Pakistani expatriate community in the world—over 2 million—which is a sustainable source of remittances for Pakistan (Siddiqa, 2017). Saudi Arabia has also been engaged in the domestic political affairs of Pakistan. After the coup in 1998, Saudi Arabia rescued former Prime Minister Nawaz Sharif and hosted him in the Kingdom for a few years. During Pervez Musharraf's era (1999–2008), as a guarantor of the deal on Sharif's exile, Saudi Arabia pressured Sharif to value the deal and keep living in the Kingdom till 2008 (Bhatti, 2017).

With the Islamic leanings of Pakistan, and the lavish economic support and overwhelming dependence on remittances from Saudi Arabia, the Kingdom's stability and security have become priorities for the Pakistani leadership. Pakistan has been seen as the second largest and strongest guarantor of the Kingdom after the US (Abbas, 2019b). Therefore, Pakistan's civil and military leadership have repeatedly assured the Saudi leadership that Pakistan will go to any extent for the security and territorial integrity of Saudi Arabia. The strong defence cooperation has manifested in practical measures with Pakistan's decision to station 15,000 troops in Saudi Arabia during the 1970s and 1980s (Mason, 2016). Bilateral defence relations were formalised through the 1982 Protocol Agreement entitling the Kingdom to request Pakistani troops when required. During the invasion of Kuwait by Iraq in 1990–1991, Pakistan sent 15,000 troops to Saudi Arabia for the protection of the holy sites and provided tanks and armoured vehicles (Ahmad and Faisal, 2016).

The two countries have been engaged in regular high-profile military exchanges and hold regular exercises such as Al-Assam I in 2004, Al-Assam II in 2006 and Al-Assam III in 2009 (Ahmad and Faisal, 2016). Further, Saudi Arabia has also been buying Pakistani defence equipment such as Al-Khalid tanks and JF-17 Thunder fighter jets (Faisal and Haider, 2014). Currently, there are 1,180 Pakistani troops stationed in Saudi Arabia, mostly as training instructors (Anis, 2016). The defence cooperation is strengthened by Pakistan's membership of the Islamic Military Alliance to Fight Terrorism (IMAFT). The Saudi-led IMAFT is a 41-nation coalition currently headed by Pakistan's former army chief, Reheel Sharif. The two countries acknowledge the potential for joint ventures in defence manufacturing and the further enhancement of defence and security cooperation at multiple levels.

The UAE

Pakistan recognised the UAE in 1971 and forged a cordial partnership based on mutual trust and a strong cultural relationship. Since then, the UAE and Pakistan enjoy cooperation at multiple levels including culture, economics, politics and defence. The UAE is one of the biggest donors of humanitarian assistance to Pakistan. At multiple times, the UAE has economically supported Pakistan during economic crises. The UAE is also one of Pakistan's largest trading partners from the GCC. The UAE hosts the second-largest expatriate community of Pakistan (Siddiqa, 2017). The relationship between the two countries is not limited to the state-to-state level. Rather, personal friendships between the leadership of the two countries have also been developed based on cultural affinity, mutual interests and trust. Emirati monarchs have close relations with Pakistan's two political parties, the Pakistan Muslim League–Nawaz (PML-N) and Pakistan Peoples Party (PPP). The UAE and Pakistan have multiple defence, security, economic and cultural agreements. High-profile visits of the civil and military leadership of Pakistan to the UAE have become an official norm in the country. However, the relationship has been witnessing a few ups and downs due to Pakistan's refusal to send its military to Yemen in 2015 and the UAE's closeness to India. These factors will be discussed below in detail.

Bahrain

Pakistan and Bahrain enjoy a strong security, political and economic relationship. Security cooperation peaked in 2011, when Pakistan helped Bahrain to curb a Shiite uprising by sending retired military officials of various ranks through the Bahria (Naval) Foundation and Fauji (Army) Foundation (*Dawn*, 2014b). The countries have also been engaged in regular state-level visits. For example, the then-Prime Minister, Yousuf Raza Gillani, visited Bahrain in 2008 with the key goal of enhancing bilateral relations. Before that, in 2006, Shaikh Salman bin Hamad Al-Khalifa visited Pakistan to negotiate a free-trade agreement. Bilateral defence cooperation has steadily improved since a visit of Pakistan's Defence Minister to Bahrain in 2008 (Ahmed and Bhatnagar, 2010). The King of Bahrain, Shaikh Hamad Bin Isa Al Khalifa, visited Pakistan in 2014. During his stay, he had a meeting at the Joint Services Headquarters in Rawalpindi and appreciated Pakistan's military support (*Dawn*, 2014a). The two countries are currently negotiating a bilateral Free-Trade Agreement and seeking out

44 *Zahid Shahab Ahmed and Khurram Abbas*

various avenues of economic cooperation. In this context, the second business-opportunities conference was organised in Islamabad in March 2017. There are 112,000 Pakistani skilled workers in Bahrain (Siddiqa, 2017).

Qatar

Pakistan and Qatar have enjoyed a consistent and sustained relationship since 1971. The bilateral relationship has been further institutionalised through regular high-profile visits, especially in the early decades of Qatar's independence in the 1970s and 1980s. Sheikh Khalifa bin Hamad Al Thani's visits to Pakistan in the 1970s and 1980s paved the way for long-term economic and security cooperation between the two countries. Pakistan reciprocated Qatar's high-profile visits. President General Zia-ul-Haq visited Doha in 1985 (Atique, 1985). In recent times, there have been frequent high-level interactions, for example, the emir of Qatar visited Pakistan in 2015, and the President of Pakistan visited Qatar in 2016. Since the start of the 21st century, there have been key agreements signed to boost bilateral economic cooperation. In 2007, the Qatari finance minister signed several agreements and memorandums of understanding for cooperation on industrial zones and energy projects in Pakistan (Ahmed and Bhatnagar, 2010).

There has also been an agreement through which Pakistan imports Liquid Natural Gas (LNG) from Qatar. The LNG project has become Pakistan's lifeline because it considerably reduces the cost of electricity production and minimises the shortfall of electricity in the country. According to a report, Pakistan imports 3.75 million tonnes of LNG annually from Qatar to add 2,000 MW of electricity (Shahid, 2017). Qatar is hosting around 115,000 Pakistani expatriates who are an important source of remittances for Pakistan (Siddiqa, 2017). The relationship between Qatar and Pakistan is not confined to the state-to-state and institution-to-institution levels. Rather, the ruling family of Qatar has a relationship with the PML-N leadership (Ahmed and Bhatnagar, 2010). A recent example is that of the participation of a Qatari royal in the corruption charges against deposed former Prime Minister Nawaz Sharif. In this whole episode of the Panamagate hearing,[1] the Sharifs' case was linked to Hamad Bin Jassim Bin Jaber Al-Thani (prime minister of Qatar during 2007–2013), who submitted two letters to the Supreme Court of Pakistan to clarify the Sharif family's business ties and money trail in the Middle East.

Kuwait

Pakistan-Kuwait relations are diverse, spanning trade, culture and security. Both countries share a vision of regional security, i.e., mediation, reconciliation and an end to conflicts. This is evident from the responses of both countries to regional conflicts such as Yemen, the Qatar/Gulf crisis, etc.

The two countries remained neutral and played an active role as mediators to defuse tensions between the wary parties. Pakistan is keen to develop its weapons market in Kuwait. In a bid to sell fighter jets, Pakistan offered to sell Pakistan Aeronautical Complex/Chengdu Aerospace Corporation (PAC/CAC) JF-17 Thunder fighter jets and PAC Super Mushshak trainer aircraft in 2016; however, Kuwait has not yet finalised the deal (Gady, 2016). Kuwait has been one of the largest contributors of emergency assistance to Pakistan during natural disasters. Kuwait was the first country to send aid to Pakistan-administered Jammu and Kashmir and pledged a generous US$100 million in aid for earthquake-affected areas (*BBC*, 2005). Kuwait had banned work and family visas for Pakistanis in 2011. After a decade-long suspension, Kuwait resumed visas for the family and business categories, which is evidence of improved bilateral cooperation (*The News*, 2021). However, Kuwait's growing relationship with India and its neutrality in the Kashmir dispute have become major factors in the relationship between Pakistan and Kuwait. The relationship was rattled when Kuwait supported the Indian stance on the Kashmir dispute, which was a political shock for Pakistan (Abbas, 2019a).

The economic cooperation between the two countries largely revolves around the oil trade between the two countries. Kuwait has been a long-time supplier of white oil products (useful in pharmaceuticals, cosmetics and chemical processing) to Pakistan and has long had ambitions to build a refinery designed specifically to use Kuwaiti crude (Shaikh, 2020). Pakistan State Oil continues to have a long-term contract under which it purchases High-Speed Diesel and other white products from Kuwait and enjoys favourable payment terms (Shaikh, 2020). The Kuwait Foreign Petroleum Exploration Company (KUFPEC) has been investing in Pakistan and, since 1987, its investment has exceeded $1 billion (Shaikh, 2020). Currently, 109,853 Pakistanis are living in Kuwait, which makes them the sixth-largest foreign community hosted by Kuwait (Toumi, 2016).

Oman

Pakistan and Oman have centuries-old cultural, economic and security cooperation. Oman is considered Pakistan's fifth neighbouring country due to Muscat's proximity to Gwadar. There is a large segment of the Omani population with ethnic links to Pakistani Balochistan. The distance between Oman and Pakistan is merely 202 nautical miles from the Gwadar seaport. Both countries share similar positions on various regional-security issues. Oman follows a policy of neutrality and peace in the GCC, while Pakistan also aspires to develop a balanced relationship with all GCC countries and Iran. Following the Saudi campaign in Yemen and the Qatar/Gulf crisis, Oman remained neutral and did not follow the Saudi-led bloc's policies. The Sultanate has followed a policy of peace and friendship with all its neighbours. It is pertinent to mention that Oman played a vital role in the

46 *Zahid Shahab Ahmed and Khurram Abbas*

culmination of the Joint Comprehensive Plan of Action (JCPOA) between the P5+1 and Iran signed in 2015 (Almajdoub, 2016).

Pakistan and Oman have strong cooperation in the naval field. Joint naval exercises, naval training and exchange of cadets at naval academies are some areas of bilateral naval cooperation between the two countries. In February 2018, Oman signed an agreement with India for providing the Duqm port to India for the refuelling and maintenance of New Delhi's naval ships (Abbas, 2019a). Pakistan had strong concerns over Oman's decision, which it privately conveyed to Oman. However, Oman has clarified to Pakistan that the Duqm port will not be handed over as a full-fledged naval base for security or surveillance to India (Abbas, 2019a). Pakistan is of the view that with the Gwadar deep seaport becoming functional and China-Pakistan Economic Corridor (CPEC) projects gaining momentum, Pakistan-Oman bilateral relations can foresee a higher level of interaction (Hafeez, 2020).

Irritants in Pakistan-Gulf relations

The above discussion reflects that the Pakistan-GCC relationship is highly cordial and the GCC states, especially Saudi Arabia, the UAE, Bahrain and Qatar, enjoy good relations with Pakistan. However, the dawn of the second decade of the 21st century has witnessed multiple irritants in the relationship of Pakistan to the GCC countries. These irritants include Pakistan's desire for neutrality and its self-assumed mediatory role in GCC conflicts with a particular emphasis on Iran, Indian growing influence in the GCC and Pakistani concerns, Pakistan's response to the Qatar-Gulf diplomatic crisis and the Abraham Peace Accords and subsequent diplomatic pressure of the GCC countries to recognise Israel. These factors will be discussed in detail to understand their impact on the Pakistan-GCC relationship.

The Iran factor

Since the Islamic Revolution in Iran, the GCC-Iran relationship has been conflictual. Though Iran enjoys a limited level of cooperation with Oman and Qatar, relations with Saudi Arabia and the UAE are conflictual in nature at the bilateral and regional levels. Multiple reasons led to this conflictual relationship. Iran does not accept Saudi Arabia as a leader of the Muslim Ummah. Tehran's proxies in the Middle East such as Hezbollah and the Houthis, threaten Saudi regional interests. Iran's explicit support to Shiite uprisings in Bahrain and Saudi Arabia has manifested Tehran's strategy of regime change in GCC countries. Iran's territorial dispute with the UAE over the control of the disputed islands of Abu Musa, Greater Tunb and Lesser Tunb has further marred its relationship with the GCC countries (Majidyar, 2018). Moreover, the Iranian aggressive policies during the Donald Trump era have injected unprecedented fear among the GCC countries.

In response to the US maximum-pressure campaign, on 4 December 2018, President Hassan Rouhani publicly declared that Iran would not allow any nation to export oil through the Strait of Hormuz if Iranian oil exports were halted (DiChristopher, 2018). This was an implicit threat to oil exports by Iran's neighbours, Saudi Arabia and the UAE. The threat created some ripple effects as 30 per cent of the world's oil exports pass through the Strait of Hormuz. Iran's threats to halt all oil exports by the Gulf countries were soon followed by military escalations in the Persian Gulf and the Gulf of Oman. There were well-coordinated military attacks on two oil tankers near the Strait of Hormuz on 13 June 2019, preceded by similar attacks on Saudi and Emirati oil tankers off the UAE coast on 12 May 2019 (Rania El Gamal, 2019). The oil-tanker attacks created tensions in the Gulf. The high level of threat perception from Iran has compelled the GCC countries to import sophisticated weapons and to modernise their militaries to make them capable of handling regional conflicts. The Abraham Accords between Israel and two GCC countries (Bahrain and the UAE) aim to strengthen regional alliances against Iran (Bowen, 2020). Iran naturally has not welcomed the peace deals and is worried that other GCC states, especially Saudi Arabia and Oman, might also normalise their relations with Israel (Hafezi, 2020).

Pakistan has adopted the self-assumed role of a mediator between the GCC and Iran. For Pakistan, choosing sides would damage its economic and political interests. On the one hand, Pakistan has strong economic and defence relations with the GCC countries, while on the other hand, it shares a 980-km border with Iran. Owing to the fact that the largest Pakistani expatriate community resides in the GCC, souring its relationship with the Gulf region is nearly impossible for Pakistan because Islamabad is dependent on remittances from the Gulf region. Likewise, the nearly 15–20 per cent Shia population of Pakistan favours a better relationship with Iran due to their sectarian leanings. The proxy war of the GCC countries and Iran led to sectarian violence in Pakistan during the 1980s and 1990s. During 1989–2018, 3,072 incidents of sectarian violence led to 5,602 casualties in Pakistan (South Asia Terrorism Portal, 2018). While Iran has successfully spread its tentacles in the Middle East through its proxies, it has also been able to create similar terrorist paraphernalia in the Afghanistan-Pakistan (Af-Pak) region in the shape of two battle-hardened groups—the Liwa Fatemiyoun (Fatemiyoun Brigade) and the Liwa Zainebeyoun (Zainebeyoun Brigade). Both the groups have fought in the Syrian theatre against the anti-Baathist regime factions and Sunni militant groups like Jabhat al-Nusra and Daesh.

As discussed above, Pakistan has been a strong supporter of pan-Islamism since its creation in 1947. For Pakistan, a united front of all Muslim countries serves its interests better, as compared to a divided and lacklustre approach of Muslim countries. For instance, the OIC has been consistently used by Pakistan to gain the Muslim world's support towards its stance on the Jammu and Kashmir dispute with India. A united voice

48 *Zahid Shahab Ahmed and Khurram Abbas*

of Muslim countries in support of Pakistan has been a long-term desire, which materialised during the initial years of the establishment of the OIC. Further, the division among two major Muslim countries, i.e., Saudi Arabia and Iran, lands Pakistan in a difficult situation, as Saudi Arabia often pressurises Pakistan to choose its side in its conflict with Iran. Therefore, it often finds ways of mediating between the two leading Muslim countries. Though Pakistan may have a tilt towards Saudi Arabia due to excessive economic reliance on the Kingdom, Islamabad has positioned itself in a way to balance the relationship between the two arch-rivals of the Gulf (Ahmed and Akbarzadeh, 2020). In 2016, after the execution of Shia Saudi cleric and activist Nimr al-Nimr, the Iranian reaction heightened tensions between Iran and Saudi Arabia. The Iranian public stormed into the Saudi mission in Tehran and set it on fire (Abbas, 2019b). In response, the Kingdom had cut all diplomatic ties with Iran. In this crisis, Pakistan played a communicator's role between the Saudi rulers and the Iranian government that eventually led to a defusing of tensions between the two countries (Abbas, 2019b). Likewise, in 2019, Prime Minister of Pakistan Imran Khan visited Iran and Saudi Arabia with the key agenda of acting as a mediator to resolve the growing differences between the two countries (Shams, 2019). Later, in August 2020, Khan claimed that his mediation between Tehran and Riyadh "played an important role in defusing tensions between Saudi Arabia and Iran" (*Al Jazeera*, 2020).

However, Pakistan's role as a mediator has not been accepted by Saudi Arabia and the UAE. Rather, they expect Islamabad to side with the Gulf countries during times of crisis with Iran. Saudi Arabia pressed Pakistan to side with Riyadh against Tehran multiple times, especially in 2016. Two high-profile visits from the Kingdom to Islamabad took place during the crisis. Within a week, MBS, who was then deputy crown prince, and Adel al-Jubeir, the foreign minister of Saudi Arabia, visited Pakistan. Moreover, the Kingdom had included Pakistan in its Islamic Military Alliance. Though Pakistan cautiously responded to its inclusion into the Islamic Military Alliance, it turned down Saudi requests to side with Riyadh against Tehran (Riedel, 2016). Despite strategic cooperation in diverse fields, these nuances in the relationship have created a stiffness in the bilateral relationship between the two countries. Riyadh has shown its displeasure to Pakistan through various gestures. For instance, it has persistently denied Pakistan's mediation and repeatedly told Pakistan to uphold its promises of the Kingdom's security and territorial integrity (Abbas, 2019b).

The India factor

As discussed earlier, contrary to the hopes of the Saudi-led bloc, Pakistan adopted neutrality and a mediatory role in the Yemen conflict and Qatar's diplomatic crisis. The response of the Saudi-led Arab bloc to Pakistan's

Pakistan and the Gulf 49

back-to-back refusals has been a major shift in the GCC's foreign policy. Pakistan's refusal was unexpected for the Saudi-led Arab bloc. The Emirati leadership was furious. The UAE deputy foreign minister, Dr Anwar Mohammed Gargash, threatened Pakistan with consequences (*Dawn*, 2015). A few months later, Saudi Arabia conferred its highest civil award on Indian Prime Minister Narendra Modi (*The Indian Express*, 2016), which was an explicit reaction of Riyadh to Islamabad's refusal. During Modi's state visit to Saudi Arabia, both countries signed a joint statement condemning cross-border terrorism and promising to cut support for states that provide safe havens to terrorists. Typically, New Delhi ascribes "cross-border terrorism" to Pakistan. Therefore, such a statement was a signal of change in the Saudi Arabian strategic thinking. Moreover, Saudi Arabia also voted in favour of the proscription of several militant groups, including Lashkar-e-Taiba, two days before Modi's visit to Saudi Arabia, which is unprecedented (Ahmad, 2016b).

In contrast to Turkey and Iran, the Saudi-led GCC bloc remained silent on Indian actions in Jammu and Kashmir. Contrary to their previous roles in Indo-Pak conflicts, Saudi Arabia and the UAE acted as passive mediators and facilitators to defuse tensions between the two South Asian nuclear arch-rivals. This is a clear manifestation of a policy shift in Saudi and Emirati foreign policy that they will no longer choose sides in Pakistan's conflicts. During a visit of the UAE crown prince Muhammad Bin Zayed, the Kashmir dispute was not mentioned in the press release owing to the UAE's hesitation due to its economic relationship with India (MOFA, 2019). Furthermore, the OIC not only invited India as "guest of honour" to its 46th ministerial session, but it has also de-hyphenated Kashmir from Palestine, which is evident from its final communiqué (OIC, 2019).

From the killing of Burhan Wani (a young freedom fighter of Jammu and Kashmir) to the revocation of Articles 370 and 35A by India, both countries did not officially condemn Indian actions. Saudi Arabia is still reluctant to hold an OIC Summit to discuss the issue. This has frustrated Pakistan, which had been counting on the Saudi-dominated OIC to back Islamabad's position on the Kashmir dispute. In August 2020, Pakistan's Foreign Minister Shah Mahmood Qureshi criticised Riyadh for not allowing the OIC to hold a meeting on the Kashmir issue (Dawn, 2020).

In response, Saudi Arabia and the UAE demanded that Pakistan repay their loans (Syed, 2018). As has often been the case, Pakistan's military stepped in to try to assist on the issue of loan repayment, with a quick visit of the country's army chief, General Qamar Javed Bajwa, to Saudi Arabia, but he was denied an audience with MBS (Basit and Ahmed, 2020). To some experts, Pakistan's policy of neutrality hurts the bilateral relationship between Pakistan and the Saudi-led bloc. Former President Musharraf believes that Pakistan should have supported Saudi Arabia and the UAE in the Qatar diplomatic crisis as both countries always supported Pakistan during good and bad times (*Dawn*, 2017). Contrary to this opinion, some

50 *Zahid Shahab Ahmed and Khurram Abbas*

experts opine that the policy of neutrality is in Pakistan's national interest, as by this policy, Pakistan will be able to retain some leverage over all the GCC countries (Abbas, 2019b).

Recent disturbances

To understand how Pakistan's relations with GCC states have been challenged by some recent events, we now present three case studies to show some hiccups in the last decade.

The Yemeni Civil War

The Yemeni Civil War that started in 2014 has created new security challenges for neighbouring states, especially Saudi Arabia. Riyadh and its other regional allies, for example, the UAE, view the Yemeni Houthis as Iran's proxies and have been aggressively trying to crush the Houthi militants. The decision to attack Yemen's Houthis through a Saudi-led coalition was orchestrated by MBS. He was appointed as Minister of Defence on 23 January 2015 (*BBC*, 2018). A series of events, including the fall of Northern Yemen, the Houthis' seizing control of Yemen's capital, and the ouster of Yemen's President Abdrabbuh Mansur Hadi, posed an enormous national-security threat to Saudi Arabia (*BBC*, 2018). As Minister of Defence, MBS took the bold decision to launch airstrikes against the Houthis (*BBC*, 2018). He had claimed that he would curb this national-security threat within six months (Hiro, 2018). Despite rigorous efforts, his claim proved wrong as the Saudi-led military alliance for Yemen continues. Scholars claim that instead of unilateralism, the Kingdom is following the path of multilateralism to attain its strategic and political objectives (Tamamy, 2012). The establishment of IMAFT in 2015 is a glaring example of Saudi-led military alliances against its adversaries in the region (Abbas, 2017). Perhaps the reason for adopting this path could be the lack of a strong military muscle (Ahmed, 2018). Therefore, the Kingdom has played a leading role in the past in establishing various multilateral organisations including the GCC, the OIC and the Arab League.

Initially, Saudi Arabia established a partnership with nine Arab states and the US. Washington has been a part of this anti-Houthi coalition for obvious reasons, for example, due to fears of disruption of the trade route and access to oil as it had previously articulated that the volatility in Yemen challenged its interests (Exum, 2015). Despite the military strength of the initial coalition, Riyadh was eager for Pakistan's participation in the coalition. This is indicative of an age-old reliance in the Kingdom on military backing from Pakistan. The Saudi demand for troops was not a surprise to Islamabad because the country has a long history of international troop contributions, especially in United Nations peacekeeping missions.

Due to Pakistan's commitments under the 1982 military agreement and being the second-largest security guarantor of the Kingdom, the demand for formally participating in the Saudi-led coalition was inevitable and natural from the GCC countries (Mason, 2016). Since 2004, there have been joint military exercises between the two countries, for example, Al-Assam I in 2004, Al-Assam II in 2006 and Al-Assam III in 2009 (Ahmad and Faisal, 2016). Saudi Arabia is a top buyer of Pakistani weapons, including Al-Khalid tanks and JF-17 fighter jets (Ahmad and Faisal, 2016). As the incumbent Defence Minister, Khawaja Asif, has confirmed, 1,180 Pakistan Army personnel are serving in Saudi Arabia as training instructors (Anis, 2016). This shows an advanced level of military cooperation between both countries. This contextual understanding is important to make sense of Saudi-led GCC demand for the contribution of Pakistani troops in Yemen's War.

Contrary to the expectations of GCC countries, Islamabad decided to remain neutral in Yemen's conflict. Islamabad further articulated its Middle East policy based on factors such as neutrality, mediation and balanced inter-state relations between Iran and the GCC countries (*The Nation*, 2017b). The decision of the parliament to refrain from participation in IMAFT demonstrated this strategy of safeguarding the country's national interests and a desire to avoid Saudi and Iranian proxies in the Middle East. In discussions on Yemen in 2015, most of the parliamentarians focused on a political and diplomatic solution. There were various compelling reasons for Pakistan's denial of the Saudi request for joining the Saudi-led coalition in Yemen's war. War fatigue of the Pakistani forces against terrorism, fear of a sectarian backlash and a desire for an improved relationship with Iran led to Islamabad's policy shift towards the GCC.

The GCC countries in general, and Saudi Arabia in particular, were not expecting Pakistan's blunt refusal. In response to Pakistan's refusal, Saudi Arabia pressured Islamabad through Kuwait and the UAE. The GCC countries viewed the Pakistani government's initial decision as a betrayal (Wasty, 2017). The editor-in-chief of *Al Seyassah*, a Kuwaiti newspaper, wrote: "The Pakistani stance [...] adopted through the parliament's decision to remain neutral has dropped the blackmail masks about protecting sacred Islamic sites and sharing a common destiny with Muslim countries" (Toumi, 2016). In addition, the UAE's Minister of State for Foreign Affairs, Dr Anwar Mohammed Gargash, said, "The Pakistani parliament's resolution, which promoted neutrality on the Yemeni conflict, and voiced support for Saudi Arabia is contradictory and dangerous and unexpected from Islamabad" (*The Express Tribune*, 2015). Pakistan's refusal to join the Saudi-led coalition in Yemen's war still haunts Pakistan-GCC relations. The mistrust persists in the GCC over Pakistan's commitments to the Kingdom's territorial security and is a major stumbling block to a cordial relationship.

52 *Zahid Shahab Ahmed and Khurram Abbas*

The Qatar-Gulf crisis

Over the past two decades, a major shift in the foreign policy of Pakistan has been observed in that Islamabad will no longer take sides in intra-Arab conflicts. This is evident with Pakistan's response to the Qatar diplomatic crisis in 2017. In the past, during the Saudi-Yemen conflict in 1969 and Saddam Hussain's attack on Kuwait in 1991, Pakistan explicitly took sides in intra-Arab conflicts and sent troops to protect Saudi Arabia (Abbas, 2019). However, the response to Qatar's diplomatic crisis was in line with the policy shift of Islamabad. The socio-economic and political transformation of the country under various governments has compelled Pakistan to remain neutral in various intra-Arab tensions or conflicts. Therefore, Prime Minister Khan argues that the country's foreign policy aims to "safeguard" its national interests "to forge cordial and friendly relations with all neighbours, Muslim countries and the larger international community" (Khan, 2015). As discussed earlier, Pakistan enjoys not only a social, cultural, political, economic, strategic and security relationship but also a certain degree of friendship among the ruling elite of the GCC countries and Pakistan. Hence, in June 2017, the government of Pakistan was perturbed by the Qatar-Gulf crisis (*The Economist*, 2017). Following the Qatar-Gulf crisis, King Salman asked Nawaz Sharif to take a side while he was visiting Saudi Arabia in June 2017. The Sharif family of Pakistan enjoys a very cordial business partnership and friendly relationship with the Qatari ruling elite. As discussed earlier, Hamad Bin Jassim bin Jaber Al-Thani (prime minister of Qatar during 2007–2013) tried to rescue Nawaz Sharif during the Supreme Court hearing in 2017. Hence, it was also a puzzle for Sharif because he did not want to be partial between the elites of the two countries, with whom he enjoys brotherly relations.

Hence, Pakistan decided to adopt a mediatory role and offered to mediate between Qatar and other actors of the diplomatic crisis (Abbas, 2019). Equally, it is important to notice that all the GCC stakeholders view Pakistan as an important country. This is evident through official exchanges, especially since 2017, and the levels of cooperation between Pakistan and Saudi Arabia, the UAE, Bahrain and Qatar. In the aftermath of the crisis, there have been regular exchanges between high-ranking officials from Pakistan and Saudi Arabia, the UAE and Qatar. Before Nawaz Sharif's short visit to Saudi Arabia on 13 June, a Qatari delegation headed by the secretary of the Qatari emir, Abdul Hadi Mana Al Hajri, had visited Islamabad on 8 June to explain the nature of the diplomatic crisis with Arab countries. A month later, on 18 July, the foreign minister of Qatar, Sheikh Mohammed bin Abdulrahman al-Thani, arrived in Islamabad to gain Pakistan's support in connection with Doha's lingering conflict (Yousaf, 2017). Simultaneously, there have been regular visits by Pakistani officials, such as Prime Minister Shahid Khaqan Abbasi and Army Chief General Qamar Javed Bajwa, to Saudi Arabia and the UAE. The recent bilateral exchanges, however, have not focused on Pakistan's mediation in the Qatar-Gulf conflict. This could be because Pakistan's earlier attempts to mediate had received a lukewarm response from the conflicting parties, especially from the Saudi-led Arab countries, because they wished to see Pakistan on their side in this conflict (Wasty, 2017).

Saudi Arabia demanded that Pakistan take a side in the Qatar-Gulf crisis (Wasty, 2017). This is not the first time that Saudi Arabia has pressured Pakistan to follow Riyadh's policy in a conflict. Since Pakistan's refusal to join the Saudi-led campaign in Yemen, the relationship between the Saudi-led bloc and Pakistan was strained, which was later improved when Pakistan decided to join the Saudi-led international Islamic force to counter terrorism. This means the foreign-policy officials of Pakistan were again facing a diplomatic puzzle. In the wake of the Qatar-Gulf rift, Pakistan faced a test of its foreign policy, which aims to maintain good relations with the conflicting parties. While Sharif and his family have businesses in Saudi Arabia and the UAE, Sharif could not distance himself from Qatar at a critical juncture in his political career, i.e., the Panamagate hearing. According to Shahid (2017), the Qatari royal family had provided Sharif with assurances to rescue him in the Panama Papers corruption charges.

Contrary to the Saudi-led Arab bloc, "neutral" and "balanced foreign policy" were the buzzwords of Pakistan's response. Pakistan's foreign office issued a statement saying, "Pakistan believes in unity among Muslim countries. We have made consistent efforts for its promotion. The situation, therefore, is a matter of concern" (MOFA, 2017). Similar was the response at the time of the diplomatic crisis between Saudi Arabia and Iran in 2016. Then Pakistan's adviser to the prime minister on foreign affairs, Sartaj Aziz, said: "Pakistan has been playing an active role in reducing tensions and promoting unity within the Muslim Ummah" (Aziz, 2016). This response explains the nature of neutrality and to some extent a desire of maintaining unity with the Muslim world.

The response of Qatar and the Saudi-led bloc to Pakistan's refusal to take sides in the diplomatic crisis led to inadvertent ramifications for Pakistan. The crisis further improved the Pakistan-Qatar relationship diplomatically and economically. The bilateral trade between the two countries substantially increased in subsequent months (SBP, 2017). In the first quarter of 2017, Qatar imported goods and services worth US$20 million from Pakistan and had exports worth US$358 million (Aziz, 2017). The new developments show positive consequences of the conflict while Qatar keeps exploring more opportunities for economic cooperation with Pakistan. Some relevant steps have been taken, for example, a Qatari shipping company (Milaha) has started a direct service between ports in Qatar and Karachi (Milaha, 2017). This is to the benefit of both countries because the new service will cut short the time and costs of trade. As the trade routes between Qatar and its GCC neighbours were blocked, Doha was eager to find alternative options. In this context, the ports of Pakistan offered connectivity and cooperation. Moreover, Qatar has relaxed its visa rules for many countries including Pakistan and now the Pakistani workforce has been benefitting from the visa-on-arrival service in Qatar (Khatri, 2017). The relaxation of the visa policy was a significant relief for the Pakistani workforce owing to the lower ranking of the Pakistani passport in terms of visa-free arrivals (Mangi, 2018). Qatar's decision has also strengthened the people-to-people relations between the two countries.

It is a positive outcome of Pakistan's decision in 2017 that Pakistan's civil and military leadership has developed a regular interaction with the Qatari rulers. Recently, the Chief of Army Staff General Qamar Javed Bajwa visited Qatar and while meeting state officials including the Emir of Qatar, he also witnessed the passing-out parade at Ahmed Bin Muhammad Military College. The defence and security cooperation between the two countries, which was stalled during the first decade of the 21st century largely due to Islamabad's treatment of Qatar as an extension of Saudi Arabia, now seems to be on the horizon. But for Saudi Arabia, it was another episode of "betrayal" from the Pakistani side in less than two years. Back-to-back refusals of Pakistan to join hands with Saudis in their conflicts led to serious mistrust in the bilateral relationship. The level of mistrust was so evident that after the Salman-Sharif Summit on 14 June 2017, the two sides could not publish a joint statement for the public.

The Abraham peace accords

As RSCT posits, actors' security concerns are primary generated in their immediate neighbourhood or regional environment. In a particular regional setting, actors are locked into a situation in which their security concerns interact, therefore, actors feel strongly about security challenges that are near them in terms of distance (Walt, 1987). It is due to this proximity of security threats that GCC states have leaned towards Israel to counter their collective threat concerning Iran. While there were informal relations between some GCC states and Israel for several years, they have now formalised through the Abraham Peace Accords. This has significance for Pakistan's relations with the Gulf.

After US mediation, the Abraham Peace Accords were signed in September 2020, paving the way for the UAE and Bahrain to establish diplomatic relations with Israel. Unlike Bahrain and the UAE, there is no formal agreement between Saudi Arabia and Israel, but there have been meetings between officials from both countries. Considering Saudi Arabia's cooperative relations with Bahrain and the UAE, it is safe to say that the Abraham Peace Accords were reached with Riyadh's approval. There is a clear geopolitical dimension here, because three GCC states and Israel are locked in a geostrategic competition with Iran and its proxies, for example, Hezbollah, Hamas and the Houthis in the Middle East. Apart from conventional security threats, several other factors, including weaknesses of the regional-security architecture, shared security concerns emanating from Iran and the dilemma of failed political and military campaigns in Yemen and Qatar, respectively, have compelled these Arab nations to shift from their longstanding confrontational policies towards Israel and engage with it to avert such challenges at a regional level.

Pakistan remained careful amid these Middle Eastern developments. Officially, unlike some Islamic countries, such as Turkey, Iran and Palestine, Pakistan's reaction was cautious concerning the Arab-Israeli normalisation process. Pakistan's Ministry of Foreign Affairs claimed the deal had far-reaching implications for the region, but did not condemn the Abraham Peace Accords (MOFA, 2020). Prime Minister Khan repeatedly denied any change in Pakistan's policy towards Israel (Gul, 2020). State Minister for Parliamentary Affairs Ali Muhammad Khan made a statement in the Parliament on Israel and termed the Jewish state as "enemy number one" of Pakistan (Alvi, 2020). The Pakistan Army also supported the government's stance on the issue and denied any rapprochement between Islamabad and Tel Aviv (Abbasi, 2020).

However, a new challenge emerged for Pakistan when Saudi Arabia and the UAE pressured it to recognise Israel. Prime Minister Khan, in a television interview, revealed that brotherly Islamic countries were pressuring the government of Pakistan to recognise Israel, which a few prominent Pakistani analysts named as Saudi Arabia and the UAE (Shahid, 2017). Khan clarified his government's position on this issue in an interview:

> There are certain things that we cannot say, because our relations with them [the Muslim countries pressuring Pakistan] are good. We don't want to upset them. Inshallah, let our country stand up on its feet, then ask me such questions.
>
> (Shahid, 2020)

This is not the first time that Saudi Arabia has tried to pressure Pakistan for its interests. Pakistan has become habituated to Saudi pressure on various regional conflicts. Apart from its direct conflicts with Arab countries or Iran, Saudi Arabia and the UAE dictate to Pakistan at international forums, too. For instance, due to pressure on Pakistan from Saudi Arabia and the UAE, Islamabad decided not to participate in a meeting of Muslim leaders in Kuala Lumpur. Foreign Minister Qureshi said that Pakistan had withdrawn over concerns that such initiatives might divide the Muslim world (Hashim, 2019).

There are various reasons for Saudi Arabia and the UAE to pressure Pakistan to recognise Israel. Pakistan is the second-largest Muslim country in the world in terms of population. Likewise, as the only Muslim nuclear country, it has played a significant role in Arab/Israeli conflicts. For Saudi Arabia, the only negative outcome of Israel's recognition might be the reduction of Riyadh's influence in the Muslim world. To avoid that, Saudi

56 Zahid Shahab Ahmed and Khurram Abbas

Arabia wants Pakistan to recognise Israel so that Islamabad may not question Saudi Arabia's leadership of the Muslim world. Likewise, Riyadh does not want to see Pakistan joining hands with Turkey and Iran against Israel. For the UAE, the security of Israeli citizens is a primary factor that has been seen as one reason for the pressure on Pakistan to recognise Israel. There are fears that the security of Israeli visitors to the UAE could be compromised by the diasporas of those Muslim countries that have not yet recognised the Jewish state.

In this context, the UAE authorities have imposed a travel ban on thirteen Muslim countries, including Pakistan, Turkey, Afghanistan, Yemen, Syria and Somalia (*Al Jazeera*, 2020). This ban is a continuation of the UAE's concerns that Iran could develop a human-intelligence network in the country to target Emirati or Israeli interests (Abbas, 2020). However, there is growing resentment within diplomatic circles about undue pressure on Pakistan by the GCC countries to recognise Israel. Prime Minister Khan has indicated in his interview that the country's economic reliance has limited Pakistan's options. Khan's remarks demonstrated his despair that the country has been economically struggling, otherwise, the government would have strongly responded to these pressure tactics.

Conclusion

RSCT helps us understand Pakistan's relations with the Gulf monarchies from a different angle. Since its independence from the British Empire in 1947, Pakistan's foreign policy and security relations have been India-centric. This dynamic has been a dominant feature also of Pakistan's foreign affairs, for example, through earlier security alliances with the United States, and currently close cooperation with China. As the Gulf states continue to enhance their economic cooperation with Pakistan's arch-rival India, Islamabad is facing a dilemma of either ignoring that or persuading its Gulf allies to support it in its disputes with India, in particular, the Jammu and Kashmir dispute. To Pakistan's disappointment, the Gulf monarchies have been hesitant to always support Islamabad's demands in connection to their relations with India. In contrast, Pakistan has consistently been keeping its relations with Iran—with whom Gulf monarchies like Saudi Arabia and the UAE have conflictual relations—on the backburner. Due to their common security concerns vis-à-vis Iran, Gulf monarchies like Bahrain and the UAE have normalised their relations with Israel through the Abraham Peace Accords. Although Pakistan has a consistent position on the Palestinian issue, the Abraham Peace Accords have not dented its relations with GCC states much. Based on RSCT, we argue that the Gulf states' security interests are linked to their immediate security environment. This is clear from how some, for example, Bahrain, Saudi Arabia and the UAE, are locked into a catch-22 situation with Iran. Their conflicts with Iran transcend ideological divisions and are linked to the overall geopolitical environment of the Middle East. This is also demonstrated through how Iran supports the Shi'as in Bahrain and Yemen. As a stronger military power in the Middle East, Israel also views Iran as its major threat. This and US mediation have played key roles in bringing Israel closer to the Gulf monarchies. Over the years, Islamabad has demonstrated a better understanding of the geopolitical dynamics of the Middle East and that has helped Pakistan deal pragmatically with other crises like the Yemeni conflict and the Qatar-Gulf crisis.

Note

1 The Panama Papers case or the Panamagate hearing was a legal corruption case before the Supreme Court of Pakistan heard between 1 November 2016 and 23 February 2017. The case was brought to the court by Pakistan Tehreek-e-Insaf chief Imran Khan following the Panama Papers leak, which disclosed links of Nawaz Sharif and his family with offshore companies. After months of investigations and court hearings, Nawaz Sharif was disqualified from the Prime Minister's seat on 28 July 2017 (Cheema, 2021).

References

Abbas, K. (2016, February 04). *Pakistan's Relations with Gulf States.* Retrieved from Islamabad Policy Research Institute (IPRI): Islamabad Policy. http://www.ipripak.org/pakistans-relations-with-gulf-states/

Abbas, K. (2017, December 10). Efficacy of Riyadh-led alliances. *Express Tribune.* https://tribune.com.pk/story/1580326/efficacy-riyadh-led-alliances

Abbas, K. (2019a). Indian Growing Influence in the GCC countries: Political, Economic and Strategic Risks for Pakistan. *IPRI Journal,* XIX(2), pp. 57–89.

Abbas, K. (2019b). Passive Mediation in Persian Gulf Conflicts: A Case Study of Pakistan's Peace Initiatives. *Journal of Middle Eastern and Islamic Studies,* 16(4), pp.1–18.

Abbas, K. (2020). How killing of top Iranian Nuclear Scientist will shape geopolitics of Persian Gulf? *Global Village Space.* https://www.globalvillagespace.com/how-killing-of-top-iranian-nuclear-scientist-will-shape-geopolitics-of-persian-gulf/ (accessed 29 May 2021).

Abbasi, A. (2020). Armed forces fully support country's stated position on Israel: DG ISPR. *The News.* https://www.thenews.com.pk/print/750941-armed-forces-fully-support-country-s-stated-position-on-israel-dg-ispr (accessed 02 June 2021).

Ahmad, N. (2016a, January 9). Pak-Saudi Relations: Friends with Benefits. *The Express Tribune.* https://tribune.com.pk/story/1024531/pak-saudi-relations-friends-with-benefits/ (accessed 10 June 2021)

Ahmad, N. (2016b, April 12). India after Modi's Saudi offensive. *The Express Tribune.* https://tribune.com.pk/story/1083500/india-after-modis-saudi-offensive/ (accessed 29 May 2021).

Ahmad, K., and Faisal, M. (2016). Pakistan-Saudi Arabia Strategic Relations: An Assessment. *CISS Insight,* 3(1), pp. 23–37.

Ahmed, Z. S. (2018). Understanding Saudi Arabia's Influence on Pakistan: The Case of the Islamic Military Alliance to Fight Terrorism. *The Muslim World,* 109(3), pp. 308–326.

58 *Zahid Shahab Ahmed and Khurram Abbas*

Ahmed, Z. S., and Akbarzadeh, S. (2020). Pakistan Caught between Iran and Saudi Arabia. *Contemporary South Asia*, 28(3), pp. 336–350.

Ahmed, Z. S., and Bhatnagar, S. (2010). Gulf States and the Conflict between India and Pakistan. *Journal of Asia Pacific Studies*, 1(2), pp. 259–291.

Al Arabiya (2016, November 18). Largest number of Umrah pilgrims came from Egypt, Pakistan. *Al Arabiya*. https://english.alarabiya.net/en/perspective/analysis/2016/11/18/Largest-number-of-Umrah-pilgrims-came-from-Egypt-Pakistan-.html (accessed 03 June 2021).

Al Jazeera (2020). UAE halts new visas to citizens of 13 mostly Muslim states. *Al Jazeera*. https://www.aljazeera.com/news/2020/11/25/uae-halts-new-visas-to-citizens-of-13-mostly-muslim-states (accessed 09 June 2021).

Ali, K. (2017, November 18). Haj quota for Pakistan increased. *Dawn*. https://www.dawn.com/news/1319562 (accessed 03 June 2021).

Almajdoub, S. (2016, April 25). Discrete diplomacy: Oman and the Iran nuclear deal. *E-International Relations*. https://www.e-ir.info/2016/04/25/discrete-diplomacy-oman-and-the-iran-nuclear-deal/ (accessed 01 June 2021).

Alvi, M. (2020). Israel enemy number one until Palestine, Masjid-e-Aqsa freed. *The News*. https://www.thenews.com.pk/print/702173-israel-enemy-number-one-until-palestine-masjid-e-aqsa-freed (accessed 03 June 2021).

Anis, M. (2016, January 20). 1,180 Pakistan army personnel present in Saudi Arabia: Kh Asif. *The News*. https://www.thenews.com.pk/print/92465-1180-Pakistan-Army-personnel-presentin-Saudi-Arabia-Kh-Asif (accessed 02 June 2021).

Atique, F. (1985). Pakistan's Foreign Policy: A Quarterly Survey. *Pakistan Horizon*, 38(4), pp. 3–18.

Aziz, M. S. (2016, June 09). *Statement by Adviser to the Prime Minister on Foreign Affairs, at a Press Conference in Islamabad.* Retrieved from Ministry of Foreign Affairs: http://www.mofa.gov.pk/pr-details.php?prID=3852 (accessed 04 June 2021).

Aziz, S. (2017, September 06). Qatar taps Pakistan market amid Gulf blockade. *Al Jazeera*. http://www.aljazeera.com/news/2017/09/qatar-taps-pakistan-market-gulf-blockade-170904143241676.html (accessed 02 June 2021).

Basit, A., and Ahmed, Z. S. (2020, August 31). Pakistan's balancing act may be failing. *Al Jazeera*. https://www.aljazeera.com/opinions/2020/8/31/pakistans-balancing-act-may-be-failing (accessed 10 June 2021)

BBC (2005, October 12). Race to save earthquake survivors. http://news.bbc.co.uk/2/hi/south_asia/4333218.stm (accessed 06 June 2021).

BBC (2018, October 22). Saudi Crown Prince Mohammed bin Salman, power behind the throne. https://www.bbc.com/news/world-middle-east-40354415 (accessed 06 June 2021).

Bhatti, H. (2017, January 26). Panamagate hearing: Second letter from Qatari Royal "Clarifies" Sharif investment in Gulf steel mills. *Dawn*. https://www.dawn.com/news/1310842 (accessed 03 June 2021).

Bowen, J. (2020, September 14). Five reasons why Israel's peace deals with the UAE and Bahrain matter. *BBC News*. https://www.bbc.com/news/world-middle-east-54151712 (accessed 06 June 2021).

Buzan, B., and Waever, O. (2003). *Regions and Powers: The Structure of International Security.* New York: Cambridge University Press.

Chaudhury, D. R. (2021, February 20). Pakistan's foreign debt & liabilities continue to surge. *Economic Times*. https://economictimes.indiatimes.com/news/international/world-news/pakistans-foreign-debt-liabilities-continue-tosurge/articleshow/81129333.cms?from=mdr (accessed 06 June 2021).

Cheema H. (2021, October 3). How Pakistan's Panama Papers probe unfolded. *Dawn*. https://www.dawn.com/news/1316531

Dawn (2014a, March 20). King of Bahrain vows to enhance military cooperation at JSHQ. https://www.dawn.com/news/1094257 (accessed 07 June 2021).

Dawn (2014b, March 20). Pakistan not sending troops to Bahrain or Saudi: PM. https://www.dawn.com/news/1094412 (accessed 07 June 2021).

Dawn (2015, April 11). UAE Minister warns Pakistan of "heavy price for ambiguous stand" on Yemen. https://www.dawn.com/news/1175284 (accessed 07 June 2021).

Dawn (2017, December 12). Musharraf urges Pakistan to back UAE, Saudi Arabia against Qatar. https://www.dawn.com/news/1376073 (accessed 06 June 2021).

Dawn (2020). Qureshi asks OIC to stop dragging feet on Kashmir meeting. https://www.dawn.com/news/1572857 (accessed 06 June 2021).

DiChristopher, T. (2018, December 04). Iranian President Hassan Rouhani threatens to close Strait of Hormuz if US blocks oil exports. *CNBC*. https://www.cnbc.com/2018/12/04/iranian-president-hassan-rouhani-threatens-to-close-strait-of-hormuz.html (accessed 05 June 2021).

Exum, A. M. (2015). *On the Knife's Edge: Yemen's Instability and the Threat to American Interests*. Washington: Center for a New American Security.

Faisal, K. A. (2016). Pakistan-Saudi Arabia Strategic Relations: An Assessment. *CISS Insight*, 3(1), pp. 23–37.

Faisal, A. A., and Haider, M. (2014, November 28). Made in Pakistan weapons being sold to 40 countries. *Dawn*. https://www.dawn.com/news/1147302 (accessed 03 June 2021).

Gady, F. S. (2016, August 08). Will Kuwait purchase Pakistan's new fighter jet? *The Diplomat*. https://thediplomat.com/2016/08/will-kuwait-purchase-pakistans-new-fighter-jet/ (accessed 05 June 2021).

Gul, A. (2020). Pakistan: No plans to recognize Israel. *Voice of America*. https://www.voanews.com/south-central-asia/pakistan-no-plans-recognize-israel (accessed 09 June 2021).

Hafeez, J. (2020, October 24). Pak-Oman defence co-operation. *Arab News*. https://arab.news/bqmhr (accessed 09 June 2021).

Hafezi, P. (2020, August 19). Iran's response to Israel-UAE pact: Tough rhetoric, no action. *Reuters*. https://www.reuters.com/article/us-israel-emirates-iran-analysis-idUSKCN25E20M (accessed 08 June 2021).

Hashim, A. (2019, December 18). Neutral' Pakistan pulls out of Malaysia summit of Muslim nations. *Al Jazeera*. https://www.aljazeera.com/news/2019/12/18/neutral-pakistan-pulls-out-of-malaysia-summit-of-muslim-nations (accessed 08 June 2021).

Hiro, D. (2018). *Cold War in the Islamic World: Saudi Arabia, Iran and the Struggle for Supremacy*. Uttar Pradesh: Harper Collins.

Karam, S. (2009, November 11). Saudi Arabia grants Pakistan $380 million loan. *Reuters*. https://www.reuters.com/article/pakistan-saudi-loan/saudi-arabia-grants-pakistan-380-million-loan-idUSLB11734320091111. (accessed 10 June 2021).

Khan, R. M. (2015). Foreign Policy of Pakistan in the Changing Regional and Global Settings. *Journal of Contemporary Studies*, 4(1), 14–29.

60   *Zahid Shahab Ahmed and Khurram Abbas*

Khatri, S. S. (2017, September 21). Qatar introduces free visa on arrival for Pakistani nationals. *Doha News*. https://dohanews.co/qatar-introduces-visa-on-arrival-for-pakistani-nationals/ (accessed 11 June 2021).

Majidyar, A. (2018, April 06). UAE official calls for international action to end "Iranian occupation" of disputed islands. *Middle East Institute*. https://www.mei.edu/publications/uae-official-calls-international-action-end-iranian-occupation-disputed-i (accessed 11 June 2021).

Mangi, A. (2018, March 04). Pakistani passport ranked fourth worst for international travel. *The Express Tribune*. https://tribune.com.pk/story/1650981/1-pakistani-passport-ranked-fourth-worst-international-travel/ (accessed 11 June 2021).

Mason, R. (2016). Saudi Arabia's Relations with South Asia. In N. Partrick (Ed.), *Saudi Arabian Foreign Policy: Conflict and Cooperation* (pp. 304–322). London: I.B. Tauris.

Milaha (2017). Milaha launches fastest container service between Pakistan and Qatar. https://www.milaha.com/2017/08/27/milaha-launches-fastest-container-service-between-pakistan-and-qatar/ (accessed 13 June 2021).

MOFA (2017, June 08). *Record of the Press Briefing by Spokesperson*. Retrieved from Ministry of Foreign Affairs: http://www.mofa.gov.pk/pr-details.php?mm=NTA1OA (accessed 10 June 2021).

MOFA (2019, January 06). *Visit of Crown Prince of UAE, 6th January, 2019*. Retrieved from Ministry of Foreign Affairs of Pakistan. http://www.mofa.gov.pk/pr-details.php (accessed 11 June 2021).

MOFA (2020). *Recognition of Israel Not under Consideration*. Retrieved from Ministry of Foreign Affairs: http://mofa.gov.pk/recognition-of-israel-not-under-consideration/ (accessed 11 June 2021).

Naviwala, N. (2015, September 04). Playing Hardball with Aid to Pakistan. *Foreign Policy*. http://foreignpolicy.com/2015/09/04/playing-hardball-with-aid-to-pakistan/ (accessed 12 June 2021).

OIC (2019, February 26). *OIC Holds 46th CFM Session in Abu Dhabi: 50 Years of Islamic Cooperation: Roadmap for Prosperity and Development*. Retrieved from Organization of Islamic Cooperation: https://www.oic-oci.org/topic/?t_id=20621&t_ref=11715&lan=en (accessed 12 June 2021).

Portal, S. A. (2018). Sectarian violence in Pakistan. Retrieved from South Asia Terrorism Portal: http://www.satp.org/satporgtp/countries/pakistan/database/sect-killing.htm (accessed 12 June 2021).

Rania El Gamal, B. S. (2019, May 13). Saudi oil tankers among those attacked off UAE amid Iran tensions. *Reuters*. https://www.reuters.com/article/us-saudi-oil-tankers-fujairah-idUSKCN1SJ088 (accessed 12 June 2021).

Riedel, B. (2016, January 11). Why do Saudi Arabia and Iran compete for Pakistani support? *Brookings*. https://www.brookings.edu/blog/markaz/2016/01/11/why-do-saudi-arabia-and-iran-compete-for-pakistani-support/ (accessed 13 June 2021).

SBP (2017). *Economic Data*. Retrieved from State Bank of Pakistan. http://www.sbp.org.pk/ecodata/index2.asp (accessed 13 June 2021).

Shahid, K. K. (2017, June 07). The Qatar crisis: A diplomatic curveball for Pakistan. *The Diplomat*. https://thediplomat.com/2017/06/the-qatar-crisis-a-diplomatic-curveball-for-pakistan/?allpages=yes&print=yes (accessed 07 June 2021).

Shahid, K. K. (2020, November 22). How Saudi Arabia is pressuring Pakistan to recognize Israel. *Haaretz*. https://www.haaretz.com/middle-east-news/.premium-how-saudi-arabia-is-pressuring-pakistan-to-recognize-israel-1.9315768 (accessed 12 June 2021).

Shaikh, N. A. (2020, November 03). Reflections on Pakistan and Kuwait. *The Gulf News*. https://arab.news/ner7n (accessed 09 June 2021).

Shams, S. (2019, October 13). Can Pakistan's Imran Khan mediate between Iran and Saudi Arabia? *DW*. https://www.dw.com/en/can-pakistans-imran-khan-mediate-between-iran-and-saudi-arabia/a-50813144 (accessed 08 June 2021).

Siddiqa, A. (2017). *The Qatar-Gulf Rift: Impacts on the Migrant Community*. Islamabad: Institute of Strategic Studies Islamabad.

Syed, B. S. (2018, October 24). Saudi Arabia pledges $6bn package to Pakistan. *Dawn*. https://www.dawn.com/news/1440974 (accessed 11 June 2021).

Tamamy, S. M. (2012). Saudi Arabia and the Arab Spring: Opportunities and Challenges of Security. *Journal of Arabian Studies*, 2(2), pp. 143–156.

The Economist (2017, October 19). *The Boycott of Qatar Is Hurting Its Enforcers*. https://www.economist.com/news/middle-east-and-africa/21730426-if-saudis-and-emiratis-will-not-trade-doha-iranians-will-boycott (accessed 13 June 2021).

The Express Tribune (2015, April 11). Yemen conflict: Pakistan's decision is dangerous and unexpected, says UAE foreign minister. *The Express Tribune*. https://tribune.com.pk/story/868076/yemen-conflict-pakistans-decision-is-dangerous-and-unexpected-slams-uae/ (accessed 11 June 2021).

The Indian Express (2016, April 03). PM Modi conferred Saudi's highest civilian honour. https://indianexpress.com/article/india/india-news-india/modi-saudi-arabia-king-abdulaziz-sash-civilian-honour/ (accessed 08 June 2021).

The Nation (2017a, May 24). Pakistan ready to help defuse tension between Saudi Arabia, Iran. https://nation.com.pk/24-May-2017/pakistan-ready-to-play-mediator-s-role-between-saudi-arabia-iran-fo (accessed 10 June 2021).

The Nation (2017b, October 26). Imam-e-Ka'aba attends cabinet meeting. *The Nation*. https://nation.com.pk/26-Oct-2017/imam-e-ka-aba-attends-cabinet-meeting (accessed 11 June 2021).

The News (2021, May 31). Kuwait lifts 11-year visa ban on Pak citizens. https://www.thenews.com.pk/print/842468-kuwait-lifts-11-year-visa-ban-on-pak-citizens (accessed 05 June 2021).

Toumi, H. (2016, October 05). 7 nationalities make up 90% of foreigners in Kuwait. *The Gulf News*. https://gulfnews.com/world/gulf/kuwait/7-nationalities-make-up-90-of-foreigners-in-kuwait-1.1907439 (accessed 06 June 2021).

Walt, S. M. (1987). *The Origins of Alliances*. New York: Cornell University Press.

Wasty, S. (2017, September 15). Pakistan and Qatar: Constraints and dilemmas. *International Policy Digest*. https://intpolicydigest.org/2017/09/17/pakistan-qatar-constraints-dilemmas/ (accessed 28 May 2021).

Yousaf, K. (2017, July 18). Qatari FM makes surprise stopover in Islamabad. *The Express Tribune*. https://tribune.com.pk/story/1460788/qatars-foreign-minister-arrive-islamabad-official-visit/ (accessed 08 June 2021).

3 The Estranged Partners
Iran's Complicated Relations with India and Pakistan

Mohammad Soltaninejad

Situated at the confluence of the two sub-regions of the Persian Gulf and the Indian sub-continent, Iran has a special place in India's Look West policy. With its abundant energy resources, Iran has been a main target of New Delhi's policy of diversifying its sources of energy. In addition to that, Iran's geostrategic location makes it an indispensable part of India's much-needed North-South Corridor that connects India to Central Asia and Russia. On the flip side, India has a lot to offer Iran. New Delhi is expected to provide the necessary capital for the development of Iran's Chabahar port and to construct the railways and other necessary infrastructures to turn it into a hub of trade in the Oman Sea and the Persian Gulf. More importantly, India was once viewed in Tehran as a political resort against US pressures. Their tightening bonds were even characterised as a strategic partnership. Despite this, the relationship between Tehran and Delhi never realised its full potential. A few years after announcement, the strategic partnership proved to be more of an empty slogan than a substantive desired state that the two sides try to achieve. In a similar way, Iran's relations with Pakistan has remained limited and bereft of a spirit of productivity and vitality. Their security interconnectedness and their potentials to meet each other's economic needs are not translated into a durable mutually-profitable cooperation. Without being able to satisfy one another's expectations, the best they have done so far is not to antagonise one another. Construction of a gas pipeline between the two countries is long overdue and other initiatives for expansion of trade have remained immaterialised. In short, Iran's relationships with India and Pakistan have remained complicated, neither leaning to a total collapse nor inclined to durable cordiality and friendship.

In this chapter, the trajectory of Iran's relations with India and Pakistan is studied, analysing varying domestic, regional and international factors that impact them. These levels of analysis are interlinked and the ebbs and flows in the relations are explained with due reference to them. At the domestic level, the respective internal developments in India and Pakistan that have begotten Iran's involvement are brought to light. At the regional level, the focus is on the interconnectedness of Iran's ties with India and Pakistan and the impact each of them leave on Iran's relations with the other. Here, the

DOI: 10.4324/9781003283058-4

The Estranged Partners 63

role Iran's arch-rival, Saudi Arabia, plays in directing Iran's relations with India and Pakistan is also discussed. It is demonstrated how the triad of Iran, India and Pakistan calibrate their policies in a balancing game. At the international level, the United States is the most important actor whose role in shaping the dynamics of Iran's relations with India and Pakistan is examined.

Iran and India: A relationship turned sour

India's relations with Iran began in 1950 and from the beginning lacked enough chemistry, mainly because Iran was a part of the Western bloc headed by the US but India was a non-aligned nation tilted towards the Soviet Union. In the heyday of the Arab nationalism, New Delhi partnered Egypt as Iran's main rival. Iran, for its part, partnered Pakistan as Tehran and Islamabad were bound together by the US-led security arrangements manifested in the Baghdad pact founded in 1955 renamed to the Central Treaty Organization (CENTO) after the collapse of the monarchical system of Iraq in 1958. India was uncomfortable with these arrangements that were, first and foremost, shaped to curb the soviet influence in the region. Delhi's discomfort with such West-oriented arrangements is best reflected in the late Indian Prime Minister, Jawaharlal Nehru's description of them as wrong, dangerous and harmful (Naaz, 2001). In spite of that, India and Iran remained at ease with one another throughout the Pahlavi dynasty.

The Iranian revolution in 1979 did not transform the nature of India-Iran relations. However, the gradual economic liberalisation policies of India and the subsequent growth of industries in the 1990s changed Delhi's attitude towards the Persian Gulf countries, including Iran, as indispensable sources of energy. In addition to the rising Indian need for energy and the markets for its manufactured products, the emergence of the Taliban in Afghanistan and the threats they posed to both Tehran and New Delhi drove the two sides even closer. The tendency to expand relations continued after the collapse of the Taliban, and the two sides found Afghanistan a fertile ground for cultivating ties, as they both desired a stable Afghanistan run by an inclusive government. Tehran and Delhi had common concerns over Pakistan's presence in Afghanistan, and they could both benefit from building roads to complete the much-desired North-South Transport Corridor (NSTC) that would connect India to Central Asia, with Iran a major beneficiary of the transit fees.

In 2001, the Indian Prime Minister, Atal Bihari Vajpayee, visited Iran expressing India's interest in developing bilateral relations focused on energy provision, completing the NSTC, Afghanistan's security and technology transfer (Khan, 2001). The Indian consulate in Bandar Abbas was established that year to promote India's trade with Iran and increase its security-monitoring ability in the Persian Gulf. The two countries also expanded military cooperation that included officer exchanges, the conduct of joint marine drills and weapons sales (Ahmed & Bhatnagar, 2018, 5).

64 *Mohammad Soltaninejad*

These were preludes to the announcement of the strategic partnership between the two sides in 2003 according to the Delhi Declaration signed by Vajpayee and Iranian President Mohammad Khatami. With this, Iran would ease the US pressures and India would get a strategic advantage over Pakistan. Two months after the declaration, Iranian and Indian warships held joint naval drills. India also agreed to train Iranian military personnel and help Iran maintain and repair its Russian-made Mig-29 fighters (Hathaway, 2004).

However, the expanding ties between the two countries received a severe blow from 2005 onwards, when Iran-US tensions increased over Iran's nuclear activities (Soltaninejad, 2017). In 2005, Washington signed a nuclear deal with New Delhi that facilitated cooperation between the two on civilian use of nuclear technology (Council on Foreign Relations, 2010). The US, though, used the deal as leverage to hinder the further development of Iranian-Indian cooperation and to ultimately reverse it. India hoped that it could continue cooperating with Iran while reassuring Washington that this cooperation did not harm US interests. In fact, India was trying to balance its position between Iran and the US. But New Delhi was ultimately obliged to take the US side on the issue of Iran's nuclear program, mainly due to intense US pressure (Pant, 2006, 26). For Washington, India's ties with the US and its cooperation with Iran were mutually exclusive. India had to choose between them. On one occasion, for example, the US ambassador to New Delhi, David Mulford, condemned a visit paid by the Iranian president Mahmoud Ahmadinejad to India in 2008, saying that "Americans, particularly members of the Congress, will view Ahmadinejad's visit as India providing a platform for an enemy of the US" (Dikshit, 2010). Such US reactions put India in a position to minimise its energy and trade cooperation with Iran. Voting for International Atomic Energy Agency (IAEA) resolutions against Iran's nuclear activities in September 2005 and February 2006 was an example of India supporting the US-led campaign of preventing Iran from becoming a nuclear power. India continued its alignment with the US in the IAEA in 2009 and voted against Iran in a resolution issued in November of that year (*The Hindu*, 2009). This Indian approach took its toll on Iran-India relations, leading to Iran's cancellation of an LNG deal with India in November 2007. The Asian Clearing Union through which India used to pay Iran's oil money also stopped working in December 2010 (Ahmed & Bhatnagar, 2018, 5).

India-Iran cooperation was revived after the signing of the Iran nuclear deal in 2015. Indian Prime Minister Narendra Modi visited Iran in 2016 and signed a number of agreements to develop Chabahar and to construct a railway that connects India to Afghanistan and Central Asia (*The Hindu*, 2016). The amount of India's investment in Chabahar was estimated to reach $500 million (*The Guardian*, 2016). The two countries also discussed a preferential trade agreement and a bilateral investment treaty (Roche, 2018). In such a transformed atmosphere, the volume of trade between the two countries increased. In the first year after the lifting of sanctions alone, India's oil imports from Iran doubled to 473,000 barrels per day. In 2016, Iran was propelled into fourth place among India's oil suppliers, up from seventh in 2015 (Verma, 2017). The short-lived removal of sanctions also renewed hopes for India's settling of its debts to Iran and making investments in Iran's energy and transportation sectors. In line with this, reports were released showing that India's refineries were ready to settle $6 billion of outstanding debts to Iran (Iranian Diplomacy, 2015). A contract was also signed between the two countries that would provide $450 million of credit for the export of steel rails to Iran and to partly fulfil India's commitment to develop Chabahar (Reuters, 2016).

This positive trend in expanding relations was reversed once again after Donald Trump withdrew from Iran's nuclear deal and tried to bring Iran's oil exports to zero in the framework of his maximum-pressure campaign. The special personal relations between Modi and Trump, combined with the traditional exposure of India to US pressure over Iran, reversed the reviving relations between Iran and India. India halted its import of oil from Iran in May 2019 (*The Hindu*, 2021a). Since then, India's exports to Iran have only been limited to food and pharmaceuticals that are allowed to be sent to Iran under humanitarian exemptions made by the US treasury (Jayaswal, 2021). India's investments in Chabahar were also hampered by the new surge of sanctions. Although the US exempted Chabahar from sanctions and allowed India to continue developing this strategic port, in practice, India's activities in Chabahar shrank considerably, best reflected in the reduction of the annual budget allocated to the development of the port to one-third in 2020 (Bhattacherjee, 2019).

As the review of the two countries' relations has showed, the geostrategic location of Iran, combined with India's ability to secure financial resources for the development of Iran's ports and railways/roads, in addition to the huge potential of trade between the two countries form the backbone of their cooperation. Here, the factor of Afghanistan in Iran-India connections should not be neglected. Guaranteeing the security and stability of Afghanistan has been a common interest of the two countries. Tehran and Delhi both supported the central government in Kabul and saw an expansion of the Taliban's influence as a source of threat. This was best reflected in a Rouhani-Modi joint statement in May 2016, when they supported a "strong, united, prosperous and independent Afghanistan" (India Ministry of External Affairs, 2016). Afghanistan is a key component of the NSTC and, therefore, India and Iran are concerned about its fate. Afghanistan is especially important for India as Delhi is keen to build alternative trade routes for the Belt and Road Initiative (BRI) and the China–Pakistan Economic Corridor (CPEC) that are initiated by India's two primary rivals, China and Pakistan. The fall of Kabul to the Taliban in August 2021 was an unfortunate incident for both Iran and India. However, India was particularly disturbed by the Taliban takeover, and Delhi's interests received a severe blow

66   *Mohammad Soltaninejad*

as a result of that. The US exit from Afghanistan sharply curtailed India's influence in Afghanistan (Kaura, 2021). With Pakistan being the most influential player in Afghanistan, India's investments in this country that reach $3 billion will not come to fruition (Subramanian, 2021). Similarly to India, Tehran favours a comprehensive government in Kabul, but Iran has secured fairly peaceful relations with the Taliban too. For Tehran, the priority is that Afghanistan does not turn into a hotbed of radical Islamist activities, and therefore it tries not to antagonise the Taliban. Iran hopes that the Talibs will be able to expel its much-hated adversary, Daesh, from Afghanistan.

Despite the fact that Iran and India have plenty of reasons to bind together, the prospects for a durable partnership between them are dim. The US influence is certainly the most important factor that disrupts Iran-India ties and, as discussed earlier, has proven to be the ultimate determinant of the two countries' relations. In addition to that, Iran's historical support of Pakistan's cause on Kashmir works against an Iranian-Indian durable partnership. Iran has been, for the most part, sympathetic towards Pakistan about the fate of Kashmir and looks at it from an ideational-religious perspective. Iran's foreign policy in general is bound by the fact that it is a great Muslim nation, and both before and after the revolution has shown varying degrees of solidarity with the Muslim peoples when they have been in conflict with their non-Muslim opponents. Although in the years after the revolution, Iran has been cautious over Kashmir not to hurt either side in the conflict, it has been, for the most part, supportive of the Organization of Islamic Countries' (OIC) stance on Kashmir, which has sided with Pakistan. After all, Iran's Supreme Leader has twice, in 2010 and 2017, addressed the people of Kashmir as being under oppression, equating them with the Yemeni and Bahraini people (Bilgrami, 2018). In addition to Kashmir, the Pakistani factor is also relevant in India-Iran relations over the issue of the origins of Iran's nuclear program. The fact that the Pakistani Abdul Qadeer Khan was the source of Iran's nuclear technology created unease in India about Iran's nuclear program and its links to Pakistan. In view of this, India talked about the necessity of disclosing the sources of Iran's nuclear program (Fair, 2007). Iran's natural response could have been to remind India that Delhi is not even a party to the Nuclear Non-Proliferation Treaty (NPT), but Tehran practised restraint, refraining from directly addressing India on this matter.

The other factor that distances Iran's vision on security and trade from that of India is the fact that for Iran, the development of Chabahar should not come at the expense of its relations with Pakistan or China. In other words, unlike the Indian perspective that Iran's Chabahar and Pakistan's Gwadar are competitors, Iran seeks opportunities to connect Chabahar to Gwadar. For Iran, the primary objective is to develop Chabahar and build the infrastructure to connect it to Pakistan and Afghanistan so that Iranian gas is exported to its eastern neighbours and the transit fees for passing goods are delivered. Put simply, while India looks at Chabahar and its presence in Iran's Sistan and Balochistan province as leverage against Pakistan, Iran aims at developing regionally integrated mechanisms of trade that include India, Pakistan and China. This is best revealed by Iran's Ambassador to Pakistan, Mehdi Honardoost, who said that from an Iranian perspective, the Chabahar port agreement is not finished and is not limited to Iran, India and Afghanistan. Even before India, the offer to cooperate on Chabahar was extended to Pakistan and then China (Tasnim, 2016). As Haji-Yousefi and Narouei (2021) discuss, Iran and India are geo-economically convergent on Chabahar as a commercial and transit hub. However, Tehran and Delhi's geopolitical views on Chabahar diverge. Iran seeks to use Chabahar as a means to neutralise the US policies to isolate it and also to strengthen its ties with China and Pakistan, but India, which is the greatest US ally in South Asia, looks at Chabahar as a strategic asset to counterbalance China and Pakistan.

In addition to such diverging intentions, there are complications inside India related to the rise of the Hindu nationalist and anti-Islamist movement of Hindutva that create doubts about the materialisation of an Iran-India strategic partnership. The increase in ultranationalist tendencies in India has caused the Indian government to feel more of an urge to pronounce the secular nature of the state, and one way to do that has been to showcase its constructive relations with the Persian Gulf Islamic nations, including Iran. The way Iran and India manage the radical Hindu affairs in their relations is best reflected in the Babri Masjid case of 1992. In that case, Iran supported the Muslims and strongly condemned the demolition of the mosque (Nayar, 2020). This came at a time of relative Arab-world silence over the issue, as Saudi Arabia and other Arab states of the Persian Gulf were concerned that taking firm positions would activate their own radical Islamists. Iran seized the opportunity, condemned the action and organised demonstrations against this incident in front of the Indian embassy in Tehran (Gupta, 2011). To curb the ramifications, India arranged its Prime Minister Narasimha Rao's visit to Iran. Before that, the Indian parliament had passed the Places of Worship Act in 1991 in a bid to freeze the status of religious places and to prevent "conversion of the places of worship of any religious denomination into one of a different denomination or section," (Venkataramanan, 2019) demonstrating that the Indian government was against the deepening of religious rifts and any damage to the Muslim sanctities. This showed how careful India was not to allow such sectarian issues to disrupt its relations with Iran. However, the tensions over what Iran regards discrimination against Muslims is recurrent. Another clear example is the Iranian Supreme Leader and Foreign Minister's objections against the attacks on Muslims in India in March 2020 after riots surged in Delhi over a new citizenship law that gave privilege to non-Muslim Pakistani, Bangladeshi and Afghan nationals to acquire Indian citizenship (Roy, 2020).

Iran and Pakistan: The uncomfortable neighbours

In 1948, Iran was the first country that congratulated Pakistan on its independence. From the beginning, Iran saw its interests best served in having a stable Pakistan in its neighbourhood. Mediating between Pakistan and Afghanistan over their border issues was a step in this direction. In the international scene, Iran and Pakistan found themselves in the Western bloc under the protection of the United States. This, combined with the other fact that they share the same religion, led to Iran's support of Pakistan's position during its disputes with India over Kashmir. The relations stayed at a steady course of cordiality for the whole duration of the Pahlavi dynasty. As Mohammadally (1979, 51) says, "A great deal of the cordiality owes its origin directly to the common heritage of the two countries. This heritage that encompasses the whole spectrum of cultural, ethnic, linguistic and religious affinities dates back centuries." Strategically speaking, what bound Iran and Pakistan further was their apprehension about Moscow and Delhi. Iran's primary foreign threat was coming from the Soviet Union that had once occupied Northern Iran during the Second World War before being forced out by the United States. For Pakistan, the main threat was emanating from Soviet-inclined India. This common vision drove Iranian Shah Mohammad Reza Pahlavi to go as far as proposing the formation of a confederation of Iran and Pakistan with a single army with the Shah as head of the Army (Vatanka, 2015, 28). Under the reign of the Shah, Iran remained committed to supporting Pakistan's cause on Kashmir even after Pakistan's poor performance in the 1965 war with India and its defeat of 1971 that, as Vatanka (2015, 81) argues, drove Shah to adopt a patronising attitude towards Pakistan. One of the main achievements of constructive Iran-Pakistan relations during the Shah reign was their successful negotiating and establishing of borders that have remained unchallenged to date (Rana, 2016). The Baloch insurgency was a matter of grave concern for the two countries that guaranteed their border-protection cooperation.

After the Iranian revolution, the antagonism between Iran and the United States distanced Tehran from Islamabad, which remained committed to the Western bloc. At the time of Iran's revolution, General Zia-ul-Haq, who was a staunch follower of the Sunni sect of Islam, came to power in Pakistan through a military coup. For him, the revolutionary and republican new Iran presented a starkly different model of government in a Shia-dominated country. Pakistan became even more wary when Iran started to export its revolution to neighbouring countries. As a result, "Pakistan began to drift away from Iran to the Sunni Arab countries of the Middle East, including Saudi Arabia" (Notezai, 2017). With Zia-ul-Haq's mandate to disseminate the Sunni sect of Islam, the divide between Shias and Sunnis became wider in Pakistan and sectarian tensions started to rise. Iranian leader Ayatollah Khomeini's issuance of a directive in 1986 to the Iranian government to protect Pakistan's Shias complicated the situation even more (Haqqani, 2020).

The Estranged Partners 69

Since then, one source of friction between Iran and Pakistan has been the Sunni/Shia divide and the insecurities that emanate from the resulting sectarian tensions. These religious rifts are combined with ethnic secessionist tendencies in the Balochistan provinces of Iran and Pakistan, leading to a rise in insurgencies and acts of terror.

Radical Salafi groups active in Pakistan have conducted terror operations against Iranian nationals. Iranian diplomat Sadegh Ganji was assassinated in Pakistan in 1990. Seven years later, Iranian air force officers were killed in Rawalpindi. Lashkar-e-Jhangvi and Sepah-e-Sahaba are the most notorious of such groups that are involved in terrorist operations. These matters have been repeatedly discussed between Iranian and Pakistani officials. For instance, in 1999, Mohammad Khatami, Iran's then-president, expressed concerns to his Pakistani counterpart Pervez Musharraf about the rise in sectarian violence in Pakistan (Alam, 2004, 533). In another case, Iran's President Mahmoud Ahmadinejad accused Pakistani security agents of cooperating with the terrorists who committed suicide bombings in south-eastern Iran (France 24, 2009). Iran claims that Pakistan provides support to the Jundallah terrorist group in Iran's Sistan and Balochistan province, whereas Pakistan complains against the activities of India's diplomatic missions in Iran.

In the aftermath of the Iranian revolution, another source of friction between Iran and Pakistan has been Afghanistan. While during the Shah's reign, Iran was more of a mediator between Afghanistan and India (Emadi, 1995, 4), after the Iranian revolution and the subsequent rise in sectarian conflicts, Afghanistan became a scene for activities of the Taliban, who were primarily trained in the Pakistani madrasas. Since the evacuation of the Soviet forces from Afghanistan, Iran and Pakistan found themselves in opposing fronts, where Pakistan was behind the Taliban and Iran stood by the Northern Alliance. Pakistan helped the Taliban to take control of most parts of north Afghanistan. Pakistani extremists under Taliban command massacred nine Iranian diplomats in Mazar-i Sharif, leading Iran to mobilise troops on the border with Afghanistan (Rubin & Batmanglich, 2008, 2). Afghanistan under the Pakistani-backed Taliban turned into such a threat to Iran that Tehran supported the US invasion of its neighbour to topple the Taliban. Even after the collapse of the Taliban in 2001, Pakistan continued to boost the shattered Taliban organisation, and after their revival, lobbied for their return to the political scene. "Pakistan has long been one of the Taliban's most important advocates, from openly supporting its regime before 2001 to allegedly providing a haven to the group during the US war" (Parkin & Bokhari, 2022). Iran, however, never trusted the Taliban, and despite improving relations with them (Daragahi, 2021), always preferred a strong central government in Afghanistan. The thaw in relations between Iran and the Taliban wasn't Iran's favourite choice. In fact, after the Taliban, thanks to Pakistan's backing, proved to be a formidable force in Afghanistan and after other interested parties, including the US,

70 *Mohammad Soltaninejad*

engaged in serious negotiations with the Taliban, Iran started to approach the Taliban preparing for the worst-case scenario of their Kabul takeover. After the Taliban captured Kabul in 2021, Pakistan's president Imran Khan welcomed their victory, saying that they had "broken the chains of slavery" (Miller, 2021). For Iran, however, the picture is more complicated. Iran cheered the US withdrawal from Afghanistan but feared what could follow (Berger, 2021). Iran found the departure from Afghanistan of the United States, of whom Tehran has always been wary, to be in its best strategic interests. However, the prospect of rising insecurity in Afghanistan with the presence of Daesh there is alarming for Iran.

Another major factor that shapes Iran's attitude towards Pakistan is Islamabad's military cooperation with the United States. Iran is alarmed by the fact that Pakistan's territory has been used twice by the United States against foreign targets. The United States used Pakistani soil once in 1980 to organise and manage anti-Soviet forces and another time in 2001 to attack the Taliban. "Pakistan's military bases and ground and lines of communication played a role in facilitating and sustaining the US-led military invasion of Afghanistan" (Gul, 2021). Pakistan is well aware of Iran's worries and has repeatedly assured Iran that its soil will not be used to launch attacks against other countries (*Arab News*, 2020). Despite this, there is news confirming that Pakistan continually provided air and ground access to the US military (Iqbal, 2021). Although their cooperation has been focused on Afghanistan, Iran is wary of where Pakistan would stand in case of a US military operation against Iran. It is certain that Pakistan strives not to be caught in the US/Iran conflict. The neutral and cautious language Pakistan used after the killing of the Iranian general Suleimani in January 2020 to urge Iran and the United States to practice maximum restraint was out of Islamabad's concern about such an eventuality (*The Express Tribune*, 2020).

These concerns are not limited to Iran. In a similar way, Pakistan is suspicious of Iran's security and military cooperation with its main competitor, India. The Pakistani authorities have accused India of whipping up terrorism in Pakistan (Khan, 2015). They regard the Indian consulate in Zahedan as a base for planning insecurities in the eastern Pakistani province of Balochistan. They refer to the case of arrested Indian navy officer Kulbhushan Jadhav as evidence of such actions (Karim, 2022). A dossier of alleged Indian involvement in the terrorist activities in Balochistan, the Federally Administered Tribal Areas (FATA) and Karachi was handed over to the UN Secretary General by Pakistan's representative to the UN (Khetran, 2017, 115). Despite this, Iran and Pakistan do not want the border incidents and sporadic acts of terror to become a source of tension in their relations. This is particularly important for Islamabad as Pakistan already has a history of hostility with its two other neighbours over border issues: with India over Kashmir and with Afghanistan over the Durand Line. In those cases, as far as Pakistan's interests are concerned, Iran has, for the most part, acted constructively. Tehran played the role of a mediator in

Pakistan's border conflict with Afghanistan in 1963 and Tehran has mostly sympathised with Islamabad on Kashmir.

Economic trade and transportation is another domain defining Iran-Pakistan relations. Before the Iranian revolution, the economic connections between the two countries were mainly defined in the framework of the Regional Cooperation for Development (RCD) signed in 1964 between Iran, Pakistan and Turkey. After the Iranian revolution and Iran's exit from West-oriented regional arrangements, the Economic Cooperation Organization (ECO) became the major setting for regionally defined economic cooperation between Iran and Pakistan. The trade and economic cooperation of Iran and Pakistan, however, has been mainly bilateral and has remained limited. In 2021, the volume of Iran's exports to Pakistan barely exceeded $1 billion and its imports from Pakistan were even less, standing at $177 million (Trade Promotion Organization of Iran, 2021). A preferential-trade agreement between the two countries signed in 2004 has remained non-operational (Donyaye Eghtesad, 2021). Although the volume of trade between the two countries is currently trivial, there is a lot of potential that remains unfulfilled. From 1995, one of the major topics of interest between Iran and Pakistan has been building a gas pipeline from Iran to Pakistan. Although they agreed to complete the pipeline, Pakistan has refrained from fulfilling its part of the deal. Iran completed its section of the pipeline in 2011 and even proposed to make an investment of $500 million to remedy Pakistan's shortage of capital, but to no avail (Sarabi, 2022). This drove Tehran in 2018 to threaten to file for arbitration with Pakistan for a loss of $1.2 billion it endured as a result of Pakistan's refusal to complete its share of the gas-pipeline project (Global Arbitration Review, 2018). This threat was not effective and Pakistanis continued to bring excuses to not do the project. According to Pakistani officials, the main reason for Pakistan's failure to do its end of the bargain is US pressure (*Arab News*, 2019).

The Persian Gulf factor: The role of Saudi Arabia

The Persian Gulf countries, particularly Saudi Arabia, have a role to play in directing Iran's relations with India and Pakistan. In fact, the dynamics of Iran's connections with South Asia are inseparable from the quality of relations between Saudi Arabia and each of India and Pakistan. The persistent tensions between Iran and Saudi Arabia that shape the security character of the Persian Gulf sub-region has its bearing on how Tehran manages its relations with India and Pakistan. Generally speaking, Iran-Pakistan relations are more prone to the Saudi Arabian influence than Iran-India relations. For India, the main factor impacting the direction of its relations with Iran is the United States, and Saudi Arabia's role is rather indirect at best. India seeks an expansion of relations with both Riyadh and Tehran, without one being sacrificed for the other. Despite this, Riyadh enjoys a superior position in India's look to the Persian Gulf in terms of volume of trade and

72   *Mohammad Soltaninejad*

security. Iran, in contrast, has an unequivocal geostrategic importance for India, but the relationship has not grown to its potential, mainly due to the disruptive role the US has played, with Saudi Arabia being mostly a neutral bystander. Conversely, Pakistan is heavily impacted by the position of Saudi Arabia to expand its ties with Iran. Here again, the bilateral relationship between Iran and Pakistan is a matter of geographical proximity and geopolitical necessity. However, the disruption comes, this time, from the other side of the Gulf, that is, Saudi Arabia. In the remainder of this chapter, the way Saudi Arabia impacts Iran's connections with India and Pakistan is explained at length.

Saudi Arabia's close relations with India started after the demise of the Soviet Union and end of the Cold War. Before that, the two countries belonged to the two opposing global camps and therefore, the relations were kept at a minimal level. With the collapse of the Soviet Union and triumph of liberal democracy over communism, India started to implement liberal economic policies at home. Economic liberalisation and privatisation made India reconsider its foreign policies to attract international investments and also get access to sources of energy. In such an atmosphere, the oil-rich and wealthy Persian Gulf nations, particularly Saudi Arabia, found their way into the radar of India's foreign policy. The Persian Gulf states also needed India as they were trying to secure markets for their energy, and they needed a labour force to implement their construction and infrastructure projects. This paved the grounds for an unprecedented expansion of their ties with India. The transformation of Indo-Saudi relations was a consequence of this economic interdependence.

From the mid-2000s onward, Saudi-Indian relations have witnessed a gradual but steady rise that is reflective of two strategic shifts the two countries are facing. On the Saudi side, the most important political force that drives it towards India is the feeling in Riyadh that the United States is no longer a reliable protector. Over the past decade, there has been a growing consensus in the United States that the Middle East is no longer the asset it used to be for securing the United States' vital interests. Barack Obama was known for his desire to relieve the United States from the region. His "pivot Asia" doctrine was formulated around shifting US attention to East Asia, where there was an urge to contain China. He was the first US president who tried to revive the traditional balancing acts in the Middle East by resolving the nuclear issue with Iran and leaving Riyadh on its own to resolve its problems with Tehran. After Obama, Donald Trump improved the US-Saudi Arabia relations but his commitment to the security of the Arab states in the Persian Gulf was shaky, at best. For him, what mattered the most was the arm deals he signed with the Gulf Arab states and also the continuation of their oil pumping into the global market. When Saudi Arabian oil installations were hit by Iran-backed Houthis, he did not interfere, assuring the Arab states that the United States was no longer a reliable security umbrella. The worst came with Joe Biden, who promised to revive the nuclear deal with Iran and heavily criticised Saudi Arabia on human rights issues and its war on Yemen. These realities have driven Riyadh to boost its relations with other great powers, most notably China and then India. Although China has got the lion's share in this Saudi strategic shift, India has its potential and has been another target for Riyadh to establish strategic relations. On the Indian side, the most important driving force to expand ties with Saudi Arabia is its desire to grow to the status of a great power that links it to the geostrategic sub-region of the Persian Gulf for securing political links and guaranteeing the flow of energy.

The constant exchange of visits at the highest echelons of government and also at the ministerial level is reflective of the durability of a blooming relationship. King Abdullah's visit to India in 2006 and issuance of the Delhi Declaration was a turning point in the expansion of ties between the two countries. In 2005, Saudi Arabia was only exporting $790 million of oil to India, which jumped to $12.2 billion in 2006 and skyrocketed to $32 billion in 2014. The total volume of bilateral trade reached $48 billion in the same year. Henceforth, India became the fourth-largest trade partner of Saudi Arabia after China, the US and the United Arab Emirates (UAE) (Quamar, 2019, 14–16). In fact, Saudi Arabia is the most reliable source of energy for India that has provided 17–18 per cent of its crude-oil needs over the past decade (Powell, Sati & Tomar, 2022). In October 2014, India's oil and gas minister, Dharmendra Pradhan, travelled to Riyadh to participate in a bilateral ministerial meeting on energy. After King Abdullah died in January 2015, India announced a day of mourning. India's vice president, Mohammad Hamid Ansari, travelled to Saudi Arabia to extend India's condolences. After the demise of King Abdullah, Modi visited the new Saudi king, Salman bin-Abdul-Aziz, twice. Adel Al-Jubeir, the foreign minister of Saudi Arabia, visited India in March 2016, paving the grounds for a subsequent visit of the Indian prime minister to Saudi Arabia, where he was warmly welcomed (Quamar, 2019).

While energy security dominates the India-Saudi Arabia agenda of growing ties, security and defence cooperation are also becoming more important in their relations (Rajagopalan, 2021). The defence cooperation between India and Saudi Arabia is expanding, informed by the fact that Delhi has little to offer in terms of defence systems to Riyadh, but it has the potential to be a hub for the cooperative development of intra-regional defence technologies (Taneja, 2022). In fact, India can only have a complementary role to play in Saudi Arabia's quest for security. Notwithstanding such facts, the shared Indian-Saudi apprehension for the security of the Persian Gulf waterways drives them to boost their defence cooperation. In the midst of the rising tensions between Iran and the Unites States, Saudi Arabian oil facilities were hit by the Houthis in 2019. Similar attacks against Saudi Aramco were conducted in 2021. These incidents have gravely affected Saudi Arabia's security calculations. At the same time, India has also felt the urge to provide security coverage for its ships passing through the Persian Gulf.

Since 2019, Operation Sankalp has provided safe passage to an average of 16 Indian-flagged merchant vessels in the Gulf region every day (*The Hindu*, 2021b). Under such common threats, the security and defence cooperation between Delhi and Riyadh is growing. The persistent fact, though, remains India's effort to maintain a balance between Riyadh and Tehran. Delhi calibrates its defence and security relations with Riyadh within a complex equilibrium that involves Washington, Tehran and Islamabad. While Washington is supportive of expanding relations between India and Saudi Arabia, Delhi expands its ties with Riyadh only in a way that does not harm its relations with Iran. After all, India's balancing act against Pakistan is heavily dependent on its ongoing cooperation with Iran.

When it comes to Pakistan, the historically most important factor that directs Pakistan's relations with the Persian Gulf countries is Kashmir, over which Islamabad has gained the support of the OIC. The importance of Kashmir in shaping Pakistan's relations with the Persian Gulf countries is reflected in Islamabad's bid to have constructive relations with both Tehran and Riyadh. Where Kashmir is concerned, a united Muslim position in support of Islamabad is the primary Pakistani interest. Apart from Kashmir, Iran and Saudi Arabia's proximity to Pakistan makes Islamabad wary of a probable military conflict between these two regional powers that would have averse security ramifications for Pakistan. At the same time, Islamabad has been trying to introduce itself as a pivot state in the Muslim world, using its position as the sole Muslim nation that has acquired nuclear weapons. Against this backdrop, Pakistan has tried to play the role of a mediator between Iran and Saudi Arabia (Al Jazeera, 2020). In fact, when it comes to Iran-Saudi Arabia relations, Pakistan's primary concern is the continuation of the support it receives from both nations on the Kashmir case and also the prevention of a military conflict between them that may drag Pakistan in.

Pakistan's relations with Iran and Saudi Arabia, however, go beyond these balancing and mediating acts. Saudi Arabia has a great deal of influence over Pakistan that affects the quality and extent of its ties with Iran. This influence comes, first and foremost, from the loans Saudi Arabia grants to Pakistan. In 2018, for instance, Saudi Arabia agreed to give Pakistan a loan of $6.2 billion that was critical to support Islamabad's balance of payments (OpIndia, 2022). In addition to that, Pakistani nationals are working in Saudi Arabia and send an abundance of annual remittances back home that is again financially significant for Islamabad. In only seven months of the fiscal year 2018, Pakistan received $18 billion of remittances from Saudi Arabia and the UAE (Ahmed, 2022). Pakistan's reliance on Saudi Arabia is not only about financial assistances but it is also a matter of Saudi Arabia's funding of the Deobandi and Ahl-al-Hadis madrasas. Saudi Arabia uses its influence with the Pashtun-based Deobandi Salafis to pressure Pakistan into compliance with its demands in the regional political and security dynamics (Afzal, 2019). Iran's revolution in 1979 and the Soviet Union's

The Estranged Partners 75

invasion of Afghanistan in that year drove Saudi Arabia to disseminate its own readings of Salafi Islam in Pakistan. The Talibs who graduated from the Saudi schools were fervent fighters against the Soviet army and founded the Taliban regime after the Soviet withdrawal from Afghanistan and the subsequent conflicts they had with the Northern Alliance.

All these factors have created powerful leverage for Saudi Arabia over Pakistan and have restricted Islamabad's margin of political and strategic manoeuvre vis-à-vis Riyadh. One clear case of how Saudi loans shape its relations with Pakistan is a visit paid by Pakistan's chief of staff to Riyadh to mend the strained ties with Saudi Arabia resulting from the criticism the Pakistani foreign minister had levelled against Saudi Arabia over Riyadh's position on the Kashmir issue, resulting in a Saudi threat of cancelling a $3 billion loan they promised to Pakistan and their intention not to extend oil credit of $2.3 billion (Batool & Thakkar, 2021). Such Saudi leverage is significant in determining the depth and breadth of Pakistan's relations with Iran. Pakistan adjusts its Iran policy in accordance with the signals it receives from Riyadh and also the dominant atmosphere of Iran-Saudi Arabia relations. The degree to which Pakistan's foreign policy is influenced by Saudi Arabia is showcased in the cancellation of Imran Khan's planned attendance at the Malaysian-engineered Kuala Lumpur summit held in December 2019 (Cafiero & Al-Jaber, 2019). This Pakistani decision came after Khan's visit to Saudi Arabia (Jamal, 2019). The reason was, as Turkish president Erdoğan later revealed, Saudi pressure (Dawn, 2019).

Despite this, Saudi Arabia-Pakistan relations are not of the patron-client type. Pakistan is not even an all-weather partner for Riyadh. All the leverage Saudi Arabia has over Pakistan has not provided Riyadh with a blank cheque to direct Islamabad's policies. In fact, Pakistan has proven able to manoeuvre between Saudi Arabia and Iran, building a balance between its two powerful neighbours. The most notable example is the Pakistani parliament's vote against the Pakistani army's involvement in the Yemen war in favour of Saudi Arabia (Boone & Dehghan, 2015). In fact, all the influence Saudi Arabia enjoys in Islamabad has failed to drag Pakistan into the Yemeni war. In 2015, Pakistan declared neutrality in the war and, under the pressure of Riyadh, agreed to send troops only on the condition that they would not cross the Saudi border into Yemen (Ghouri, 2018). The best Pakistan has pledged to do for Saudi Arabia in Yemen is to play the role of a mediator between the conflicting parties.

After all, Iran is Pakistan's immediate neighbour with their securities intertwined. Pakistan has a border of 832 kilometres with Iran and, therefore, cannot adopt policies that antagonise Tehran. The Shias of Pakistan look favourably at Iran and Iran has become a point of reference for them (Akbarzadeh, Ahmed & Ibrahimi, 2021). They comprise 15–25 per cent of the total Pakistani population and receive support from Iran (Vatanka, 2012). The most apparent case was Ayatollah Khomeini's order to the Iranian government to protect the Shia in Pakistan against General

76 *Mohammad Soltaninejad*

Zia-ul-Haq's sectarian politics. "The Shia community believes that had it not been for Ayatollah Khomeini's intercession and pressures from Iran the Zia regime would have effectively marginalised the community" (Nasr, 1999, 313). Therefore, the Shia have the potential to pressure Islamabad not to succumb to the Saudi demands against Iran. Iran has already proved able to mobilise and recruit them. The Zainabiyoun Brigade fighting in Syria is comprised of two to five thousand Pakistani Shias organised and funded by Iran (Guven, 2020). The Shia elements among the ruling elites and within political parties sympathise with Iran and they are against the unlimited expansion of Pakistan's relations with Saudi Arabia when such relations undermine Pakistan's ties with Iran or endanger Iran's interests (Batool & Thakkar, 2021). Finally, it should be borne in mind that there is a lot of potential for cooperation between Iran and Pakistan. The outstanding gas pipeline and rail and road connection projects between the two countries can yield a lot of interests. Pakistan awaits the elimination of the obstacles for their fulfilment. This explains Pakistan's decision not to throw all its weight behind Riyadh and will most probably continue to define the scope of Pakistan-Saudi Arabia relations in the years to come.

Conclusion

There is a great potential for the expansion Iran's relations with India and Pakistan. However, their bids to bond together have faced a number of challenges and, therefore, the scope of Tehran's relations with these two South Asian nations has remained limited. The first challenge is the enduring conflict between India and Pakistan over Kashmir and their security competition in the Persian Gulf. This has squeezed Iran's capacity to maintain balanced and constructive relations with them. Tehran's interest in involving India in its infrastructure development projects in Chabahar has created problems in its relations with Islamabad, best reflected in their exchange of accusations over the insecurities in their common border areas. Pakistan cannot shut its eyes to India's placing pressures on its western flank. On the Indian side, Iran's support of Pakistan in the Kashmir case and also its advocacy of the Indian Muslim population is irritating. This predicament provides its own opportunities for Iran and expands Tehran's margin of manoeuvre vis-à-vis India and Pakistan. Iran's involving of India in Chabahar gives it an undisputable leverage over Pakistan. At the same time, Iran's strategic location on Pakistan's doorstep makes it an unparalleled asset for India. After all, India and Pakistan remain to be Iran's potential partners and not competitors. Iran is keen to see Chabahar developed by Indian enterprises. Rail and road construction projects in Iran's Sistan and Balochistan also await India's action. Pakistan has a similar huge potential that Iran tries to make use of. Iran cannot let go of the gas pipeline to Pakistan on which millions of dollars have already been spent.

The Estranged Partners 77

All this potential, however, has remained under-materialised due to the presence of third parties that disrupt Iran's plans to work with India and Pakistan. The most important of such obstacles is the United States. Washington has successfully hampered India and Pakistan's cooperation with Iran. Iran's energy exports to India have been halted, mainly due to direct US pressure. Chabahar has also fallen victim to the Iran/US dispute over the nuclear issue. In a similar way, Pakistan has refrained from executing its end of the deal with Iran to build the gas pipeline. The United States is apparently behind this. As the Iran/US conflict intensifies, Iran becomes more suspicious of the close Indian and Pakistani relations with the US. There is no guarantee that Pakistan's territory will not be used to launch attacks against Iran. On the other way around, the security of India and Pakistan would be compromised in case of an escalation between Iran and the US. Pakistan is Iran's immediate neighbour and the instabilities arising from Iran undermine its security. India's economy is heavily dependent on the security of the Persian Gulf waterways and any military confrontation between Iran and the US would endanger the already shaky security structure in the Persian Gulf, hampering the flow of energy to India. The security interconnectedness between Iran and South Asia comes to light better when the role Saudi Arabia plays in this respect is revealed. Riyadh is relevant in the balancing acts between Tehran, Delhi and Islamabad. Saudi Arabia has made up for the loss of Iran's oil exports to India. The expanding energy and trade ties between Saudi Arabia and India make it possible for Delhi to forget its plans for lucrative business with Iran. The Saudi factor, however, is best reflected in Pakistan's relations with Iran, where Riyadh has powerful and effective leverage to direct Islamabad's Iran policy. Islamabad, in turn, tries to strike a balance in its relations with Tehran and Riyadh so as not to be dragged into any dispute between its two powerful neighbours. In short, the security game in the Persian Gulf with the participation of India and Pakistan is a complicated one in which no actor is bereft of its tools to balance others. Iran uses the India/Pakistan conflict to preserve its relations with each of them. India and Pakistan, for their part, work with Iran to balance one another and they each moderate Iran's influence using their own effective leverages. Iran needs Pakistan's cooperation to maintain security and stability in its province of Sistan and Balochistan. Similarly, Iran needs to keep India as a potential investor in its infrastructure projects and a client for its oil and gas.

References

Afzal, Madiha. 2019. Saudi Arabia's hold on Pakistan. Brookings. https://www.brookings.edu/research/saudi-arabias-hold-on-pakistan/

Ahmed, Khurshid. 2022. Saudi Arabia, UAE largest contributors to Pakistan's $18 billion remittances—SBP. Arab News. https://www.arabnews.pk/node/2022926/pakistan

Ahmed, Z. Shahab and Bhatnagar Stuti. 2018. The India-Iran-Pakistan Triad: Comprehending the Correlation of Geo-Economics and Geopolitics, *Asian Studies Review* 42 (3): 517–536.

Akbarzadeh, Shahram, Ahmed, Z Shahab and Ibrahimi, Niamatullah. 2021. Iran's Soft Power in Pakistan, *Asian Politics and Policy* 13 (3): 305–325.

Al Jazeera. 2020. Pakistan's Khan says mediation prevented Saudi-Iran escalation. https://www.aljazeera.com/news/2020/8/3/pakistans-khan-says-mediation-prevented-saudi-iran-escalation

Alam, Shah. 2004. Iran-Pakistan Relations: Political and Strategic Dimensions. *Strategic Analysis* 28 (4): 526–545.

Arab News. 2019. Gas pipeline project impossible under US sanctions, Pakistan tells Iran. https://www.arabnews.pk/node/1495251/pakistan

Arab News. 2020. Pakistan says won't allow its soil to be used against any other state. https://www.arabnews.pk/node/1608621/pakistan

Batool, Fizza and Thakkar, Chirayu. 2021. Comparing India and Pakistan's Approaches to a Possible Iran-Saudi Rapprochement. South Asian Voices. https://southasianvoices.org/comparing-india-and-pakistans-approaches-to-possible-iran-saudi-rapprochement/

Berger, Miriam. 2021. Iran cheers US withdrawal from Afghanistan—but fears what could follow. The Washington Post. https://www.washingtonpost.com/world/2021/07/10/iran-taliban-afghanistan-us-troop-withdrawal/

Bhattacherjee, Kallol. 2019. Union Budget 2019–20: Bhutan gains, Chabahar loses in Budget pie. The Hindu. https://www.thehindu.com/business/budget/union-budget-2019-20-bhutan-gains-chabahar-loses-in-budget-pie/article28298680.ece

Bilgrami, M. Pervez (2018) Iran's conflicting stand on the Kashmir issue. Center for Iranian Studies in Ankara (IRAM). https://iramcenter.org/en/irans-conflicting-stand-on-the-kashmir-issue/

Boone, Jon and Dehghan, S Kamali. 2015. Pakistan's parliament votes against entering Yemen conflict. The Guardian. https://www.theguardian.com/world/2015/apr/10/pakistans-parliament-votes-against-entering-yemen-conflict

Cafiero, Giorgio and Al-Jaber, Khalid. 2019. Kuala Lumpur summit: A challenge to Saudi leadership? Middle East Institute. https://www.mei.edu/publications/kuala-lumpur-summit-challenge-saudi-leadership

Council on Foreign Relations. 2010. The US-India nuclear deal. https://www.cfr.org/backgrounder/us-india-nuclear-deal

Daragahi, Borzou. 2021. Iran spent years preparing for a Taliban victory. It may still get stung. Atlantic Council. https://www.atlanticcouncil.org/blogs/iransource/iran-spent-years-preparing-for-a-taliban-victory-it-may-still-get-stung/

Dawn. 2019. Erdogan says Saudi "put pressure" on Pakistan to withdraw from Malaysia summit: Turkish media. https://www.dawn.com/news/print/1523364

Dikshit, Sandeep. 2010. U.S. tried to put the screws on India over Iran. The Hindu. https://www.thehindu.com/news/national//article60548341.ece

Donyaye Eghtesad. The double standards of the trade officials. https://donya-e-eqtesad.com/%D8%A8%D8%AE%D8%B4-%D8%A8%D8%A7%D8%B2%D8%B1%DA%AF%D8%A7%D9%86%DB%8C-4/3823175-%D8%B1%D9%81%D8%AA%D8%A7%D8%B1-%D8%AF%D9%88%DA%AF%D8%A7%D9%86%D9%87-%D9%85%D8%AA%D9%88%D9%84%DB%8C-%D8%AA%D8%AC%D8%A7%D8%B1%D8%AA (in Persian).

The Estranged Partners 79

Emadi, Hafizullah. 1995. Exporting Iran's Revolution: The Radicalization of the Shiite Movement in Afghanistan, *Middle Eastern Studies* 31 (1): 1–12.

Fair, Christine. (2007). India and Iran: New Delhi's New Balancing Act, *The Washington Quarterly* 30: 145–159.

France 24. 2009. Tehran to demand Pakistan hand over alleged attack mastermind. https://www.france24.com/en/20091019-tehran-demand-pakistan-hand-over-alleged-attack-mastermind

Ghouri, Ahmad. 2018. Pakistan's role in Yemen crisis. The Express Tribune. https://tribune.com.pk/story/1835370/pakistans-role-yemen-crisis

Global Arbitration Review. 2018. Iran threatens Pakistan with claim over stalled pipeline. https://globalarbitrationreview.com/article/iran-threatens-pakistan-claim-over-stalled-pipeline

Gul, Ayaz. 2021. Pakistan: No more military bases for US Afghan mission. VOA. https://www.voanews.com/a/south-central-asia_pakistan-no-more-military-bases-us-afghan-mission/6205700.html

Gupta, Shekhar. 2011. Babri Masjid demolition 1992: How the world reacted. India Today. https://www.indiatoday.in/india/story/babri-masjid-demolition-1992-ayodhya-pakistan-international-community-147820-2011-12-05

Guven, Aydin. 2020. ANALYSIS—Iran-backed Zainabiyoun Brigade could become Pakistan's new national security problem, Anadolu Agency. https://www.aa.com.tr/en/analysis/analysis-iran-backed-zainabiyoun-brigade-could-become-pakistan-s-new-national-security-problem/2033585#

Haji-Yousefi, A. Mohammad and Narouei, Hadi. 2021. Geopolitics, Geoeconomics and the Prospects of Iran-India Cooperation in Chabahar, *Geopolitics Quarterly* 17 (3): 61–87 (in Persian).

Haqqani, Husain. 2020. Iran's revolutionary influence in South Asia. Hudson Institute. https://www.hudson.org/research/16472-iran-s-revolutionary-influence-in-south-asia

Hathaway, Robert. 2004. The "strategic partnership" between India and Iran. Woodrow Wilson Center Asia Program. https://www.wilsoncenter.org/publication/the-strategic-partnership-between-india-and-iran-pdf

India Ministry of External Affairs. 2016. India–Iran Joint Statement—"civilizational connect, contemporary context" during the visit of Prime Minister to Iran. https://www.mea.gov.in/bilateral-documents.htm?dtl/26843/India__Iran_Joint_Statement_quot_Civilisational_Connect_Contemporary_Contextquot_during_the_visit_of_Prime_Minister_to_Iran

Iqbal, Anwar. 2021. Pakistan to continue giving air, ground access, says Pentagon. Dawn. https://www.dawn.com/news/1625310/pakistan-to-continue-giving-air-ground-access-says-pentagon

Iranian Diplomacy. 2015. India prepares for settling debt to Iran. Iranian Diplomacy. http://irdiplomacy.ir/en/news/1949384/india-prepares-for-settling-debt-to-iran-

Jamal, Umair. 2019. The Kuala Lumpur Summit 2019 shows Pakistan's diplomatic subservience to Saudi Arabia. The Diplomat. https://thediplomat.com/2019/12/the-kuala-lumpur-summit-2019-shows-pakistans-diplomatic-subservience-to-saudi-arabia/

Jayaswal, Rajeev. 2021. With Biden at helm in US, India-Iran trade prospects may improve: Exporters. Hindustan Times. https://www.hindustantimes.com/business/with-biden-at-helm-in-us-india-iran-trade-prospects-may-improve-exporters-101613013612675.html

80 *Mohammad Soltaninejad*

Karim, Umar. 2022. Pakistan-Iran relations and the security situation in Balochistan. Arab News. https://www.arabnews.pk/node/2020356

Kaura, Vinay. 2021. India's search for a new role in Afghanistan. Middle East Institute. https://www.mei.edu/publications/indias-search-new-role-afghanistan

Khan, M. Naseem. 2001. Vajpayee's Visit to Iran: Indo-Iranian Relations and Prospects of Bilateral Cooperation, *Strategic Analysis* 25 (6) 765–779.

Khan, Ilyas. 2015. What lies behind Pakistani charges of Indian terrorism. BBC. https://www.bbc.com/news/world-asia-32604137

Khetran, M. Sherbaz. 2017. Indian Interference in Balochistan: Analysing the Evidence and Implications for Pakistan, *Strategic Studies* 37 (3): 112–125.

Miller, M. Chatterjee. 2021. Pakistan's Support for the Taliban: What to Know. Council on Foreign Relations. https://www.cfr.org/article/pakistans-support-taliban-what-know

Mohammadally, Safia. 1979. Iran-Pakistan Relations (1947–1979), *Pakistan Horizon* 32 (4): 51–63.

Naaz, Farah. 2001. Indo-Iranian relations 1947–2000. *Strategic Analysis* 24 (10): 1911–1926.

Nasr, Vali. 1999. Sectarianism and Shia politics in Pakistan, 1979–present. CEMOTI. https://www.persee.fr/doc/cemot_0764-9878_1999_num_28_1_1503

Nayar, Mandira. 2020. Iran's criticism of Delhi violence unlikely to affect bilateral ties. The Week. https://www.theweek.in/news/india/2020/03/04/irans-criticism-of-delhi-violence-unlikely-to-affect-bilateral-ties.html

Notezai, M. Akbar. 2017. Iran-Pakistan at the Crossroads? A tradition of cooperation is giving way to a much more complicated relationship. The Diplomat. https://thediplomat.com/2017/07/iran-pakistan-at-the-crossroads/

OpIndia. 2022. Patriotic Pakistanis are hating Saudi Arabia, and they have solutions for all problems: Nukes and opium. https://www.opindia.com/2022/01/patriotic-pakistanis-are-hating-saudi-arabia-over-loan-payback-turkey-nukes-oil/

Pant, Harsh. 2006. India and US-Iran Imbroglio: Difficult Choices Ahead, *Journal of Asian Affairs* 19 (01): 25–38.

Parkin, Benjamin and Bokhari, Farhan. 2022. Taliban victory unleashes hardline forces in Pakistan. https://www.ft.com/content/6c1ac211-df0f-4607-9f1e-c9b15e16d609

Powell, Lydia, Sati, Akhilesh and Tomar, V. Kumar. 2022. India's oil imports: Trends in diversification. Observer Research Foundation. https://www.orfonline.org/expert-speak/indias-oil-imports/

Quamar, Muddassir. 2019. Indo-Saudi relations emerging strategic dimensions. Middle East Institute, New Delhi. http://www.mei.org.in/uploads/content/173-1566929735-analyses-monograph.pdf

Rajagopalan, Pillai. 2021. India-Saudi Arabia defense cooperation. The Diplomat. https://thediplomat.com/tag/india-saudi-arabia-defense-cooperation/

Rana, M. Amir. 2016. Iran and Pakistan's intertwined history. Dawn. https://www.dawn.com/news/print/1272879

Reuters. 2016. India raises Iran credit line to $450 million. Reuters. https://www.reuters.com/article/india-iran-credit-idINKCN0X31DJ

Roche, Elizabeth. 2018. PM Modi meets Hassan Rouhani, India Iran sign pacts after substantive talks. Mint. https://www.livemint.com/Politics/CHAmyDgX0de6OYFlhCSKjJ/Narendra-Modi-Hassan-Rouhani-hold-substantive-talks-to-bo.html

Roy, Shubhajit. 2020. Explained: Reading the criticism from Iran. The India Express. https://indianexpress.com/article/explained/iran-on-delhi-violence-javad-zarif-6305705/

Rubin, Barnett and Batmanglich, Sara. 2008. The U.S. and Iran in Afghanistan: Policy gone awry. MIT Center for International Studies. https://www.files.ethz.ch/isn/93911/Audit_10_08_Rubin.pdf

Sarabi, Kazem. 2022. Iran begins talks to export gas to Pakistan. Caspian News. https://caspiannews.com/news-detail/iran-begins-talks-to-export-gas-to-pakistan-2022-5-29-45/

Soltaninejad, Mohammad. 2017. Iran–India Relations: The Unfulfilled Strategic Partnership, *India Quarterly: A Journal of International Affairs* 73 (1): 21–35.

Subramanian, Nirupama, 2021. Explained: What are India's investments in Afghanistan? The Indian Express. https://indianexpress.com/article/explained/explained-indias-afghan-investment-7406795/

Taneja, Kabir. 2022. India–Saudi Arabia military cooperation takes a step forward. Observer Research Foundation. https://www.orfonline.org/expert-speak/india-saudi-arabia-military-cooperation-takes-a-step-forward/

Tasnim. 2016. Iran welcomes China, Pakistan to join Chabahar Project: Envoy. https://www.tasnimnews.com/en/news/2016/05/29/1087127/iran-welcomes-china-pakistan-to-join-chabahar-project-envoy

The Express Tribune. 2020. COAS calls for "maximum restraint" after Iranian general's killing by US. https://tribune.com.pk/story/2129853/pompeo-reaches-gen-qamar-amid-us-iran-standoff

The Guardian. 2016. India to invest $500m in Iranian port of Chabahar. The Guardian. https://www.theguardian.com/world/2016/may/23/india-invest-500m-iran-port-chabahar-modi-transit-accord-afghanistan

The Hindu. 2009. India votes against Iran in IAEA resolution. The Hindu. https://www.thehindu.com/news/national//article60630495.ece

The Hindu. 2016. Modi's Iran visit: Key takeaways. The Hindu. https://www.the-hindu.com/news/national/Modis-Iran-visit-key-takeaways/article14335305.ece

The Hindu. 2021a. India to resume buying oil from Iran once U.S. sanctions ease. The Hindu. https://www.thehindu.com/business/Industry/india-to-resume-buying-oil-from-iran-once-us-sanctions-ease/article34271888.ece

The Hindu. 2021b. Operation Sankalp: Sixteen Indian-flagged vessels provided safe passage everyday. https://www.thehindu.com/news/national/operation-sankalp-sixteen-indian-flagged-vessels-provided-safe-passage-everyday/article61442282.ece

Trade Promotion Organization of Iran. 2021. Pakistan trade statistics. https://tpo.ir/countries/%D9%BE%D8%A7%DA%A9%D8%B3%D8%AA%D8%A7%D9%86 (in Persian).

Vatanka, Alex. 2012. The Guardian of Pakistan's Shia. Hudson Institute. https://www.hudson.org/research/9863-the-guardian-of-pakistan-s-shia

Vatanka. Alex. 2015. *Iran and Pakistan: Security, Diplomacy and American Influence.* London and New York: Tauris.

Venkataramanan, K. 2019. What does the Places of Worship Act protect? The Hindu. https://www.thehindu.com/news/national/what-does-the-places-of-worship-act-protect/article61615043.ece

Verma, Nidhi. 2017. India's 2016 Iran oil imports hit record high—trade. Reuters. https://www.reuters.com/article/india-iran-oil-idINKBN15G3XR

4 Complex Interdependence and Security Architecture

Charting Bangladesh-Gulf Ties and Political Engagements

Lailufar Yasmin

The security architecture in the 21st century is going through a rapid transformation. The century unfolded with a massive shift in terms of the global centre of power being shifted from the West to the East with question marks on the durability of the postwar liberal order and global leadership. A stable international order provides a location of power in the system as well as at least a semblance of structural peace. In the absence of such clear directions, we have seen systemic instabilities, and pockets of tensions rising globally. The SARS-COVID-19 or coronavirus pandemic, since its onset in 2020 has undoubtedly made the security concerns of states more complex. It clearly showed how integrated and interdependent economies are all around the world. The butterfly effect, a mathematical model of chaos theory coined in the 1970s, could not have been proven more effectively in the social world than with the unfolding of the pandemic. The idea of complex interdependence to understand global trade and dependence entered the lexicon of international relations (IR) in the 1970s too. It was, however, the pandemic that made us realise the breadth and vulnerability of the *global village* where physical connections came to a halt and were yet to be fully functional in mid-2021. Nonetheless, Asia's security structure and geopolitical thrust in the 21st century also saw tremendous attention with four clear security hotspots emerging—the South China Sea, the Korean Peninsula, the South Asian region and last but not least the Middle East—all as a historical continuum of geopolitical tussles of previous eras. States in Asia came under closer scrutiny, not only due to security issues but also due to the meteoric rise of China along with the rise of regional actors like India, Iran, Turkey and Bangladesh, with their assertive international policies, as well as economic resources to back up their assertiveness.

This chapter discusses Bangladesh's relationship with Gulf countries—Saudi Arabia, Kuwait, the United Arab Emirates (UAE), Qatar, Bahrain and Oman—keeping this general overview in mind. Despite a topsy-turvy beginning surrounding the Cold War politics during the birth of Bangladesh while it was fighting its War of Independence in 1971, Bangladesh-Gulf relations hit off positively soon in the early 1970s. Bangladesh's need for aid to address its war-ravaged economy in the post-independence period

DOI: 10.4324/9781003283058-5

Complex Interdependence and Security Architecture 83

was readily met by the wealthy nations of the Gulf. Bangladesh has also been a steady supplier of migrant labour in the region. Bangladesh has been globally the 11th-highest remittance earning country in 2019, primarily due to a stronger US economy and a rise in oil prices that generated outward remittances, particularly from the Gulf Cooperation Council (GCC) (Bangladesh 3rd in South Asia, 11th globally: WB, 2019; Bangladesh continues to see robust remittance inflow, 2020). In this chapter, I articulate different stages of the relationship between Bangladesh and the GCC countries. In a globalised world of complex interdependence, the GCC countries and Bangladesh can develop stronger ties by emphasising each other's strengths and exploring new areas of engagement. While the pandemic has temporarily put an embargo on people's transfer from one country to the other, Bangladesh holds a particular strength in terms of providing an uninterrupted labour supply once the channels reopen. Bangladesh's strength in providing unskilled and semi-skilled labour is unparalleled, not only in terms of numbers, but also in terms of the familiarity of religion and culture, and thus bears a geopolitical implication for the region. Moreover, Bangladesh has developed strong bilateral ties with individual Gulf countries, where the trajectory of the relationship is shifting gradually from Bangladesh only being an aid-dependent and underdeveloped country to a country full of possibilities for the Gulf countries to tap. Bangladesh is also a potent security partner of the region, aptly demonstrated during the Kuwait crisis in 1991 and later on, by being a part of security alliances in the Middle East region.

In the context of the changing international architecture, this chapter makes two central contributions to the existing scholarship. It argues how, theoretically, the nexus between economy and security is changing in the 21st century. Strategic calculations are done not solely based on security imperatives; rather, resources and connectivity are being prioritised as states are more aware of how interdependence has assumed a new meaning with time. The increasing complexities of interdependence have significantly manoeuvred the contemporary security architecture. This theoretical underpinning is backed by discussing Bangladesh's relationship with the Gulf countries to reveal its practical implications. There is already a dearth of academic literature on understanding the patterns of the relationship between the Gulf countries and Bangladesh. This chapter aims to fill the lacuna using a scholarly analysis of the proposed theoretical framework to explore different patterns and aspects of the relationship between Bangladesh and the Gulf countries to comprehend the geopolitical impacts and security implications of such a relationship.

The chapter begins with a discussion on the theoretical underpinnings of security and complex interdependence and how they are intertwined in the 21st century. Drawing on several examples, this section asserts that 21st-century politics can hardly draw a clear line between security and economic issues. Rather, the changing nature of complex interdependence

84 *Lailufar Yasmin*

has established ties between security and economy that are driving political considerations in contemporary political calculations. The next section outlines the regional security architecture of the Gulf region. Bangladesh's relationship with the Gulf region is articulated in the next broad section divided into two sub-sections—economic relations and security relations. This section, overall, articulates the areas of cooperation, challenges and possible areas of expansion of the relationship from bilateral and multilateral perspectives. In the end, this chapter, taking a comprehensive approach, summarises why complex interdependence drives the relationship stronger in the 21st century despite security concerns that may seem intractable.

Security and complex interdependence in the 21st century

In the study of IR, realists argue that survival is the primary goal of a state, for which the struggle for power defines relationships among states. As there is no central authority in the international system, states are on their own for ensuring their survival, which is often manifested in the policy of a zero-sum game—the gain of X is considered as the loss of Y and vice versa. Realism, thus, seldom prescribes any cooperation among states, except security alliances that might be needed to achieve a greater objective of national security. The North Atlantic Treaty Organization (NATO) and the Warsaw Pact during the Cold War period are examples of such competing security alliances led by the United States (US) and the former Soviet Union to counter each other. Liberalism, on the other hand, strategises relationships through the lens of the prisoner's dilemma game, where relative gain matters more than absolute gain. Through cooperation and the creation of more such areas, states will have a stake to sustain the framework for the benefit of each other. Thus, the idea of the European Union gradually took shape, built on the European Coal and Steel Community (ECSC), when the then-French Foreign Minister Robert Schuman claimed that this economic arrangement would make war between France and Germany "materially impossible" (Schuman, 1994: 12). Although scholars argue that "trade can prevent war" or "war is unprofitable" are banal arguments, in the new era of globalisation where the nature of trade and interdependence have assumed a complex nature, one might argue that this "complex interdependence" has brought about a fundamental shift in the way states interact with each other. As stated before—the flap of a butterfly can stir a systemic change—and this idea of the "butterfly effect" drew scholarly attention as to how it can create a "defect" in the system as well (Dizikes, 2011; Vernon, 2017; Goldin and Mariathasan, 2014)—to explain the complex nature of interdependence. Often, the nature of interdependence is also explained as "unintended interdependence" or "competitive interdependence"—but the onset of the pandemic and the consequent closure of borders all around the world have taught the world how it is ever-so interdependent (Eriksson, 2017; Krieken, 2019; Hass, 2021).

Complex Interdependence and Security Architecture 85

In the theoretical discussion of security and complex interdependence, scholars generally view them as located on two different spectrums and mutually exclusive. However, "complex interdependence" does not qualify as a theory in itself, as it outlines, according to Keohane and Nye, "the goals and instruments of state policy" (Keohane and Nye, 1987). IR scholars generally consider this as an offshoot of neoliberalism. Nonetheless, complex interdependence has fanned out differently since the idea was first introduced in IR. In the 21st century, it is no longer considered a goal and instrument of state policy; rather, it comprehensively dominates international trade and connectivity. In the systemic analysis of IR, where states act as the central actor of decision-making, cities are increasingly emerging as key to advancing a state's appeal, attraction and ability to draw in more investments (Sassen, 1991; 2005; Khanna, 2016). Under the neoliberal economic system, the rush to connectivity has added a unique pattern of complex interdependence for which security consideration and choosing allies for security partnerships are often driven by geopolitical and economic considerations.

By asserting so, I am in no way placing more significance on complex interdependence than security aspects; rather drawing attention to the fact that politics in the 21st century is not *only* security-centric as it used to be in previous eras; it takes geopolitical and geoeconomic considerations while making decisions about security alliances. Several examples of how international politics is influenced and decisions are shaped can be traced in support of this assertion. While Quad was first proposed in 2007, it failed to gain momentum in terms of not only lack of interest by its member countries but also due to lack of relevance in the absence of any clear so-called security threat that the alliance would work to counter. China's rise was still on pen and paper than being a reality until Xi Jingpin's ascension to power and shedding of China's passive role in international politics by declaring a massive Belt and Road Initiatives (BRI)—an economic plan to spread China's wings to the rest of the world. BRI has generally been considered by Western countries, as well as Japan, and China's neighbouring India as a tool to promote China's supremacy to the world, which made them devise counter plans to check China's rising influence. BRI, often seen as a tool of not only economic statecraft but also a tool to promote China's soft power, thus, gave rise to Japan devising its own plans to promote "Quality Infrastructure" projects. Gradually, the US first adopted an *Asia-Pivot policy* under the Obama Administration, promoted the Indian Ocean as one of the priority oceans in its two-ocean maritime strategy, introduced Free and Open Indo-Pacific (FOIP) under the Trump Administration, and issued its first Indo-Pacific Strategy (IPS) and Quad was revived as Quad 2.0. The latest G-7 meeting is set to unveil its own infrastructure project to counter China's BRI. This short account of the international strategic environment in the first quarter of the 21st century shows the interplay between security and economy has become more interconnected than ever and their divide

86 *Lailufar Yasmin*

has rather become blurry. That is why we need to take into account how complex interdependence is creating a new world of strategy where security and economic considerations are going hand in hand—these may be unintended, unintentional, or competitive but they do exist in this interconnected fashion. With this theoretical underpinning, I discuss the security architecture of the Gulf region in the next section.

The regional security architecture in the Gulf region

Region building generally is a process of social, historical and political connections based on geographical contiguity, overlappings and landmarks. The idea of region as a part of political interest is a product of various international developments that took place in the 20th century and particularly during the Second World War. The immediate concern was to divide the world into different strategic sectors for warfighting purposes, especially in Asia (Brewster, 2015). Since the postwar period, IR as a discipline was seriously pursued in the US and subsequently the need for understanding regional diversities also emerged to enrich the US decision-making process concerning different parts of the world (Carleton, 1948; Morgenthau, 1952; Schäfer, 2010; Guilhot, 2011; Khosrowjah, 2011). The Gulf Region, however, has a richer and longer historical existence than many other *political* regions, although contestation in terms of its naming emerged in the modern era. The political landscape of the Middle East, colonialism and the gradual establishment of statehood in the region have made such a contestation a reality. The Persian Gulf, a major water body of the region, is considered the defining marker for Iran, while the Arab countries of the region and beyond located in the greater Middle East made it compulsory to use it as Arabian Gulf and so does the United Nations (UN). The semantic use of the term is interesting as the US government names the region as the Persian Gulf, while the US Navy used Arabian Gulf till the 1991 Gulf War. Iran, on the other hand, officially does not allow the Arab usage of the name for the region in its official documents (Zraick, 2016). The political region-building has adopted the title of GCC involving Arab states of the region.

The Middle East is rife with the Palestine crisis since the statehood of Israel was announced on 15 May 1948. The political relations between the Arab states and Israel have undergone a remarkable transformation in the recent period. Despite Israel and Arab states fighting several conventional wars, the trajectory of the relationship in the past few years has shifted and has been influenced by the regional power calculations within the Middle East (Shlaim, 1977; Lewin, 2016; Rabi and Mueller, 2017; Siniver, 2018; Abadi, 2019; Quamar, 2020; Rynhold and Yaari, 2020; Strategic Comments, 2020; Hitman and Zwilling, 2021). The signing of the Abraham Accord and the thawing of the relationship between Israel and Bahrain gradually followed by some Arab countries according formal recognition to Israel have been seen as a positive step in creating peace in the Middle East region

Complex Interdependence and Security Architecture 87

(Vohra, 2021). The region has also seen a sectarian conflict evolving between the Sunni-dominated Saudi Arabia and Shiite Iran and the regional security architecture accordingly was affected (Tzemprin, Jozić and Lambaré, 2015; Fatima, Zehraa and Malik, 2017; Abuelghanam and Tahboub, 2018; Hiro, 2019). Some of the Arab countries found a new value in cultivating a relationship with the arch-rival Israel to check Iran's ambition for claiming regional hegemony. Iran's nuclear ambition, in particular, was seen to make an already unstable region even more vulnerable and undoubtedly, a violation of the Nuclear Non-Proliferation Treaty (NPT). However, there has been a rapid shift in the regional political scene since 2020–2021 as the world is witnessing a thaw in the Saudi Arabia-Iran relationship as well (Ahmadian and Mohseni, 2021; Ibish, 2021). Despite a promising future, the Gulf region remains a tinderbox in the near future, till the Palestine issue is resolved and the international community puts a check on Iran's nuclear ambition. The next section discusses Bangladesh's geopolitical significance and areas of cooperation between Bangladesh and Gulf countries.

Bangladesh: The standard-bearer of South Asia

Kaushik Basu, the former Chief Economist of the World Bank, has long been predicting a phenomenal economic prospect waiting for Bangladesh. Outlining the areas which would enhance Bangladesh's economic performance and growth, he saw a bright future for the country and termed Bangladesh the "next Asian Tiger" (Bangladesh poised to be the next Asian Tiger, 2015; Halder, 2015). Sadanand Dhume wrote in 2012—"Bangladesh is South Asia's Standard-Bearer" (Dhume, 2012). Very few Bangladeshi or international scholars paid any serious attention to such predictions. In two years, the phrase "Bangladesh Surprise" caught international attention given Bangladesh's economy continued the path of sure and steady economic growth (Asadullah, Savoia and Mahmud, 2013; 2014; Al-Muti, 2014; Hossain, 2017). Several joint collaborative research projects conducted by Bangladeshi and international scholars outlined and explained how Bangladesh's economy, despite having very few natural resources continued with its economic miracle. It is no surprise that in 2021, Bangladesh has graduated to being a "developing country," while it was categorised as a "lower underdeveloped country" in 2015. The Covid-SARS pandemic has slowed its rate of economic growth and under the current rate of growth, Bangladesh would emerge as the 28th largest economy in the world by 2030. By many economic indicators, it has surpassed its South Asian neighbours, especially the economic giant of the subcontinent India. In terms of per capita income, Bangladesh is earning USD280 more than India making it a gross total of USD 2227 (Bangladesh's per capita income rises to $2,227, 2021; Bangladesh surpasses India on per capita income, 2021). Bangladesh is now richer than both India and Pakistan, whereas it started with a 0 foreign currency reserve when it emerged as an independent country in 1971. In only

88 *Lailufar Yasmin*

50 years, no other country in the world has achieved what Bangladesh has been able to—by increasing its foreign reserve to USD 45.1 billion. In only 50 years, Bangladesh has emerged as a Lending country—by extending its generous helping hand to Sri Lanka with USD200 million from its foreign reserve (Basu, 2021; Explained: What Bangla-Lanka currency swap means, 2021). Certainly, Bangladesh has a lot to learn from Sri Lanka's experience whose external debt has skyrocketed, and therefore, this has provided a cautionary note for Bangladeshi policymakers about how to proceed and re-evaluate its strengths and weaknesses. This is where Bangladesh's formidable relationship with Gulf countries plays a significant role, which I discuss elaborately in the next section.

Bangladesh and the Gulf countries: The beginning of the relationship

Bangladesh's journey with the Gulf countries has not started smoothly. A country, which fought its War of Liberation against a postcolonial country—Pakistan, had to play it on two fronts. First, it was on the fields— the war where Bangladeshis living in then East Pakistan had to lead the resistance movement against the Pakistan Armed Forces, and the second— at the normative and ideational level, where Bangladesh was internationally painted by Pakistan being under a "Hindu" influence and generated a disinformation campaign. It shrouded the fact that the war was not only of the majority Muslim-dominated population fighting to establish a secular identity based on their ethnic and cultural identity, which by no means relegated their religious identity but also against West Pakistan's economic exploitation of East Pakistan, that is Bangladesh's resources to its benefit. By the 1960s, it was clear how East Pakistanis were exploited in various quarters such as in terms of access to government jobs to how the money earned from exporting East Pakistan's goods was spent to decorate West Pakistani establishments (Jahan, 1972). The colonial cartographical massacre that created the state of Pakistan into two separate wings with 1,000 miles of Indian territory separating them made national integration virtually impossible. The rise of Bengali nationalism and the realisation that East Pakistan has turned into an internal colony of the state of Pakistan—that there emerged two economies within one country—led the Bengalis to realise their age-old dream of establishing a *Sonar Bangla*—Golden Bengal—depicted in the literature of Bengali writers over the years.

Bangladesh started with a war-ravaged economy which needed immediate economic assistance to feed its people and run its wheel of the economy. The wartime allies—India and the Soviet Union—were unable to meet such huge economic commitments owing to the state of their financial situation. It was time for Bangladesh to look towards the international community based on its foreign policy principle of "Friendship with all, malice to none," proudly proclaimed by Bangabandhu Sheikh Mujibur Rahman. Bangladesh's history of its war against an oppressor also acted as its fundamental guide

Complex Interdependence and Security Architecture 89

Table 4.1 The timeline of Bangladesh receiving diplomatic recognition from the gulf countries

Saudi Arabia	1975
Kuwait	1973
The United Arab Emirates (UAE)	1973
Qatar	1978
Bahrain	1974
Oman	1974

when it declared in the Conference of the Non-Alignment Movement in 1973, "The world is divided into two halves, the oppressed and the oppressors. I am with the oppressed" (Trivedi, 1999: 398). Thus, Bangladesh laid out the ideological foundation of its foreign policy where it provided unwavering support to the cause of Palestine and other such places that were fighting to establish their right to self-determination. This brought Bangladesh to the limelight in terms of creating a positive image and countering the negative propaganda that was run against it in 1971 (Huque and Akhter, 1987: 202). By 1972 and 1973, many Muslim-majority countries accorded diplomatic recognition to Bangladesh, emerging as the fourth largest Muslim-majority country at the time of its independence (now the third-largest Muslim-majority country), such as Algeria, Egypt, Iraq, the UAE and Kuwait. As a result of this, Bangabandhu was able to participate in the Non-Aligned Movement (NAM) summit held at Algiers in 1973. It formally joined the Organisation of Islamic Countries (OIC) and participated in its summit held in Pakistan in 1974. Bangladesh's relationship with the Arabian Gulf countries began to warm up immediately as Bangladesh's goodwill gesture of sending a 28-member army medical unit during the 1973 Arab-Israeli War did not go unnoticed. Bangladesh also sent 50 tons of tea to Egypt during this period. Additionally, a "five thousand strong volunteer brigade [*sic*], composed of former freedom fighters, was ready to join with the Arab countries in their fight against Israel" during the war (Hossain, 1997: 43). Gradually, Arab Gulf countries recognised Bangladesh as an independent country, a timeline of which is shown in Table 4.1.

The UAE being one of the first Arab countries to accord formal diplomatic recognition to Bangladesh, played an instrumental role in ensuring Bangladesh's membership in the OIC (Imran, 2017). Keeping in mind Bangladesh's diplomatic manoeuvring and eagerness to connect with the Middle East region as a whole, several other Arab states also conferred diplomatic recognition although it took some time to establish formal channels of communication. Gradually, Bangladesh's relationship with Gulf countries flourished to an extent where normative shifts took place as Bangladesh was able to cogently create affinity and bondage in terms of religious identity as well as its ideological stances pursued on the Palestine issue. The longstanding socio-cultural relations between East Bengal and the Middle East were once again revived in the modern era by establishing

90 *Lailufar Yasmin*

formal relations. Materially, Bangladesh has set itself as a cheap source of labour market both internationally and for the expanding economies of the region.

The development of Bangladesh's bilateral relations with the Gulf countries: The economic sector

Bangladesh has developed cordial bilateral relations with each of the countries of the Gulf region. Manpower export is seen as an alternative development strategy for countries of the Southern Hemisphere that have an edge in this area. With the greying of the great powers (Ray, Sinha and Chaudhuri 2007; Jackson and Howe, 2008), and alternately, Southern countries enjoying a demographic dividend, it is the movement of people unprecedented since the 1970s that has changed the face of globalisation. Bangladesh joined this new globalised economy in 1976 when the total number was only 6,087 (Ahmed and Karim, not dated). Since then, foreign remittance has figured as one of the greatest strengths of its economic miracle, gradually reducing its dependence on foreign aid, overseas development assistance (ODA) and other sorts of financial assistance and rather emerged as a Lender itself. At present, foreign remittances sent by migrant workers stand as 6.6 per cent of its gross domestic product (GDP) despite the raging pandemic. Bangladesh has been one of the three larger recipient-earning countries in 2020 earning USD21.75 billion, which was an 18.4 per cent increase from 2019 (Rise in Remittance in 2020: Bangladesh one of three large recipients, 2021; Hasan, 2021; Rahman, and Al-Hasan, 2021). Such an earning has been able to contribute to a stable economic condition throughout 2020 and 2021. While manpower export was halted during the pandemic, it has started to resume. There are many areas where Bangladeshi labour is required and therefore, big prospects are waiting for Bangladesh as globally vaccination programs widen and succeed. Bangladesh's strength in terms of its relationship with the Gulf countries lies in its ability to supply cheap labour for which it requires a stable Gulf region. This particular issue is also its vulnerability as Bangladesh's shinning economy would be affected severely in the case of a dent in manpower export to the region. A recent analysis reveals that Bangladesh's connection to the Gulf region in terms of labour export is going to emerge as vital given the kind of services Bangladeshi labourers provide (Siddiqui, 2021).

Labour export figures are a key economic incentive for developing Bangladesh's relations with the Gulf countries in general, while bilateral relations have also flourished in other areas as well. With Saudi Arabia, forging a meaningful economic relationship suffered a setback initially although gained momentum in the mid-1970s. With a majority Muslim population, Bangladesh holds religious and cultural appeal to Saudi Arabia. It has been keen to improve bilateral relations as well as develop its cultural influence through endowments to establish mosques and other religious institutions, which created many internal and external concerns about the import of a particular type of Islamic tradition in Bangladesh (Bangladesh to build hundreds of mosques with Saudi cash, 2017; Saudi mosque funding concerns Bangladeshi minorities, 2017). It was publicised that Saudi Arabia would be a part of Bangladesh's USD1 billion project to build 560 mosques throughout the country and cultural centres with libraries and other related facilities (Abedin, 2017). The Saudi donation to build "Model Mosques" in Bangladesh for which funding commitments were made in 2017 raised many controversies as there was denial from the Saudi sources regarding its commitments (Hasan, 2017). However, it was revealed in 2020 that Saudi Arabia would indeed be a part of the project and especially with a plan to build eight iconic mosques (PM says eight "iconic mosques" will be built with Saudi assistance, 2020).

Since the establishment of a formal relationship, Saudi Arabia invests in Bangladesh through the Saudi Fund for Development (SFD), under which Bangladesh has received a total of SR. 1,166.31 million in economic assistance from 1975 to 2012. This money was disbursed under economic assistance which was distributed to different sectors such as infrastructure development, road and railways, irrigation, rural electrification, fertiliser and health sector, among others, according to the Economic Relations Division of the Government of Bangladesh (GoB) (Functions of Economic Wing: Riyadh, 2014). The nature of bilateral relations seems to be shifting as now the country is showing active interest in foreign direct investments (FDI) in Bangladesh. Saudi interest to invest lies in the areas of oil and gas, fertiliser, cement, power plants, solar energy and physical infrastructures whereas Bangladesh is interested to bifurcate the cooperative scheme through its stock market and private sector (Byron and Habib, 2019). On part of Saudi Arabia as well, its public and private sector companies have expressed similar interests (Bhuiyan, 2020a). Bangladesh expects a whopping USD30 billion to USD50 billion in investments from Saudi Arabia as charted out in the 13th session of Bangladesh–Saudi Arabia Joint Economic Commission (JEC), as the latter has created a USD250 billion Public Investment Fund under its "Look East" investment policy (Bangladesh eyeing $50b in investment from Saudis, 2020; Sumon, 2020). It seems Bangladesh's growing economic success has not escaped being noticed by Saudi Arabia, which has termed Bangladesh as a "True Asian Tiger" (A new chapter of Saudi-Bangladesh ties, 2019; Saudi delegation "serious" about starting new chapter with Bangladesh, 2019).

Bilateral relations with UAE have a deeper historical connection as UAE played an instrumental role in Bangladesh's accession to the OIC. Being the second-largest economy in the Gulf region, UAE has a lot to offer to Bangladesh and vice versa. The two countries pursued concrete steps to establish a solid bilateral relationship by signing several agreements on areas of cultural and economic cooperation. An agreement on cultural cooperation was signed between the two countries in March 1978, followed

92 *Lailufar Yasmin*

by a General Trade Agreement in 1984. There are a few other agreements on economic cooperation that were signed bilaterally such as the Agreement on the Avoidance of Double Taxation, and the Promotion and Reciprocal Protection of Investment in January 2011 (Ahmed, 2020). Being one of the major aviation hubs of the Gulf region, the UAE signed an Air Services Agreement with Bangladesh in October 2017 as well.

The UAE has been a longstanding development partner of Bangladesh by providing economic assistance and project loans. It has emerged as one of the key investors in Bangladesh with USD7 billion (*Ibid*). Bilateral trade between the two countries has reached about USD1.3 billion per annum where certain Bangladeshi products have strong possibilities to create appeal in UAE's market, such as readymade garments (RMG), pharmaceuticals, jute products, fabrics, home textile, bicycles, plastic products, processed food, furniture, among others (Belal, 2019). To promote trade, several Bangladeshi companies regularly participate in different trade fairs held in UAE, such as Gulf Information Technology Exhibition (GITEX), Gulf Food, Textile fair, Autumn fair and Dubai Shopping Festival, among others (Imran, *Ibid*). From Bangladesh's point of view, trade between the two countries is expected to reach "$2 billion by 2021, $5 billion by 2025, and $10 billion by 2030" (Belal, *Ibid*).

Bangladesh-UAE bilateral relations, however, experienced a setback over Bangladesh's strategic miscalculation of supporting Russia's bid in the first round of voting to hold the World Expo 2020 over the UAE's bid. In the second round of voting, Bangladesh quickly corrected its strategic mistake and voted for UAE but it left a negative imprint on the bilateral relations that was reflected later surrounding the controversy on Bangladeshi workers working in the country (Rashid, 2014). UAE imposed a ban on recruiting Bangladeshi workers due to some Bangladeshi workers' fraudulent practices since October 2012, which has left 700,000 Bangladeshi workers in UAE stranded in their current jobs and no new workers have been recruited since then (UAE ban on Bangladeshi workers to be lifted—report, 2017; Bhuiyan, 2020b). Bangladeshi workers from UAE used to be the second-largest senders of foreign remittances, which are now replaced by remittances sent from the US (US overtakes UAE as second biggest remittance hotspot for Bangladeshis, 2020). Since then, Bangladesh has been working with UAE authorities to resolve the issue to no avail so far, although it seems a glimmer of hope is visible.

Bangladesh's foreign policy goals and objectives prioritise developing strong economic and strategic bonds with the rest of the world. As the Qatar crisis broke out in the Gulf region, Bangladesh pursued a policy of neutrality, as will be discussed in greater depth in the next section, but it did not make Bangladesh shy away from developing stronger bilateral ties with the country. As Bangladesh aims to diversify its export destination and attract FDI for its development, Qatar can be one of the significant partners to these ends. Also, 400,000 Bangladeshis living in Qatar who

Complex Interdependence and Security Architecture 93

have sent $1.1 billion in remittances in 2019 (6.03 per cent of the total remittance) is another calculation for Bangladesh to keep in mind in the evaluation of bilateral relations (Bangladesh, Qatar to sign MoU to promote trade relations, 2020). As Qatar opens up to invest in other countries and Bangladesh is developing 100 special economic zones (SEZs), Bangladesh has requested Qatar to take advantage of such economic opportunities and be a partner in Bangladesh's growing economy (Shoeb, 2020). Several MoUs on furthering economic cooperation between the two countries have been signed (Qatar urged to recruit more skilled Bangladeshi manpower, 2020). Qatar Petroleum has already entered Bangladesh's liquified natural gas (LNG) sector via a Dutch company to ensure a steady supply of the product on a long-term basis (Qatar Petroleum to supply 1.25 m tonnes LNG to Bangladesh, 2021). Bangladesh-Qatar relations, thus, are moving towards a bilateral partnership and are expected to flourish in the coming years.

Bangladesh-Kuwait relations solidified over the years, especially after Bangladesh's unwavering support during its annexation by Iraq in 1990. Bangladesh did not hesitate to stand by Kuwait for the restoration of its sovereignty during the Gulf War of 1991. It deployed 2,300 troops for logistical support in Saudi Arabia which was seen as a valuable contribution by Bangladesh (Hossain, 1997: 42). Bangladesh's contribution was recognised by Saudi Prince Khalid bin Sultan, who observed, "Bangladesh made a most valuable contribution to our logistics, sending us some of their best support units which, at that stage, I needed more urgently than combat troops" (Chowdhury, 2020). The strategic decision to support Kuwait created prolonged cooperation between Kuwait and Bangladesh both in the military and economic areas. The two countries signed a Trade and Economic Cooperation Agreement in 1979 and a Technical Cooperation Agreement in 2000 to generate more expatriate manpower from Bangladesh (Chowdhury, 2000). Later on, areas of cooperation expanded to include road communications, investment protections and diplomatic visa exemptions where deals were signed between the two countries in 2016. Under the Kuwait Fund, as per two agreements signed in 2012 and 2016, respectively, Bangladesh is to receive USD 50 million (in 2012) and USD 48 million (in 2016) in the road communication sector (Bangladesh signs four deals with Kuwait, 2016). For Bangladesh, Kuwait is one of the top foreign remittance-earning countries. However, there is a fear of the dent in remittance flow from Kuwait as the country proposes an expatriate quota on a country basis under which from around 350,000 Bangladeshis living there, about 150,000 may have to return (Mahmud and Hasan, 2020).

Since its inception, the Bangladesh-Bahrain relationship started by prioritising each other's economic and strategic considerations. Although the formal relationship was established in the mid-1970s, it took some time to establish consulate services. Later on, from the 1990s, the relationship started to assume institutional form through the signing of some agreements such as an agreement on Economic, Commercial and Technical

94 *Lailufar Yasmin*

Relations, an agreement on Cultural Cooperation and bilateral air services agreement, Reciprocal Protection and Promotion of Investment and on the Avoidance of Double Taxation (Bangladesh–Bahrain bilateral relations, not dated; Bangladesh-Bahrain ties improve, many agreements signed, 2015), among others. Bilateral trade between the two countries reached USD26.4 million in 2020 (Bahrain, Bangladesh share keenness to boost trade, bolster cooperation, 2021). The two countries have started dialogues to boost areas of investment, where Bahrain has expressed interest in investing in pharmaceuticals, light engineering, solar power and renewable energy projects in Bangladesh (Bid to boost Bangladesh and Bahrain ties, 2020).

Bangladesh-Oman bilateral relations are also bold and have a historic connection. While UAE facilitated Bangladesh's membership in OIC, Oman was the first Arab country to promote Bangladesh's membership in the UN. The country is a huge market for Bangladesh to earn foreign remittances as Bangladeshi workers have been able to create a good reputation through their hard work (Hassan, 2018). As Bangladesh's potential is being recognised globally, it has not escaped Oman's notice as well. The first-ever Foreign Office Consultation (FOC) between the two countries was held on 8 June 2021, where the two countries identified key areas of cooperation such as the formation of a Joint Business Council as well as identifying "new areas of cooperation which [would] includes [sic] maritime affairs, diplomatic academies, think-tanks and start-ups and desalinization" (Bangladesh, Oman keen to expand economic partnership, 2021).

The Gulf region is of paramount importance for Bangladesh as most of its foreign remittance earnings originate from this region, as shown in Table 4.2 (Rahman and Al-Hasan, 2021).

Table 4.2 The remittances Bangladesh receives from different parts of the world

Country	Share in July–June	Share (July–June)		% share in incremental remittance
	FY 2015	FY 2020	FY 2021	
Saudi Arabia	21.8%	21.0%	23.7%	30.4%
United States (US)	18.4%	11.6%	12.5%	14.8%
United Arab Emirates (UAE)	15.7%	14.3%	10.8%	2.3%
Malaysia	9.0%	6.9%	9.0%	14.3%
United Kingdom (UK)	5.3%	7.8%	8.0%	8.3%
Kuwait	7.0%	7.9%	7.1%	5.2%
Oman	6.0%	6.8%	7.1%	7.6%
Qatar	2.0%	5.9%	5.2%	3.3%
Italy	1.7%	4.4%	3.2%	0.5%
Singapore	2.9%	2.4%	2.7%	3.3%
Others	10.2%	11%	10.7%	10.0%
Total	100%	100%	100%	100%
(In Million USD)	(15,316.9)	(7,716.3)	(10,894.1)	(3,177.8)

Bangladesh, therefore, is keen to develop bilateral relationships with the Gulf states. One must note in this context that the Bangladesh of the 1970s and the Bangladesh celebrating its 50th year of independence are two different entities, as identified earlier in this chapter. Today's Bangladesh has been able to develop itself as one of the key destinations of investments globally due to it being a large market of 160 million people along with its locational endowment accrued from its lynchpin position at the mouth of the Bay of Bengal (Yasmin, 2016b, Yasmin and Rahman, 2019). Several countries, including China and Japan, are keen to be Bangladesh's development partners. At the same time, due to its positional reality (Zaman, 2017), Great Powers like the US, the United Kingdom (UK), Russia and Australia, to name a few, are also interested to make their footprints visible in Bangladesh (Yasmin, 2016a; Yasmin, 2019). Bangladesh's rising capacity-building and economic growth has earned it to be one of the fastest-growing economies in the world. Bangladesh has been able to create its standing vis-à-vis the Gulf countries in the contemporary political scenario. In the next section, I discuss the strategic issues that bind Bangladesh and Gulf countries on the same thread.

The development of Bangladesh's bilateral relations with the Gulf countries: Strategic concerns

Bangladesh is located miles away from the Gulf region, which does not diminish its strategic appeal to the Gulf regional security architecture for multifarious reasons. Its Sunni-majority Muslim population provides a strategic incentive for Saudi Arabia to develop a closer tie with Bangladesh. The identity struggle between Saudi Arabia and Iran or in other words, the Sunni-Shiite rivalry has broader implications for the countries with a Muslim majority than just Saudi Arabia and Iran. Bangladesh's Sunni-majority demographic provides Saudi Arabia to identify Bangladesh as one of its key security partners. Developing a defence relationship with Saudi Arabia began in the early 1980s when Saudi Arabia sent members of its Armed Forces to Bangladesh's Defence Services Command & Staff College (DSCSC). Defence Cooperation between the two countries, especially in terms of participating in Bangladesh Armed Forces' National Defence College (NDC) and DSCSC for undertaking various training courses. Bangladesh's robust participation during the Gulf War of 1991 was seen as its commitment not only towards Islamic solidarity but also to Saudi Arabia itself. Bangladesh and Saudi Arabia signed a defence Memorandum of Understanding (MoU) under which 1,600 Bangladeshi troops would clear minefields on the Saudi-Yemen border and take part in civilian constructions (Bhuiyan, 2019; Hossain, 2019; Marsdon, 2019). However, Bangladesh has taken a cautious step in this proxy war and pursued a neutral posture in the Yemen crisis between Saudi Arabia and Iran-backed Houthi rebels.

96 *Lailufar Yasmin*

Bangladesh-Kuwait defence relationship was also emboldened by Bangladesh's steadfast commitment to Kuwait's independence and sovereignty. Bangladesh Army assisted in removing landmines after the end of the Gulf War in which 270 Bangladeshi soldiers lost their lives (Chowdhury, 2020). As part of Operation Reconstruction Kuwait (ORK), a Bangladeshi military contingent is deployed in the country and working with five other countries in landmine sweeping and other associated work to rebuild a war-torn Kuwait (Rahman, 2015). Bangladesh and Kuwait have recently signed an agreement on Cooperation in Military Fields of Training and other areas to enhance their bilateral defence relationship (Bangladesh signs four deals with Kuwait, 2016).

Bangladesh has been hosting 1.1 million Rohingyas, an influx that originally began in the mid-1970s. The latest influx starting on 26 August 2017, put Bangladesh in a tricky situation in which it had to open its border and host fleeing Rohingyas from being tortured by Tatmadaw, Myanmar's Army. Bangladesh has received worldwide acclamation for its generous and humanitarian act but for the country alone, it is difficult to manage such a big refugee crisis. It is during this difficult time, that the countries of the Gulf region, alongside other countries, extended their unfailing support for Bangladesh to manage such a big humanitarian crisis. The King Salman Humanitarian Aid and Relief Center (KSrelief) alone is providing relief for 120,000 Rohingyas living in different camps (Alhamawi, 2021). Saudi Arabia is also working with the US in integrating a multi-sectoral refugee support program in Bangladesh (Saudi Arabia, US sign Rohingya aid deal, 2020). However, in 2020, a media report emerged that Saudi Arabia was to deport some 55,000 Rohingyas living in the country whose passports had expired. Later, it was resolved as Bangladesh proposed to form a joint committee to investigate and resolve the matter involving officials of both countries (Sakib, 2021). Besides Saudi Arabia, UAE and other Gulf countries are also actively assisting Bangladesh in managing this humongous crisis through providing financial aid, food aid and other humanitarian assistance (UAE performing effective role in supporting Rohingya refugees, 2018; Qatar Charity's relief aid for Rohingya refugees in Ramadan, 2021).

The transnational threat emerging from the Rohingya crisis and fall-out of this if sustainable repatriation cannot be ensured is recognised at the international level. Similarly, one cannot but remain oblivious to the emerging threat of terrorism worldwide. To combat terrorist threats in the Muslim World, Saudi Arabia proposed a coalition of 34 states in 2015 and Bangladesh has joined as a member. The Islamic military coalition has announced "a duty to protect the Islamic nation from the evils of all terrorist groups and organizations whatever their sect and name which wreak death and corruption on earth and aim to terrorize the innocent" (Browning and Irish, 2015). Bangladesh, with several geopolitical considerations of its own, has become a strong member of the group. In the meantime, however, a rift in Saudi-Pakistan relations has led to the formation of an alternative bloc of Islamic nations, spearheaded by countries like Malaysia and Turkey (Qader, 2020). However, Bangladesh's policy of neutrality remains strong and it has also become a part of the alliance without it letting affect its robust relationship with Saudi Arabia. In a similar vein, Bangladesh has remained neutral in the ongoing Qatar crisis among the Gulf countries as Bangladesh's primary concern is to advance its economic growth and development. Bangladesh's economic success is built upon the mantra of "growth without enmity"—a phrase popularised in Bangladesh's scholarly and policy level circle.

Concluding observation: Bangladesh as an emerging middle power

In this chapter, the major thrust has been given to understanding the nature of the relationship between Bangladesh and Gulf countries through the prism of complex interdependence and regional security architecture. The chapter has shown how the framework of understanding the international strategic environment is shifting rapidly. In today's world, security and interdependence cannot be considered situating in two different spectrums but rather increasingly interconnected and dependent in terms of policy formations and framings. In this context, the world is connected in a manner that physical distance matters less as hotspots emerging in any corner of the world have the potential to affect the whole world. The pandemic that we are living through is a glaring example of this. Similarly, the strategic scenario is shifting in such a manner that countries that used to remain at the periphery are emerging as significant and creating a new kind of appeal to the rest of the world. Bangladesh falls into this category which has transformed itself phenomenally in only 50 years of its independence. Its rise has caught international attention in a manner that scholars are titling Bangladesh as one of the "emerging middle powers" (Brewster, 2021). Its potential is recognised by Gulf countries too and a number of these countries see Bangladesh as a place to invest and be part of Bangladesh's development partner. A secure and stable Bangladesh, with a Muslim-majority population, is in the security interest of the Gulf countries too for which Bangladesh has emerged as a solid security partner of the region as well. In conclusion, the chapter argues that the new century requires a new perspective to consider while making strategies. This is aptly demonstrated in Bangladesh-Gulf relations and will gradually heighten the mutual relationship towards a strategic partnership.

References

A new chapter of Saudi-Bangladesh ties. *The Daily Star*, March 7, 2019 [Online] https://www.thedailystar.net/business/saudi-arabia-bangladesh-relationship-new-chapter-opened-1711720 (Accessed: June 8, 2021).

Abadi, J. (2019) Saudi Arabia's Rapprochement with Israel: The National Security Imperatives. *Middle Eastern Studies*, Vol. 55, No. 3, pp. 433–449.

98 *Lailufar Yasmin*

Abedin, S.A. (2017) Saudi to pay big money for mosques. *Dhaka Tribune*, April 20 [Online] https://www.dhakatribune.com/bangladesh/nation/2017/04/20/saudi-pay-big-money-mosques (Accessed: June 8, 2021).

Abuelghanam, D. and Tahboub, N. (2018) Mixed Messages: Iran versus Saudi Arabia and GCC. *Contemporary Review of the Middle East*, Vol. 5, No. 4, pp. 365–386, DOI: 10.1177/2347798918795937.

Ahmadian, H. and Mohseni, P. (2021) From Detente to Containment: The Emergence of Iran's New Saudi Strategy. *International Affairs*, Vol. 97, No. 3, May, pp. 779–799, DOI: https://doi.org/10.1093/ia/iiab014.

Ahmed, K.U. (2020) Bangladesh-UAE: deepening relations. *The Financial Express*, January 20 [Online] https://thefinancialexpress.com.bd/public/views/bangladesh-uae-deepening-relations-1579535613 (Accessed: June 9, 2021).

Ahmed, S.S. and Karim, M.R. (not dated) Manpower export in Bangladesh: problems and prospects. *Bangladesh Economic Association* [Online] https://bea-bd.org/site/images/pdf/011.pdf (Accessed: June 9, 2021).

Alhamawi, L. (2021), Saudi aid agency helps thousands of Rohingya refugees in Bangladesh. *Arab News*, June 6 [Online] https://www.arabnews.com/node/1871596/saudi-arabia (Accessed: June 15, 2021).

Al-Muti, S.A. (2014) Bangladesh's development surprise: a model for developing countries. *The Asia Foundation*, June 25 [Online] https://asiafoundation.org/2014/06/25/bangladeshs-development-surprise-a-model-for-developing-countries/ (Accessed: June 15, 2021).

Asadullah, M.N., Savoia, A. and Mahmud, W. (2013) "Paths to Development: Is There a Bangladesh Surprise?" *BWPI Working Paper 189*, November. Manchester, United Kingdom: University of Manchester.

Asadullah, M.N., Savoia, A. and Mahmud, W. (2014) Paths to Development: Is There a Bangladesh Surprise? *World Development*, Vol. 62, pp. 138–154.

Bahrain, Bangladesh share keenness to boost trade, bolster cooperation. *Bahrain News Agency*, March 10, 2021 [Online] https://www.bna.bh/en/BahrainBangladesh sharekeennesstoboosttradebolstercooperation.aspx?cms=q8FmFJgiscL2fwIz ON1%2BDgQrzcNeu4Oori68oBRHK5Y%3D (Accessed: June 14, 2021).

Bangladesh 3rd in South Asia, 11th globally: WB. *The Daily Star*, April 10, 2019 [Online] https://www.thedailystar.net/business/news/bangladesh-3rd-south-asia-11th-globally-wb-1727731 (Accessed June 11, 2021).

Bangladesh continues to see robust remittance inflow. *Dhaka Tribune*, September 14, 2020 [Online] https://www.dhakatribune.com/business/economy/2020/09/14/bangladesh-continues-to-see-robust-remittance-inflow (Accessed June 11, 2021).

Bangladesh eyeing $50b in investment from Saudis. *The Daily Star*, February 12, 2020 [Online] https://www.thedailystar.net/business/news/bangladesh-eyeing-50b-investment-saudis-1866766 (Accessed: June 8, 2021).

Bangladesh in 34-state Islamic military alliance. *The Daily Star*, December 15, 2015 [Online] https://www.thedailystar.net/city/bangladesh-%E2%80%98joins%E2%80%99-riyadh-based-anti-terrorism-coalition-187609 (Accessed: June 15, 2021).

Bangladesh poised to be the next Asian Tiger. *The Daily Star*, December 14, 2015 [Online] https://www.thedailystar.net/business/bangladesh-poised-be-the-next-asian-tiger-186874 (Accessed: June 8, 2021).

Bangladesh signs four deals with Kuwait. *The Daily Star*, May 4, 2016 [Online] https://www.thedailystar.net/country/bangladesh-signs-four-deals-kuwait-1218490 (Accessed: June 14, 2021).

Complex Interdependence and Security Architecture 99

Bangladesh surpasses India on per capita income. *The Financial Express*, May 21, 2021 [Online] https://thefinancialexpress.com.bd/economy/bangladesh-surpasses-india-on-per-capita-income-1621610135 (Accessed: June 8, 2021).

Bangladesh to build hundreds of mosques with Saudi cash. *Dawn*, April 27, 2017, [Online] https://www.dawn.com/news/1329553 (Accessed: June 8, 2021).

Bangladesh's per capita income rises to $2,227. *Dhaka Tribune*, May 17, 2021 [Online] https://www.dhakatribune.com/business/2021/05/17/planning-minister-bangladesh-s-per-capita-income-increased-to-2-227 (Accessed: June 8, 2021).

Bangladesh, Oman keen to expand economic partnership. *The Daily Star*, June 9, 2021 [Online] https://www.thedailystar.net/business/news/bangladesh-oman-keen-expand-economic-partnership-2107669 (Accessed: June 9, 2021).

Bangladesh, Qatar to sign MoU to promote trade relations. *The Daily Star*, November 18, 2020 [Online] https://www.thedailystar.net/bangladesh-qatar-sign-mou-promote-trade-relations-1996985 (Accessed: June 9, 2021).

Bangladesh–Bahrain bilateral relations. *Embassy of Bangladesh*, Manama, Bahrain (not dated) [Online] http://www.banglaembassy.com.bh/relation/relation.htm (Accessed: June 14, 2021).

Bangladesh-Bahrain ties improve, many agreements signed. *BDNews24.com*, December 23, 2015 [Online] https://bdnews24.com/bangladesh/2015/12/23/bang-ladesh-bahrain-ties-improve-many-agreements-signed (Accessed: June 14, 2021).

Bangladesh-UAE relations moving towards partnership. *Khaleej Times*, March 26, 2021 [Online] https://www.khaleejtimes.com/supplements/bangladesh-uae-relations-moving-towards-partnership (Accessed: June 9, 2021).

Basu, N. (2021) Covid aid to India, financial help to Sri Lanka—Bangladesh is showcasing its economic rise. *The Print*, May 28 [Online] https://theprint.in/diplomacy/covid-aid-to-india-financial-help-to-sri-lanka-bangladesh-is-showcasing-its-economic-rise/667019/ (Accessed: June 15, 2021).

Bhuiyan, H.K. (2019) Dhaka, Riyadh sign defense MoU. *Dhaka Tribune*, February 15 [Online] https://www.dhakatribune.com/bangladesh/foreign-affairs/2019/02/15/dhaka-riyadh-sign-defense-mou (Accessed: June 8, 2021).

Bhuiyan, H.K. (2020a) Saudi Arabia wants to invest in Bangladesh. *Dhaka Tribune*, November 22 [Online] https://www.dhakatribune.com/bangladesh/2020/11/22/saudi-arabia-wants-to-invest-in-bangladesh (Accessed: June 8, 2021).

Bhuiyan, H.K. (2020b) UAE job market all but shut for over 7 years. *Dhaka Tribune*, January 14 [Online] https://www.dhakatribune.com/bangladesh/foreign-affairs/2020/01/14/uae-job-market-all-but-shut-for-over-7-years (Accessed: June 9, 2021).

Bid to boost Bangladesh and Bahrain ties. *Gulf Daily News*, September 20, 2020 [Online] https://www.zawya.com/mena/en/economy/story/Bid_to_boost_Bangladesh_and_Bahrain_ties-SNG_185095010/ (Accessed: June 14, 2021).

Brewster, D. (2015) The Rise of the Bengal Tigers: The Growing Strategic Importance of the Bay of Bengal. *Journal of Defence Studies*, Vol. 9, No. 2, April–June, pp. 81–104.

Brewster, D (2021) A rising Bangladesh starts to exert its regional power. *The Interpreter*, Lowy Institute, June 10 [Online] https://www.lowyinstitute.org/the-interpreter/rising-bangladesh-starts-exert-its-regional-power (Accessed: June 10, 2021).

Browning, Noah and Irish, John (2015) Saudi Arabia announces 34-state Islamic military alliance against terrorism. *Reuters*, December 15 [Online] https://www.reuters.com/article/us-saudi-security-idUSKBN0TX2PG20151215 (Accessed: July 11, 2021).

100 *Lailufar Yasmin*

Byron, R.K. and Habib, W.B. (2019), Saudi to invest in 30 big projects. *The Daily Star*, February 19 [Online] https://www.thedailystar.net/frontpage/news/saudi-invest-30-big-projects-1704205 (Accessed: June 8, 2021).

Carleton, W.G. (1948) Review. *The Journal of Politics*, Vol. 10, No. 3, August, pp. 579–581.

Chowdhury, R. (2000) Bangladesh, Kuwait sign agreement. *Gulf News*, November 1 [Online] https://gulfnews.com/uae/bangladesh-kuwait-sign-agreement-1.434052 (Accessed: June 14, 2021).

Chowdhury, U. (2020) OP-ED: Bangladesh and the first Gulf War. *Dhaka Tribune*, October 24 [Online] https://www.dhakatribune.com/opinion/op-ed/2020/10/24/op-ed-bangladesh-and-the-first-gulf-war (Accessed: June 14, 2021).

Dhume, S. (2012) Bangladesh is South Asia's standard-bearer. *Wall Street Journal*, May 4 [Online] https://www.wsj.com/articles/SB10001424052702304746604577381671411071762 (Accessed: June 8, 2021).

Dizikes, P. (2011) When the butterfly effect took flight. *MIT News Magazine*, February 22 [Online] https://www.technologyreview.com/2011/02/22/196987/when-the-butterfly-effect-took-flight/ (Accessed: June 15, 2021).

Eriksson, A. (2017) Unintended interdependence: conflict-driven cooperation in Northeast Asia. *Interdependence in the Asia Pacific Century/Region*, ISA Pacific, Hong Kong.

Explained: what Bangla-Lanka currency swap means. *The Indian Express*, May 29, 2021 [Online] https://indianexpress.com/article/explained/explained-significance-of-the-200-million-currency-swap-bangladesh-has-approved-for-sri-lanka-7333158/ (Accessed: June 15, 2021).

Fatima, N., Zehraa, S. and Malik, M.S. (2017) Saudi Arabia, Iran and Middle East—A Dilemma. *Global Political Review*, Vol. II, No. 1, pp. 72–80.

Functions of Economic Wing: Riyadh. *Economic Relations Division*, Government of Bangladesh, October 28, 2014 [Online] https://erd.gov.bd/site/page/8af74816-c350-4eb0-82c4-6c627e22dda3 (Accessed: June 8, 2021).

Goldin, I., and Mariathasan, M. (2014) *The Butterfly Defect: How Globalization Creates Systemic Risks, and What to Do About It*. Princeton, NJ: Princeton University Press.

Guilhot, N. (Ed.) (2011) *The Invention of International Relations Theory: Realism, the Rockefeller Foundation, and the 1954 Conference on Theory*. New York: Cambridge University Press.

Halder, N. (2015) Bangladesh poised to be next Asian Tiger. *The Financial Express*, December 17 [Online] https://www.thefinancialexpress.com.bd/views/bangladesh-poised-to-be-next-asian-tiger (Accessed: June 8, 2021).

Hasan, R. (2017) Confusion over KSA $1b fund to build 560 mosques. *The Daily Star*, May 18 [Online] https://www.thedailystar.net/city/saudis-backtracked-1b-mosque-project-funding-1406866 (Accessed: June 8, 2021).

Hasan, M. (2021) Remittance inflow to Bangladesh accounted for 6.6% of GDP in 2020. *Dhaka Tribune*, May 18 [Online] https://www.dhakatribune.com/business/2021/05/18/remittance-inflow-to-bangladesh-accounted-for-6-6-of-gdp-in-2020 (Accessed: June 9, 2021).

Hass, R. (2021) *Stronger: Adapting America's China Strategy in an Age of Competitive Interdependence*. Yale University Press, London.

Hassan, M.E. (2018) Oman keen to deepen ties with Bangladesh. *Daily Sun*, December 21 [Online] https://www.daily-sun.com/arcprint/details/358455/Oman-keen-to-deepen-ties-with-Bangladesh/2018-12-21 (Accessed: June 14, 2021).

Complex Interdependence and Security Architecture 101

Hiro, D. (2019) *Cold War in the Islamic World: Saudi Arabia, Iran and the Struggle for Supremacy.* Oxford: Oxford University Press.

Hitman, G. and Zwilling, M. (2021) Normalization with Israel: An Analysis of Social Networks Discourse within Gulf States. *Ethnopolitics*, Vol. 20, DOI: https://doi.org/10.1080/17449057.2021.1901380.

Hossain, I (1997) Bangladesh and the Gulf War: Response of a Small State. *Pakistan Horizon*, Vol. 50, No. 2, April, pp. 39–55.

Hossain, N (2017) *The Aid Lab: Understanding Bangladesh's Unexpected Success.* Oxford: Oxford University Press.

Hossain, S. (2019) Bangladesh to send 1,600 minesweepers to KSA. *New Age*, February 5 [Online] http://www.newagebd.net/article/63866/army-to-send-1600-minesweepers-to-ksa (Accessed: June 8, 2021).

Huque, A.S. and Akhter, M.Y. (1987) The Ubiquity of Islam: Religion and Society in Bangladesh. *Pacific Affairs*, Vol. 60, No. 2, Summer, pp. 200–225.

Ibish, H. (2021) Saudi Arabia's new dialogue with Iran was long in the making. The Arab Gulf States Institute in Washington, May 4 [Online] https://agsiw.org/saudi-arabias-new-dialogue-with-iran-was-long-in-the-making/ (Accessed June 11, 2021).

Imran, M. (2017) Bangladesh and UAE are working together to take bilateral ties to new heights. *Khaleej Times*, March 26 [Online] https://www.khaleejtimes.com/20170326/khaleej-times-dubai-uae-bangladesh (Accessed: June 8, 2021).

Jackson, R. and Howe, N. (2008) *The Graying of the Great Powers: Demography and Geopolitics in the 21st Century.* Washington DC: Center for International & Strategic Studies.

Jahan, R. (1972) *Pakistan: Failure in National Integration.* Dhaka: The University Press Limited.

Keohane, R.O. and Nye, J.S. (1987) Power and Interdependence Revisited. *International Organization*, Vol. 41, pp. 725–753, DOI: 10.1017/S0020818300027661.

Khanna, P. (2016) *Connectography: Mapping the Future of Global Civilization.* New York: Random House.

Khosrowjah, H. (2011) A Brief History of Area Studies and International Studies. *Arab Studies Quarterly*, Vol. 33, No. 3/4, Summer/Fall, pp. 131–142.

Krieken, R.V. (2019) Nobert Elias and organizational analysis: towards process-figurational theory. In Clegg, S. and Cunha, M.P.E. (Eds.) *Management, Organizations and Contemporary Social Theory*, London: Routledge.

Lewin, E. (2016) The Inevitable Dead End of the Arab-Israeli Conflict. *Cogent Social Sciences*, Vol. 2, No. 1, 1227294, DOI: 10.1080/23311886.2016.1227294.

Mahmud, J. and Hasan, R. (2020) Bangladeshi workers: around 2 lakh may have to leave Kuwait. *The Daily Star*, July 15 [Online] https://www.thedailystar.net/backpage/news/bangladeshi-workers-around-2-lakh-may-have-leave-kuwait-1930549 (Accessed: June 14, 2021).

Marsdon, K. (2019) Current Saudi Arabian interest in Bangladesh: what is its key motivator? *Future Directions*, March 20 [Online] https://www.futuredirections.org.au/publication/current-saudi-arabian-interest-in-bangladesh-what-is-its-key-motivator/ (Accessed: June 8, 2021).

Morgenthau, H.J. (1952) Area Studies and the Study of International Relations. *UNESCO International Social Science Bulletin*, Vol. IV, No. 4, pp. 647–654.

Muntasir, Belal. (2019) UAE keen to grow bilateral trade to $10bn by 2030. *Dhaka Tribune*, March 24 [Online] https://www.dhakatribune.com/business/2019/03/24/uae-keen-to-grow-bilateral-trade-to-10bn-by-2030 (Accessed: July 11, 2021).

102 *Lailufar Yasmin*

PM says eight "iconic mosques" will be built with Saudi assistance. *The Financial Express*, November 26, 2020 [Online] https://www.thefinancialexpress.com.bd/national/pm-says-eight-iconic-mosques-will-be-build-with-saudi-assistance-1606409076 (Accessed: June 8, 2021).

Qader, M. (2020) OIC, a new emerging Muslim alliance and Bangladesh. *The Independent*, September 20 [Online] https://www.theindependentbd.com/post/253494 (Accessed: June 15, 2021).

Qatar Charity's relief aid for Rohingya refugees in Ramadan. *Gulf Times*, April 13, 2021 [Online] https://www.gulf-times.com/story/688861/Qatar-Charity-s-relief-aid-for-Rohingya-refugees-i (Accessed: June 15, 2021).

Qatar Petroleum to supply 1.25m tonnes LNG to Bangladesh. *The Daily Star*, February 24, 2021 [Online] https://www.thedailystar.net/business/news/qatar-petroleum-supply-125m-tonnes-lng-bangladesh-2050113 (Accessed: June 15, 2021).

Qatar urged to recruit more skilled Bangladeshi manpower. *Dhaka Tribune*, November 18, 2020 [Online] https://www.dhakatribune.com/bangladesh/migration/2020/11/18/qatar-urged-to-recruit-more-skilled (Accessed: June 9, 2021).

Quamar, M.M. (2020) Changing Regional Geopolitics and the Foundations of a Rapprochement between Arab Gulf and Israel. *Global Affairs*, Vol. 6, No. 4–5, pp. 593–608.

Rabi, U. and Mueller, C. (2017) The Gulf Arab States and Israel since 1967: From "No Negotiation" to Tacit Cooperation. *British Journal of Middle Eastern Studies*, Vol. 44, No. 4: The Six-Day War: 50 Years on, pp. 576–592.

Rahman, Z. (2015) Bangladesh helps reconstruct Kuwait. *Bangla News*, December 7 [Online] https://www.banglanews24.com/english/national/news/bd/47638.details (Accessed: June 14, 2021).

Rahman, M. and Al-Hasan, M. (2021) Remittance flows in recent times: wherefrom is so much money coming? *The Financial Express*, February 9 [Online] https://thefinancialexpress.com.bd/views/remittance-flows-in-recent-times-wherefrom-is-so-much-money-coming-1612880545 (Accessed: June 9, 2021).

Rashid, H.U. (2014) Is Bangladesh's foreign policy becoming India and Russia-centric? *Institute of Peace and Conflict Studies*, April 15 [Online] http://www.ipcs.org/comm_select.php?articleNo=4390 (Accessed: June 9, 2021).

Ray, S., Sinha, A.K. and Chaudhuri, S. (2007), Making Bangladesh a Leading Manpower Exporter: Chasing a Dream of US $30 Billion Annual Migrant Remittances by 2015. Paper Presented at the seminar of Strategy for Increasing Annual Migrant Remittances for Bangladesh, organized by Bangladesh Enterprise Institute, Dhaka, Bangladesh, June [Online] file:///C:/Users/User/Downloads/Migrant%20Workers%20Remittances%20in%20Bangladesh.pdf (Accessed: June 9, 2021).

Rise in remittance in 2020: Bangladesh one of three large recipients. *The Daily Star*, February 20, 2021 [Online] https://www.thedailystar.net/backpage/news/remittance-2020-bangladesh-third-largest-recipient-2047861 (Accessed: June 15, 2021).

Rynhold, J. and Yaari, M. (2020) The Transformation of Saudi-Israeli Relations. *Israel Affairs*, DOI: https://doi.org/10.1080/13537121.2020.1832320.

Sakib, S.M.N. (2021) Saudi Arabia won't send Rohingya back to Bangladesh. *Anadolu Agency*, March 12 [Online] https://www.aa.com.tr/en/middle-east/-saudi-arabia-wont-send-rohingya-back-to-bangladesh/2173654 (Accessed: June 15, 2021).

Sassen, S. (1991) *The Global City: New York, London, Tokyo*. Princeton, NJ: Princeton University Press.

Sassen, S. (2005) The Global City: Introducing a Concept. *Brown Journal of World Affairs*, Vol. 11, No. 2, pp. 27–43.

Saudi Arabia, US sign Rohingya aid deal. *Arab News*, November 13, 2020 [Online] https://www.arabnews.com/node/1762571/saudi-arabia (Accessed: June 15, 2021).

Saudi delegation "serious" about starting new chapter with Bangladesh. *BDNews24. com*, March 7, 2019 [Online] https://bdnews24.com/economy/2019/03/07/saudi-delegation-serious-about-starting-new-chapter-with-bangladesh (Accessed: June 8, 2021).

Saudi mosque funding concerns Bangladeshi minorities. *Union of Catholic Asian News (UCA News)*, May 2, 2017 [Online] https://www.ucanews.com/news/saudi-mosque-funding-concerns-bangladeshi-minorities/79098# (Accessed: June 8, 2021).

Schäfer, W. (2010) Reconfiguring Area Studies for the Global Age. *Globality Studies Journal*, No. 22, December, pp. 1–18.

Schuman, R. (1994) The Schuman declaration. In Nelsen B.F. and Stubb A.CG. (Eds.) *The European Union*. London: Palgrave, pp. 11–12.

Shlaim, A. (1977) The Study of the Arab-Israeli Conflict. *British Journal of International Studies*, Vol. 3, No. 1, April, pp. 97–118.

Shoeb, M. (2020) Qatar-Bangladesh economic ties to witness major boost. *The Peninsula*, February 3 [Online] https://thepeninsulaqatar.com/article/03/02/2020/Qatar-Bangladesh-economic-ties-to-witness-major-boost (Accessed: June 9, 2021).

Siddiqui, K. (2021), Manpower export: jobs there but takers few. *The Business Standard*, February 9 [Online] https://www.tbsnews.net/bangladesh/migration/manpower-export-jobs-there-few-takers-199330 (Accessed: June 9, 2021).

Siniver, A. (2018), Arab–Israeli conflict. In Martel, G. (Ed.) *The Encyclopedia of Diplomacy*. Hoboken, New Jersey: John Wiley & Sons, Ltd., pp. 1–10, DOI: 10.1002/9781118885154.dipl0337.

Sumon, S. (2020) Saudi Arabia reportedly set to invest $30bn in Bangladesh, *Arab News*, February 12 [Online] https://www.arabnews.com/node/1626891/world (Accessed: June 8, 2021).

The Abraham Accords. (2020). Israel–Gulf Arab Normalisation *Strategic Comments*, Vol. 26, No. 8, pp. iv–v, DOI: 10.1080/13567888.2020.1853892.

Trivedi, R. (1999) *International Relations of Bangladesh and Bangabandhu Sheikh Mujibur Rahman [Documents, Messages and Speeches] 1971–1973*, Volume 1. Dhaka: Parama.

Tzemprin, A., Jozić, J. and Lambaré, H. (2015) The Middle East Cold War: Iran-Saudi Arabia and the Way Ahead. *Croatian Political Science Review*, Vol. 52, No. 4–5, pp. 187–202.

UAE ban on Bangladeshi workers to be lifted—report. *Gulf Business*, May 18, 2017 [Online] https://gulfbusiness.com/uae-ban-bangladeshi-workers-lifted-report/ (Accessed: June 9, 2021).

UAE performing effective role in supporting Rohingya refugees. *Relief Web*, May 11, 2018 [Online] https://reliefweb.int/report/bangladesh/uae-performing-effective-role-supporting-rohingya-refugees (Accessed: June 15, 2021).

US overtakes UAE as second biggest remittance hotspot for Bangladeshis. *The Financial Express*, August 17, 2020 [Online] https://thefinancialexpress.com.bd/economy/us-overtakes-uae-as-second-biggest-remittance-hotspot-for-bangladeshis-1597673388 (Accessed: June 9, 2021).

Vernon, J.L. (2017) Understanding the Butterfly Effect. *American Scientist*, Vol. 105, No. 3, p. 130.

104 *Lailufar Yasmin*

Vohra, A. (2021) The Abraham Accords passed their first big test. *Foreign Policy*, June 8 [Online] https://foreignpolicy.com/2021/06/08/the-abraham-accords-passed-their-first-big-test/ (Accessed June 11, 2021).

Yasmin, L. (2016a) Bangladesh and the great powers. In Riaz, A. and Rahman, M.S. (Eds.) *Handbook on Contemporary Bangladesh*. London and New York: Routledge, pp. 389–401.

Yasmin, L. (2016b) Thalatta! Thalatta! Bangladesh finds the sea. In *Cooperative Partnership and Sustainable Development: A Strategy through Blue Economy among BIMSTEC Countries*. Dhaka: Coastal Association for Social Transformation (COAST), pp. 11–23.

Yasmin, L. (2019) India and China in South Asia: Bangladesh's Opportunities and Challenges. *Millennial Asia*, Vol. 10, No. 3, pp. 322–336, DOI: https://doi.org/10.1177/0976399619879864.

Yasmin, L. and Rahman, M.A. (2019) Linking Development and Diplomacy in the Context of Bangladesh in 21st Century. *Mirpur Papers*, Defense Services Command and Staff College (DSCSC), Vol. 25, No. 29, pp. 1–16.

Zaman, R.U. (2017) Can Bangladesh turn its burdensome geography into a blessing? *East Asia Forum*, September 1 [Online] https://www.eastasiaforum.org/2017/09/01/can-bangladesh-turn-its-burdensome-geography-into-a-blessing/#:~:text=While%20it%20is%20not%20possible,International%20Relations%2C%20University%20of%20Dhaka (Accessed: June 15, 2021).

Zraick, K. (2016) Persian (or Arabian) Gulf is caught in the middle of regional rivalries. *The New York Times*, January 12 [Online] https://www.nytimes.com/2016/01/13/world/middleeast/persian-gulf-arabian-gulf-iran-saudi-arabia.html (Accessed: June 4, 2021).

5 Sri Lanka and the Gulf States

Shakthi De Silva and Robin Vochelet

The underlying theme of this publication is to explore the linkages between the South Asian regional security complex (RSC) and the Gulf subcomplex, drawing on insights from regional security complex theory (RSCT). This chapter analyses the degree of security interdependence and securitisation between the Gulf, Iran and Israel (GII) on the one hand and the South Asian Island of Sri Lanka. By examining the degree of security independence between the two—from a Sri Lankan standpoint—the authors conclude that Sri Lanka and the GII differ in their perceptions of threats and tend to politicise—more often than securitise—common threats. The chapter delves into several types of security threats ranging from global threats (climate change) to regional threats (terrorism within the region).

Securitisation and regional security complex theory

Securitisation, a product of the Copenhagen school of thought, finds its clearest expression in the work of Barry Buzan, Ole Wæver and Jaap de Wilde (1998). In their view, securitisation occurs "when a securitizing actor uses a rhetoric of existential threat and thereby takes an issue out of what under those conditions is 'normal politics'" (1998, pp. 24–25). A securitised issue is framed either as a special kind of "politics" or as above politics. A spectrum can therefore be drawn, ranging from "non-politicised public issues ('the state does not deal with it and it is not in any other way made an issue of public debate and decision'), through politicised ('the issue is part of public policy, requiring government decision and resource allocations or, more rarely, some other form of communal governance') to *securitisation*" (in which case an issue is no longer debated as a political question, but dealt with at an accelerated pace and in ways that may violate normal legal and social rules) (Buzan et al., 1998, p.23). Simply put, securitisation, refers to the process of presenting an issue as an existential threat, thereby justifying extraordinary measures to deal with it.

DOI: 10.4324/9781003283058-6

106 *Shakthi De Silva and Robin Vochelet*

Securitisation is often associated with political discourse. For the process of securitisation to succeed, a securitising actor (for instance, a head of state) needs to effectively convince the target audience (often the public of the state) of the necessity to perceive a referent object (such as sovereignty or territorial integrity) as being existentially threatened (Buzan and Hansen, 2009, p. 214). Through the process of securitisation, an issue is then "dramatized as [one of] supreme priority, so that an agent [securitizing actor] can legitimately claim a need to raise the issue above the constraints of regular political rules and procedure and open debate to treat it by 'extraordinary measures'" (Stritzel, 2014, p. 15). Scholars argue that "if by means of an argument about the priority and urgency of an existential threat, the securitizing actor has managed to break free of procedures or rules he or she would otherwise be bound by, we are witnessing a case of securitization" (Buzan et al., 1998, p. 25).

In sum, the distinguishing feature of securitisation is a specific "rhetorical structure (survival, priority of action) because if the problem is not handled now, it will be too late, and we will not exist to remedy our failure" (Buzan et al., 1998, p. 26). This urgency must win the assent of the target audience, thereby enabling the securitising actor to authorise "whatever means they deem most appropriate" (Balzacq et al., 2016, p. 495) to protect the referent object.

RSCT contends that "security interdependence is normally patterned into regionally based" security complexes as threats travel more easily in geographically contiguous regions (Buzan and Waever, 2003, p. 4). The tendency to securitise issues is "more intense between the actors inside such complexes" (p. 4). Lake and Morgan (1997, p. 12) echo this point, highlighting that, members of a RSC "are so interrelated in terms of their security, that actions by any member and significant security-related developments inside any member have a major impact on the others." Thus, RSCs are characterised by "durable patterns of amity and enmity taking the forms of ... coherent patterns of security interdependence" (Buzan and Waever, 2003, p. 45). Regional and international issues are often securitised by the actors within a RSC, thus solidifying a tightly knit network of security interdependence.

Frazier and Stewart-Ingersoll (2010), building on the work of Buzan and Waever (2003), contend that there are five types of RSC. In their view, these include:

1 A **hegemonic security order**, where one state exercises preponderant power to establish the "essential rules, norms and modes of operation" of the RSC (Frazier and Stewart-Ingersoll, 2010, p. 735)
2 A **collective security order**, where states agree to norms and rules of stability and collectively address certain security threats that any member state may face. Over time, a common identity may develop among the members of the region

3 An RSC of **power restraining power** operates when states build "conventional strength through arms and/or coalitions" so that "no state has sufficient strength to make aggression rationally feasible" (p. 736)
4 Regional powers banding together to address common security threats while still engaged in competition against one another is a **concert security order**
5 And finally, an **unstructured security order** reflects a situation where minimum-security interdependence exists and there exists no means to create or maintain any order within the RSC.

Although scholars have discussed numerous ways to categorise state-power (Barnett and Duvall, 2005; Snider, 1987), for the sake of simplicity, we classify hegemonic potential by measuring the state's military expenditure. The GII, as a multipolar RSC encompassing several aspirant regional hegemons including Iran, Saudi Arabia and Israel, currently operates as a "power restraining power" regional complex.[1] Saudi Arabia consistently spends a significant portion of its GDP on defence expenditure enabling it to maintain its position among the top ten states in terms of military expenditure. Israel slots into the top 20, alongside the Islamic Republic of Iran (Da Silva et al., 2021). Sri Lanka, on the other hand, operates in a "hegemonic security order" in which India exercises predominance over smaller South Asian states. Thus, the discrepancy between the types of regional orders provides us with an initial impression of the way in which both regional orders securitise threats. This will be discussed in greater detail in the next section.

Although Buzan and Waever contend that RSCT is best applied in the post-Cold War period (post 1991), the authors—by examining the period from 1948 to the contemporary era—adopts RSCT to interrogate whether it is felicitous to claim that the securitisation patterns of Sri Lanka and the GII, justify a combination of the two into a larger RSC. The types of security threats analysed in this chapter range from global threats (climate change) to regional threats (terrorism within the region).

Sri Lanka and the GII

Sri Lanka has historically maintained close trade links with the Middle East. The island, as a well-known Indian Ocean entrepôt for spices and silk in the ancient maritime silk road, routinely traded with Persian and other Middle Eastern traders. For instance, Ptolemy's maps depicted Sri Lanka considerably larger than many other neighbouring countries, indicating the island's significance among the trading community at the time. Evidence of Arabic coins minted using copper and silver were uncovered as far back as the Anuradhapura Kingdom, which lasted from 377BC-1017AD. Other trading items such as ceramics transported by Middle Eastern merchants

108   *Shakthi De Silva and Robin Vochelet*

have also been dug up in ancient archaeological sites dating as far back as the 2nd century BC.

Bohingamuwa (2017), in an exposition on Sri Lanka's Mannar harbour, states that Middle Eastern ceramics "originating largely from Iran, Iraq and Saudi Arabia that are datable from the 11th … to the 15th centuries account for 11.5% of total middle eastern assemblage" in the Port of Mannar alone. In addition, cargo carrying silk, spices and sandalwood from the Middle East frequented other harbours located on the island's western seaboard. Historical records also document the degree of inter-regional links between the Middle East and Sri Lanka. For example, in his article on the importance of the Mannar port, Kiribamune (1991) argues that a monk by the name of Vajrabodhi documented the presence of 35 Persian ships at the Mannar harbour and that he travelled with Middle East traders to the Chinese port of Canton.

Ali's (1984) work on the Sri Lankan Muslim community's origins reveals that "ethnologically, the Muslim community … is a complex of Moors and the Malay's [together with] the Arab's, Persians, and Afghans and other converted individuals." According to some scholars, Arab settlements were constructed around Colombo for trading purposes and may have triggered a growth in the number of the Muslim community in Sri Lanka (Jayasuriya, 1949). Thus, trade became a precursor to deepening Sri Lanka's ties with the Gulf and broader Middle East. The onset of Western colonialism and imperialism damaged these ties which were rekindled after Sri Lanka's independence in 1948.

As Sri Lanka borders the unipolar South Asian regional power—India—it tends to formulate its foreign and security policy keeping New Delhi's interests in mind. Bishku (2020) adds that Sri Lanka's Middle East policy "in general has been in line with that of India, with the exception of military ties with Israel during the Cold War …. the Arab Gulf states care less about Sri Lanka's ties with Israel, while Iran is in no position to exert political pressure on Sri Lanka" (p. 117). While this does not imply that Sri Lanka maintains a sense of obeisance to the regional power, it does demonstrate how the island's policymakers—at times reflexively—refrain from stepping on New Delhi's toes when devising security ties with extra-regional states. The GII, on the other hand, manifests starkly different dynamics. Saudi Arabia operates as a regional hegemon in the Gulf. Israel and Iran, to a certain degree, rival Saudi Arabia's claim and, in the case of the latter, utilises regional proxy wars to offset Saudi Arabia's hegemony. Two out of the three also possess capabilities to launch a nuclear missile.

Buzan and Waever (2003) contest the claim that the Middle East/West Asia falls within the Asian supercomplex and maintain that the security interdependence characteristics of the GII can be distinguished from that of the rest of Asia. They also subdivide the Middle Eastern RSC. In their view,

Sri Lanka and the Gulf States 109

it comprises of a Maghreb subcomplex, a Levant Subcomplex and the Gulf Subcomplex each of which manifest somewhat different security orders.

However, as this book examines whether commonalities exist in the securitisation strategies of South Asian and Middle Eastern nations in the interest of identifying a larger RSC, we begin our exploration to find out whether this holds true using the case of Sri Lanka and the GII. The GII includes the Gulf subcomplex (Iran, Iraq and the Gulf states) and Israel (which, according to Buzan and Waever, belongs to the Levant subcomplex). Israel has been included in the GII in this chapter as it has strong links with Sri Lanka in each of the domains analysed below and, as a consequence, helps us examine whether securitisation patterns can be observed between the GII and Sri Lanka.

The next section surveys the nature of interaction between the GII and Sri Lanka in several domains and explores the tendency of both regions to securitise common issues and concerns. This section also helps extrapolate whether security interdependence is evident by the way in which issues are/ are not securitised by Sri Lanka and the GII.

Trade

Inter-regional exchanges and engagement can be measured by several indicators, a key variable being the trade of goods and services. Geographical contiguity—which tends to engender ethnic, religious and ideological commonalities—coupled with political enthusiasm to deepen ties often spurs strong trade relations between regions. The geographic proximity between Sri Lanka and the GII, however, has not translated into deep bilateral trade links. None of the GII countries rank among the top ten export destinations for the island and, as Table 5.1 indicates, bilateral trade in some instances remains heavily asymmetrical.

Table 5.1 Sri Lanka's trade relations with the GII

GII country	Exports (million USD) as of 2020	Imports (million USD) as of 2020	Trade balance (million USD) as of 2020
Bahrain	7.23	36.40	−29.17
Iran	78.87	7.79	71.08
Iraq	110.17	12.11	98.06
Israel	89.18	67.13	22.05
Kuwait	22.28	65.59	−43.31
Oman	12.44	175.68	−163.24
Qatar	26.24	31.79	−7.55
Saudi Arabia	75.77	187.55	−111.78
United Arab Emirates	188.90	868.01	−680.11

Source: Sri Lanka Export Development Board (2021), *Export Performance Indicators,* https://www.srilankabusiness.com/ebooks/export-performance-indicators-of-sri-lanka-2011-2020.pdf

Table 5.2 The main export products of Sri Lanka to the GII

Exported product	2016 value in USD millions	2017 value in USD millions	2018 value in USD millions	2019 value in USD millions	2020 value in USD millions	2020 share value in USD millions	Percentage average growth
Tea packets	224.04	247.34	227.54	206.44	188.06	25.43	−5.31
Tea in bulk	252.01	270.76	255.74	207.05	180.46	24.41	−9.36
Diamonds	70.37	53.23	73.09	92.09	64.13	8.67	3.62
Apparel	67.96	70.54	55.95	53.02	35.03	4.74	−16.11

Source: Sri Lanka Export Development Board (2021), *Export Performance Indicators,* https://www.srilankabusiness.com/ebooks/export-performance-indicators-of-sri-lanka-2011-2020.pdf

Sri Lanka's trade statistics demonstrate a negative trade balance with several nations in the Arabian Peninsula, chiefly because the island imports a substantial quantity of oil from the region. Sri Lanka's sizable export volume, in the case of Iraq, UAE and Saudi Arabia, comprises tea, and to a lesser degree, food and other beverages (Sri Lanka Export Development Board, 2021). Collectively, the Middle East consists of 7.36% of Sri Lanka's export earnings share in 2020. Export revenue to the region, however, has seen a relative decline in recent years, mainly owing to the rise of alternative cheaper exporters in other parts of the world (see Table 5.2).

A country-by-country breakdown of Sri Lanka's largest export product to each of the GII countries shows the gradual decline in volume, particularly since 2018.

The drop in Sri Lanka's main export revenue, as shown in Table 5.3, clearly indicates that the island's exports have been underperforming prior to the outbreak of Coronavirus, which began to significantly impact global supply chains after early 2020. In sum, none of the GII countries rank among the top Sri Lankan export destinations and there exists a substantial negative trade balance between the GII and Sri Lanka in favour of the former.

Since independence, the island has chiefly been governed by two major parties: the Sri Lanka Freedom Party which tends to adopt nationalistic left-leaning ideological positions and the United National Party (UNP) which espouses more liberal economic and political stances. The island's ties with Israel witnessed significant vicissitudes during the Cold War owing to the change in power between the two parties. Sri Lanka's first Prime Minister, D.S. Senanayake of the UNP, commenced the first military vessel purchase from Israel and welcomed Israeli agriculture technical advisors to the country (Amarasinghe, 2021). Ties with Israel saw a downturn during the Sri Lanka Freedom Party administration of Prime Minister S.W.R.D. Bandaranaike (1956–1959) and was terminated by his widow— Mrs. Bandaranaike—in the 1970s.

Table 5.3 Breakdown of the main Sri Lankan export product to each GII country

Exported product	2016	2017	2018	2019	2020	2020 percentage share	Percentage average growth
			Country/value in USD millions				
Iran							
Tea in bulk	128.98	149.69	123.72	97.81	71.61	90.79	−16.02
Iraq							
Tea packets	63.75	86.48	78.06	59.45	54.13	32.77	−1.58
Israel							
Diamonds	70.34	53.21	73.09	92.09	64.13	71.91	3.64
Kuwait							
Tea packets	12.64	13.88	13.61	13.65	11.30	50.72	−2.42
Oman							
Petroleum oils	0.12	4.13	6.70	4.49	3.28	26.37	66.35
Qatar							
Bananas	3.28	3.95	5.97	5.78	3.77	15.55	6.60
Saudi Arabia							
Tea packets	16.78	19.46	25.90	31.08	35.69	47.10	19.78
United Arab Emirates							
Petroleum oils	30.20	44.72	80.35	72.07	33.55	17.76	6.87

Source: Sri Lanka Export Development Board (2021), *Export Performance Indicators,* https://www.srilankabusiness.com/ebooks/export-performance-indicators-of-sri-lanka-2011-2020.pdf

In contrast, UNP governments have tended to demonstrate a notable indulgence towards Israel. For example, Prime Minister Dudley Senanayake of the UNP "refused to label Israel as an aggressor" during the 1967 Arab-Israel Wars while UNP President J.R. Jayewardena openly courted Israeli support to win the internal armed conflict in Sri Lanka (Bishku, 2020, pp. 120–121). The Jayewardena administration, however, appointed A.C.S Hameed, a Muslim politician, as the country's first Foreign Minister (previously the portfolio of Foreign Minister was held with the Prime Minister) hoping to appease Gulf nations and demonstrate Sri Lanka's desire to balance ties with both parties. Full diplomatic relations with Israel, however, were not instituted until after the end of the Cold War. Sri Lanka continues to expand its bilateral ties with countries of the GII—and as recently as December 2021, Sri Lanka inked eight agreements with the United Arab Emirates, one of which dealt with augmenting bilateral security cooperation (Newswire, 2021).

Although attempts to enhance trade ties have been espoused, they remain piecemeal and dependent on the foreign policy approach of the Sri Lankan government in power at the time. Despite Sri Lanka's current forex crisis, policymakers have refrained from securitising and politicising the asymmetric trade balance with the GII. This demonstrates the significance

112 *Shakthi De Silva and Robin Vochelet*

Table 5.4 Sri Lanka's labour migration to countries of the GII

| Country | 2016 | | 2017 | | 2018 | | 2019 | | 2020 | |
	Number	Percentage	No	%	No	%	No	%	No	%
Saudi Arabia	63,293	26.07	37,745	17.80	35,733	16.92	35,415	17.44	9,407	17.46
Kuwait	32,400	13.34	37,410	17.65	46,914	22.21	43,073	21.21	8,040	14.92
UAE	40,117	16.52	36,667	17.30	32,821	15.54	32,860	16.18	10,714	19.89
Qatar	59,523	24.51	56,637	26.72	50,749	24.03	40,783	20.08	9,689	17.98
Bahrain	3,225	1.33	3,002	1.42	2,922	1.38	3,017	1.486	1,050	1.95
Iraq	171	0.07	162	0.08	262	0.12	183	0.09	160	0.30
Israel	2,271	0.94	2,487	1.17	2,033	0.96	1,559	0.768	778	1.44

Source: Sri Lanka Bureau of Foreign Employment 2021, *Outward Labour Migration in Sri Lanka,* http://www.slbfe.lk/file.php?FID=588

ascribed to maintaining amicable ties with the region although substantive measures are yet to be adopted to enhance Sri Lanka's trade ties with the GII.

Migration

Another domain of engagement between the GII and Sri Lanka pertains to the migrant workforce residing in the GII. Migrant worker remittances traditionally account for the second largest share of the country's foreign exchange earnings, after merchandise exports (Weeraratne, 2020). Migrant labour, particularly female domestic helpers, is a major source of external income for Sri Lanka. Moreover, over 60% of the domestic helper demand is supplied from South and Southeast Asian economies (Addleton, 1991). According to Sri Lanka's Bureau of Foreign Employment (see Tables 5.4 and 5.5), over

Table 5.5 Remittances received by Sri Lanka

| | Remittances | | Remittances received from the Middle East as a percentage of total remittances |
| | Middle East | Total | |
Year	USD millions	USD millions	
2020	51.7	7,104	51.7
2019	51.5	6,717	51.5
2018	51.2	7,015	51.2
2017	51.8	7,164	51.8
2016	53.7	7,242	53.7

Source: Sri Lanka Bureau of Foreign Employment 2021, *Outward Labour Migration in Sri Lanka,* http://www.slbfe.lk/file.php?FID=588

Sri Lanka and the Gulf States 113

90% of those employed in the Middle East are concentrated in Saudi Arabia, Kuwait and Qatar.

Consequently, the GII constitutes the most important region for private remittances received to Sri Lanka:

Although female domestic workers constitute the largest group among migrant workers and are correspondingly the largest contributors of remittances received, Sri Lanka has had significant issues with regard to their treatment in the GII. Before delving into the hazards and problems migrant workers face in the GII, we begin by briefly outlining why Sri Lankans travel to the GII for employment as domestic workers/helpers.

Research into the "push and pull factors" contributing to house worker migration shows that low salaries, the lack of social security and absence of employment opportunities in the home country account for the push factors. In other words, economic and socio-political conditions in the home country drive outward migration. GII immigration policies, as well as attractive wages (when GII currencies are converted into Sri Lankan rupee) and the presence of a high demand for domestic household workers are often pull factors (Ekanayake and Amirthalingam, 2021) influencing Sri Lankan women to seek employment as housemaids in the GII.

The well-being of such workers, or the lack thereof, is often a major cause of friction between GII nations and Sri Lanka. A study by Wickramage et al. (2017) underscores the gravity of crimes committed against female housemaids. 60% of the houseworkers surveyed, complained of violence and other physical harassment during their period of service. To test the veracity of their claims, the researchers conducted clinical investigations which proved that 60% of all housemaids scrutinised in their survey had been subject to physical violence. Injuries include permanent disabilities, disfiguration and other non-lethal forms of physical abuse. Other forms of punishment included "deprivation of food and water, deprivation of sleep and inadequate sleeping conditions" (2017, p. 3). Their research also unearthed evidence of human trafficking and sexual abuse meted out against women employed in the GII, some of which resulted in pregnancies during their employment period (also see Abu-Habib, 1998; Cox, 1997; Haddad, 1999).

Thus, "housemaid migration," as Shaw (2010) terms it, constitutes a very sensitive issue, particularly if a housemaid dies during her period of employment, either as a result of government-sanctioned punishment or abuse by her GII employer. Advocacy groups and human rights organisations within Sri Lanka point to such events, arguing that the Sri Lankan government must limit or ban the outflow of housemaids to the GII on the basis that many Middle East nations do not adequately safeguard the human rights of foreign workers, particularly those in the housemaid category (Aneez, 2016). Although, Sri Lankan political authorities have promised to gradually ban/limit the outflow of such migrants to the GII on several occasions, no

114 *Shakthi De Silva and Robin Vochelet*

tangible action has been implemented as yet. Therefore, despite being politicised ("the issue is part of public policy, requiring government decision and resource allocations or, more rarely, some other form of communal governance"), it remains to be seen whether a Sri Lankan government gives in to civil society pressure and bans/limits housemaid migration. Public demands for GII houseworker migration to be securitised have therefore fallen on deaf ears; largely owing to the substantial revenue earned from remittances and the disinclination among Sri Lankan politicians to disconcert their GII counterparts.

Terrorism

Terrorism, or the threat or actual use of violence by a non-state actor to attain a political and/or religious goal, is a major concern for the GII and Sri Lanka. The island, since the late 1970s, was engaged in a protracted intra-state conflict against the Liberation Tigers of Tamil Eelam (LTTE) which demanded a separate territorial enclave to establish an independent nation for the Tamil minority in the island.

Decades of British favouritism of the Tamil community, most notably through the provision of professional job opportunities, were radically altered by the Sinhala Only Act of 1956. This piece of legislation, hurriedly enacted, made Sinhala (the language spoken by the majority Sinhalese community) the only official language of Sri Lanka. The Sinhala Only Act was coupled with measures to improve tertiary educational opportunities for Sinhalese students by forcing Tamil students to attain higher marks in national exams to stand a chance to enter local Universities. "Thus, this legislation passed by a Sinhalese-dominated government...tilted the odds in the other direction and effectively discriminated against Tamil students" (Anandakugan, 2020). Decades of prejudice culminated with the Black July Pogroms where at least a thousand Tamil citizens were murdered by mobs as a reprisal against the death of 13 Sri Lankan soldiers at the hands of the LTTE. The LTTE engaged in a guerrilla war against the Sri Lankan armed forces and carried out numerous terror attacks including bombing the Sri Lankan Bandaranaike Airport (1986), murdering Buddhist monks who were travelling in a bus (1987) and other suicide bomb attacks, one of which resulted in the death of President Ranasinghe Premadasa.

The LTTE received funding from several nations with large Tamil Diaspora communities until it was militarily defeated in 2009. It is also known to have received advanced military training from Palestinian factions in the Middle East from 1978 to 1980. Some analysts also believe that the LTTE may have developed the art of suicide terrorism from the Palestinian factions operating in the GII (Bloom, 2003). During the war, successive Sri Lankan governments securitised the conflict, permitting substantial discretion concerning information that is relayed to the public of the armed forces activities and justifying these and other emergency measures on the basis of safeguarding national security.

Having militarily defeated the LTTE in 2009, Sri Lanka adopted a lax security policy towards combatting terrorism. The island's complacent political and security atmosphere was upended following the Easter terror bombings carried out on the 21st of April 2019 by individuals inspired by the Islamic State in Iraq and Syria (ISIS) terrorist network. A series of suicide bombings in several hotels and Catholic churches resulted in the death of over 260 civilians, injuring 500 more. Although ISIS has now largely been militarily defeated in the Middle East, the prospect of lone-wolf attacks by those inspired by the group continues to be a source of concern for Sri Lanka. In contrast to the LTTE, however, Sri Lankan politicians have not securitised the threat from ISIS and other Islamic fundamentalist groups. Instead, the government's attention and resources are currently devoted to tackle the financial problems affecting the country.

Since the end of the Second World War, the Middle East has been a hotbed for many terrorist organisations. Several factors contributed towards the emergence of such networks, including the presence of repressive regimes, the influence and involvement of extra-regional powers in the region, poor socioeconomic conditions and the pervasiveness of inter-state conflicts.

In his *Analytical History of Terrorism*, Shughart II (2006) argues that the dynamics characterising modern-day terrorism can be traced to the "post-colonial or anti-colonial wave of terror" that began in the 1920s (p. 15). Terrorist activities were carried out during this time "in the service of nationalism and ethnic separatism" leading up to the creation of new states in Asia and Africa (p. 15). Rebellions and clashes against the British colonial government, instigated in Egypt, Afghanistan and Iraq gradually spread throughout Asia. Anti-British violence reached noteworthy levels of brutality in the Palestinian Mandate where bombings of immigration offices, attacks against British officials, and the detonation of explosives near British offices housed in the King David Hotel were carried out to influence Britain to fully open borders to all Jewish individuals desiring to arrive in Israel (Shughart II, 2006, p. 19). With the consolidation of the state of Israel, some Palestinian groups took up radical measures to reclaim the land. Israel's victory in the six-day war against the combined forces of UAR Egypt, Jordan and Syria in particular, strengthened their resolve that terrorism was the only way to dent Israel's status and power.

The Palestine Liberation Organization (PLO), founded in the 1960s for the purpose of restoring an independent state of Palestine, collaborated with other terrorist groups (Hoffman, 1998, pp. 67, 82) to carry out attacks against Jewish citizens. Evidence of such partnerships surfaced following the Black September attacks against Israeli athletes at the 1972 Olympics

(Shughart II, 2006, p. 22). The Black September Organization operated as a clandestine wing of Al-Fatah in the 1970s. According to Sullivan (n.a), it was "founded with the objective to avenge the expulsion of the Palestine Liberation Organization (PLO) from Jordan in September 1970. This time [period] was referred to as Black September, hence the name chosen by the Black September Organization."

The Al-Fatah movement was formed in the early 1960s by Yasser Arafat. "Backed by Syria, Fatah began carrying out terrorist raids against Israeli targets in 1965, launched from Jordan, Lebanon and, at the time, Egyptian occupied Gaza" (Ashley, 2011, p. 168). Many of these raids were carried out against civilian targets. Al Fatah later joined the PLO in 1968 and by the 1980s, following Israel's invasion of Lebanon, the group dispersed across the Middle East. A splinter group by the name of Abu Musa or Fatah Al-Intifada emerged in the 1980s and operated as the military wing of the Fatah. The PLO thus developed into an umbrella organisation encompassing several other groups and movements. Although its original goal was to dismantle the state of Israel, it has now shifted to accept a two-state solution provided that the historic lands of Palestine are returned to constitute a state of Palestine.

Divisions between Muslim communities also spawned fundamentalist networks. Muhammad Abd al-Wahhab's (1703–1787) brand of puritan Islamic theology ideologised a "return ... to the pure authentic Islam of the Prophet, removing and, where necessary, destroying all later accretions" (Lewis, 2001, p. 59). Wahabism, as it was later known, merited terrorist brutalities as necessary to purify the Muslim religion and remove elements that may challenge its ascendency. Additionally, the House of Saud's decision to openly embrace Wahabism and "generously fund fundamentalist religious schools and terrorist groups throughout the region" also contributed towards the spread of other terror networks (Shughart II, 2006, p. 28).

The Iranian Revolution of 1979 added a novel dynamic into the growing pool of terrorist organisations, seeking to export the Shia revolution throughout the Middle East. The Shia militant group Hezbollah, literally translated as the Party of God, was founded in 1982 as a "direct response to Israel's 1982 invasion of Lebanon" (Ashley, 2011, p. 187), with significant support from Iran. Hezbollah began operations in Lebanon, training assassins, kidnappers and suicide bombers to carry out attacks against Israel. Notable suicide bombings include one in April 1983 in front of the US embassy in Beirut which killed over 50 American and Lebanese citizens. Kindt (2009) maintains that the historical persecution faced by the Shia community in Lebanon and elsewhere as a result of British and French colonisation, as well as Sunni dominant governments, created a "profound sense of alienation" among the community. This, together with the military occupation of Lebanon

Sri Lanka and the Gulf States 117

by Israel, spurred an increase in the ranks of the Hezbollah group in the 1980–1990s.

According to Ganor and Azani (2019),

> Hezbollah also employed active methods and means of psychological warfare against Israel and against enemies of the organization and, in doing so, became one of the first to develop a complex and effective propaganda system that included—even back in the 1980s and 1990s— radio and television stations, newspapers, internet sites, and more. Hezbollah understood the importance of psychological warfare and the use of the media.
>
> (p. 579)

With the outbreak of the Intifada, whereby Palestinians protested the Israeli occupation of West Bank and Gaza following the 1967 war, the terrorist group Hamas began to play an active role in the violent attacks against Israel. Hamas, an outgrowth of the Muslim Brotherhood, is a Sunni, Islamist, religious movement which sprang from Egypt intending, as per its charter, to endow the land of Palestine to Islam and "liberate Palestine through violent Jihad" (p. 586). Ganor and Azani (2019) contend that Hamas' terrorist attacks were justified as necessary in order "to strike a harsh moral blow to Israeli society and to destabilize Israel from within in a way that would cause it to change positions and withdraw from the Gaza Strip and West Bank" (p. 581). Post (2007) adds that Hamas became "increasingly radical as Palestinians became frustrated with Fatah, angry with Israel and willing to accept more hostile tactics" following the Intifadas in the late 1980s. Similar to the ISIS and Al Qaeda, Hamas "has [also] proven particularly effective at mobilizing the new media to support recruitment, information sharing, and coordination of logistics" (Post, p. 158)

The Soviet invasion of Afghanistan bred substantial resentment and anger in the Middle East, spawning the emergence of Al-Qaeda under Osama Bin Laden. Al-Qaeda, literally translated as "The Base," was formed in 1988 and undertook the arduous task of fighting against the Soviet troops in Afghanistan. After Afghanistan witnessed the withdrawal of Soviet soldiers, Bin Laden's priority shifted to ridding American soldiers from the Arabian Peninsula—thereby "liberating Islam's holy sites." He subsequently announced to the world his desire "for every American and every Jew everywhere on Earth to be killed" (Ganor and Azani, 2019, p. 584). His gaze also centred on overthrowing "heretic regimes" such as the Saudi Arabian, Egyptian and Israeli governments which are closely associated with the United States.

The 9/11 attacks demonstrated the global reach of Al-Qaeda. The subsequent US retaliation engendered the rise of splinter groups, such as the

118 *Shakthi De Silva and Robin Vochelet*

Al-Qaeda in the Arabian Peninsula, Al-Qaeda in the Islamic Maghreb, Al-Qaeda in Iraq and other terrorist sleeper cells in the Middle East. The death of Bin Laden generated hope that Middle East terrorism would subsequently diminish in scale, but the rise of the ISIS as well as the role played by lone wolf attackers and ISIS-inspired terrorist bombers in parts of Europe and Asia continues to make that prospect unlikely.

"The success of ISIS's ground operation in Iraq and Syria, and the establishment of the Caliphate in the second half of 2014, were a magnet not only for young people in Syria and Iraq but also for people in the Arab and Muslim world who surged in the thousands to join the ranks of ISIS." (Ganor and Azani, 2019, p. 587). The territory it occupied before it was militarily defeated had "its own army, police force, judicial system and an annual budget of approximately 2 billion USD. To all intents and purposes, ISIS had a de facto state" (Solomon and Tausch, 2021, p. 21) within the borders of occupied Iraq and Syria.

This non-exhaustive overview of the terrorist groups operating in Sri Lanka and the GII expounds on the reasons why each group emerged, and the degree of threat posed by terrorism in Asia. While the treatment meted out to the Tamil minority community led to the rise of the LTTE; the advent of an ISIS-inspired terror network in the island was not necessary a result of the treatment of Sri Lanka's Muslim minority. Moreover, the fact that the attacks took place within a span of ten years since the LTTE's military defeat showcased the necessity for the country's intelligence community to maintain cognisance of regional and international terror network operations. Sri Lanka's lax policy towards intelligence gathering and political dysfunction under the National Unity Government also served as an opportune breeding ground for the spread of radical fundamentalist ideologies. As the Easter bombings constituted suicide attacks which were carried out by the leaders of the group, the government was unable to capture or interrogate any mastermind related to the bombings. The inability to foresee that regional terror networks could inspire lone wolf or coordinated bombings of this nature is also reflective of the weakness within the security apparatus of the island. While the attacks led to heightened reflection on the emergence of such terrorist outfits—the issue was not securitised—and instead, under the current Gotabaya administration, security has once again taken a back seat owing to Sri Lanka's financial crisis.

With regard to the GII, the emergence of terrorist networks can be traced as far back as the colonial period. The antipathy towards the state of Israel, the activities by the Islamic Republic of Iran, extra-regional intervention, namely from the Soviet Union and the US, as well as the dictatorial/autocratic regimes in the region are some of the factors which contributed to the rise of terror networks. Middle East governments have attempted to securitise terrorism, but as Berger (2021) argues

Sri Lanka and the Gulf States 119

only in Egypt, Libya, and Tunisia has the 'securitization of terrorism' been successful in the sense that it comes close to the level of concern the predominant issue areas receive ... Despite the 'crowding out' of terrorism by other issues, Arab regimes still employ securitization of terrorism with the aim of justifying legislation mostly aimed at silencing non-violent political opposition.

(pp. 819–820)

Terrorism, therefore, is a common security threat in the GII and Sri Lanka. ISIS-inspired Easter bombings in Sri Lanka underscores the possibility that individuals inspired by terrorist groups operating in the GII can carry out attacks in the island. In that sense, the terrorist dynamics of Sri Lanka and the GII are comparable. The inability to build on these common security issues through information sharing and other concerted diplomatic and security efforts to tackle terrorism or even holistically securitise terrorism, demonstrates the absence of sufficient will to engage with the issue by both parties.

RSCT argues that states which are geographically close to one another, and which share certain commonalities are more likely to witness the emergence of common security concerns. In situations where security interdependence emerges, such RSC tend to securitise regional/global security threats. Reflecting on the GII, Jarząbek (2018) argues that it is characterised by a substantial number of local conflicts and a strong US presence. Local conflicts involve terrorist non-state actors as well as inter-state conflicts. For example, the tendency of Israel to securitise the "nuclear threat" from Iran is manifest through Israeli Prime Minister Benjamin Netanyahu's accusation at the United Nations General Assembly in 2018 (and earlier in 2012) that Iran is planning/or intends to launch an aerial nuclear attack against Israel. Having successfully securitised the threat of Iran internally, Netanyahu believed that he could galvanise the international community to adopt his position towards Iran. To a certain degree, his efforts have been successful in derailing the P5+1 Nuclear Agreement as US President Biden continues to be reluctant on re-entering the agreement after his predecessor withdrew under the influence of the Israeli lobby. Similarly, King Salman bin Abdulaziz of Saudi Arabia and his regime attempted to securitise the threat from Iran among the global community through speeches at the United Nations General Assembly (Al-Jazeera, 2020). Efforts to securitise terrorism, similar to the successful securitisation of Iran in Israel and Saudi Arabia however, has not effectively trickled down to the securitisation of terrorism in the GII except in the case of a few states.

Shared historical, ethnic, religious and cultural ties constitute important variables in increasing cooperation among nations. The same applies to the GII. Colonisation by Western imperialists (except in the case of Iran and

120   *Shakthi De Silva and Robin Vochelet*

parts of the Arabian Peninsula) followed by tensions between the Sunni and Shia communities, and the antipathy generated after the creation of the state of Israel engendered common security dynamics within the GII. The aforementioned nuclear threat from Iran is an issue that Saudi Arabia and Israel continue to securitise to the internal, regional and international audiences. Non-state terrorist actors with the tacit support of regional governments continue to engage in terrorist activities against the state of Israel. Meanwhile, Israel has intervened in the internal affairs of neighbouring countries to counter the influence from terrorist groups and has successfully repelled previous attacks against its territory.

When compared with Sri Lanka, however, we do not see similarities to the extent that would justify merging South Asia and the Middle East into a larger security complex. Despite the devastation and political pledges made to prevent the recurrence of another ISIS-inspired attack in future, ISIS and other Islamic fundamentalist terrorism has not been securitised in Sri Lanka. Moreover, while maintaining favourable ties with Arab governments, Sri Lanka continues to try to forge strong bonds with Iran, as Tehran is among the largest importers of Sri Lankan tea. Although bilateral ties with Israel have seen several reverses, this is, in large part, due to the administration in power at particular moments in Sri Lanka's history. The UNP, owing to its inclination to side with Western governments, has tended to be more accommodative and welcoming of Israel compared to Sri Lanka Freedom Party administrations.

In sum, terrorism and the inter-state tensions in the GII and larger Middle East context fail to make a sufficiently large impression on Sri Lanka's policymakers. While taking note of GII inter-state tensions, Sri Lanka continues to maintain amicable ties with Israel and Iran as well as other Arab nations. Although the threat of terrorism has re-emerged in Sri Lanka, it has not led to the securitisation of terrorist groups operating in the Middle East. Therefore, exploring the domain of terrorism leads to the conclusion that neither inter-state tensions nor the threat of terrorism is securitised in the same manner in the GII and Sri Lanka. Security interdependence is consequently insufficient to constitute a merging of the two regions into a larger RSC.

Climate change

Climate change and the impact it has on human security and inter-state conflict is another domain of importance for the GII and Sri Lanka. The Middle East continues to experience water scarcity—as illustrated by a 2018 World Bank report which stated that over 60% of the Middle East and North African population live in areas with high or very high-water stress (World Bank, 2018). The report went on to posit that between 6% and 14% of the region's GDP would decline owing to the shortage of water by

2050. A 2019 SIPRI report adds that "increasing competition over natural resources, particularly water, may add to existing tensions and cause new conflicts" (Stockholm International Peace Research Institute, 2019, p. 3). While the Middle East and North African states often share natural aquifers, the interdependence this generates "is not matched by corresponding agreements for joint management of transboundary water" (p. 4), which adds to the possibility that tensions may erupt over the distribution of water between states.

The prevalence of droughts and high temperatures in the GII are likely to exacerbate as a result of climate change. As the GII oil-producing rentier states tend to depend on the revenue earned from oil, scholars contend that these economies underemphasise the importance of developing a diversified economy with effective tax collection as a form of state income generation. Consequently, the pressure from taxpayers to establish accountable bureaucracy decreases. Lack of democracy in the Gulf states and Iran further complicates the task of bringing environmental issues onto the political agenda. The weakness or absence of feedback channels between civil society and government units makes it harder for Non-Governmental Organisations and activists to call for climate action. Effective climate change action in the GII therefore necessitates the regimes in power to take measures of their own accord.

Climate change has also exacerbated inter-state conflicts. According to Krampe and Gignoux (2018) most rural conflicts in Yemen during 2013 were water related. Schwartzstein (2017) claims that ISIS recruitment was bolstered by the fact that the Iraqi government did not assist rural Sunnis during the droughts of 2017. Iraq also witnessed violent protests related to the breakdown of water and energy services (United Nations Assistance Mission for Iraq, 2020).

Similarly, natural resources have come to occupy a central role in Israeli-Palestinian relations, particularly as it comes to water resources. As of 2020, it was estimated that 92% of the water in the Gaza Strip, an "open-air prison" (Chebab, 2007, p. 182)[2] under Israeli blockade since the Gaza wars of 2014, is undrinkable. Water resources in the West Bank, on the other hand, were the focal point of the Oslo II Agreements signed between both parties in 1995. The agreements resulted in the creation of a Joint Water Committee (JWC) responsible for the management of water desalination infrastructure in Areas A and B of the West Bank (EcoPeace Middle East, 2019, p. 27). While the JWC was intended as a temporary measure, the committee remains in place over 20 years later.

In spite of these cases, evidence of GII efforts to securitise climate change is scant. Although many GII nations recognise and acknowledge the scientific claims concerning the gravity of climate change and forecasts for the region, "governments have avoided framing climate change as a threat to security and/or as a problem justifying exceptional measures" (Mason, 2013, p. 303).

122   *Shakthi De Silva and Robin Vochelet*

As a small developing nation in the Indian Ocean, Sri Lanka is highly vulnerable to the adverse impact of climate change. The 2004 Tsunami made clear the degree to which the low-lying plains and coastal region can be susceptible to natural disasters and sea level rise. The latter, followed by the erosion of the beach, threatens the livelihoods of fishermen residing along the coastline. Changes in temperature, rainfall variability, droughts and flash floods—exacerbated by climate change—can also adversely affect Sri Lanka's agriculture sector, upon which many base their sustenance. In addition, a substantial share of foreign income is also generated by exporting crops such as cinnamon and tea which are highly sensitive to fluctuations in the soil makeup and rainfall pattern. Beyond the threat that climate change poses to food security, there is also a threat to the uneasy peace that followed the end of the civil war in 2009. Sri Lanka's most at-risk regions in terms of food security are concentrated in the northern and northwestern provinces of Sri Lanka (Punyawardena et al., 2015), which have been the main battlefield of the 30-year internal armed conflict between the Sri Lankan government and the LTTE. These same regions are also considered at high risk of rising sea levels which threaten to erode the country's northern coastline, thereby adding geographic implications to the climate crisis looming upon Sri Lanka.

The GII and Sri Lanka have publicly expressed their commitment to addressing climate change as reflected in Table 5.6.

Iran stands as an outlier, as per Table 5.6, because it continues to refuse to sign the Paris Climate accords until the United States lifts the sanctions imposed on the country. Climate change mitigation plans set out by Sri Lanka and the GII target several areas including minimising greenhouse gas (GHG) emissions, furthering the development of renewable energy generation projects, building resilience among vulnerable communities and adapting new techniques and technology to protect critical sectors such as human security, water and endangered ecosystems.

For countries in the Middle East—including Israel and Iran—the issue of climate change bears significant influence over regional stability. The creation of the state of Israel in 1947 has been a major point of contention with Arab states in the region, at times exacerbated by civil wars and political instability. As the climate crisis unfolds, environmental disasters are likely to act as "threat multipliers," showing the deep linkage between environmental and political stability in the region, and the need to address climate change as a security issue. Despite regional tensions, all countries are threatened by climate change, particularly with regard to water resources in the region.

Since the early 1950s, several bilateral water-sharing agreements have been initiated, mainly between Jordan and Israel, Israel and Palestine, as well as Jordan and Syria. Additionally, Egypt signed the Nile Waters Agreement with neighbouring Sudan in 1959, owing to the country's geographical location in Africa. While these agreements illustrate efforts to

Sri Lanka and the Gulf States   123

Table 5.6 Country and climate change agreements signed

Country	Party to
Bahrain	**Paris Agreement** Date of signature—22 April 2016 Date of ratification—23 December 2016 **Kyoto Protocol** Date of ratification—31 January 2006
Iraq	**Paris Agreement** Date of signature—08 December 2016 Date of ratification—01 December 2021 **Kyoto Protocol** Date of ratification—28 July 2009
Kuwait	**Paris Agreement** Date of signature—22 April 2016 Date of ratification—23 April 2018 **Kyoto Protocol** Date of ratification—11 March 2005
Oman	**Paris Agreement** Date of signature—22 April 2016 Date of ratification—24 April 2019 **Kyoto Protocol** Date of ratification—09 January 2005
Qatar	**Paris Agreement** Date of signature—22 April 2016 Date of ratification—23 June 2017 **Kyoto Protocol** Date of ratification—11 January 2005
Saudi Arabia	**Paris Agreement** Date of signature—03 November 2016 Date of ratification—03 November 2016 **Kyoto Protocol** Date of ratification—31 January 2005
United Arab Emirates	**Paris Agreement** Date of signature—22 April 2016 Date of ratification—21 September 2016 **Kyoto Protocol** Date of ratification—26 January 2005
Israel	**Paris Agreement** Date of signature—22 April 2016 Date of ratification—22 November 2016 **Kyoto Protocol** Date of signature—16 December 1998 Date of ratification—15 March 2004
Iran	**Paris Agreement** Date of signature—22 April 2016 **Kyoto Protocol** Date of ratification—20 August 2005
Sri Lanka	**Paris Agreement** Date of signature—22 April 2016 Date of ratification—21 September 2016 **Kyoto Protocol** Date of ratification—03 September 2002

Source: United Nations Climate Change (n.a), https://unfccc.int/process/parties-non-party-stakeholders/parties-convention-and-observer-states?op=Clear

124   Shakthi De Silva and Robin Vochelet

address access to natural resources, they remain constrained to two parties at a time, thereby considerably fragmenting a regional response to climate issues (Feimuth et al., 2007, p. 10).

There have been loose attempts from politicians in Israel to securitise the issue by placing climate change on the same level of concern as traditional security threats. Despite unveiling a National GHG Emissions Reduction Plan in 2010, Israel omitted any policy suggestions addressing dependence on oil and other fossil fuels. In 2014, Israel accounted for 0.2% of global GHG emissions, the large part of which are generated by fossil fuel power plants and oil refineries (Michaels and Tal, 2015, p. 482). However, Israel's Plan shows that policy actions have failed to match these discourses, instead avoiding addressing energy transition and tackling fossil fuel dependency. Concretely, this also means that the Israeli public opinion remains ambivalent with regard to the climate crisis, focusing instead on security threats such as suicide bombings and rocket launches (Times of Israel, 2022).

Owing to the GII's dependence on fossil fuels for energy generation, Sri Lanka ranks substantially lower in terms of CO_2 emissions and per capita GHG emissions. Reports by Sri Lankan ministries state that, out of the annual electricity demand (over 13,000 Giga Watt hours), approximately 1,500–2,000 Mega Watts are produced through renewable energy, the bulk of which is generated from hydropower (Ministry of Mahaweli Development and Environment, 2018). Several blueprints have been laid out by the government and line ministries to tackle climate change, including the National Climate Change Adaptation Strategy for Sri Lanka in 2010, seeking to bring about the many stakeholders impacted by the climate change to develop sustainable policies addressing collective environmental concerns (Ministry of Mahaweli Development and Environment, 2010, p. 3; Ministry of Environment, 2010). Nearly a dozen plans were then announced by the Government of Sri Lanka in the following year, targeting industries such as agriculture and fisheries, urban development, technology assessment, national transport and long-term electricity generation.

However, the vague language used in such plans, the lack of concrete environmental goals to be achieved and transparency surrounding their implementation, as well as the multiplication of overlapping plans only produced sluggish progress. This lack of commitment to climate pledges demonstrates that climate change has not been securitised by Sri Lanka. The GII and South Asia have already begun experiencing the adverse ramifications of climate change including tapering rainfall volumes, increasing humidity, dwindling water supplies and diminishing agricultural yields. The Gulf nations' high annual CO_2 emissions rates (particularly in the case of Iran and Saudi Arabia) and high per capita GHG emissions demonstrate that sufficient action to combat climate change has not been undertaken by political elites. While Sri Lanka is not a major emitter, it often encounters the negative ramifications of a warming climate. Nevertheless, this has not prompted the island to wholeheartedly commit to a transition into less carbon inducive means of energy generation. In fact, a substantial portion of the island's energy is still generated through coal and oil imported from the GII and elsewhere. In sum, while Sri Lanka's food production and the livelihoods of many are directly dependent on favourable weather conditions, it has not securitised initiatives to prevent global warming, nor has it publicly called for GII nations to drastically cut down on GHG emissions. Thus, while the climate unifies the GII and Sri Lanka in the sense that a drastic reduction in emissions would aid efforts to combat climate change, no substantial effort has been made in this regard.

In this sense, our analysis demonstrated that while securitisation is evident in certain cases (i.e. LTTE terrorism and Sri Lanka), evidence of common security threats such as climate change, ISIS and other Islamic fundamentalist terrorist groups have not been securitised. Contentious issues relating to migration and trade have also not moved beyond the level of politicisation.

Conclusion

This chapter examined the extent to which common threats are securitised by the GII and Sri Lanka and the degree of security independence between the two. Based on the degree of security independence and geographical contiguity, it also explored whether the GII and Sri Lanka can be classified into a larger RSC. By delving into how Sri Lanka and GII nations dealt with global challenges (climate change) and regional threats (terrorism) and issues concerning nations in the GII and Sri Lanka in particular (migration and trade) it came to the conclusion that they have not effectively securitised common security issues. While some GII nations securitise terrorism, Sri Lanka has not done so since the defeat of the LTTE. Although GII nations and Sri Lanka face the looming threat of climate change and have assented to conventions and agreements to limit carbon emissions, they have not, as of yet, taken substantial steps to drastically shift to alternative forms of energy generation or substantially cut emissions. Trade and migration are notably sticking points for Sri Lanka particularly owing to the imbalance of trade ties with the GII and the harassment and violence meted out to domestic houseworkers travelling to GII nations. In both cases, however, the issue has not been securitised by policymakers. Consequently, this chapter concludes that efforts to incorporate Sri Lanka and the GII into a larger RSC based on the degree of securitisation is untenable. Although Sri Lanka and the GII face similar region and global challenges and have strong bilateral socio-economic ties, the degree of securitisation of common threats is minimal.

126 *Shakthi De Silva and Robin Vochelet*

Notes

1 Although Buzan and Waever (2003, p. 51) ascribe Israel to the Levant sub-complex, owing to Israel's historical engagements with the Gulf nations and its relationship with Sri Lanka, the authors included Israel into a larger GII subcomplex. Moreover, despite classifying Israel in the Levant, Buzan and Waever admit that "there is so much overlap and interplay that [they] cannot be disentangled" (pp. 51–52).
2 Scholars, politicians and journalists such as David Cameron, Noam Chomsky and Jonathan Cook later reused the term "open-air prison" to describe Gaza. Zaki Chebab is the first one to have used it in a published work.

References

Abu-Habib, L. 1998, The Use and Abuse of Female Domestic Workers from Sri Lanka in Lebanon, *Gender & Development*, vol. 6, no. 1, pp. 52–56.

Addleton J. 1991, The Impact of the Gulf War on Migration and Remittances in Asia and the Middle East, *International Migration*, vol. 29, no. 4, pp. 509–526.

Al-Jazeera. 2020, Saudi King denounces Iran's expansionism in fiery UN speech, https://www.aljazeera.com/news/2020/9/23/saudi-king-calls-for-comprehensive-solution-on-iran-in-un-speech

Ali, A. 1984, The Genesis of the Muslim Community in Ceylon (Sri Lanka): A Historical Summary, *Asian Studies Association of Australia Review*, vol. 19, pp. 65–82.

Amarasinghe, P. 2021, The Israeli Sri Lankan relationship, *The Begin Sadat Center for Strategic Studies*, https://besacenter.org/israel-sri-lanka-relationship/

Anandakugan, N. 2020, The Sri Lankan Civil War and its history, *Harvard International Review*, https://hir.harvard.edu/sri-lankan-civil-war/ (Accessed 05 April 2022).

Aneez, S. 2016, Sri Lanka to gradually ban housemaids abroad amid abuses, social cost, *Reuters*, https://www.reuters.com/article/us-sri-lanka-housemaids-ban-idUSKCN0YN5UK

Ashley, P. 2011, *The Complete Encyclopaedia of Terrorist Organizations*. Casemate, Philadephia.

Balzacq, T., Léonard, S., and Ruzicka, J. 2016, "Securitization" Revisited: Theory and Cases, *International Relations*, vol. 30, no. 4, pp. 494–531.

Barnett, M. and Duvall, R. 2005, Power in International Politics, *International Organization*, vol. 59, no.1, pp. 39–75.

Berger, L. 2021, Securitization Across Borders–Commonalities and Contradictions in European and Arab Counterterrorism Discourses, *Global Affairs*, vol. 7, no. 5, pp. 813–830.

Bishku, M.B. 2020, Sri Lanka and the Middle East, *Middle Eastern Studies*, vol. 56, no. 1, pp. 116–130.

Bloom, M.M. 2003, Ethnic Conflict, State Terror and Suicide Bombing in Sri Lanka, *Civil Wars*, vol. 6, no. 1, pp. 54–84.

Bohingamuwa, W. 2017, Ancient Mahatitta in Sri Lanka: A Historical Biography, *Journal of the Royal Asiatic Society of Sri Lanka*, vol. 62, no. 2, pp. 23–50.

Buzan, B. and Hansen, L. 2009, *The Evolution of International Security Studies*, Cambridge University Press, Cambridge.

Buzan, B. and Waever, O. 2003, *Regions and Powers: The Structure of International Security*, Cambridge University Press, Cambridge.

Sri Lanka and the Gulf States 127

Buzan, B., Waever O., and de Wilde, J. 1998, *Security: A New Framework for Analysis*, Lynne Rienner, Boulder.

Chebab, Z. 2007, *Inside Hamas: The Untold Story of Militants, Martyrs, and Spies*, I.B. Tauris. *Google Books* [online]. https://books.google.com/books?id=V-8BAwAAQBAJ&pg=PT194&redir_esc=y (Accessed 28 March 2022)

Cox, D. 1997, The Vulnerability of Asian Women Migrant Workers to a Lack of Protection and to Violence, *Asian and Pacific Migration Journal*, vol. 6, no. 1, pp. 59–75.

Da Silva, D., Tian, N., Marksteiner, A. 2021, *Trends in World Military Expenditure 2020*, Stockholm International Peace Research Institute, Stockholm.

EcoPeace Middle East. 2019, *Climate Change, Water Security, and National Security for Jordan, Palestine, and Israel* [online]. Amman, Jordan; Tel Aviv, Israel; Ramallah, Palestine: Carry, Inga (ed.). Available at: https://hidropolitikakademi.org/uploads/wp/2019/07/climate-change-web.pdf (Accessed 28 March 2022)

Ekanayake, A.P. and Amirthalingam, K. 2021, An Empirical Study of the Factors That Motivate Sri Lankan Professionals to Migrate to Qatar. *Migration and Development*, vol. 10, no. 3, pp. 403–420.

Freimuth, L., Bromberg, G., Mehyar, M., and Al Khateeb, N. 2007, *Climate Change a New Threat to Middle East*, Friends of the Earth-Middle East, Jordan.

Frazier, D. and Stewart-Ingersoll, R. 2010, Regional Powers and Security: A Framework for Understanding Order Within Regional Security Complexes. *European Journal of International Relations*, vol. 16, no. 4, pp. 731–753.

Ganor, B. and Azani, E. 2019, "Terrorism in the Middle East" in Chenoweth, E., English, R., Gofas, A., Kalyvas, S. (eds). *The Oxford Handbook of Terrorism*, Oxford University Press, Oxford. pp. 569-589

Haddad, R. 1999, A Modern-Day "Slave Trade": Sri Lankan Workers in Lebanon, *Middle East Report*, vol. 211, pp. 39–41.

Hoffman, B. 1998, *Inside Terrorism*, Columbia University Press, New York.

Jarzabek, J. 2018, The Theory of Regional Security Complexes in the Middle Eastern Dimension, *Wschodnioznawstwo*, vol. 12, pp. 155–170.

Jayasuriya, C. 1949, A Historical Survey of Ceylon Trade, *Journal of the Royal Society of Arts*, vol. 97, no. 4802, pp. 757–768.

Kindt, M.T. 2009, "Hezbollah: A State within a State" in Kindt, M.T., Post, J.M., Schneider, B.R. (eds). *The World's Most Threatening Terrorist Networks and Criminal Gangs*. Palgrave Macmillan, New York, pp. 123–144.

Kiribamune, S. 1991, The Role of the Port City of Mahatitta in the Trade Networks of the Indian Ocean, *Sri Lankan Journal of Humanities*, vol 17, pp. 171–192.

Krampe, F. and Gignoux, S. 2018, Water Service Provision and Peacebuilding in East Timor: Exploring the Socioecological Determinants for Sustaining peace, *Journal of Intervention and Statebuilding*, vol. 12, no. 2, pp. 185–207.

Lake, D. and Morgan, P. (eds). 1997, *Regional Orders: Building Security in a New World*, Pennsylvania State University Press, University Park.

Lewis, B. 2001, The Revolt of Islam. *New Yorker*, vol. 77, no. 36, pp. 50–63.

Mason, M. 2013, Climate Change, Securitisation and the Israeli-Paliestinan Conflict, *The Geographical Journal*, vol. 179, no. 4, pp. 298–308.

Michaels, L. and Tal, A. 2015, Convergence and Conflict with the "National Interest": Why Israel Abandoned Its Climate Policy, *Energy Policy*, vol. 87, pp. 480–485, [online] http://dx.doi.org/10.1016/j.enpol.2015.09.040 (Accessed 28 March 2022).

128 *Shakthi De Silva and Robin Vochelet*

Ministry of Environment. 2010, National Climate Change Adaptation Strategy for Sri Lanka, [online] https://www.climatechange.lk/adaptation/Files/Strategy_Booklet-Final_for_Print_Low_res(1).pdf (Accessed 28 March 2022)

Ministry of Mahaweli Development and Environment. 2010, *National Adaptation plan for climate change impacts in Sri Lanka* 2016–2025, Ministry of Mahaweli Development and Environment, Battaramulla.

Ministry of Mahaweli Development and Environment. 2018, *Nationally Determined Contributions under the Paris Agreement for Climate Change Sri Lanka*, Ministry of Mahaweli Development and Environment, Battaramulla.

Newswire. 2021, UAE to sign 8 agreements with Sri Lanka, https://www.newswire.lk/2021/12/19/uae-to-sign-eight-agreements-with-sri-lanka/

Post, J. 2007, *The Mind of the Terrorist: The Psychology of Terrorism from the IRA to Al Qaeda*, Palgrave Macmillan, New York.

Punyawardena, R., Marambe, B., Silva, P., Premalal, S., Rathnabharathie, V., Kekulandala, B., Nidumolu, U., and Howden, M. 2015, "Climate, Climate Risk, and Food Security in Sri Lanka: The Need for Strengthening Adaptation Strategies" in Filho, W.L. (ed.). *Handbook of Climate Change Adaptation*, 1st edition, Springer, Berlin, pp. 1759–1789.

Schwartzstein, P. 2017, Climate change and water woes drove ISIS recruiting in Iraq, *National Geographic*, https://www.nationalgeographic.com/science/article/climate-change-drought-drove-isis-terrorist-recruiting-iraq

Shaw, J. 2010, Making housemaid remittances work for low-income families in Sri Lanka, *Development in Practice*, vol. 20, no. 1, pp. 18–30.

Shughart II, W.F. 2006, An Analytical History of Terrorism, 1945–2000, *Public Choice*, vol. 128, no. 1, pp. 7–39.

Snider, L.W. 1987, Identifying the Elements of State Power: Where Do We Begin? *Comparative Political Studies*, vol. 20 no. 3, pp. 314–356.

Solomon, H. and Tausch, A. 2021, *Arab MENA Countries: Vulnerabilities and Constraints against Democracy on the Eve of the Global Covid-19 Crisis*, Springer, Singapore.

Sri Lanka Export Development Board. 2021, Export performance indicators, https://www.srilankabusiness.com/ebooks/export-performance-indicators-of-sri-lanka-2011-2020.pdf

Stockholm International Peace Research Institute—SIPRI. 2019, *The World Food Programme's Contribution to Improving the Prospects for Peace*, SIPRI, Stockholm [online], https://sipri.org/sites/default/files/2019-06/wfp_global_report.pdf (Accessed 28 March 2022)

Stritzel, H. 2014, *Security in Translation: Securitization Theory and the Localization of Threat*, Palgrave Macmillan, New York.

Sullivan, D. n.a, The Black September Attacks, *The 1972 Munich Olympics: The Darkest Day in Olympic History*, [online] http://75286874.weebly.com/the-black-september-terrorists.html

Times of Israel. 2022, After terror attacks, poll finds bleak security outlook among Israelis, https://www.timesofisrael.com/after-terror-attacks-poll-finds-bleak-security-outlook-among-israelis/ (Accessed 07 May 2022).

United Nations Assistance Mission for Iraq. 2020, *Human Rights Violations and Abuses in the Context of Demonstrations in Iraq October 2019 to April 2020, Office of the United Nations High Commissioner for Human Rights*, Baghdad, Iraq.

Weeraratne, B. 2020, COVID-19 and migrant works: the economics of repatriation, *Talking Economics*, https://www.ips.lk/talkingeconomics/2020/12/16/covid-19-and-migrant-workers-the-economics-of-repatriation/

Wickramage, K., De Silva, M., and Peiris, S. 2017, Patterns of abuse amongst Sri Lankan omen returning home after working as domestic maids in the Middle East: An exploratory study of medico-legal referrals, *Journal of Forensic and Legal Medicine*, vol. 45, pp. 1–6.

World Bank. 2018, *Beyond Scarcity: Water Security in the Middle East and North Africa*, International Bank for Reconstruction and Development, Washington D.C.

6 Oman's Relations with Pakistan and India

Mehmet Rakipoğlu and Gökhan Ereli

Introduction

Located on the edge of the Middle East and across the Indian Ocean and South Asian countries, Oman's geographic position attaches special importance to the country in terms of maritime, trade, and naval power (Tekir 2022, 512). Therefore, geography has been critical in the making of Oman's foreign policy as well (Kechichian 1995a, 15). The geopolitics of the country caused Oman to experience challenges and rivalries in its historical trajectory. First, the Portuguese considered Oman as a vital base for controlling the maritime route to India. Second, the British were concerned to protect the trade flow to India that was threatened by the French since Napoleon invaded Egypt, and sending letters to Muscat caused concern in London (Riphenburg 1998, 36). Then, the US kept its strategic reservation on Oman due to its strategic location. Contrary to this negative impact, Oman's favourable geography allowed Muscat to interact with many countries such as the African countries and the South Asian countries. This geographical aspect has rendered the Sultanate to pursue a multi-sectoral or multi-directional foreign policy.

Geographically, being the closest Gulf country to India and Pakistan, Oman prioritised economic gains in its relations with these countries. As Lefebvre argues, Oman has been trying to keep close ties with South Asian countries for benefitting from its location (Lefebvre 2010, 105). This also means that Oman does not seem to be willing to take a strict position when the regional rivalry is at its peak. Therefore, the Sultanate has strategic room for foreign policy manoeuvrings. In this sense, Oman has been paying special attention to India and Pakistan. This chapter seeks to locate Oman's special relationship with India and Pakistan within the concept of regional cooperation and rivalries. In this context, Oman's relations with India and Pakistan are also related to the security complex that has been established by these two Asian countries. In the security complex theory, which tries to explain relations between neighbouring countries with similar security tendencies, the South Asian Security Complex (SASC) is seen as a structure with India and Pakistan forming the majority.

DOI: 10.4324/9781003283058-7

India

Historically, trade and economy have been vital in Oman-India ties. Since the third millennium BC, trade has been sustained between rulers in India and the Gulf (Pradhan 2013, 107). The eleventh century witnessed progress in terms of trade between India and Oman by transforming Khais island into a trade centre (Ahamed 2015, 133). In this sense, traditionally, merchants have played a critical role in Oman-India relations. Many Indian merchants conducted commercial activities in Oman under the control of the British as well (Hanieh 2011,9). For example, Khimji Ramdas' founder of an Indian company headed for trade to Oman in 1870. In this regard, Indian merchants internationalised trade activities in Oman (Pradhan 2013, 114). The commercial relations were deep-rooted that Indian traders were not adversely affected by the civil war in the 1740s (Pradhan 2013, 110). However, during the time of the Sayyid Sultan, some Indian merchants threatened Oman's interest in maritime domains, therefore, Sayyid Sultan authorised his pirate to go after them. Subsequently, these tensions were replaced with constructive cooperation (Kechichian 1995b, 70). The cooperation was deepened to the degree the Indian rupee was accepted as the valid currency in Oman until 1976.

Therefore, there has been an introversion between India and Oman in terms of economy. In addition, the rise of South Asian countries in time offered economic opportunities to Oman. Oman has been investing in many initiatives in the petrol-chemical industry to prepare the Sultanate for a post-oil economy. Signing a memorandum of understanding (MoU) in 1993, Oman started to cooperate with India on joint refining and fertiliser projects (O'Reilly 1998, 78). Similarly, Oman signed several agreements with Indian-based companies to develop high-tech renewable energy facilities to convert non-potable water into drinking water (Lefebvre 2010, 107). Therefore, cooperation with India serves the core of Oman's post-oil projects. In that respect, Indian investment in Oman costs nearly 7 billion dollars. With these figures, India is the leading country in terms of foreign direct investment (FDI) in Oman.

Even though the government in India refused to help Oman during the 1850s to defend territorial integrity in the fight against Wahhabis (Al-Khalili 2005, 81), the economy paved the way for cooperation for both sides. In this sense, Indians have played a crucial role in reviving Oman's trade. Some travellers noted that Indian merchants during the 17th century were around 5,000, meaning the Indians were dominating the commercial life in Oman but their role in politics was strictly limited since Omanis labelled them as foreigners (Pradhan 2013, 110–113). Utub—the rival of Imam Sultan ibn Ahmad who ruled Oman between 1792 and 1804—directly traded with India to gain control of the economy (Al-Khalili 2005, 17–18). Even though India and Oman share traditional linkages in terms of the politics of the British, the priority for the British has been its dominant status over the route to India. In this

132 *Mehmet Rakipoğlu and Gökhan Ereli*

sense, in time Oman became more dependent on the British government in India. Therefore, there was a hierarchical relationship between Oman and India (Kechichian 1995a, 5). Moreover, during the period of the British colony, Indians were considered agents of British interest since a law was enacted aiming to protect Indians and give unique advantages to the Indians in Omani jurisdiction (Ahamed 2015, 135). Therefore, British-controlled India and Oman relations were strained due to colonial practices till the 20th century. In fact, according to a British regulation during this period, people who immigrated to Oman from British India were considered to be under the authority of Britain, rather than Oman (Ahamed 2015, 135). Naturally, such developments continued the upset the process of relations.

The Sultan of Oman made a diplomatic visit to India in 1932 welcomed warmly by the Viceroy of India (Bailey 1988, 425). After gaining independence from the UK, India-Oman political ties were repaired by terminating the 1939 Treaty of Commerce dictated by the British. Both sides recognised each other and established consulates. Moreover, the new agreement on commerce and navigation was signed during the 1950s (Ahamed 2015, 136). The political cooperation continued when Oman gained its independence. India has sided with Oman on several occasions despite many Arab countries opposed to Muscat. After the Cold War, diplomatic ties grew. Indian leader Shri Rajiv Gandhi visited Muscat in 1985 and this development led to an increase in diplomatic contacts in the coming years (Kechichian 1995a, 220). In 1996, the Indian President visited Oman. In 1997, Sultan Qaboos made an official visit to India lasting four days. In 1998, the Indian Prime Minister visited Oman (Ahamed 2015, 137). Therefore, a gradual increase happened in the bilateral relations stemming from the frequent upper-level contacts.

Expatriates

Oman, like the other Gulf countries, has been subjected to migrant workers from various cultures. Immigrant workers have been playing a crucial role in trade and administration (Allen 1987). According to Oman National Centre for Statistics and Information, the Indian workforce in Oman is the second largest with the number standing at nearly 500,000 at the end of 2021, just after Bangladeshis (Kutty 2022).

The Indian community is very active in Omani daily life and economic activities (Kechichian 1995a, 222). It is known that Oman has been witnessing Indian workers influx whether skilled or not. Therefore, Indians became the key players in Oman's economic development process. There are at least three reasons why foreign workers flourished after the 1970s that are considered vital for industrialisation projects to succeed (Okruhlik 2011, 125). Firstly, Omanis, those who could work in industry, departed their country before the discovery of oil due to the poor quality and living conditions such as the low salaries, and underdeveloped educational system. Secondly,

Omanis have been skilful in terms of agriculture and fishing. They are non-professional in the urban labour force, whereas Indians have experience (Pradhan 2013, 115). Thirdly, the discovery of oil brought lots of opportunities triggering an influx of foreign workers. Therefore, the discovery of oil increased the need for workers. Since the early 1970s, Indians have chosen Oman or other Gulf countries for wealth and prosperity fuelled by the discovery of oil. Therefore, India's migration to Gulf was spared right after the oil discovery (Pradhan 2013, 108). Since the oil discovery, the workers' population increased noticeably and reached nearly 70 per cent of the labour force in Oman (Hanieh 2013, 63). The growing migrant worker population created social class differences in Oman society. But it is argued that the "Zubair"—one of the important capitalist classes of Oman—is originally from Baluchi (Peterson 2004, 36). On the other hand, migrants of the labour force to Oman are described as a positive-sum game in which both Oman and foreign workers both win (Hanieh 2013, 126).

Considering that Indian expatriates have been joining the production process, it can be stated that Oman always pays great regard to India, as Indians have played a crucial role in developing the Omani economy. Pradhan argues that the role of the Indian community in transforming Oman's undeveloped economy into a modern and innovative model is pivotal (Pradhan 2013, 108). Moreover, Indians were in different important sectors. Pradhan categorised Indian expatriates working in Oman into four categories. The first group includes unskilled workers such as workers in construction companies. The second includes skilled and semi-skilled workers. The third group includes professionals such as doctors. The last includes the private sector such as businessmen (Pradhan 2013, 116). Omanis generally tend to work in the government sector, due to the huge wage gaps compared with the private sector. This situation makes it convenient for the private sector to be dominated by foreign workers, highly Indians (Pradhan 2013, 119). To illustrate the importance of the Indian workforce in the health sector, in 1976, out of 200, only 20 doctors were from Oman, the rest of them were Indians and Pakistanis (Nyrop 1977, 365). Similarly, in 2010 the official statistics have shown that the majority of 12,000 nurses were from India.[1] In addition, Omanis have been choosing India for joint replacement surgery of kidneys (Beaudevin 2013, 97–100). Therefore, there has been traditional, deep-ties cooperation in the field of medicine and health care. During the 1990s, most Indian expatriates were employed in the health field (Kechichian 1995a, 222).

To exemplify that Indians have been playing a critical role in the Omani economy, the Lulu hypermarket—one of the most widespread hypermarkets in the Gulf and Oman—is owned and run by Indians. Due to Indians' critical role in Oman's economy, Oman does not take a strict position against the Indian government and tries to pursue a non-interventionist policy towards regional escalations. That's why Oman has been following a hedging strategy in regional politics. Moreover, if Oman sides with India against Pakistan or vice versa, this clash will directly trigger Omani society

134 *Mehmet Rakipoğlu and Gökhan Ereli*

(Kechichian 1995a, vi). For that reason, Oman's position was neutral during Bangladesh's membership in the UN. The Sultanate voted to abstain which Pradhan considered a pro-Indian stance (Pradhan 1999, 77). Oman is generally inclined to support a peaceful resolution to the India-Pakistan problem (Kechichian 1995a, 225), since it considered the India-Pakistan or Kashmir problem as a threat to its national security (Kechichian 1995a, v). Despite strained relations and conflicts between India and Pakistan, tensions between communities residing in the Gulf region are rare. Because Oman, like the United Arab Emirates (UAE), is trying to prevent conflicts between India and Pakistan, with which it maintains close and friendly relations, between its immigrant communities. Therefore, it develops close economic and political relations with both states (Hellyer 2001, 162).

Moreover, Oman tried to play a mediator role in the India-Pakistan conflict in 1985 (Valeri 2014, 51; Szalai 2018, 221) since Muscat has been considering that political instability in the neighbouring countries will directly affect its stability. Thanks to the mediation attempts, both sides agreed not to attack each other's nuclear power facilities. However, the conflict was not solved entirely. Because India interpreted that any attempts to solve Kashmir or other problems are interference in her internal hegemony (Ahmed and Bhatnagar 2010, 288).

On the other hand, since the Sultanate welcomes other cultural ethnicities, the social structure of Oman is highly cosmopolitan and heterogeneous. Ibadi religious tradition has been providing a culture of tolerance to Hindu religious practices, creating a positive atmosphere in bilateral relations and easing the integration of Indians into Omani society (Lefebvre 2010, 111). For example, Hindus were able to practise their religious duties under the protection of the ruler Ahmad Abu Sa'id during the 1740s civil war. The ruler Ahmad did not only protect them but also allowed them to build their temples (Pradhan 2013, 110). Similarly, allowing to operate Indian schools, Oman helps them to integrate into daily life. Moreover, later on, Indians were given land to build a social centre consisting of their traditional buildings (Pradhan 2013, 117–118).

Growing political and military ties

Ports of Oman have been hosting global and regional competitions both for global (such as the US, China, and the UK) and regional powers (such as India and Iran). India too has illustrated the intrigue in these ports. Official visits and MoUs have been taking place between India and Oman on this point. In August 1971, Oman signed treaties of friendship and cooperation with India (Khalili 2005, 145). Herein, military cooperation commenced between the two countries. Sultan Qaboos from the early years of his reign encouraged Indians to settle in Oman. Moreover, to cope with possible coup attempts or any threats, the Sultan enrolled officers from Baluchistan for his equipped powers. It was the same ruler that looked for military advice from the government of India. On that note, many Indians have found a special vacancy in Oman's security staff (Weiner 1982). For example, the Sultan employed Indians in police service, technical advisory, and construction. Moreover, Indians were granted privileged positions such as special permission to trade without a local partner (Pradhan 2013, 115). Similarly, Indian merchants were exempted from certain taxes for the period (Kechichian 1995a, 215). Even though Sultan trusted India for providing security, India did not assist Oman to suppress the Dhofar rebellion (Ahamed 2015, 137) since India considered Oman as an active actor in the Western block. During that time, India inclined towards the Soviet bloc due to the political environment embracing socialist ideals, despite its commitments to the Non-Alignment Movement. Therefore, India as a member of a part of the non-Western world deliberately abandoned Oman in the face of the Dhofar rebellion.

After the Soviet invasion of Afghanistan in 1979, Omani officials visited India. Deputy Prime Minister for Foreign Affairs Sayyid Fahar bin Taymur met with Indian Prime Minister Indira Gandhi to discuss and strengthen military ties. For Oman, deep and close military ties with India aimed to balance the Soviet threat (Pradhan 1999, 83). India signed MoU on military cooperation with Oman in 2005. Starting in 2009, joint air defence exercises with India and Oman renewed the MoU in 2016. With the help of these close ties, India had an opportunity to use the Port of Duqm for limited military purposes. Both countries signed an agreement in 2018 enabling India to access the Port of Duqm which is strategically vital for military purposes and logistical support. India considers that having access to the Port of Duqm helps to prevent China from enlarging its influence over the Indian Ocean. Therefore, it is argued that India intends to balance China by using Duqm as a military base (Dedeoğlu 2022, 82). In 2019, a maritime transport agreement was signed between the two countries, empowering India's presence near Oman to balance China. In 2021, both countries started to conduct joint military exercises (Tekir 2022, 530). Aiming at providing operational exposure and to enhance interoperability of both the Air Forces, India and Oman conducted Joint Air Force Exercise in 2022, reaffirming close ties.

Port of Duqm also serves as a logistic hub for India (Roy 2018). In this sense, the investment of India in the port of Duqm has recently been consolidated. For example, under the Little India tourism project, Indian companies have been developing multi-million-dollar worth private complexes and lodgings in the port of Duqm that can attract nearly a billion dollars in a decade (Dedeoğlu 2022, 82). Therefore, Oman constitutes a critical point for India's geopolitical ambitions and national interests. Cooperation has institutionalised when Oman joins the Indian Ocean Rim Association for Regional Cooperation in 1997 by which the Sultanate aims to increase trade volume with member countries including India. Therefore, Oman prioritises the Indian Ocean and therefore India. In this sense, relations with India have been considered important (O'Reilly 1998, 79–80).

136 *Mehmet Rakipoğlu and Gökhan Ereli*

Pakistan

The very early period of Omani-Pakistan relations in the 18th century was full of tensions. Baluchistan region, which is a part of modern Pakistan, had been ruled by Oman since 1792 (Nicolini 2009, 239–267). The Sultan of Oman was appointing a governor to Baluchistan to have the administrational control. Moreover, Oman had sent a small garrison to the Makran coast city proving its military dominance. In this regard, it can be stated that for Oman, Gwadar has been considered a critical point. Geographically being near to the Makran coast, Oman moved its troops there to control the lands. In 1798, Omani forces seized some parts of the Bandar Abbas district including the islands of Hormuz, Qishm, Hanjam, and Minab (Kechichian 1995a, 252). This military dominance raised uneasiness in Oman's relations with the region. Further, Salim bin Thuwayni and his religious practices resulted in annoyance among people living in Gwadar. Moreover, the decision to ban on slave trade further accelerated political polarisation and social separation due to some Baluchi tribes operating the slave trade. Omani Sultan Turki bin Said freed all slaves taking refuge in Gwadar bothering some Baluchi tribes such as Rinds. Therefore, Omani rulers did not only occupy the land but also controlled and diverted the administration in Gwadar.

When the British entered the political scene over Baluchistan, Oman's control strengthened after 1886 (Kechichian 1995a, 228). Both Oman and the British were interested in projecting power over Gwadar due to different reasons. For example, Oman was considering that Gwadar would house oil whereas the British mainly focused on taking advantage of its logistics and strategic position. For the British, Oman was important for the security of the route through the Indian colony (Ataman 2005, 375). The discussion between Oman and England about the fate of Gwadar was suspended due to the breakout of the Second World War. In the 1950s, Pakistan expressed the will to control Gwadar, but the ruler of Oman consistently refused despite the British advice to sell it. In this regard, Islamabad persistently claimed that Gwadar must be handed over to Pakistan. Moreover, Pakistan threatened Oman that if Gwadar is not given to Islamabad, Pakistan will not support Oman in any case (Joyce 1995, 77). Oman's apprehensions were mainly due to Pakistan's policy. In this regard, Oman did not accept Pakistan due to the idea that Pakistan is not an equal country but rather a domain that can deal with Oman only through the British (Bailey 1988, 615). Therefore, Pakistan's pressure on London was reflected negatively in Oman. However, rebellion or uprising in Dhofar province forced and compelled Oman to find new economic resources (Khalili 2005, 95). In this sense, in 1955 Sultan Said rejected the lease draft of Pakistan but he also implied the will to negotiate with one condition which is the presence of the British. There are at least two reasons for answering the change in Oman's decision. The first one is about Oman's will to join Arab League. The second one is about dealing with the

Oman's Relations with Pakistan and India 137

rebellion in Dhofar. Oman was geographically close to Pakistan's Gwadar port which is a small enclave on the Makran coast. During the 17th century, Imam Sultan bin Sayf acquired control of Gwadar and Balochistan. Therefore, losing control of Gwadar weakened Oman's capabilities in terms of geopolitics (Kechichian 1995a, 5).

In the post-war period, Oman decided to join the Arab League. London's assistance, lobbying, and permission were almost an obligation for Oman to become a member of the Arab League. The British were supporting Pakistan on the issue of Gwadar. On the other hand, Oman knew that if Pakistan stops paying, Oman could not force them to pay. Therefore, Oman understood that cooperation with the British is an obligation for advocating national interests. In this sense, to become a member of the Arab League and for protecting its interest Oman accepted London's advice to sell Gwadar. Owing to this development, it is claimed that the main reason for the sale of Gwadar is not due to Pakistani concerns, but British incentives (Joyce 1995, 79). Secondly, to overcome the uprising, Oman needed to strengthen its army. Islamabad wanted to buy Gwadar. Without any choice, Oman had to accept it. Pakistan paid 3 million pounds sterling and the Gwadar enclave was sold to Pakistan in July 1958 (Khalili 2005, 5).

Gwadar port is located at the heart of the China-Pakistan Economic Corridor, boosting Muscat's strategic importance for both Beijing and Islamabad (Tekir 2022, 513). Even though Oman lost Gwadar, it kept in contact with Baluchis. For example, Baluchi tribesmen were the main parts of the newly organised Sultan's army in the late 1950s. The Sultan was fully trusting Baluchis because they were known as loyal (Kechichian 1995a, 229). In this sense, Peterson alleged that the first record of recruitment of Baluchis soldiers into Oman's army dates back to the 16th century with the Yarubi imams (Peterson 2013, 230).

Moreover, allocating Baluchi-origin soldiers into the army became a tradition passed on to other successors. In this regard, the Baluchi people have served in the army with the incentives of the British officers (Hanieh 2011, 9). During the establishment phase, the Baluchi forces were composing 70 per cent of the army (Kaylani 1979, 574). Due to their loyalty to the Sultanate, Oman demanded the continued supply of recruits from Gwadar to the army even though Gwadar was sold to Pakistan. Therefore, integrating Baluchi-origin people into the security system of Oman has been vital. Moreover, Sultan Said was a shrewd statesman because he demanded 10 per cent of the profit from a possible discovery of oil for 25 years from Gwadar (Khalili 2005, 95).

Contrary to its relations with India, initially, Oman's relations with Pakistan were not good. As explained, Oman's political stance on Bangladesh was the main issue of contention. The Sultanate did not support Pakistan over Bangladesh. By abstaining from the vote at the UN, Oman was the only Muslim country that did not side with Pakistan despite British advice (Ahamed 2015, 137). Therefore, it can be argued that religion has never been

138 *Mehmet Rakipoğlu and Gökhan Ereli*

a determinant of Oman's foreign policy (Pradhan 1999, 82). Oman refused it and the Sultan proved that Oman follows a principle-based foreign policy. In this regard, Oman aimed not to be a stakeholder. This political stand hampered the development or improving ties between Oman and Pakistan. Therefore, Oman's political position negatively affected its relations with Pakistan. On the other hand, Pakistan took a more conservative turn socially and adopted and started implementing Shariah law. Even though Omanis were not directly affected by Pakistan's Shariah law, Ibadhi values and practices became a target. Despite the political and religious divergencies, Oman tried to alter the chaotic atmosphere in bilateral relations because the top priority for Oman's foreign policy has been maintaining good relations with all neighbouring countries. In addition, Pakistan was one of the few countries sending troops to Oman for fighting against rebellions (Kechichian 1995a, 229). In this sense, Oman launched a new campaign to improve its ties with Pakistan.

Growing ties

After deciding to repair broken ties with Pakistan, Oman has taken several steps in foreign policy. In this sense, Yusuf bin Alawi—Minister Responsible for Foreign Affairs—visited Pakistan several times. Alawi's visits to Islamabad paved the way for normalisation. Moreover, these visits prepared the ground for high-level meetings between two leaders. Sultan Qaboos and the President of Pakistan Zia ul-Haq met in 1981 indicating that normalisation is underway. They both agreed to repair ties and built communication channels by which they could cooperate on several issues. Zia and Sultan Qaboos expressed that Pakistan and Oman have traditional ties in terms of culture and history. These close ties helped the two leaders to improve bilateral relations.

Soviet invasion of Afghanistan also contributed to the normalisation process. Pakistan and Oman shared the same concerns about regional security and the impact of the Soviet invasion over it. Therefore, both countries were against the invasion, and they cooperated to deal with the possible security challenges. Even though it has never been public, the Kashmir crisis could have been discussed by Sultan Qaboos and Zia due to the crisis directly affects bilateral relations between Pakistan and Oman. Therefore, it can be stated that regional security has been complex and directly affected Oman-Pakistan relations. Improving ties was not only about security. Relations were improved when the two countries signed an agreement in the media field after Zia offered to do so. This agreement expanded into many fields, such as economy, trade, and education. Moreover, it was decided that both countries establish a joint ministerial committee (Kechichian 1995a, 231).

The pace of development in bilateral relations continued during the 1980s. Both Omani and Pakistani foreign ministers met several times to discuss international and regional issues. These visits and talks marked that Oman

Oman's Relations with Pakistan and India 139

and Pakistan managed to keep communication channels open despite the security challenges. For example, both countries adhered to the principle that expresses non-alignment. Moreover, Oman and Pakistan shared the same objection to foreign interventions. Therefore, even though the balance of power was challenged due to the Soviet invasion of Afghanistan, and the Iraq-Iran war, both countries found a suitable ground on which to continue cooperating (Kechichian 1995a, 231). To illustrate their objection to the Soviet invasion of Afghanistan, both condemned Moscow and sided with Afghanistan by advocating the territorial integrity of Afghanistan.

Security-related issues became more prominent during the 1980s. Oman's Chief of the Armed Forces visited his Pakistani counterpart in 1983 (Al-Khalili 2005, 231). They discussed furthering the defence cooperation. The visit accelerated the strengthening of security ties. In this regard, just a few months after that visit, the Special Envoy of Sultan Qaboos visited Islamabad and conveyed a message from Sultan Qaboos to President Zia. In 1984, Yusuf bin Alawi made another official visit to Pakistan proving that Oman and Pakistan are on the way to building an alliance. Alawi met his counterpart and discussed the current situation in the region. Pakistani Foreign Minister warmly welcomed and thanked Alawi due to Oman's support to Pakistan on the Afghanistan issue. Developing relations was not limited to politics and security. Both foreign ministers agreed to increase trade volume. In this regard, Oman and Pakistan were eager to provide a platform where the private sectors could come together and discuss the way for enhancing cooperation in the economic domain. It can be stated that both sides were also expressing their will to cooperate in education and cultural fields (Kechichian 1995a, 232). During his visit to Pakistan in 1984, Alawi and his counterpart signed many agreements bolstering bilateral relations in various fields such as education and arts.

Oman's neutral stance over several international or regional conflicts emerged with lots of opportunities. For example, when Sultan Qaboos invited the President of Pakistan General Zia, and the Prime Minister of India Rajiv Gandhi, both leaders found a ground to exchange their views in Oman (Kechichian 1995a, 230). Therefore, even though India-Pakistan bilateral relations remained tense, Oman's efforts were helpful in terms of keeping communication channels open. Moreover, Zia and Gandhi expressed their commitments to the peace. On the other hand, although Oman was neutral in the crisis between India and Pakistan, neither Pakistan nor India desired to punish Muscat. Rather, Pakistan proposed a non-aggression pact with Oman, while India proposed a friendship. Therefore, Oman successfully pursued hedging towards both countries (Kechichian 1995a, 232). In this regard, Oman remained silent and avoided announcing official policy towards the decision of the Indian parliament to end the autonomy of Kashmir in 2019 (Dedeoğlu 2022, 68). Oman comprehended that any conflict between India and Pakistan would be directly played out in the country. That's why Oman did not allow Pakistanis to protest India when the Babri Masjid in Ayodhya

140 *Mehmet Rakipoğlu and Gökhan Ereli*

was demolished by Hindu extremists in 1992. Therefore, Oman has avoided becoming part of the conflict. Rather, Oman chose to obstruct the spill-over effect of the India-Pakistan conflict to reflect on the country. In this regard, Oman has been playing a mediator and facilitator role in ending the disputes between India and Pakistan. Moreover, Oman was searching for a way for defusing the tension through diplomatic visits.

To end the Iraq-Iran war, Muscat sent Yusuf bin Alawi in 1986–1987 to Pakistan aiming to limit arms sales to both belligerents (Khalili 2005, 182). With intensified cooperation focusing on the Iraq-Iran war, Pakistan and Oman became closer. In 1989, both countries agreed to sign an MoU bolstering and fostering bilateral relations. This MoU included a wide range of fields such as agriculture and fisheries. A month later, an agreement was signed on media relations. Even though these developments created a positive atmosphere in bilateral relations, regional developments such as Iraq's invasion of Kuwait deaccelerated the pace of improving ties. But both countries decided to work together towards the Iraqi invasion of Kuwait. In this sense, the foreign minister of Pakistan made an official visit conveying his president's message to the Sultan. Pakistan sought to assist in the security of oil by joining the US-led political decision and UN sanctions on Iraq. Moreover, Pakistan sided with Kuwait by deploying 5,000 troops in consultation with Oman (Khalili 2005, 234). In this regard, Pakistani forces were deployed to Saudi Arabia and Kuwait to encounter the Iraqi threat (Kechichian 1995a, 234). In this sense, it can be argued that Pakistan-the GCC military ties empowered. For example, in 1990, Pakistan's high-ranked military officials such as the Director-General of Pakistan's Armed Forces Training Establishment visited Oman. After this visit, both countries became familiar with each other's military equipment since the visit enabled military cooperation (Kechichian 1995a, 235). Moreover, the positive perception that Pakistan contributes to the Gulf security has increased once more in the eyes of Oman. This is directly reflected in trade ties. In this sense, once security ties became stronger, Oman and Pakistan started to increase trade volume. For example, the import of rice and cotton from Islamabad increased considerably during the 1990s. Moreover, Pakistan started providing consultation to Oman on some development projects inside the Kingdom. For example, Nespak (the National Engineering Services) was involved in the Nizwa power station project expansion. Similarly, it was the same company that helped to rebuild the highway called Liwa-to-Shinas (Kechichian 1995a, 236). These commercial initiatives spilled over into the security ties. In this regard, Oman decided to cooperate with Pakistan on light observation aircraft in 1994 to acquire them (Kechichian 1995a, 236).

Oman signed a continental shelf agreement with Pakistan in 2000 to build trust. In this regard, maritime boundaries with Pakistan were determined by signing an agreement (Wippel 2013a, 323). Moreover, it is stated that Oman and Pakistan are considering signing a free trade deal. The Gulf Cooperation Council has been negotiating with Pakistan in terms of a free trade deal since 2006. As a member of the GCC, Oman has been carrying on these talks (Wippel 2013b, 167). Therefore, Oman prioritises economic ties with Pakistan. In this regard, Pakistan is the second destination in terms of Oman's direct investment (Wippel 2013b, 174–175).

Expatriates

Expatriates are a vital topic concerning Oman-Pakistan relations. It has been widely known that since the 1970s, Oman has become a popular destination for foreign workers. In this regard, along with Indians, Pakistanis began to work in Oman. The current figures have shown that Pakistanis are the third-largest expatriate group in Oman. In this sense, according to official data Pakistani workforce number stood at nearly 200,000 (Kutty 2021). These expatriates have been considered vital for both sides enabling diplomatic contacts. For example, President Zia visited Oman in 1981 partly due to the rise in the number of Pakistani expatriates (Kechichian 1995a, 230).

Even though Pakistani expatriates are Muslim originated, their religious identity never granted them privileges. A significant part of the Baluchi population in Pakistan was transferred to Oman. Most of these people were brought to Oman for protecting the ruling family. They were loyal to the Sultanate and primarily lived in Muscat. Even though the sultans have been depending on the Baluchi people for protection, Oman could not assimilate them due to their belonging to the Sunni sect (Kechichian 1995a, 236). On the other hand, when one considers that Oman is a house of Ibadi tradition protected by Sunni Muslims, it is no surprise that the sultans have been tolerant towards other religious understanding (Kechichian 1995a, 236).

Oman's relations with the South Asian Security Complex after the 2000s

The SASC is best defined by India and Pakistan's long-running military and political rivalry (Buzan 1988, 1–2). Along with them, there are several small states, middle powers, and failed states, such as Afghanistan, Iran on the West and Nepal on the north, and Myanmar (Burma), Bhutan, Bangladesh, and Sri Lanka to the East and the South. Also, Malaysia, Singapore, Philippines, Indonesia, and states in Indochina; Vietnam, Laos, and Cambodia could be grouped under a regional security complex (Buzan 1988, 4). The Gulf, Arabian Sea, and the Bay of Bengal have long been entwined with the security of the region and the well-being of India and Pakistan. Attempts to guarantee the safety of these three seabeds, as well as the cycles of collaboration and confrontation, would need to be examined in a larger context that encompassed the Gulf states.

In that respect, having direct, close, and open maritime contact with both India and Pakistan, Oman has carefully mastered to get both political and scholarly attention in security studies as well. Although India and Pakistan

142 *Mehmet Rakipoğlu and Gökhan Ereli*

became independent and enmeshed in a security dilemma environment with each other at the beginning of the Cold War, the area began to be referred to as a security complex in the 1990s and 2000s (Takahashi 2000, 1–2). In this context, the fact that the two nations neighbouring each other have grown to play a prominent role in regional security patterns mandated a degree of similarity in their security and defence interactions with other countries in the region. In certain ways, the security complex formed by the nature of the conflict between India and Pakistan illustrates that post-Cold War security has taken on a more regional character. As one of the theory's architects, Barry Buzan put it, security, and insecurity in the members of the complexes are frequently defined by geographical proximity (Buzan 1988, 2–3).

Not only the geographical proximity between India and Pakistan but also their proximity to the conflict-ridden regions deteriorated the resilience and integrity of the SASC, leading it to face various problems in the post-Cold War period. After the 2000s, with sectarianism began to flame foreign policy discourses, Saudi and Iran rivalry created a problem environment in which India and Pakistan faced an unwilling dilemma of choosing an ally. Also in Afghanistan, years-long political instability under the US invasion and military confrontations resulted in the Taliban capturing Kabul, and the dramatic withdrawal of the US forces stationed in the region in August 2021. While political and military developments in the North and West of the SASC did not do much to promise regional stability, the developments in the Indochina countries (Cambodia, Laos, Myanmar, Thailand, Vietnam) were also bleak. In 2021, the democratically elected government of Myanmar was deposed by Myanmar's military, threatening to further escalate regional political and military instability in the surrounding regions of the SASC. Also, another factor that affects the SASC has been the economic rise of China and the Chinese political, economic, and military ventures both into India and Pakistan and also into other regions. All of these affected the way the SASC has been formed, interacted with, and moulded.

Along with the problems facing the SASC relating to China, the Gulf region has been an important crossroads at which Indian, Pakistani, and Chinese interests are converged (Tapan 2021). Both India and Pakistan have been in economic collaboration with the Gulf states, particularly with Saudi Arabia, the UAE, and Qatar, most often to create lucrative trade relations and to counter Chinese economic and trade initiatives in the region. One of the forerunners in terms of trade with India and Pakistan has been the UAE, which signed a CEPA with India in 2022, promising to uplift the existing $60billion in trades to $100 billion in five years. Considering these changes, it is also said that owing to its growing economic potential, India is in direct rivalry with China instead of Pakistan, and that the SASC should be modified to include China and India as the main countries.

The geographical proximity between the Gulf countries and the commonalities in the security relations between the Gulf countries have given enough indicators to refer to the Gulf as a security complex much as the

Oman's Relations with Pakistan and India   143

security linkages between India and Pakistan demonstrate South Asia as a security complex. Nearly after the 1970s, all the Gulf states were already independent nations with a growing need for a security umbrella which would later be provided by the US. Also, the growing Saudi Iranian rivalry and pan-Arabist regional whims of Saddam Hussein, caused a foreign policy environment to be shaped in the Gulf region that could be called a security complex.

In this context, Oman's bilateral security, defence, and other interactions with India and Pakistan need a review of both the waterways that connect all three nations, as well as challenges in the land and air security domains. Even when they had not yet officially declared their independence from Britain, Oman's relations with India and Pakistan developed especially at the level of the political elite. Sultan Taimur bin Faisal bin Turki, who was the Sultan of Muscat and Oman between 1913 and 1932 spent considerable time in Mumbai, present-day India, and Karachi, present-day Pakistan after abdicating his throne in 1932 (Ahamed 2015, 136). The fact that India and Pakistan were preferred instead of any Arab country by the Sultan emphasises Oman's historical and socio-cultural bonds with these countries.

The fundamentals of Omani foreign policy in the post-2000s period

As previously stated, Oman has long been linked with neutrality, both in its Middle East policy and as a conventional foreign policy stance. Kechichian lists Oman's foreign policy principles as non-intervention, respect for international law, adherence to the non-alignment, and peaceful resolution of conflicts. As early as the 1980s, Oman's neutrality strategy and mediation policy could be seen at play in its relations with the countries of South Asia such as India and Pakistan, and the Gulf states. In 1985, Oman assumed the role of accelerating diplomatic talks between India and Pakistan, and in 1986 Oman assumed the role of mediator in the crisis between Qatar and Bahrain (Valeri 2014, 1). In that respect, the mediation role of Oman in the case of the India and Pakistan dispute in 1985 may have stemmed from the solid bilateral relations between the two countries with Oman. In other words, the fact that Oman had established fruitful historical and conjectural relations with both India and Pakistan allowed Oman to play a mediation role in the 1985 dispute. Also, in the 1986 dispute between Qatar and Bahrain, two Gulf neighbours of Oman, Sultan Qaboos bin Said led the Omani mediation role as one of the shrewd and wise statesmen in the region.

Apart from the concept of neutrality, there have been various ascriptions made to Omani foreign policy. O'Reilly has referred to traditional Omani foreign policy strategy as "Omanibalancing" (O'Reilly 1998, 70). O'Reilly in his paper refers to the theory of "omnibalancing," which is a theory of regime security and balance of power developed by political scientist Stephen David. In this context, Omanibalancing refers to the capability of establishing political, economic, and military relations with all of the rival countries of Saudi Arabia/Iran, Israel/Iran, and India and Pakistan (O'Reilly 1998, 70–71). Under these circumstances, it can be said that Oman has developed good relations with Saudi Arabia and Iran, and to a certain extent, has achieved autonomy—in time—in its relations with Israel, unlike many other Arab countries.

In the concerned literature, Omani foreign policy is categorised as follows. 1970–1975 period is about recognition in Omani foreign policy. In these years, Omani statesmen yearned for building relations with their Arab partners and with the states that were around the wider Arab world. The second phase is generally categorised as 1976–1980 when Oman needed greater "financial attention" due to domestic turmoil stemming from Dhofar Rebellion. The third phase is the post-1980s when Oman built a tradition of neutrality and intensified its efforts towards making it more permanent (Kechichian 1995b).

Against the backdrop of neutrality, Oman has maintained ties with Egypt, which recognised Israel in 1979 following the Camp David Accords, Iraq which annexed Kuwait in 1991, and Syria, which started a horrific war against its people in 2011. In the post-2000 period, Oman has become an important mediator between the warring parties in the region after Saudi Arabia and the UAE were involved in the war in Yemen in 2015, due to its neutrality policy. However, during the land, sea, and air blockade against Qatar by Saudi Arabia, UAE, Bahrain, and Egypt in 2017, Oman, along with Kuwait did not follow this trend as a policy preference and was able to use its mediation card in regional politics within this framework (Ereli 2019). Although this wise diplomacy in regional crises is generally attributed to Sultan Qaboos being a state leader who had been in office since 1970, these political tendencies have continued under the reign of Haitham bin Tariq, who took office after the death of Sultan Qaboos in 2020.

In the literature, Oman has often been referred to as "the Switzerland of the Middle East/Arabia" due to its strategy of political neutrality and a policy to mediate between conflicting parties (Worrall 2021, 135). Worrall also states that the way neutrality policy is being pursued by Switzerland and Oman is different (Worrall 2021, 138). One important consequence of Oman's neutrality policy is that the country's defence expenditures are very high relative to its GDP. On a global scale, Oman has the highest per capita defence expenditure standing at $2500, which is a quite serious ratio for a country that allocates as much as 12 per cent of its GDP to defence expenditures (Dudley 2020). The fact that Oman has certain security arrangements and cooperation with both US and the UK, the largest security, weapons, and equipment providers to the Gulf, does not mean that Oman has official alliances with the US and UK. By way of not signing into formal alliances, Oman has had relaxed foreign policy manoeuvrability, therefore presiding over a room for action (Worrall 2021, 139). In all this context, it shows that Oman can benefit from the strategic relations

Oman's Relations with Pakistan and India 145

of these alliances without being a direct member of the military alliances. This issue mainly stems from both the activities of Omani diplomats and, to a greater extent, Oman's geopolitical significance.

Oman and India after the 2000s

While India was one of Oman's most ardent political backers during the country's bid to join the UN in 1971, Oman sided with India throughout the Bangladesh War of Independence (Ahamed 2015, 136). In this context, it is clear that the two nations came to an agreement in the 1970s on international institutions and defence concerns. Oman's relationship with India has evolved since the 1970s when Sultan Qaboos began his rule after his father, Said bin Taimur and involves the country's objective of greater recognition in international affairs and efforts to minimise its reliance on Britain (Kechichian 1995b). This partnership between India and Oman in the 1970s turned into a more intense security partnership, especially after the Soviet Invasion of Afghanistan (Ahamed 2015, 138). The Soviet Invasion of Afghanistan in 1979, the Iranian revolution that took place in the same year, and the Iran-Iraq war that followed, required Oman to make difficult choices as a balance-leaning, mediator, and neutral actor in the region.

After the 2000s, the security partnership of India and Oman has developed to fight against piracy in the Indian Ocean, counter-terrorism efforts, and struggle against non-state armed actors. In addition, an increasing number of agreements on military equipment, partnerships on information technologies, cooperation on military training, and joint naval exercises have been taking place between India and Oman. In 2005, an MoU on defence cooperation between India and Oman was signed, facilitating the way the two countries are cooperating in military education and military technology (Lefebvre 2010, 111). While an MoU was signed in the field of defence cooperation between Oman and India in 2006, the two countries agreed to increase joint naval exercises in 2008 (Singh 2017). India and Oman renewed the MoU on military cooperation in 2021 and the Indian Navy and the Royal Navy of Oman signed a memorandum of understanding in September 2021 on the exchange of white shipping formation (Chaudhury 2021). Especially with the start of Prime Minister Narendra Modi's period in India in 2014, security and strategy consensus between India and Oman has intensified. This strategic maritime cooperation between Oman and India can also be explained by the importance that India's maritime strategy gives to Oman and the Gulf countries (Singh 2017).

Oman, which, like other Gulf countries, is trying to diversify an economy dependent on hydrocarbon resources, sees improving its economic relations with India as a basic need. In this context, India's need to build economic, security, and defence partnerships with Oman is necessitated by the presence of almost 700,000 Pakistani workers in Oman, the hydrocarbon resources that India is obtaining from Oman, and the balancing of the

146 *Mehmet Rakipoğlu and Gökhan Ereli*

India-Pakistan problem with the Gulf nations (Cafiero 2016). In 2018, the development of military relations between India and Oman continued, and, in a way, India's potential to benefit from Oman's ports emerged. In this context, especially after the 2000s, it has emerged that one of the most important issues in the relations between India and Oman—in a way to eliminate the threat elements of the SASC—is the field of maritime security and defence cooperation (Quamar 2018). India's maritime security and defence cooperation actions with Oman also provide it leverage to counter China's ambitions in the Indian Ocean and elsewhere (Quamar 2018). Oman and India inked an agreement to increase their maritime security cooperation just last year, in 2021. The deal was signed in Muscat, the capital of Oman by Indian Chief of Navy Staff Admiral Karambir Singh and Oman Chief of Navy Staff Admiral Saif bin Nasser bin Mohsen Al-Rahbi (*Wionews* 2021).

The evolution of bilateral relations in the context of maritime and security cooperation does not preclude the formation of difficulties on a variety of subjects. The attitude of Oman's religious leaders, particularly the Grand Mufti of Oman, Ahmad bin Hamad al-Khalili, to the situation of Muslims in India and some statements made by Indian officials regarding Islam, is one of the most critical concerns. In this context, the recent derogatory remarks of officials of India's Bharathiya Janata Party (BJP) towards the Prophet Mohammed drew intense backlash from many Muslim-majority countries. The Grand Mufti of Oman has also reacted to the Indian officials about their over-the-line remarks. Al-Khalili condemned "the insolent and obscene rudeness of the official spokesman for the ruling extremist party in India against the messenger of Islam" (Ellis-Petersen 2022). Having condemned the Indian officials, Al-Khalili went on to call for a boycott of Indian products as well.

This is not the first time Oman's Grand Mufti talked about India. In February, al-Khalili demanded an end to the oppressive policies of the Indian government against Muslims and the resulting social discrimination. Earlier, in a school in the Karnataka region of India, most Muslim women who were wearing hijab were prevented from continuing their education because of their appearance, and it was stated that this was based on a ministry decision. In this context, although there is cooperation on security and political issues in bilateral relations, it is seen that different actors within countries have conflicts about social sensitivities.

Oman and Pakistan after the 2000s

Oman's strong connections with the security complex established by India and Pakistan are partly a result of Oman's maritime proximity and neighbourliness to these two nations, which has exposed it to overlapping challenges (Habib 2017). Following the 2000s, the evolution of Oman and Pakistan, as well as Oman-India ties, is influenced by a variety of cultural, socio-economic, and geographical factors. Apart from the Pakistani worker population in Oman, the presence of citizens from Pakistan's Baluchistan region in Oman, as well as Oman's position as the closest Gulf state to Pakistan, promoted the development of social and cultural ties between the two countries. Within the framework of defence and security cooperation, it is seen that Oman improved its relations with Pakistan in the 1970s and 1980s. In addition, after the 2000s, the security cooperation between Oman and Pakistan was expanded to include cooperation in maritime security (Habib 2017, 105–106.) With the MoU signed between Oman and Pakistan in 2005, a political consultation mechanism was established between the two countries under the foreign ministries (Ahmed and Bhatnagar 2010, 275).

Close security and defence cooperation between Oman and Pakistan continue as recently as 2020. In this respect, Oman and Pakistan inked a military cooperation pact in October 2021. The pact was concluded at the Ministry of Defence of Oman in Muscat. Also, the rising maritime security and defence cooperation between the two nations would be noticeable in this context, with the Pakistani navy and Omani navy contributing to joint exercises (Jamal 2020). In February 2022, the media wing of the Pakistan Armed Forces, Inter-Services Public Relations—ISPR stated that Oman and Pakistan agreed to increase their military cooperation (Tribune 2022). As a result, it is reasonable to predict that the two nations' security cooperation would increase in counter-terrorism measures in response to the instability produced by the situation in Afghanistan.

Oman's diplomatic relations with China, which it has built since 1978, are just as important for the SASC as its contacts with India and Pakistan (The Diplomat 2014). When it is remembered that Oman was the first Arab country to export oil to China in 1983, it can be seen that Oman attaches importance to trade and energy relations with China as well as India and Pakistan (The Diplomat 2014). The likelihood of China acquiring influence in the Indian Ocean through Oman's strategic position makes the strategic partnerships built by Oman and China with India and Pakistan relevant (Chaziza 2019, 33). Oman is developing its political, military, and economic cooperation with China, India, and Pakistan. Within this framework, the fact that the three Asian powers China, India, and Pakistan trying to articulate economically fruitful and politically low-profile relations with Oman, has given Oman foreign policy flexibility (Cafiero 2016).

Conclusion

Oman's geographical position, on the route to the Indian Ocean, and the Bay of Bengal, has required it to enter into important commercial, economic, political, and security relations with South Asian countries throughout history. This position of Oman, which has established commercial and political relations with the state structures established in the geography where India and Pakistan are located throughout history, makes Oman important both for these two countries and the Gulf region. Moreover, Oman has been hosting an important number of expatriates including from Pakistan and

148 *Mehmet Rakipoğlu and Gökhan Ereli*

India. After the end of the colonial period, Oman's social, commercial, and economic relations with both India and Pakistan increased, and with the end of the Cold War, defence and security relations peaked.

It is seen that Oman has established partnerships with India and Pakistan to ensure maritime security in the Gulf, the security of the Strait of Hormuz, the security of the Arabian Sea, and the advantage these two countries can take from Oman's ports. In this regard, Oman has succeeded in preserving good relations with both Pakistan and India. With the various MoUs signed after the 2000s, it can be stated that Oman exchanged military equipment and conducted joint naval exercises with the Indian and Pakistani navies. In this framework, the relations of the three countries until modern times were realised within the framework of British sovereignty and protection. After the emergence of India and Pakistan as independent countries, the tensions in the Cold War environment and the multi-polar nature of 21st-century international relations have shaped Oman's relations with the security complex in the region.

The fact that India and Pakistan formed the SASC has given these two countries to articulate their relations with the Gulf countries in terms of security primarily. In this context, Oman's cooperation with India and Pakistan on issues such as ensuring maritime security, fighting against piracy, fighting against terrorism, and preventing non-state actors from creating instability in the seas remains a fulcrum of Oman's engagement with its South Asian partners.

Note

1 For a more detailed study, see Percot, M. (2006). "Indian Nurses in the Gulf: Two Generations of Female Migration", *South Asia Research* 26 (1). pp. 41–62.

References

Ahamad, Mohd Firoz. (2015). "Security Issues in the Indian Ocean and the India-Oman Relationship", *World Affairs: The Journal of International Issues* 19 (4). pp. 130–143.

Ahmed, Zaid Shabab and Stuti Bhatnagar. (2010). "Gulf States and the Conflict between India and Pakistan", *Journal of Asia Pacific Studies* 1 (2). pp. 259–291.

Al-Khalili, Majid. (2005). "Oman's Foreign Policy: Foundations and Practice", *Ph.D. Thesis in International Relations*, Florida International University.

Allen, Calvin Hayes Junior. (1987). *Oman: Modernization of the Sultanate.* London: Westview Press/Croom Helm.

Ataman, Muhittin. (2005) "Sultanate of Oman", in *Foreign Policy of States: A Handbook on World Affairs.* Wolfgang Gieler, Kemal Inat and Claudio Kullmann (eds), Istanbul: TASAM Publications.

Bailey, R. W. (1988). *Records of Oman 1867–1947.* Farnham Common: Archive Editions.

Beaudevin, Claire. (2013). "Of Red Cells, Translocality and Origins: Inherited Blood Disorders in Oman", in *Regionalizing Oman: Political, Economic and Social Dynamics.* Steffen Wippel (ed), New York and London: Springer.

Buzan, Barry. (1988). "The Southeast Asian Security Complex", *Contemporary South Asia* 10 (1). pp. 1–16.

Cafiero, Giorgio. (2016). "Oman Diversifies Allies with Closer India Ties", *Middle East Institute*, 5 October 2016. https://www.mei.edu/publications/oman-diversifies-allies-closer-india-ties

Chaudhury, Dipanjan Roy. (2021). "Oman Desires India's Partnership in Materialising Its Vision-2040", *The Economic Times*, 18 November 2021. https://economictimes.indiatimes.com/news/india/oman-desires-indias-partnership-in-materialising-its-vision-2040/articleshow/87770462.cms?utm_source=contentofinterest&utm_medium=text&utm_campaign=cppst

Chaziza, Mordechai. (2019). "China's Economic Diplomacy Approach in the Middle East Conflicts", *China Report* 55 (1). pp. 24–39.

Dedeoğlu, Müge. (2022). "Dynamics of Oman's Foreign Policy Under Sultan Qaboos's Reign Through the Lenses of Neo-Classical Realism", *Master's Thesis*, Middle East Technical University.

Dudley, Dominic. (2020). "Which Country Spends Most Per Person On Defense? It Might Not Be The One You Think", *Forbes*, 19 February 2020. https://www.forbes.com/sites/dominicdudley/2020/02/19/country-spends-most-on-defense/?sh=48cc97e212f8

Ellis-Petersen, Hannah. (2022). "Prophet Muhammed Remarks Embroil India in Row with Gulf States", *The Guardian*, 6 June 2022.

Ereli, Gökhan. (2019). "Körfez krizi sonrası Umman dış politikasındaki arayışlar", *Anadolu Ajansı*, 26 July 2019. https://www.aa.com.tr/tr/analiz/korfez-krizi-sonrasi-umman-dis-politikasindaki-arayislar/1542181

"Exploring the China and Oman Relationship", *The Diplomat*, 10 May 2014. https://thediplomat.com/2014/05/exploring-the-china-and-oman-relationship/

Habib, Fatima. (2017). "The Maritime Neighbor: Pakistan's Relations with Oman— A Review", *Policy Perspectives* 14 (1).

Hanieh, Adam. (2011). *Capitalism, and Class in the Gulf Arab States*. New York: Palgrave Macmillan.

Hanieh, Adam. (2013). *Lineages of Revolt: Issues of Contemporary Capitalism in the Middle East*, Chicago: Haymarket Books.

Hellyer, Peter. (2001). "The Evolution of UAE Foreign Policy", in *United Arab Emirates: A New Perspective*. Ibrahim Abed and Peter Hellyer (ed.), London: Trident Press Ltd.

Hussein, Muawya Ahmed and Ahmed, Hanaa Mahmoud Sid. (2019). "The Impact of Foreign Direct Investment on Economic Growth in Oman (1990–2014)", *Global Journal of Economics and Business* 6 (3). pp. 551–563.

"India, Oman Ink Pact to Boost Maritime Security Cooperation", *Wionews*, 27 September 2021. https://www.wionews.com/india-news/india-oman-ink-pact-to-boost-maritime-security-cooperation-416424

Jamal, Sana. (2020). "Pakistan and Oman Sign Military Cooperation Agreement", *Gulf News*, 22 October 2020. https://gulfnews.com/world/asia/pakistan/pakistan-and-oman-sign-military-cooperation-agreement-1.74748286

Joyce, Miriam. (1995). *The Sultanate of Oman: A Twentieth-Century History*. Westport and London: Praeger.

Kaylani, Nabil. (1979). "Politics and Religion in 'Uman: A Historical Overview", *International Journal of Middle East Studies* 10 (4). pp. 567–579.

Kechichian, Joseph A. (1995b). "A Unique Foreign Policy Produces a Key Player in Middle Eastern and Global Diplomacy", *RAND Corporation Research Brief.* https://www.rand.org/pubs/research_briefs/RB2501.html

Kechichian, Joseph A. (1995a). *Oman and the World: The Emergence of an Independent Foreign Policy.* Santa Monica: RAND Monograph Reports.

Kutty, Samuel. (2021). "Expatriate Population in Oman Drops to 37% Amid Pandemic", *Zawya,* 5 September 2021. https://www.zawya.com/en/economy/expatriate-population-in-oman-drops-to-37-amid-pandemic-rlcsc4tu

Kutty, Samuel. (2022). "Fall in Expat Workers in the Sultanate of Oman", *Oman Observer,* 10 February 2022. https://www.omanobserver.om/article/1114029/oman/community/fall-in-expat-workers-in-the-sultanate-of-oman

Lefebvre, Jeffrey Alan. (2010). "Oman's Foreign Policy in the Twenty-First Century", *Middle East Policy Council* 17 (1). https://mepc.org/omansforeign-policy-twenty-first-century

Nicolini, Beatrice. (2009). "The Myth of the Sultans in the Western Indian Ocean during the Nineteenth Century: A New Hypothesis", *African and Asian Studies* 8 (3). pp. 239–267.

Nyrop, F. Richard. (1977). "Oman", in *Area Handbook for the Persian Gulf States.* Washington, DC: Government Printing Office.

O'Reilly, Marc J. (1998). "Omanibalancing: Oman Confronts an Uncertain Future", *Middle East Journal* 52 (1). pp. 70–84.

Okruhlik, Gween. (2011). "Dependence, Disdain, and Distance: State, Labor, and Citizenship in the Arab Gulf States", *in Industrialization in the Gulf: A Socioeconomic Revolution.* Jean-François Seznec and Mimi Kirk (eds), London and New York: Routledge.

"Pakistan, Oman Vow to Enhance Military Engagements, Strategic Ties", *Tribune,* 10 February 2022. https://tribune.com.pk/story/2342951/pakistan-oman-vow-to-enhance-military-engagements-strategic-ties

Peterson, John E. (2004). "Oman's Diverse Society: Northern Oman", *Middle East Journal* 58 (1). pp. 32–51.

Peterson, John E. (2013). "The Baluch Presence in the Persian Gulf", in *Sectarian Politics in the Persian Gulf.* G. Potter Lawrence (ed), London: Hurst.

Pradhan, Samir (1999). "Indo-Omani Relations: Political, Security and Socio-Cultural Dimensions", in *India and Oman: History, State, Economy and Foreign Policy.* Aftab Kemal Pasha (ed), New Delhi: Gyan Sagar Publications.

Pradhan, Samir. (2013). "Oman-India Relations: Exploring the Long-Term Migration Dynamics", in *Regionalizing Oman: Political, Economic and Social Dynamics.* Steffen Wippel (ed), New York and London: Springer.

Quamar, Muddassir Md. (2018). "Locating Oman in India's Strategic Engagements with the Gulf", *Middle East Institute,* 19 June 2018. https://www.mei.edu/publications/locating-oman-indias-strategic-engagements-gulf

Riphenburg, Carol J. (1998). *Oman: Political Development in a Changing World.* Westport and London: Praeger.

Roy, S. (2018). "India Gets Access to Strategic Oman Port Duqm for Military Use, Chabahar-Gwadar Insight", *The Indian EXPRESS,* February 13 2018. https://indianexpress.com/article/india/india-gets-access-to-strategic-oman-port-formilitary-use-chabahar-gwadar-in-sight-5061573/

Singh, Abhijit. (2017). "India's Middle Eastern Naval Diplomacy", *Middle East Institute,* 27 July 2017. https://www.mei.edu/publications/indias-middle-eastern-naval-diplomacy

Szalai, Máté. (2018). "The Small States in the Middle East: The Foundations and Application of the Complex Model of Size", *Doctoral Thesis*, Corvinus University of Budapest.

Takahashi, Sugio. (2000). "Redefinition of Cooperative Security and -Regional-Security in the Asia-Pacific", *NIDS Security Reports* 1. pp. 101–115. http://www.nids.mod.go.jp/english/publication/kiyo/pdf/bulletin_e1999_5.pdf

Tapan, Oorja. (2021). "How Relevant Is Barry Buzan's Regional Security Complex Theory in Today's South Asia and Beyond?", *Thekootneeti.in*, 19 August 2021. https://thekootneeti.in/2021/08/19/how-relevant-is-barry-buzans-regional-security-complex-theory-in-todays-south-asia-and-beyond/

Tekir, Gökhan. (2022). "The Maritime Silk Road: Implications for Oman's Foreign Policy", *Middle Eastern Studies* 13 (4). pp. 465–492.

Valeri, Marc. (2014). "Oman's Mediatory Efforts in Regional Crises", *Norwegian Institute of International Affairs*, March 2014. https://ore.exeter.ac.uk/repository/handle/10871/14682

Weiner, Myron. (1982). "International Migration and Development: Indians in the Persian Gulf", *Population and Development Review* 8 (1). pp. 1–36.

Wippel, Steffen. (2013a). "Concluding Remarks: Regionalizing Oman Beyond Conventional Metageographies", in *Regionalizing Oman: Political, Economic and Social Dynamics*. Steffen Wippel (ed), New York and London: Springer.

Wippel, Steffen. (2013b). "Oman and the Indian Ocean Rim—Economic Integration Across Conventional Meta-Regions", in *Regionalizing Oman: Political, Economic and Social Dynamics*. Steffen Wippel (ed), New York and London: Springer.

Worrall, James. (2021). "'Switzerland of Arabia': Omani Foreign Policy and Mediation Efforts in the Middle East", *The International Spectator-Italian Journal of International Affairs* 56 (4). pp. 134–150.

7 Pakistan and Saudi Ties

An Overview of Political, Strategic, Economic and Defence Linkages

Umer Karim

Pakistan and Saudi Arabia remain key political and security stakeholders in their respective regional environs of South Asia and the Middle East. Both countries have attained a leading stature in the entire Muslim world. Sitting at critical geopolitical flashpoints, both countries have had a large impact on the political, economic and security climate of the two regions. Over time, the bilateral relationship has evolved into a multi-dimensional engagement that has not only translated into an aligned foreign policy outlook but also resulted in a collaboration in security and economics. This has essentially meant that the Saudi corridors of power have built formidable connections with the political and non-political power brokers in Pakistan. The mutual partnership finds its origins in the bond of a shared religion, which has brought the two sides closer to each other. Yet over the years, a unique level of trust has been established among the leaderships and people on both sides, which has then been translated into the emergence of a resolute strategic association.

This has essentially meant that in terms of their respective foreign policy approaches, particularly towards South Asia and the Middle East, both Saudi Arabia and Pakistan give considerable importance to the political and strategic concerns of the other side. Saudi Arabia has always supported Pakistan's stance on Kashmir and urged a peaceful resolution of the conflict. Pakistan in turn has reiterated its resolve to defend the geographical integrity and sovereignty of the Kingdom. The two countries also have stood together to respond to the plight of Muslims, particularly in the case of Palestine, and have been the founding members of the Organisation of Islamic Cooperation (OIC), a forum that gives the Muslim world a platform to project its voice. The political and strategic significance of this relationship has withstood the test of time. The transformation of the international political order, particularly the Soviet invasion of Afghanistan in 1979, has had a positive impact on the ties between the two countries, with interpersonal ties devolving into institutional partnerships. Similarly, even in the case of occasional strains in the relationship, both sides have kept open a line of communication, and they have eventually resolved the conflict.

DOI: 10.4324/9781003283058-8

Pakistan and Saudi Ties   153

To map out this special relationship and understand the functionalities impinging on the trajectory of bilateral ties, this research paper investigates the historical nature of the ties and their evolution by looking at the progression of external and internal political developments while also detailing the extent of concurrence in the strategic sphere.

Historical backdrop and interpersonal ties among leaderships (1947–2018)

The Arabian Peninsula and the Indian subcontinent are not alien to each other. Well before the advent of Islam, both regions were connected through trade and commerce. Arab traders were frequent visitors to the Indian ports and constituted a crucial link in east-west maritime trade. These Arab merchants then became the first to bring Islam into the Indian subcontinent. Not long afterwards, the western parts of the region (which constitute present-day Pakistan) saw Arab rule during the Umayyad caliphate, accompanied by the population's embrace of Islam. With the entry of Central Asian Muslim invaders into the political scene of the region, South Asia was further integrated into the Islamic world and forged new connections with the successive caliphate centres. Local Muslim rulers had great reverence for the two Holy Cities and contributed towards their development as well as commissioning the construction of dormitories for the pilgrims (Hussain 2016, 153–158). The spiritual connection of South Asian Muslims with the twin cities was physically manifested as pilgrims travelled to take part in Hajj every year.

These dynamics have connected these two lands, and the Saudi leadership was not only aware of the political situation in the Indian subcontinent but also keenly supported the Muslim struggle for a separate homeland. As the state of Bengal in the Indian subcontinent, which at the time was ruled by the Muslim League, faced a dire famine, Saudi King Abdul Aziz Al-Saud donated the generous sum of £10,000 ($12,500) to the Muslim League Bengal Relief Fund, which was set up by Quaid-e-Azam Muhammad Ali Jinnah, who would later become the founder of Pakistan (Ahmad 1982).

In 1946, as the All India Muslim League sent its delegation to the first meeting of the United Nations, it was Prince Faisal who supported them over the obstructions orchestrated by representatives of the Indian Congress, inviting them to the official reception that he held in honour of all the other UN delegations. Here the prince introduced the All India Muslim League and explained the struggle for independence of the Muslims of the Indian subcontinent to the international audience (Ahmad 2016). When Pakistan gained its independence, the Kingdom was one of the first states to recognise it. Pakistan also highly valued its relations with the Muslim countries more generally, and soon after independence, the country's founder, Jinnah, sent his special envoy, Malik Feroz Khan Noon, on a visit to several Muslim nations including Saudi Arabia. Noon was personally received by

154   *Umer Karim*

King Abdul Aziz and offered his personal plane to take him to Dhahran on his way back to Karachi (Pirzada 1976).

Interestingly, the first trip of Indian Premier Jawaharlal Nehru to Saudi Arabia was followed by a rise in misunderstandings between Pakistan and the Kingdom. This most likely was due to the Indian perception of Pakistan as a new colonial project of Great Britain in the Islamic world. This meant that Pakistan only had a Hajj Mission in Jeddah while diplomatic matters were still managed by the High Commission in Cairo. To reverse this situation, the Pakistani premier sent a secret delegation to the Kingdom in May 1951. The key person in this group was Muhammad Asad, an Austrian convert to Islam who not only knew the Middle East inside out but also had served for several years in the court of King Abdul Aziz, who referred to him as a son (Ahmad 2013). It was Asad's presence in the meetings alongside Prince Faisal (the then foreign minister of the Kingdom) and Faisal's love for Pakistan that eventually helped to resolve the existing misunderstandings (Arshad 2016). Asad was an iconic figure who played a central role in bringing the two nations together. On the one hand, he executed missions for the Saudi Royal Court, and on the other hand, he had been instrumental in drawing out the ideological foundations of Pakistan. This also shows that the Indian factor in the relationship had an impact from very early on, something that will be discussed in detail in Section 2, on the strategic relationship.

Against this backdrop, the first official trip of a Pakistani head of state took place in 1953 when governor-general Ghulam Muhammad toured Saudi Arabia and met with King Abdul Aziz (The Citizens Archive of Pakistan 2018). In a rare hint of the closeness of the Pakistani-Saudi leadership, Ghulam Muhammad suggested, in a communication with the American ambassador, that if the United States were to give direct military aid to Pakistan, he might be able to convince Saudi King Saud, with whom he maintained cordial ties, to join any future military agreement along with Turkey and Iran (Hildreth 1952–1954). The following year, King Saud visited Pakistan on a state visit and loaned his support to the Islamic foundations of Pakistan and efforts to unite the Islamic world (*Pakistan Horizon* 1954). He also laid down the foundation of a new housing scheme in Karachi, which was named after him and is known as "Saudabad" (Munir 2017). Afterwards, however, the bilateral relationship experienced a downturn.

Saudi Arabia was not pleased by Pakistan's decision to become part of the Baghdad Pact in 1955 and reacted sharply. The Saudi embassy in Riyadh issued a statement criticising the move as a stab in the heart of the Arab and Muslim states (Bishku 1992). Here it is also pertinent to remember that in the 1950s, Saudi Arabia had adopted a rather accommodative stance towards Egypt and was less inclined to confront the Nasserite-led movement (Pande 2014, 139). On Pakistan's part, the move was mainly an attempt to shore up its precarious defence capabilities vis-à-vis India by joining a pro-Western alliance and to acquiesce to receiving much-need defence equipment. Pakistan was also eager to garner support from the Arab world for its conflict with India (Hashmi 2011). The bilateral ties gradually started to improve owing to Iraq's departure from the Baghdad Pact and geopolitical changes that affected the foreign policy outlook of both countries. The critical factor behind this shift was a change of guard in both Pakistan and Saudi Arabia. As a result of a military coup, General Ayub Khan took the helm of affairs in Pakistan, and although he did not opt-out of Western-supported alliances, and in particular the Baghdad Pact, he started to engage with the Soviet Union, China, and the Islamic countries. His 1960 visit to Saudi Arabia was a success and put the relationship back on track. Meanwhile, as Prince Faisal ultimately ascended the Saudi throne, there was a marked shift in Saudi foreign policy from supporting Arab nationalism to focusing on Islamic unity. During the Indo-Pakistani war of 1965, Saudi Arabia fully supported Pakistan and provided monetary assistance as well. The following year, King Faisal visited Pakistan for the first time since his ascension to the throne, which initiated the Pakistani-Saudi security relationship. Both sides also agreed on the need to institute a political body that would represent the Muslim Ummah on a global level.

The OIC was finally formed in 1969, with both states as its founding members. Saudi Arabia stood with Pakistan in the Indo-Pakistani war of 1971 and expressed grief and shock at the events that resulted in the breakup of the two wings of Pakistan and the creation of Bangladesh.

Saudi Arabia did not recognise Bangladesh for a long time (Rizvi 1981). As a new political order emerged in Pakistan under Zulfiqar Ali Bhutto, the Saudi leadership was initially apprehensive owing to Bhutto's socialist ideals and strong support for Arab radical movements. However, these concerns subsided when Pakistan fully supported the Arab bloc during the Yom Kippur war against Israel in 1973, as well as the Saudi-led oil embargo. This led to the development of a strong personal bond between King Faisal and Bhutto and was manifested during the Islamic Summit of 1974, which was held in Lahore (Baghat 2012, 191). Under Bhutto, for the first time, Pakistani labourers started arriving in Saudi Arabia and a steady stream of foreign remittances was sent back home (Talbot 1998, 41).

After the tragic death of King Faisal and the removal of Zulfiqar Ali Bhutto in a military coup, the relationship was developed further by the succeeding regimes. King Khalid had visited Pakistan in 1976 (*Nytimes. com* 1976), while General Zia-ul-Haq, who had toppled Bhutto's government, visited Saudi Arabia in 1977, roughly two months into the government. One thing to note is that President Ayub, Prime Minister Bhutto and later General Zia all maintained Pakistan's strategic engagement with Saudi Arabia and the Islamic world. In 1980 Crown Prince Fahd paid a landmark visit, which had strategic implications (Weinbaum and Khurram 2014). After succeeding Bhutto, General Zia cultivated a very personal bond with the Saudi royal family, and simultaneously, Pakistan's military strengthened

156   *Umer Karim*

its strategic partnership with Saudi security forces and intelligence (Sinha 1980). Meanwhile, General Zia also kept the channels of communication open with the new Iranian regime and allegedly sold the Iranians US-made small arms and shoulder-fired stinger missiles during the last years of the Iraq-Iran conflict (Shah 1997, 30).

As Pakistan progressed towards democracy after the death of General Zia-ul-Haq in 1988, Benazir Bhutto (Zulfiqar Ali Bhutto's daughter), the chairperson of Pakistan Peoples Party (PPP), won the 1988 election and was sworn in as the country's prime minister. Saudi Arabia feared that her government would favour Iran, so to quell these doubts, PM Bhutto made Saudi Arabia her first destination abroad, bringing with her the seasoned foreign minister Sahibzada Yaqub Khan, who succeeded in developing a good rapport with King Fahd. In a two-hour-long meeting, Foreign Minister Khan emphasised that Pakistan would honour its strategic commitments with the Kingdom, especially vis-à-vis the Afghan conflict. The visit prompted an improvement in bilateral ties (Maitra 1989). With the dismissal of the government of PM Bhutto, there was a decision-making apparatus in place that was more inclined to take steps to satisfy Saudi security concerns against the backdrop of the Iraqi invasion of Kuwait. It is interesting that the civilian components of the interim setup, and especially the president, were in favour of this move, while the army chief remained sceptical (Crossette 1990).

The elections of October 1990 saw Nawaz Sharif come to power. The new government decided to send additional troops to Saudi Arabia despite resentment and protests from within its own circles and popular anti-Sharif sentiment on the street (Evans 1991). After General Zia, it was Sharif who became truly connected on a personal level with the Saudi leadership and cultivated considerable influence in Saudi Royal circles (Siddiqa 2017). The government of Nawaz Sharif was short-lived and was dismissed in 1993. Once again, Benazir Bhutto came into power, adopting a rather dynamic foreign policy towards the Middle East and engaging extensively with Iran. Bhutto visited Iran and bilateral negotiations led to the construction of a gas pipeline from the Iranian South Pars gas field to Pakistan (Haroon 2016). Bhutto's government was subsequently dismissed on charges of corruption, and following the new elections, Sharif returned to power. Sharif's second term revitalised the ties with Saudi Arabia, which had cooled during Bhutto's reign. Saudi Crown Prince Abdullah visited the country twice, first in 1997, when he attended a special Islamic summit in Islamabad, and then on a state visit in 1998 (Saudiembassay.net 1998).

Saudi Arabia was one of the countries that fully supported Pakistan after it incurred international sanctions owing to its nuclear tests. The Kingdom also provided Pakistan with $2 billion worth of oil in 1998–1999, and later changed this arrangement from a deferred payment to that of a grant to help stabilise the country's economic situation (Munir 2017). After the 1999 military coup in Pakistan, Saudi Arabia played an instrumental role in resolving the political crisis and brokered a deal resulting in Sharif and his family members being exiled to Saudi Arabia.

The strategic nature of Pakistani-Saudi ties was not affected by these developments, and from the very start, Musharaf maintained an excellent relationship with the Saudis. It was in this period that bilateral ties reached a new height and new avenues of cooperation opened, especially in the security sector. According to some of the leaked diplomatic cables, Saudi decision-makers have had such an important relationship with Musharaf that they considered him a guarantor of stability in Pakistan and believed that neither Sharif nor Benazir was a viable replacement (*The Guardian* 2010). Therefore, when General Musharaf resigned in 2008 as a result of a strong political movement in opposition to his rule, the bilateral ties were weakened again. One important reason was the emergence of Asif Ali Zardari, the widower of former PM Benazir Bhutto, as a new political power. Indeed, in 2008, he became the president of Pakistan after the PPP won the elections. Zardari was seen as someone trying to undermine the country's long-established ties with Saudi Arabia while simultaneously cosying up with Iran. It was under his government that Pakistan signed a gas pipeline deal with Iran in 2013 (Sial 2015). The bilateral relationship saw a rehabilitation after the PPP government was replaced by the Pakistan Muslim League Nawaz (PML-N), which was set up by Nawaz Sharif in 2013. This dynamic was echoed further by the statement of Prince Waleed Bin Talal regarding Nawaz Sharif as a preferable entity in Pakistani politics for Saudi Arabia (Kaminski 2013). This proximity was manifest in Sharif's first visit to Saudi Arabia and then the arrival of Crown Prince Salman in Pakistan in 2014. During the crown prince's visit, both countries reemphasised their commitment to promoting peace in Kashmir and Palestine and reiterated their support for the process of intra-Afghan reconciliation. It was in the aftermath of this visit that Pakistan got a financial donation of $1.5 billion that the country's finance minister termed a gift from friends (Farooq 2019).

Strategic relationship

After Pakistani gained its independence, both sides had a good start. Yet the bilateral ties were marred by a deficit of trust owing to Pakistan's decision to join the British-sponsored Baghdad Pact. On the Pakistani side, the Saudi engagement with India under Prime Minister Jawahar Lal Nehru was seen with concern, and the Pakistani press was particularly critical when on his arrival in the Kingdom, PM Nehru was greeted with chants of "Marhaba Rasool al-salam (Welcome, Prophet of peace)" and advised its readers to tone down their expectations from the so-called Muslim world (Mudiam 1994, 87). This estrangement in the bilateral relationship occurred because both sides had shown a lack of understanding about their respective insecurities, which played a key role even regarding the current state of bilateral relations.[1] This equation only changed when the two sides and their foreign policy outlook came into better alignment. This happened under General Ayub Khan and King Faisal, when the first notable security pact was penned in August 1967 during a visit of the former Saudi crown prince and

158   *Umer Karim*

current minister of defence, Prince Sultan Bin Abdul Aziz, visited Pakistan in the aftermath of the 1967 Arab-Israeli war. This defence agreement officiated the role of Pakistan's military trainers in Saudi Arabia and resulted in the sending of nearly one Pakistani military and air force officers to Saudi Arabia (Staudenmaier and Tahir-Kheli 1981, 3). In 1969, this military cooperation experienced first-hand exposure as Pakistani pilots flying Saudi jets repelled a military column of the Peoples Democratic Republic of Yemen that had attacked the Saudi southern border post of Wadi'a (Abbir 2002, 60). The relationship continued its positive progression as Pakistan, under Prime Minister Zulfiqar Ali Bhutto, further institutionalised a policy of "bilateralism" and of engaging equally with all the major international and regional actors (Bhutto 1976). Saudi Arabia emerged as one of the biggest financial donors to Pakistan during these years, and in 1976 Saudi financial aid reached a high peak of $500 million (Staudenmaier and Tahir-Kheli 1981, 3).

Another important episode that highlighted Pakistan's security ties to the Kingdom was the takeover of Kaaba in Makkah by religious fundamentalists in 1979. During the crisis, Saudi authorities were advised by a team of the French National Gendarmerie's GIGN and Pakistani troops. The assertions regarding the presence of Pakistani troops during the operation have been confirmed by some of the available sources available (Miller 2015, 67).[2] Yet according to journalist Yaroslav Trofimov, once the rebels inside the Holy Mosque moved into the basement, "Pakistani civilian workers" were brought in to drill perforations in the thick floor of the mosque (Trofimov 2008). It seems highly unlikely that in a situation where offensive action is being taken, unarmed workers would have been given such a task. Therefore, it seems probable that the Pakistani civilian workers mentioned by Trofimov in his book were actually special services personnel.

The Afghan conflict and the first Gulf War

As the Islamic Revolution of Iran and the Soviet invasion of Afghanistan in 1979 led to the collapse of the United States' twin pillar containment policy against the Soviet Union, Saudi Arabia and Pakistan emerged as key strategic partners for the US in the broader Middle East and South Asia. This dynamic further strengthened the strategic alignment of the two countries and initiated a unique bilateral relationship which Prince Turki Al-Faisal, the former head of Saudi Intelligence, described as "probably one of the closest relationships in the world between any two countries without any official treaty" (Rafiq 2015). The Afghan war proved to be a key arena of strategic cooperation and military intelligence sharing between the two sides (Matthiesen 2018, 231). Saudi Arabia became a principal financer of this resistance while the logistical and operational aspects were handled by the Pakistani intelligence agency, Inter-Services Intelligence (ISI). It is estimated that funds from both official and private sources in Saudi Arabia totalling around $4 billion was funnelled into the Afghan theatre during this time (Bruno 2008).[3]

The start of the Iran-Iraq war in 1980 created further instability in the region. During Crown Prince Fahd's visit to Pakistan, the defence ties were strengthened as Pakistan principally decided to send its troops to the Kingdom (Honsa 1981). It was decided under the auspices of a bilateral agreement formalised in 1982 and titled "Protocol Agreement Regarding the Deputation of Pakistan Armed Personnel and Military Training" (Government Archives 2014). This agreement has been the legal basis of all future deployments to Saudi Arabia as well. The exact number of troops sent to the Kingdom remains a matter of debate and speculation among different analysts, but a more conservative estimate puts the number at 15,000–20,000 troops, which remained in the Kingdom until 1987. These units were positioned in both training and operational roles during their stay (Baxter 1991, 143).

With the departure of Soviet troops from Afghanistan and the end of the Iran-Iraq war, the threat picture for Gulf changed and Pakistan's strategic relevance for Saudi Arabia was considerably reduced (Amin 1998). However, the mutual interests in Afghanistan and a generally aligned strategic outlook kept the two sides connected, and Saudi Arabia along with the United Arab Emirates (UAE) recognised that Pakistan supported the Taliban government in Afghanistan (Steinberg and Woermer 2013).

In such circumstances, Pakistan's ties with Saudi Arabia remained firmly intact and it received full support from Saudi Arabia following the nuclear tests of 1998. Afterwards, the visit of Prince Sultan bin Abdul Aziz, the Kingdom's defence minister, to Pakistan's nuclear and missile facilities in Kahuta signified a crucial development in the bilateral ties (Perlez 1999). The fact that the prince was the only foreigner allowed to see these sensitive installations emphasised the level of bilateral trust between the two nations.

Bilateral ties and the impact of the Yemen and Qatar crises

The bilateral strategic relationship faced a major challenge when Pakistan refused to send its troops to support the Saud-led military intervention in Yemen. The parliament session summoned to discuss the Yemen situation soon descended into a state of sheer commotion. Both the government and the opposition started hurling political diatribes and jibes at each other, and in all the ruckus, the real topic of debate was set aside (Mukhtar 2015). The government members of parliament essentially used the Yemen debate session to settle scores with the main opposition party, Pakistan Tehreek-e-Insaf (PTI), which has led to an anti-government sit-in in the capital that lasted for months.[4] This ended the chances of a compromise between the government and the opposition that could have led to a course of positive action towards the Saudi request. It is also pertinent to mention here that just as with certain pro-Saudi constituencies, an anti-Saudi constituency has also emerged within Pakistan, which is quick to vehemently attack any development in the Pakistani-Saudi relationship. Traditionally, this block

160 *Umer Karim*

mainly constituted of Shia outlets, but now it also includes Pakistan's liberal intelligentsia, who are quick to denounce any policy initiative with religious undertones (Jaffrelot 2017). All these groupings have depicted Saudi Arabia as a negative influence on Pakistan. As the debate on the Saudi request to join the military campaign in Yemen started, two narratives quickly emerged within the media and the public sphere. The narrative advanced by certain religious groupings fervently supported the Saudi initiative. On the other hand, Shia activists, liberal journalists and opposition politicians strongly denounced any such move. In this war of narratives, the latter group prevailed. The public discourse within Pakistan was averse to the idea of any military initiative that would create divisions within the Muslim world but also had very little understanding of the conflicts engulfing the Middle East, which received inadequate coverage in the national media. This discursive unanimity in the public sphere also brought the government under pressure not to join the campaign, in addition to its own desire not to get involved in Middle Eastern power politics. When it comes to the public face of Saudi Arabia in Pakistan, it is mainly represented by religious leaders hailing from the Deobandi and Ahle Hadith sects, which essentially do not appeal to a large majority of Pakistanis.

From a military perspective, it was difficult for Pakistan to contribute troops for the Yemen campaign, mainly due to the overarching domestic commitments of the security forces. For more than eight years, the Pakistan military had been involved in a counterinsurgency campaign in the northwestern tribal areas of the country against insurgents of the Tehreek-e-Taliban Pakistan (TTP). The Pakistan military had also been active within Balochistan, where the system of law and order had deteriorated owing to a Baloch separatist insurgency and sectarian killings (Alam and Al-Othaimin 2018). With the military still involved in counterterror operations across the country, it was difficult for Pakistan's military leadership to now allocate troops for the Yemen war effort. Sensing the breakdown between the two sides from the decision on Yemen, the Pakistani military's highest command scaled up its engagement with Saudi decision-makers. At the same time, it took two vital steps to assuage the Saudi concerns. First, it fully backed the Saudi initiative creating an Islamic Military Counter Terrorism Coalition (IMCTC) and complied with the Saudi request that Pakistan's former army chief General Raheel Sharif lead the coalition (Masood and Hubbard 2017). The second important step taken by Pakistan's security establishment to shore up bilateral trust was the dispatch of over 1,000 Pakistani troops to the Kingdom in early 2018 under the auspices of the 1982 agreement.[5] These troops joined 1,600 Pakistani troops already stationed there (Karim 2018). The deployment of these additional troops further sent a strong message from Pakistan that while it may not be part of any military campaign outside Saudi borders, it would be ready to defend Saudi territorial integrity and any attack that impinges on the Kingdom's national security. Additionally, the serving chief of army staff of Pakistan, General

Qamar Javed Bajwa has also been instrumental in initiating this new paradigm in the bilateral ties. Having served for three years on deputation in Saudi Arabia, he remains well versed in Saudi domestic affairs. Bajwa has successfully developed a working relationship with the new and powerful Saudi crown prince, Mohammad Bin Salman, through extensively engaging with the Saudi royal on his more than half-dozen visits to the Kingdom (Karim 2019). This was made apparent by his visible prominence during the Pakistan visit by the Saudi crown prince in early 2019 and his crucial role in stabilising the ties after the cold patch of 2020.

The Yemen question was not the only crisis that has rocked bilateral ties in recent years. Both countries again failed to see eye to eye when Saudi Arabia, standing alongside Bahrain, the UAE, and Egypt, boycotted Qatar and severed diplomatic relations with the peninsula state. Some news reports suggested that as Pakistan's then-premier Nawaz Sharif flew to Riyadh in an attempt to mediate between the two Gulf States, he was put in a catch-22 situation when the King Salman of Saudi Arabia asked him whether he was with the Kingdom or not (O'Connor 2017). The situation within Pakistan became more complex due to the Saudi demand. At that time, Nawaz Sharif was in the midst of a court investigation into the Panama Papers scandal, and his sole defence rested on the letters sent by former Qatari prime minister Sheikh Hamad Bin Jasim to exonerate him from the charge of buying properties in London through laundered money (*Dawn* 2018). In an interesting turn of events, the final letters from the Qatari prince in support of Nawaz Sharif were received by the Pakistani Supreme Court at the same time that the Arabian Peninsula was witnessing a political earthquake as Saudi Arabia and its allies cut their ties with Qatar and initiated a boycott of the Gulf nation. For Sharif, taking a position in favour of Saudi Arabia would have come at a great cost and breached his only line of defence. Additionally, the Sharif government had inked a major liquid natural gas (LNG) agreement with Qatar that had played a crucial role in alleviating the country's dire need for energy resources. Additionally, some 115,000 Pakistanis work in Qatar, mostly in relatively better job positions compared to those in the other Gulf States (Shams 2017).

Pakistan's neutrality in the geopolitical context was understandable, but its resolve to mediate between the two sides portrayed a lack of understanding of the roots of the Gulf feud as well as the general political trends that had been prevalent within the Middle East since the emergence of the Arab Spring. With the arrival of the new Pakistani prime minister Imran Khan after the elections of July 2018 and the government's extensive attempts to court and rehabilitate ties with the Kingdom, the bitterness caused by Pakistan's position on the Qatar issue was reduced. There also was an attempt specifically by Pakistan's security apparatus to try to involve Saudi Arabia and the UAE in the Afghan peace process. In the hopes of doing so, Pakistan brokered a meeting between the Taliban and the US special peace envoy, Zalmay Khalilzad, in Abu Dhabi (Syed 2018). This brought back

162　*Umer Karim*

both Riyadh and Abu Dhabi to the Afghan talks, but apparently owing to some objectionable conditions being imposed on the Taliban, this initiative did not succeed.

The India and Iran factors

It would be reasonable to suggest that India and Iran remain arch-rivals of Pakistan and Saudi Arabia, respectively. Yet there are a few points that should be kept in mind when analysing these rivalries and their impact on Pakistani-Saudi ties. In the case of Pakistan, both Iran and India are its closest neighbours by land. Pakistan has fought three wars with India, and the two states are still deadlocked with each other on the issue of Kashmir. On the other hand, Saudi Arabia has been vying for regional power with Iran. Iranian proxies have been ascendant in the region, carving out a dominant political role for themselves in several Arab capitals. Still, the two states do not share a land border and Iran may not be preparing to launch a direct military assault on Kingdom, nonetheless, it has been a patron of the Houthi rebels in Yemen, who have targeted Saudi population centres and installations with ballistic missiles and drones (*Iran Primer* 2019).

Iran-Pakistan relations: A cautious reset

In this broader context, both Pakistan and Saudi Arabia have strategic expectations of each other vis-à-vis their enemies. However, owing to geopolitical complexities, economic priorities and national security concerns, it can be difficult for the two nations to fully back their stances and initiatives. Since the uptake in Middle Eastern power wrangling after the Arab uprisings of 2011, Saudi Arabia had expected Pakistan to become part of anti-Iran initiatives politically and security-wise. Pakistan has helped its Gulf ally in certain theatres where the presence of its operatives did not involve a direct confrontation with Iran. Some reports have alleged that former Pakistan armed forces personnel were part of Bahrain's security setup and contributed towards maintaining the security of the country in the wake of protests in 2011 (Black 2011). Yet the possibility of Pakistan joining any anti-Iran political or security coalition or initiative remains highly unlikely. Pakistan's policy towards Iran is an epitome of reluctance to create new enemies and although previously it was not geared towards balancing between the Kingdom and Iran in recent years it increasingly looks like a balancing act (Karim 2017).

Pakistan's eternal nemesis India has been financing the development of the Port of Chahbahar in Iran and has significant intelligence assets deployed across the Pakistan-Iran border. Pakistani Balochistan, which borders Iran, has witnessed a rather less intense insurgency by Baloch separatist organisations. These separatists as well as sectarian organisations active within Balochistan have been involved in attacks targeting both security forces and civilians, resulting in a large loss of lives. Pakistani security sees all these activities as regulated operations orchestrated by the Indian Intelligence Agency Research and Analysis Wing (RAW) (Iqbal 2012). The arrest of a senior RAW agent, Kulbushan Yadav, while he was entering from Iran into Pakistan, has not only affirmed the apprehension of Pakistan's security apparatus apprehensions but has also raised questions regarding the Iranian complicity in these activities (Ahmed 2016). This has prompted the Pakistani government and security institutions to demand Iran to investigate the activities of Indian intelligence operatives on its soil and curb them (Raza 2016).

Pakistani security circles have also expressed concern about Iran's recruitment drive in Pakistan for the Zainabiyoun brigade operating in Syria. Light action has been taken against a local outlet involved in organising the recruitment in the restive tribal area of Kurram Agency, which is home to a significant number of Pakistani Shias (Tanoli 2017). Yet Pakistan is unwilling to raise the stakes with Iran further owing to several factors. Pakistan continually faces an active threat from India on its eastern border and the presence of an Afghani government that is friendly to India further adds to the level of insecurity. Additionally, Pakistan's ties with the United States have not been fully restored and the strategic outlooks of the two sides vis-à-vis South Asia do not necessarily run in parallel. Pakistan also wants to avoid any repeat of the scenario of the 1990s, when sectarian violence became the norm and a toxic social environment prevailed in the country.

Owing to these complications, Pakistan is attempting to engage with Iran to solve bilateral issues and trying to avoid any further complications in the bilateral ties. The multiple visits of current Pakistani premier Imran Khan to Iran are a clear indication that the political importance of Iran has significantly increased in the Pakistani political sphere. In a sign of times, Pakistan's Prime Minister Imran Khan became the first Pakistani official to publicly acknowledge during his trip to Tehran that terrorist groups operating from Pakistani had carried out attacks against Iran (Syed 2019). This was an attempt to reset ties with Iran and to enhance the level of bilateral trust something that has remained amiss in the bilateral relationship. Even the posture of Pakistan's military towards Iran has been undergoing a shift with the current military chief General Bajwa becoming the first Army Chief of Pakistan to visit Iran in over two decades (Syed 2017). This visit was then followed by the visit of the Iranian Army Chief to Pakistan, also a first in over forty years (*Tehran Times* 2018). Regardless of these improvements in bilateral relationship Pakistan's decision to formally inform Iran regarding the non-viability of the Iran-Pakistani gas pipeline under the US sanctions depicts the limitations of this new reset (Saeed 2019). These developments make it clear that the geopolitical cost of an antagonist Tehran is too much for Islamabad and the traditional hostile posture of Pakistan's security establishment towards Iran remains untenable. As opposed to their predecessors, Pakistan's current decision-makers are ready to follow this path even when it visibly reduces the country's security leverage further with the Saudi Kingdom.

164 *Umer Karim*

India-Saudi ties

On the other hand, ties between India and Saudi Arabia have seen a significant improvement in the past fifteen years (starting around 2005). To begin with, Saudi Arabia had remained largely ambivalent towards India during the cold war years due to its proximity to the Soviet Union. Indian political support for Iraq during the first Gulf war did not help the cause of Saudi-Indian ties and the relationship remained a tacit one, in which the bilateral engagement never attained a strategic outlook.

Things started to change with King Abdullah's tour of India in 2006 when he was the chief guest at India's Republic Day ceremony (Ahmed and Bhatnagar 2010). Perhaps this was a sign that with the sharp rise in India's global profile and its emergence as one of the world's biggest economies, the Saudis decided to initiate a more proactive engagement. Saudi ties with India also witnessed another uptake in the defence realm. Starting with the talks held in Riyadh in 2010 between the then-Indian prime minister Manmohan Singh and King Abdullah of Saudi Arabia, both sides agreed to set up a road map to further increase bilateral cooperation. This led to the first meeting of a Saudi-Indian Joint Committee on Defense Cooperation (JCDC) in 2012, where enhancing defence exchanges and military-to-military contacts were discussed. Building on these engagements, an eventual Memorandum of Understanding (MoU) on Defense Cooperation was signed in 2014 in India as the then Saudi Crown Prince and Defense Minister Prince Salman toured the country. The terms of the agreement included enabling joint exercises and training Saudi forces as well as sharing defence-related information (Pande 2014). The JCDC has held four meetings since its inception. Further evidence of enhanced Indo-Saudi defence engagement came when Indian Army Chief General N.M. Naravane visited Saudi Arabia in 2020. He was the first Indian Army Chief to visit the Kingdom and delivered a lecture at the King Abdul Aziz Military Academy (Philip 2020).

In wider South Asia, traditionally Pakistan has remained the principal Saudi point of contact within security and defence domains. This new Saudi-Indian security partnership has been viewed with a considerable degree of scepticism within Islamabad's political and security circles. But this also affirms the point that nations with a diverging strategic outlook gradually care less about the geopolitical sensitivities of their traditional allies and resultantly losing leverage upon them.

On the economic front, India has a significantly strong connection with the Kingdom, which has become home to a large number of Indian expatriate workers who are playing an important role in several vital sectors. They also send a hefty sum of $11 billion in remittances home every year. India imports an estimated 800,000 barrels of crude oil every day from Saudi Arabia. With the termination of India-specific waivers from the United States allowing it to import oil from Iran, Saudi oil exports to India were expected to rise even further (Handjani 2019). In 2019, Saudi Arabia started a line of negotiations with Reliance Industries Ltd. to buy a 20 per cent stake in India's biggest refinery, which would make Saudi Arabia a vital player in India's petrochemical sector (El Gamal 2019).

During Crown Prince Mohammad Bin Salman's visit to India in 2019, Saudi Minister of State for Foreign Affairs Adel Al-Jubeir refused to accept India's claim of Pakistani involvement in the suicide attack on Indian forces in Kashmir. Jubeir's statement was received with great excitement, not only within Pakistan's government circles but also by common Pakistani (*Dunya News* 2019). Yet the traditional Saudi support for Pakistan's stance over Kashmir has seen a gradual transformation. As India abrogated the special status of its administered Kashmir, the reaction from Saudi Arabia against Pakistani expectations was rather muted. Saudi Arabia did express concern over the developments in Kashmir but has not been receptive to Pakistan's demands of holding a special session of the Organization of Islamic Conference (OIC) foreign ministers on Kashmir (Aamir 2020). This has further dented the bilateral relationship something that has been discussed under the section on Saudi-Pak relations under Imran Khan. These developments further show that traditional goodwill for Saudi Arabia within Pakistan that has been there since the time of King Faisal is weakening up. This will further lessen the effectiveness of any soft power measures that the Kingdom uses in future to exert leverage on Pakistan leaving it only with hard power choices that do translate into leverage but essentially of a negative kind.

Cooperation in the security and economic domains

Defence cooperation

Defence and security cooperation between the two nations remains a field where institutional interests have been pursued to achieve national strategic objectives instead of personal goals, which are a hallmark of the political domain. The personalisation of the political domain, whereby political elites accrued personal favours in return for supporting the Kingdom, hindered the institutionalisation of bilateral ties beyond party and sectarian lines. In the defence and security sectors, an institutional pathway has been pursued, mainly due to the professional and non-personal nature of the Pakistani Armed forces. Personal relationships between military leaderships and the Saudi royalty cannot be ignored, and the dynamic was particularly prominent during the Zia and Musharaf eras. Yet it was mainly due to the political actions of the two military chiefs and subsequent involvement of the Kingdom in Pakistan's complex politics, but throughout this process, the bilateral defence relationship remained non-personal and was carried out by successive military leaders.

This unique relationship of trust between the security hierarchies on both sides has created a regional partnership that addresses changing political and

166 *Umer Karim*

security challenges but also impacts interregional alignment patterns. The modern-day nature of Pakistani-Saudi defence and security cooperation signifies their depth and diversity. The three components of the armed forces of both nations collaborate with each other. In particular, in a detailed response submitted to Pakistan's national assembly in 2014, the foreign minister explained that Pakistan has three specific defence and security cooperation agreements with the Kingdom: one concerning the 1982 troop deployment protocol; a Military Cooperation Agreement, which was signed in July 2005; and an Accord for the Provision of Military Training Services between the Ministry of Interior of Saudi Arabia and Pakistan, which was agreed to in 2007. The details of the latter two agreements remain confidential, but it can be speculated that these agreements entail cooperation between the two militaries through holding regular joint exercises and organising joint training initiatives. Pakistan's traditional role as a training hub for Saudi military cadets has only increased over the years. From 1967 to 2014, approximately 8,255 Saudi armed forces officials received training in Pakistan (Government Archives 2014). Saudi cadets arrive at Pakistani training courses every year to receive training at the army, air force and naval academies. In 2018, a batch of forty-six Saudi cadets graduated from the Pakistan Military Academy Kakul and joined the Saudi Armed Forces (*Arab News PK* 2018). Many Saudi cadets also graduated from the Pakistan Air Force Academy Risalpur (*Radio Pakistan* 2018) and also a multitude of Saudi Naval officers every year graduate from Pakistan Naval Academy (Arhama 2021).

The militaries of both nations also have established operational associations with each other and meet regularly for military exercises. The most significant in this regard has been the Al-Samsam military exercise, which is conducted by both land forces every few years. The special forces of both countries conduct joint drills with a focus on counterterrorism operations called the Al-Shihab exercises. Additionally, joint exercises have also been taking place between the naval forces since 1993, including one called Naseem Al-Bahr. Both naval forces have further increased their coordination by conducting joint operation drills (Shay 2018). In February 2018, the Aff'aa Al Sahil exercise, which was conducted in Karachi, brought together the special force wings of the two navies while simultaneously the navy Marines from both sides conducted their own exercise, termed Dera Al Sahil, in Saudi Arabia (*The Express Tribune* 2018). Pakistan also participated in the North Thunder Military exercise, held in the military city of Hafr-e-batin in Saudi Arabia, which amassed the troops of 21 Muslim countries. The Pakistani contingent included Special Services Group (SSG) commandos as well as JF-17 Thunder fighter jets from the Pakistani Air Force (Baabar 2016). Saudi Arabia has also been one of the largest importers of arms from Pakistan. For example, in 2016, Pakistan received an order of arms worth $81 million from Saudi Arabia, which mainly comprised of automatic weapons and gear carried by foot soldiers. This export of weaponry to the Kingdom adds to the strategic nature of the bilateral ties, but there remains considerable room for improvement, especially when considering the overall budget of Saudi arms imports (Haider 2016).

The inter-military ties have also been institutionalised by the creation of a Joint Military Cooperation Committee (JMCC) and a Military Cooperation Committee (MCC) in 2014 during the trip of Saudi deputy defence minister Prince Salman bin Sultan to Pakistan (Imaduddin 2014). This military coordination has occurred at the level of Joint Staff Headquarters of the Pakistan military, which incorporates all three armed components of Pakistan's security forces.

Economic cooperation

Both countries have also maintained long-standing ties in the economic sector. Saudi Arabia has remained the dominant partner here and has delivered huge amounts of foreign aid to Pakistan during crises. Saudi Arabia started to provide financial assistance to Pakistan in the 1970s. During 1979–1990, Pakistan got a special aid package of $200 million from the Kingdom. As the earthquake of 2005 rattled Pakistan, the Kingdom was at the forefront of providing aid to the country and stood out as the largest donor with an aid package of $573 million (Sengupta and Rohde 2005). The Kingdom also created a special Office of Saudi Public Assistance for Pakistan Earthquake Victims (SPAPEV) to oversee the relief and rehabilitation activities. Saudi Arabia expended similar efforts after the disastrous floods that affected all of Pakistan during 2010. This time Saudi Arabia pledged a figure of $105 million in aid alongside funds amounting to $19 million raised separately by the Saudi public (Shah 2010). The Kingdom remained the largest international donor during both of these humanitarian crises.

Saudi Arabia has also repeatedly helped to stabilise Pakistan's foreign currency reserves by depositing dollars in the State Bank of Pakistan. In 2009, the Kingdom deposited $200 million, followed by $1.5 billion in 2014. Saudi Arabia also provided Pakistan with two soft loans, to the tune of $100 million and $123 million, respectively, in 2009 and then in 2014 to help its agricultural sector. Additionally, the Saudi Development Fund has also remained a credit source for hydropower projects in Pakistan. It provided credit to the tune of $80 million for the construction of the Neelum-Jhelum hydropower project and as well as $58 million for the Golen Gol hydropower project in Chitral (Ahmad 2014). In early 2019 both sides reached an understanding to sign a MoU whereby the Saudi Development Fund is to provide funding of about $322 million for five power projects within Pakistan (Albilad 2019). The approval of a loan for the Jagran-IV Hydropower Project has already been granted but as of fall 2019, work on the other projects had not yet been initiated (Ansari 2018).

In addition to Saudi support in the infrastructure and energy sectors, the Kingdom has also remained an active contributor to Pakistan's educational sector. In particular, the International Islamic University (IIU) was

168   *Umer Karim*

established in Islamabad with a Saudi grant of $10 million and remains one of the top educational institutes of the country, especially in Shariah studies. The Faisal Mosque in Islamabad, which is sometimes considered among the wonders of the world, was also constructed with a generous amount of funding and support from King Faisal (Jamil 2017).

The fact that Saudi Arabia and Pakistan remain economically connected is also demonstrated by the presence of a large number of Pakistani expatriates. Pakistani workers started arriving in the Kingdom in the 1970s, and according to a statement by the Pakistani minister of foreign affairs to the national assembly, the number had reached 2.7 million by 2018 (*Arynews* 2018). These expatriates play an instrumental role in the economy of the country through their remittances. In the fiscal year 2020–2021, Pakistani expatriates in Saudi Arabia alone sent $7 Billion in terms of remittances (*Dawn* 2021).

Bilateral economic engagement is regulated by a Joint Ministerial Commission (JMC) compromising the cabinet members of both nations. In 2018 JMC held its eleventh session in Islamabad and formed a Joint Working Group (JWG) on Trade and Investment to further economic ties in trade and investment arenas (*The News* 2018). The current trade volume between the two sides hovers at around $3.7 billion (*Money Control* 2019). Pakistani exports to the Kingdom include agricultural produce such as rice, fruits and juices and textile products such as cotton, yarn, woollen products, towels and synthetic fabrics. In addition, leather products are also a major export. Saudi Arabia for its part exports petroleum products ranging from crude oil to petrochemical commodities (Alam, et al. 2013). During the years 2012–2017, the mutual trade volume experienced a relative decline. The trade balance has remained in favour of Saudi Arabia, but as oil imports from the Kingdom have seen a decline, the net deficit value has gone down as well. From the Pakistani perspective, a major problem remains the drop in the economic value of its export commodities, which are mainly textile and agricultural products, even when their net volume has increased. This resulted in the reduction of Pakistan's net export bill to Saudi Arabia in 2018 to $316 million, down from $335 million in 2017. In contrast, the Kingdom's total exports to Pakistan increased in 2018, rising to $3.24 billion (*Trading Economics* 2018).

Current trends

Bilateral ties took a new turn after the electoral victory of Imran Khan in the July 2018 elections. Unlike previous Pakistani rulers, Khan had no previous personal or political connection with the royals in the Gulf States. Thus, it was a test of his diplomatic and political skills to develop new relationships, particularly with Saudi Arabia, given the souring of relations following the Yemen episode. Furthermore, the election of Imran Khan changed two critical variables that had a bearing on Pakistan's foreign outlook and bilateral ties with the Kingdom. One was the nature of civil-military relations, which had reached a breaking point during the premiership of former

Pakistan and Saudi Ties   169

Prime Minister Nawaz Sharif. The other factor was a gradual erosion of trust between Pakistan's civil leadership and the Kingdom's decision-makers, particularly after the Yemen episode. With Imran Khan in power, there was the possibility of a fresh start on both accounts since unlike Nawaz Sharif, who had always been viewed with considerable scepticism, Imran Khan had no history with the military. This offered the possibility of redrawing the nature of civil-military ties and led to a unique build-up of trust between the prime minister and Army Chief General Bajwa. This was apparent in the vehemence with which the army chief defended the government's tough economic measures. The decision by the prime minister to give General Bajwa an extension of three years in his post also shows that the two men retain a good working relationship, unlike past civil-military setups, which were generally marked by a struggle for power (Jamal 2019b).

As the country faced a financing gap of more than $12 billion, Khan's government was compelled to reengage with Pakistan's traditional allies, particularly Saudi Arabia. This led to Khan's repeated visits to the Kingdom and the Saudi royals' eventual agreement to provide Pakistan with a $6 billion aid package with $3 billion as balance-of-payments support along with another one-year deferred payment option of up to $3 billion for oil imports to provide breathing space to an economy in dire straits (Haider and Dilawar 2018). This financial aid package might have been a sign of the warm ties between the new leaderships but only came after the Pakistani premier attended the Future Investment Initiative (FII) summit in Riyadh that had been marred by boycotts (Algot and Wintour 2018) owing to the murder of Saudi journalist Jamal Khashoggi. Bilateral ties relationship moved towards new heights as the Saudi Crown Prince embarked upon his trip to Pakistan. In this trip, the Saudi leader announced an investment package worth $20 billion that included the construction of an oil refinery in the Arabian Sea port of Gwada that happens to be the centre point also of the China-Pakistan Economic Corridor (Sayeed 2019). Even more important was the formation of a Supreme Coordination Council to streamline bilateral engagement and to facilitate Saudi projects within Pakistan. This visit was a unique high moment in the bilateral relationship, and it could be argued that finally, the bilateral ties recovered from the strain caused by the Yemen Crisis. However, this newfound positivity didn't last long.

Bilateral ties in crisis

In August 2019, India revoked the special status of the State of Jammu and Kashmir in its constitution and made it a formal part of the Indian Union. This development provoked a strong reaction from the Pakistani side that also reached out to its friends and allies worldwide to pressurise India diplomatically. Although Saudi Arabia expressed its concern regarding the developments yet, there was no active condemnation of the Indian move due to the extensive and strategic nature of the kingdom's economic and energy

170   *Umer Karim*

ties with India (Batrawy 2019). The visit of the Indian PM to Riyadh within a couple of months of the Kashmir move also suggested that the Kingdom has decided to remain out of the Kashmir debate and instead wants to focus on its bilateral ties with India (Chaudhary 2019). On the other hand, Turkey, whose relationship with Saudi Arabia has become increasingly contentious, came out strongly in support of Pakistan's position even at the expense of its relationship with India (Basu 2019).

Pakistan and Saudi Arabia approached the brink of a diplomatic crisis when Islamabad agreed with Turkey and Malaysia to hold a summit of Islamic countries in Kuala Lumpur to address issues concerning the Islamic world (Gul 2019). With the inclusion of Qatar and Iran in the platform, Saudi Arabia increasingly viewed the summit as a challenge to its leadership of the Muslim world and an alternative to the Saudi-led Organization of Islamic Cooperation. This was a unique moment in the history of bilateral ties as Saudi Arabia exerted pressure upon Pakistan to withdraw from the proposed summit in Kuala Lumpur, Malaysia. Since Pakistan remained dependent upon Saudi largesse, it didn't have many options. In this manner, Saudi Arabia successfully translated its economic hard power into political leverage over Pakistan's foreign policy outlook (Jamal 2019a).

This episode put a dent in the personal relationship between Khan and Mohammed bin Salman resulting in a closure of channels of communication between the two sides. As ties with Saudi Arabia became tense, Pakistan's relationship with Turkey blossomed as did the personal chemistry between Khan and Turkish President Recep Tayyip Erdogan. In his February 2020 visit to Pakistan, Erdogan fully backed Pakistan's stance on Kashmir quadrupling his popularity within every quarter of Pakistan (Morrow and Zorlu 2020). Pakistan's decision to broadcast Turkish TV series glorifying the Ottoman Empire and a personal endorsement in this regard by the Prime Minister (Haider 2020) also sent negative signals towards Saudi Arabia. For Saudi Arabia, these developments depicted Islamabad's attempts to aggrandise and court new power centres in the Muslim World. Yet this only happened once Saudi Arabia backed out of its traditional role as the champion of Muslim causes worldwide and others attempted to undermine the Kingdom in this domain. The bilateral relationship continued the downwards movement as Saudi Arabia scrapped its financial package to Pakistan and asked Islamabad to return the $3 billion loan. Pakistan managed to return $2 billion of the Saudi loan by getting alternative Chinese financial support (*Dawn* 2020a). This crisis was further exacerbated by the comments of Pakistan's Foreign Minister Qureshi who lamented the lack of Saudi support on the Kashmir issue and signalled to hold a meeting of like-minded powers outside the ambit of the Saudi-based OIC (*Dawn* 2020b).

Saudi Crown Prince declined to meet Pakistan's Army Chief General Bajwa as he tried to stabilise the relationship in the wake of FM Qureshi's outburst (*The Quint* 2020). All of these were extremely dangerous signs for Pakistan's decision-makers, and they fully understood the economic

Pakistan and Saudi Ties 171

implications of a total Saudi disconnect with Pakistan. Pakistan's political stakeholders responded by upping their engagement with the Saudi envoy in Islamabad and all the elite cadres of government, armed forces and civil society held consecutive meetings with the Saudi ambassador to smoothen up the rift and foster communication between the two sides (*Arab News Pakistan* 2020). In a goodwill, gesture government made Molana Tahir Ashrafi, head of Pakistan Ulema Council as Prime Minister's special envoy for the Middle East. Known for his close connections with Saudi Royal Court, Ashrafi was given the task to plead Pakistan's case within Saudi Arabia and the foreign ministry took a back seat on this matter (*The Express Tribune* 2020).

Rapprochement

The bilateral relationship has shown signs of improvement after the visit of Imran Khan to Saudi Arabia in May 2021. Saudi Arabia has also decided to roll over the remaining $1 billion loan to Pakistan and the Supreme Coordination Council has also been reformulated that will oversee the nature of bilateral engagement (*Arab News Pakistan* 2021). However, in a major shock for Pakistan, the proposed Saudi investment in an oil refinery in the city of Gwadar is faltering and the Saudis may be willing to move this refinery project to the urban metropolis of Karachi (Aamir 2021). This shows that even though a general rapprochement is happening between the two sides, but they are also re-calibrating their commitments.

This re-engagement needs to be viewed in the context of political changes on the global and regional level and an attempt by Saudi Arabia to engage with regional stakeholders for the peaceful settlement of conflicts. From a Pakistani perspective, it remains clear that the government battered by political and economic challenges both internally and externally has realised its limitations on the foreign policy front and a total lack of leverage with regard to the Saudi Kingdom. Moreover, with the economic challenges posed by the COVID-19 pandemic, the criticalness of expatriate remittances has increased manifold. Something which that wouldn't come from Turkey even if it can support Pakistan resolutely on foreign policy affairs.

Conclusion

The current trajectory of Pak-Saudi ties remains positive but structural issues that have been causing the two sides to drift apart are very much still there. Evolving regional security picture has been impacting upon both sides' respective strategic outlooks and the ever-increasing strategic divergence is posing the most significant challenge to the functionality of the bilateral ties. Within the ruling cadres in Pakistan, there is no appetite to start a confrontation with Iran even after the continued presence of Indian operatives on Iranian soil and the recruitment of Shia militiamen from Pakistan. Similarly, for Saudi Arabia, India remains a most lucrative

172 *Umer Karim*

energy market and establishing strategic ties with one of the biggest economies of the world remains a priority for the Kingdom. In this manner, the soft power leverage of both sides on each other is nearly negligible. The Pakistani nuclear bomb is only meant for Pakistan and old assumptions of the bomb available to Saudi Arabia in time of need may not be true anymore. The historical weightage of Saudi Arabia being the land of two Holy Mosques has suffered a setback owing to its reluctance to champion Muslim causes and this has also impacted upon the discourse vis-à-vis Kingdom in Pakistan. Since Kingdom's traditional supporters within Pakistan were all religious outfits, a changing Saudi Arabia no longer eager to support such elements will lose this soft power variable even more. On the other hand, Saudi Arabia continues to dominate Pakistan in the economic domain quite comprehensively and this economic dependence of Pakistan is not changing in the shorter term. Therefore, Saudi Arabia will remain critical for Pakistan's development and economic progression. For Pakistan, its leverage upon Saudi Arabia that came in the security domain has weakened. Even though Pakistani troops are still stationed within the Kingdom, these deployments are not of some high strategic value and thus even a departure of these troops will not alter the Saudi security picture to a great extent. This shows that currently, Saudi Arabia is the bigger partner in the bilateral relationship and Pakistan's dependency has only increased.

Notes

1 In Pakistan's case, the security policy remains India-centric. However, in the Saudi case, even though at that time the threat was more from Arab nationalist regimes than the Iranian regime, ever since the Islamic revolution, that nation's perception of threats has been primarily Iran-centric. In their bilateral engagement, both nations generally appreciate this situation, they also sometimes overlook this key variable and want the other country to support them against an enemy that is not considered a threat.

2 The involvement of Pakistani security forces in the operation has also been asserted in Simon Ross Valentine, *Force and Fanaticism: Wahhabism in Saudi Arabia and Beyond* (London: Hurst, 2015), p. 231. Hodna Gharsallah adopted a similar historical perspective in her investigative piece for *Inside Arabia* of July 2, 2018, http://insidearabia.com/historical-perspectives-siege-grand-mosque/.

3 "Saudi Arabia and the Future of Afghanistan," Council on Foreign Relations, December 10, 2008, https://www.cfr.org/backgrounder/saudi-arabia-and-future-afghanistan (Bruno 2008). Bruce Riedel, in his book *What We Won— America's Secret War in Afghanistan 1979–89* (Washington, DC: Brookings Institution, 2014), also mentions a sum of about \$20–25 million being sent for the Afghan resistance from private sources monthly. He also mentions that in 1985 William Casey, then director of the US CIA, requested that the Ronald Reagan administration increase US funding of its Afghan covert action program to \$250 million and the Saudis approved a similar raise.

4 It was quite clear from the start that a parliamentary session that was called in to debate the Yemen situation was hijacked by political agendas on both the government and opposition sides. This meant that no meaningful debate

on the Saudi request to send troops or the actual security situation in Yemen ever took place. Since the public discourse was overwhelmingly against sending troops to Yemen, the government was forced to end the matter by accepting the opposition's narrative. If the government had engaged the opposition before the parliamentary session and kept the domestic political agenda out of the debate, a more balanced resolution would have been eventually passed. The facts that the current government of PTI was the most active opposition at that time and today the government boasts strong ties with Saudi Arabia show that the debate in parliament was never issue focused but rather was a political one.

5 The parliament was informed by Pakistan's defense minister in early 2018 that Pakistan had decided to deploy a composite brigade of troops within Saudi Arabia for training and advisory purposes. Apparently, this move was made by the Pakistan military unilaterally in order to shore up ties with the Kingdom, which have seen a downturn since Pakistan refused to participate in the Yemen war. The deployment of a composite brigade including different units explains that this force was intended to help increase the capacity of Saudi forces in various fields.

References

Aamir, Adnan. 2020. "Saudi Arabia Pulls Support for Pakistan as Kashmir Tiff Widens." *Nikkei Asia*. 10 August. https://asia.nikkei.com/Politics/International-relations/Saudi-Arabia-pulls-support-for-Pakistan-as-Kashmir-tiff-widens.

————. 2021. "Pakistan's Gwadar Loses Luster as Saudis Shift $10bn Deal to Karachi." *Nikkei Asia*. 13 June. https://asia.nikkei.com/Politics/International-relations/Pakistan-s-Gwadar-loses-luster-as-Saudis-shift-10bn-deal-to-Karachi.

Abbir, Mordekay. 2002. *Saudi Arabia: Government, Society and the Gulf Crisis*. London: Routledge.

Ahmad, Khushboo, and Muhammad Faisal. 2014. "Pakistan-Saudi Arabia Strategic Relations: An Assessment." *CISS Insight* 2 (2–3): 23–37. https://ojs.ciss.org.pk/index.php/ciss-insight-journal/issue/view/Insight-Vol.2-No.2-3-2014.

Ahmad, Naveed. 1982. "Pakistan-Saudi Relations." *Pakistan Horizon The Middle East* 35 (4): 51–67. https://www.jstor.org/stable/41394170?seq=1#metadata_info_tab_contents.

————. 2016. "Pak-Saudi Relations: Friends with Benefits." 11 January. https://tribune.com.pk/story/1024531/pak-saudi-relations-friends-with-benefits/.

Ahmad, Toheed. 2013. "Muhammad Asad: The Story of a Story of a Story." *Criterion Quarterly* 6 (1). http://www.criterion-quarterly.com/muhammad-asad-the-story-of-a-story-of-a-story/.

Ahmed, Ayaz. 2016. "Uri Attack and the Doval Doctrine." *Defence Journal* 20 (3): 13–8. https://search.proquest.com/docview/1838920569?accountid=8630.

Ahmed, Zahid Shahab, and Stuti Bhatnagar. 2010. "Gulf States and the Conflict between India and Pakistan." *Journal of Asia Pacific Studies* 1 (2). https://www.humanitarianlibrary.org/sites/default/files/2014/02/8.Zahid.pdf.

Alam, Aftab, Mohammad Almotairi, Kamisan Gadar, and Omair Mujahid Malik. 2013. "An Economic Analysis of Pak-Saudi Trade Relation between 2000 and 2011." *American Journal of Research Communication* 1 (5): 209–18. http://www.usa-journals.com/wp-content/uploads/2013/04/Alam_Vol15.pdf.

Alam, Kamal, and Ibrahim Al-Othaimin. 2018. "Saudi Arabia and Pakistan: Moving from the Personal to the Strategic Domain." *Royal United Services Institute.* 18 June. https://rusi.org/commentary/saudi-arabia-and-pakistan-moving-personal-strategic-domain.

Albilad. 2019. "KSA to Invest $322m in Five Hydro-Power Projects in Pakistan." *Albilad Daily.* 15 February. http://www.albiladdailyeng.com/ksa-invest-322m-five-hydro-power-projects-pakistan/.

Algot, Jessica, and Patrick Wintour. 2018. "UK and US Pull out of Saudi Event over Alleged Murder of Jamal Khashoggi." *The Guardian.* 18 October. https://www.theguardian.com/world/2018/oct/18/liam-fox-pulls-out-of-saudi-event-over-alleged-of-jamal-khashoggi.

Amin, Shahid M. 1998. "Security in the Gulf: Pakistan's Role and Interest." *Pakistan Horizon* 51 (1): 17–28. https://www.jstor.org/stable/41394642?seq=1#metadata_info_tab_contents.

Ansari, Irshad. 2018. "Saudi Arabia Agrees to Finance Pakistan's Jagran Hydropower Project." *The Express Tribune.* 9 October. https://tribune.com.pk/story/2075223/2-saudi-arabia-agrees-finance-jagran-hydropower-project/.

Arab News Pakistan. 2020. "Ambassador Al-Malki Discusses Saudi-Pak Relations with Punjab Leaders." *Arab News PK.* 15 August. https://www.arabnews.pk/node/1719801/pakistan.

———. 2021. "Saudi Arabia, Pakistan Sign Agreement to Establish Saudi-Pakistani Supreme Coordination Council." *Arab News Pakistan.* 9 May. https://www.arabnews.pk/node/1855561/pakistan.

Arab News PK. 2018. "Saudi Cadets Complete Military Training in Pakistan." *Arab News Pakistan.* 10 November. http://www.arabnews.pk/node/1387096/pakistan.

Arhama, Altaf. 2021. "31 Saudi Officers Graduate from Pakistan Naval Academy." *Bolnews.* 28 June. https://www.bolnews.com/pakistan/2021/06/31-saudi-officers-graduate-from-pakistan-naval-academy/.

Arshad, Muhammad. 2016. "Muhammad Asad and Pola Hamida Asad: Twenty-Two Unpublished Letters." *Islamic Sciences* 14 (2): 158–86. http://www.cis-ca.org/jol/JIS-14-2/JIS-14-2-Asad-ltrs-2.pdf.

Arynews. 2018. "2.7 Million Pakistanis Living in Saudi Arabia, Minister Tells NA." *Arynews.* 9 March. https://arynews.tv/en/2-7-million-pakistanis-living-saudi-arabia/.

Baabar, Mariana. 2016. "Pakistan Participating in Counter-Terrorism Exercise in Saudi Arabia: FO." *The News.* 17 February.

Baghat, Gawdat. 2012. "Pakistan–Saudi Arabia Relations—An Assessment." In *Pakistan: The US, Geopolitics and Grand Strategies,* by Usama Butt and Julian Schofield, 188–205. London: Pluto Press.

Basu, Nayanima. 2019. "Erdogan Support for Pakistan on Kashmir at UN an Outcome of Downswing in India-Turkey Ties." *The Print.* 26 September. https://theprint.in/diplomacy/erdogan-support-for-pakistan-on-kashmir-at-un-an-outcome-of-downswing-in-india-turkey-ties/297376/.

Batrawy, Aya. 2019. "Indian Business Ties Underpin Muted Arab Response to Kashmir." *Associated Press.* 16 August. https://apnews.com/article/ap-top-news-india-global-trade-qatar-international-news-50c0012ce1c445db955a09b86732ce69.

Baxter, Craig. 1991. "Pakistan Becomes Prominent in the International Arena." *In Pakistan under the Military: Eleven Years of Zia Ul-Haq,* by Shahid Javed Burki and Craig Baxter, 137–54. Boulder: Westview Press.

Bhutto, Zulfiqar Ali. 1976. "Bilateralism: New Directions." *Pakistan Horizon* 29 (4): 3–59. https://www.jstor.org/stable/41393324?seq=1#metadata_info_tab_contents.

Bishku, Michael B. 1992. "In Search of Identity and Security: Pakistan and the Middle East, 1947–77." *Journal of Conflict Studies* 12 (3): 30–51. https://journals.lib.unb.ca/index.php/JCS/article/view/15047/16116.

Black, Ian. 2011. "Bahrain Security Forces Accused of Deliberately Recruiting Foreign Nationals." *The Guardian.* 17 February. https://www.theguardian.com/world/2011/feb/17/bahrain-security-forces-sunni-foreign.

Bruno, Greg. 2008. "Saudi Arabia and the Future of Afghanistan." *Council on Foreign Relations.* 10 December. https://www.cfr.org/backgrounder/saudi-arabia-and-future-afghanistan.

Chaudhary, Archana. 2019. "India PM to Meet King Salman in Saudi Arabia." *Bloomberg.* 24 October. https://www.bloomberg.com/news/articles/2019-10-24/india-pm-modi-to-meet-king-salman-in-saudi-arabia-on-oct-29.

Crossette, Barbara. 1990. "Pakistan Agree to Join Defense of Saudi Arabia." *New York Times.* 14 August. https://www.nytimes.com/1990/08/14/world/confrontation-in-the-gulf-pakistanis-agree-to-join-defense-of-saudi-arabia.html.

———. 2018. "PML-N Papers: Purchase of London Flats and the Al-Thani Connection." *Dawn.* 4 July. https://www.dawn.com/news/1298572/pml-n-papers-purchase-of-london-flats-and-the-al-thani-connection.

Dawn. 2020a. "Pakistan Returns $1 Billion of Saudi Arabia's Soft Loan, Officials Say." *Dawn.* 17 December. https://www.dawn.com/news/1596109.

———. 2020b. "Qureshi Asks OIC to Stop Dragging Feet on Kashmir Meeting." *Dawn.* 6 August. https://www.dawn.com/news/1572857.

———. 2021. "Remittances Exceed $2bn for 12th Straight Month with Highest Inflows from Saudi Arabia, UAE." *Dawn.* 10 June. https://www.dawn.com/news/1628615.

Dunya News. 2019. "Saudi FM Shuts Down Indian Journalist, Refuses to Condemn Pakistan." *Dunya News.* 20 February. https://dunyanews.tv/en/World/479359-Saudi-FM-shuts-down-Indian-journalist-refuses-condemn-Pakistan.

El Gamal, Rania. 2019. "Aramco in Talks to Buy Stake in Refining Business of India's Reliance." *Reuters.* 17 April. https://www.reuters.com/article/us-saudi-aramco-india-reliance/aramco-in-talks-to-buy-stake-in-refining-business-of-indias-reliance-idUSKCN1RT0H3.

Evans, Kathy. 1991. "Pakistan Doubles Forces in Saudi Arabia Despite Public Opposition." *The Guardian.* 8 January.

Farooq, Asad. 2019. "An Overview of Pak-Saudi Relations." *Dawn.* 18 February. https://www.dawn.com/news/1463802.

Government Archives. 2014. "Questions for Oral Answers and Their Replies." National Assembly Secretariat, Pakistan. 4 August. http://www.na.gov.pk/uploads/documents/questions/1407160619_854.pdf.

Gul, Ayaz. 2019. "Pakistan, Turkey, Malaysia to Jointly Launch Anti-Islamophobia TV." *Voice of America.* 26 September. https://www.voanews.com/south-central-asia/pakistan-turkey-malaysia-jointly-launch-anti-islamophobia-tv.

Haider, Kamran, and Ismail Dilawar. 2018. "Pakistan Secures $6 Billion Aid Package from Saudi Arabia." *Bloomberg.* 23 October. https://www.bloomberg.com/news/articles/2018-10-23/pakistan-says-saudi-arabia-agrees-to-6-billion-support-package.

Haider, Mateen. 2016. "Saudi Arabia Largest Importer of Pakistani Arms." *Dawn.* 6 May. https://www.dawn.com/news/1256712.

176   *Umer Karim*

Haider, Sadaf. 2020. "What Is Dirilis Ertugrul and Why Does Imran Khan Want Pakistanis to Watch It?" *Dawn Images.* 9 May. https://images.dawn.com/news/1183827.

Handjani, Amir. 2019. "Saudi Arabia Has Big Plans in India." *Foreign Policy.* 10 May. https://foreignpolicy.com/2019/05/10/saudi-arabia-has-big-plans-in-india/.

Haroon, Sana. 2016. "Pakistan between Saudi Arabia and Iran: Islam in the Politics and Economics of Western Asia." In *Pakistan at the Crossroads: Domestic Dynamics and External Pressures Religion, Culture, and Public Life*, by Christophe Jaffrelot, 301–34. New York: Columbia University Press.

Hashmi, Sohail H. 2011. "'Zero Plus Zero Plus Zero': Pakistan, the Baghdad Pact, and the Suez Crisis." *International History Review* 33 (3): 525–44. doi:10.1080/07075332.2011.615184.

Hildreth, Horace. 1952–1954. "Memorandum of Conversation, by the Ambassador in Pakistan." *Foreign Relations of the United States, 1952–1954, Africa and South Asia.* Vol. 11. Office of the Historian, Foreign Service Institute, United States Department of State. 1143. https://history.state.gov/historicaldocuments/frus1952-54v11p2/d1143.

Honsa, Carol. 1981. "Pakistan Boosting Its Gulf Security Force." *Christian Science Monitor.* 5 March. https://www.csmonitor.com/1981/0305/030541.html.

Hussain, Zakir. 2016. *Saudi Arabia in a Multipolar: Changing Dynamics.* New Delhi: Routledge India.

Imaduddin. 2014. "JMCC, MCC to Improve Pak-Saudi Defence Cooperation: Saudi Minister." *Business Recorder.* 20 January. https://www.brecorder.com/2014/01/20/154013/.

Iqbal, Abdul Rauf. 2012. *Internal and External Factors in the Balochistan Conflict.* Islamabad, Pakistan: National Defence University, Institute for Strategic Studies, Research and Analysis, 79–102.

Iran Primer. 2019. "Timeline of Houthi Attacks on Saudi Arabia." *Iran Primer.* 16 September. https://iranprimer.usip.org/blog/2019/sep/16/timeline-houthi-attacks-saudi-arabia.

Jaffrelot, Christophe. 2017. "Pakistan, Saudi Arabia, and Them." *Carnegie Endowment for International Peace.* 24 January. https://carnegieendowment.org/2017/01/24/pakistan-saudi-arabia-and-them-pub-67779.

Jamal, Umair. 2019a. "The Kuala Lumpur Summit 2019 Shows Pakistan's Diplomatic Subservience to Saudi Arabia." *The Diplomat.* 24 December. https://thediplomat.com/2019/12/the-kuala-lumpur-summit-2019-shows-pakistans-diplomatic-subservience-to-saudi-arab.

———.2019b."WhatArmyChiefGeneralBajwa'sTermExtensionMeansforPakistan." *The Diplomat.* 22 August. https://thediplomat.com/2019/08/what-army-chief-general-bajwas-term-extension-means-for-pakistan/.

Jamil, Rehan. 2017. "Role of a Dome-Less Mosque in Conserving the Religious and Traditional Values of Muslims: An Innovative Architecture of Shah Faisal Mosque, Islamabad." *International Journal of Architecture, Engineering and Construction* 6 (2): 40–5. doi:10.7492/IJAEC.2017.010.

Kaminski, Matthew. 2013. "Prince Alwaleed Bin Talal: An Ally Frets about American Retreat." *Wall Street Journal.* 13 November. https://www.wsj.com/articles/prince-alwaleed-bin-talal-an-ally-frets-about-american-retreat-1385165879.

Karim, Umer. 2022. "The Pakistan–Iran relationship and the changing nature of regional and domestic security and strategic interests". *Global Discourse* (Early View). 1–19. doi: 10.1332/204378921X16585144068826.

Pakistan and Saudi Ties   177

———. 2018. "Why Pakistan Has Troops in Saudi Arabia—and What It Means for the Middle East." *The Conversation.* 19 September. https://theconversation.com/why-pakistan-has-troops-in-saudi-arabia-and-what-it-means-for-the-middle-east-92613.

———. 2019. "New Economic Ties Deepen the Saudi-Pakistani Strategic Partnership." *Washington Institute for Near East Policy.* 27 February. https://www.washington-institute.org/fikraforum/view/new-economic-ties-deepen-the-saudi-pakistani-strategic-partnership.

Maitra, Ramatanu. 1989. "Benazir Bhutto Visit Removes Saudi Doubts." *Executive Intelligence Review* 16 (6): 52–3. https://larouchepub.com/eiw/public/1989/eirv16n06-19890203/eirv16n06-19890203.pdf.

Masood, Salman, and Ben Hubbard. 2017. "Pakistan Approves Military Hero to Head Tricky Saudi-Led Alliance." *New York Times.* 2 April. https://www.nytimes.com/2017/04/02/world/asia/pakistan-general-saudi-alliance-raheel-sharif.html.

Matthiesen, Toby. 2018. "Saudi Arabia and the Cold War." In *Salman's Legacy: The Dilemmas of a New Era in Saudi Arabia,* by Madawi Al-Rasheed, 217–34. London: Hurst.

Miller, Flagg. 2015. *The Audacious Ascetic: What the Bin Laden Tapes Reveal about Al-Qaida.* New York: Oxford University Press.

Money Control. 2019. "Pakistan Saudi Arabia Hold Business Conference to Boost Economic Ties." *Money Control.* 18 February. https://www.moneycontrol.com/news/world/pakistan-saudi-arabia-hold-business-conference-to-boost-economic-ties-3552101.html.

Morrow, Sibel, and Faruk Zorlu. 2020. "Kashmir as Important to Turkey as It Is to Pakistan." *Anadolu Ajansi.* 14 February. https://www.aa.com.tr/en/asia-pacific/-kashmir-as-important-to-turkey-as-it-is-to-pakistan-/1733770.

Mudiam, Prithvi Ram. 1994. *India and the Middle East.* London: British Academic Press.

Mukhtar, Imran. 2015. "PTI's Resistance Sidelines Asif: Dar Moves Resolution." *The Nation.* 10 April. https://nation.com.pk/11-Apr-2015/pti-s-resistance-sidelines-asif-dar-moves-resolution.

Munir, M Arshad. 2017. "Pak-Saudi Relations: A History of Goodwill." *Saudi Gazette.* 23 March. http://saudigazette.com.sa/article/175372.

Nytimes.com. 1976. "Saudi King in Pakistan." *New York Times.* 11 October. https://www.nytimes.com/1976/10/11/archives/saudi-king-in-pakistan.html.

O'Connor, Tom. 2017. "Saudis Give Pakistan One Choice: 'Are You with Us or with Qatar?'" *Newsweek.* 16 June. https://www.newsweek.com/saudi-arabia-pakistan-choice-us-qatar-626915.

Pakistan Horizon. 1954. "Chronology January 1, 1954–December 31, 1954." *Pakistan Horizon* 7 (4): 238–46. https://www.jstor.org/stable/41403761?seq=3#metadata_info_tab_contents.

Pande, Ankit. 2014. "India and Saudi Arabia Sign Defense Cooperation Pact." *The Diplomat.* 27 February. https://thediplomat.com/2014/02/india-and-saudi-arabia-sign-defense-cooperation-pact/.

Pande, Aparna. 2014. *Explaining Pakistan's Foreign Policy: Escaping India.* London: Routledge.

Perlez, Jane. 1999. "Saudi's Visit to Arms Site in Pakistan Worries U.S." *New York Times.* 10 July. https://www.nytimes.com/1999/07/10/world/saudi-s-visit-to-arms-site-in-pakistan-worries-us.html?mtrref=www.google.co.uk&gwh=C0EA8EE0C0BEEF28147C5F2D1542A357&gwt=pa.

Philip, Snehesh Alex. 2020. "What India, Saudi, UAE Look to Gain from Gen. Naravane Trip, a First by an Indian Army Chief." *The Print.* 8 December. https://theprint.in/defence/what-india-saudi-uae-look-to-gain-from-gen-naravane-trip-a-first-by-an-indian-army-chief/562866/.

Pirzada, Syed Sharifuddin. 1976. "Quaid-i-Azam and Islamic Solidarity." *Pakistan Horizon* 29 (4): 60–72. https://www.jstor.org/stable/41393325.

Radio Pakistan. 2018. "Pak-China Enjoy Strategic Relations: Chinese Air Chief." *Radio Pakistan.* 13 April. http://www.radio.gov.pk/13-04-2018/pak-china-enjoy-strategic-relations-cooperation-bw-two-armed-forces-to-be-promoted-chinese-air-chief.

Rafiq, Arif. 2015. "The Dangerous, Delicate Saudi-Pakistan Alliance." *Foreign Policy.* 01 April. https://foreignpolicy.com/2015/04/01/the-dangerous-delicate-saudi-pakistan-alliance-yemen-iran/.

Raza, Syed Irfan. 2016. "Reference Will Be Sent to Iran Calling for Probe into RAW Presence in Chabahar." *Dawn.* 28 March. https://www.dawn.com/news/1248417.

Rizvi, Mujtaba. 1981. "Pak-Saudi Arabian Relations: An Example of Entente Cordiale." *Pakistan Horizon, the Inter-Relation of Muslim States and Pakistan* 34 (1): 81–92. https://www.jstor.org/stable/41393647.

Saeed, Aamir. 2019. "Gas Pipeline Project 'Impossible' under US Sanctions, Pakistan Tells Iran." *Arab News Pakistan.* 11 May. http://www.arabnews.pk/node/1495251/pakistan.

Saudiembassay.net. 1998. "Joint Saudi-Pakistani Statement on Crown Prince's Visit." 27 October. https://web.archive.org/web/20041013072438/http://www.saudiembassy.net/1998News/Statements/StateDetail.asp?cIndex=318.

Sayeed, Saad. 2019. "Pakistan Expects 8 Investment Deals during Saudi Prince's Visit." *Reuters.* 13 February. https://www.reuters.com/article/us-asia-saudi-pakistan/pakistan-expects-8-investment-deals-during-saudi-princes-visit-idUSKCN1Q223T.

Sengupta, Somini, and David Rohde. 2005. "Pledges Exceed Goal for Pakistan Quake Aid." *New York Times.* 20 November. https://www.nytimes.com/2005/11/20/world/asia/pledges-exceed-goal-for-pakistan-quake-aid.html?mtrref=www.google.co.uk&gwh=AA5126F892837FB4EAC990E43C091BFD&gwt=pay.

Shah, Mehtab Ali. 1997. *The Foreign Policy of Pakistan: Ethnic Impacts on Diplomacy: 1971–1994.* London: I. B. Tauris.

Shah, Saeed. 2010. "Pakistan Floods: Saudi Arabia Pledges $100m." *The Guardian.* 18 August. https://www.theguardian.com/world/2010/aug/18/pakistan-floods-saudi-arabia-pledges.

Shams, Shamil. 2017. "Pakistan Faces a Diplomatic Conundrum over the Gulf Crisis." *Deutsche Welle.* 12 June. https://www.dw.com/en/pakistan-faces-a-diplomatic-conundrum-over-the-gulf-crisis/a-39209645.

Shay, Shaul. 2018. "Saudi Arabia and Pakistan—Strategic Alliance," Proceedings of the Herzliya Conference, April 2018. *Herzliya Conference Papers.* Herzliya: Interdisciplinary Center Herzliya. 1–9. https://www.idc.ac.il/en/research/ips/2018/Documents/ShaulShaySaudi.ArabiaPakistanEN17.4.2018.pdf.

Sial, Safdar. 2015. "Emerging Dynamics in Pakistani-Saudi Relations." Norwegian Peacebuilding Resource Centre. https://www.files.ethz.ch/isn/195227/202d14d49238cab72b99e625383101d3.pdf.

Siddiqa, Ayesha. 2017. "A Friendship Fit for a King." *Friday Times.* 28 April. https://www.thefridaytimes.com/a-friendship-fit-for-a-king/.

Sinha, Prem Bahadur. 1980. "Pak-Saudi Military Cooperation." *Strategic Analysis* 4 (8): 357–61. doi:10.1080/09700168009425772.

Staudenmaier, William O, and Shireen Tahir-Kheli. 1981. *The Saudi-Pakistani Military Relationship and Its Implications for US Strategy in Southwest Asia.* Carlisle, PA: US Army War College, Strategic Studies Institute.

Steinberg, Guido, and Nils Woermer. 2013. *Exploring Iran & Saudi Arabia's Interests in Afghanistan & Pakistan: Stakeholders or Spoilers—A Zero Sum Game? Part 1: Saudi Arabia.* Barcelona Centre for International Affairs.

Syed, Baqir Sajjad. 2017. "Pakistan Determined to Expand Ties with Iran: Bajwa." *Dawn.* 7 November. https://www.dawn.com/news/1368817.

———. 2018. "First Pak-Aided US-Taliban Talks held in UAE." *Dawn.* 18 December. https://www.dawn.com/news/1452076.

———. 2019. "Pakistan Soil Used for Attacks in Iran: Imran." *Dawn.* 23 April. https://www.dawn.com/news/1477837.

Talbot, Ian. 1998. *Pakistan: A Modern History.* London: Hurst Publications.

Tanoli, Qadeer. 2017. "Recruitment for Syria: Interior Ministry Bans Sectarian Outfit." *The Express Tribune.* 22 January. https://tribune.com.pk/story/1303150/recruitment-syria-interior-ministry-bans-sectarian-outfit/.

Tehran Times. 2018. "Iranian Military Chief's First Visit to Pakistan." *Tehran Times.* 16 July. https://www.tehrantimes.com/news/425437/Iranian-military-chief-s-first-visit-to-Pakistan.

The Citizens Archive of Pakistan. 2018. "The Citizens Archive of Pakistan, 'Banquet Hosted by King Ibn-e-Saud for the Pakistani Governor General Ghulam Muhammad' (digital image)." Twitter.com. 15 January. https://twitter.com/citizensarchive/status/952773238215663616?lang=en.

The Express Tribune. 2018. "Pakistan, Saudi Naval Forces Complete First Phase of Aff'aa Al Sahil Exercise." *The Express Tribune.* 14 February. https://tribune.com.pk/story/1635061/1-pakistan-saudi-naval-forces-complete-first-phase-affaa-al-sahil-exercise/.

———. 2020. "Maulana Tahir Ashrafi Given Additional Charge of Middle East Affairs." *The Express Tribune.* 22 October. https://tribune.com.pk/story/2269502/maulana-tahir-ashrafi-given-additional-charge-of-middle-east-affairs.

The Guardian. 2010. "US Embassy Cables: Saudi Influence in Pakistan." *The Guardian.* 01 December. https://www.theguardian.com/world/us-embassy-cables-documents/130876.

The News. 2018. "Second Meeting of Pak-Saudi JWG on Trade Held in Islamabad." *The News.* 7 September. https://www.thenews.com.pk/print/365315-second-meeting-of-pak-saudi-jwg-on-trade-held-in-islamabad.

The Quint. 2020. "Pak-Saudi Ties in Trouble as Army Chief Fails to Meet Crown Prince." *The Quint.* 19 August. https://www.thequint.com/news/world/pakistan-saudi-ties-trouble-army-chief-snubbed-by-crown-prince-mbs-significance.

Trading Economics. 2018. "Pakistan Imports from Saudi Arabia." *Trading Economics.* 12 November. https://tradingeconomics.com/pakistan/imports/saudi-arabia.

Trofimov, Yaroslav. 2008. *The Siege of Mecca: The Forgotten Uprising in Islam's Holiest Shrine.* London: Penguin Books.

Weinbaum, Marvin G, and Abdullah B Khurram. 2014. "Pakistan and Saudi Arabia: Deference, Dependence and Deterrence." *Middle East Journal* 68 (2): 211–28. doi:10.3751/68.2.12.

8 India and the United Arab Emirates

Upgrading the Strategic Partnership

Rhea Abraham

Introduction

To understand the current regional security dynamics in the Middle East,[1] we must look at the Iraq War of 2003, the Arab Spring of 2011, and the US-Iran conflict, which have altered inter-regional competition and influenced foreign-policy initiatives in the region. Further, the Qatar blockade in 2017 and the rapprochement in 2021 have also added to the changing pattern of relations in the region (Vakil and Quilliam, 2021). Along with regional conflicts, individually, the countries in the Middle East face the challenges of terrorism, cybersecurity and maritime piracy (Saab, 2021). In the Persian Gulf, the current security complex has undergone internal transformations due to the changing patterns of territorial disputes, change in leadership and competition (Grabowski, 2020).

Under the *"Look West Policy,"* the Indian leadership has made strenuous efforts to build better relationships with its extended neighbours, the Arab Gulf countries, particularly the United Arab Emirates (UAE), in response to the shifting balance of power. India has also welcomed the normalisation of ties between Israel and the UAE, seeing as it maintains good relations with both countries, while continuing to speak up publicly for the rights of the Palestinians. Similarly, the UAE has also shifted its focus to play a power-centric role in the region by aligning with other rising players such as India and attempting to bring peace to South Asia. Alternatively, India and the UAE continue to stress issue-based regional and global engagement, which allows diplomatic flexibility and strategic autonomy. It is therefore evident that the dynamics of national security are highly interdependent between states and can only be fully understood when considered in relation to each other (Koch and Stivachtis, 2019).

Therefore, the regional shifts and realignment of strategies in the Middle East have a spillover effect on its extended neighbourhood and mandate a study that focuses on the renewing of India-UAE relations at the inter-regional level. This is defined by collaborative and cooperative relations between them and marked by interdependencies to maintain security in the region. The chapter aims to offer a broad overview of India-UAE

DOI: 10.4324/9781003283058-9

relations under the leadership of Prime Minister Narendra Modi and Sheikh Mohammed Bin Zayed Al Nahyan—their historical origins, accomplishments, as well as prospects for a renewed and robust policy amidst the involvement of external heavyweight China and regional ally Pakistan—and concludes with the implications for the Indian-UAE rendezvous and recommendations for policymakers of the Middle East. The chapter aims to highlight the upgrading of India-UAE relations from bilateral relations to partners in multi-lateral, regional and global forums, grounded on security interdependency and geographical coherence. In doing so, the theory of regional security by Barry Buzan and Ole Weaver can be applied to these strategic geopolitical trajectories in the Middle Eastern and South Asian regions. It attempts to understand the interaction of the regional security complexes mainly through the prism of interaction between the UAE and India, and whether a merged West Asian regional security complex is the way forward.

Theoretical understanding

Regional security

The Regional Security Complex theory by Barry Buzan and Ole Weaver groups security issues around geographically separated regional complexes that are created due to security interdependence, and which links them internally and creates a sense of solidarity among these security interactions (Jarząbek, 2018). The theory justifies the degree of enmity and amity between existing states; amity relating to friendship and support mainly promoted through historical ties, and enmity arising from border disputes to ideological differences. This allows the interdependency between states and their national security, entwining them into a notional security complex based on rivalry or shared interests.

In the contemporary security environment, challenges have been emanating from non-traditional sources ranging from challenges of human migration to cross-border threats. Traditional security remains focused on the securitisation of the state, both internally and externally.

India and regional security in the Gulf

The regional security dynamics in South Asia mainly revolve around the relations between India and Pakistan and their power struggle over Kashmir. However, the economic rise of India, its military capabilities and soft power have allowed India to seek to play a greater role and take on greater responsibility in the management of regional security. India's key objectives have been to maintain regional stability and provide security. This reflects India's aspiration to play a strategic role in the Indian Ocean realm (Brewster, 2013).

182 *Rhea Abraham*

Energy dependence on Gulf countries such as the UAE, increasing remittances, trade and the presence of thriving migrants, continue to dictate the strategic and diplomatic ambitions of India in the region. The Gulf region forms part of India's extended neighbourhood and India maintains strategic ties with all the Gulf states. The Indians working in the Gulf mostly contribute to India's economic development through their remittances and play a greater role in exporting India's culture to the region. Indian migrants continue to be the largest foreign force employed in various sectors of the Gulf development process and continue to be present in all arenas of modernisation in the region. The export of manpower and skilled labour, and transfer of science and technological know-how have contributed to the promotion of India's soft-power status in the region, mainly through cooperation and collaboration with the locals. Unlike the United States, which promotes democratisation in West Asia and elsewhere, India never involves itself in the domestic affairs of any country in the region. Although American initiatives have strengthened civil-society movements in the region over the years, the US image in the region has diminished considerably, thereby leaving space for Asian powers such as India to engage more with the Gulf countries. The role of the UAE for India in the present context extends beyond a strategic one to micro-level engagements. The experience of Indian migrants (especially Muslim migrants) goes beyond remittances as the incursions of the Indian diaspora in the religious sphere are discernible with all the religious organisations that maintain cross-cultural ties with their counterparts in the Gulf.

The UAE's need for regional security

The UAE's security perspective has been mainly influenced by its vulnerability in the changing domestic and international security environment and regional conflicts, and its subsequent rise or determination to become a rising regional power (Ammar, 2020). The UAE's regional policy has also been influenced by its national population, the presence of foreigners, Arab nationalism and recently *Khaleeji* identity. Against this background, throughout the 2010s, the UAE has attempted to cast itself as a significant regional player with its impact on the geopolitics of the region and in countries beyond its geography through a recalibration of bilateral relations including those with India. It has succeeded in becoming an assertive regional player by combining energy revenues and planned economic diversification in Africa and Asia. It has been pursuing parallel engagements and employing diplomatic equity with countries, to secure its interests in the region and the extended neighbourhood (Taneja, 2021). The UAE is also focusing on building its economic and diplomatic relations amidst a perceived US withdrawal, by aligning with global powers such as China, Russia and India simultaneously (Salisbury, 2020). At the regional level, the UAE is part of the Arab Security Complex in the form of regional associations

India and the United Arab Emirates 183

such as the Gulf Cooperation Council (GCC), the Organization of Islamic Countries, the Oil Producing and Exporting Countries, the Arab League and the Non-Aligned Movement. Along with a pragmatic approach, military cooperation has been a key element in the UAE's foreign policy since 2011. The transfer of capacity building and training has helped the UAE support its network of alliances in the region and abroad (Ardemagni, 2020). The UAE has upgraded its military capabilities and engaged in military interventions in the region, in Yemen in 2015.

Historical ties

History is a reminder of the cultural relationship that India and the countries of the Arabian Peninsula uphold, and which has cemented political and economic ties even today. The economic relationship has been based on oil, trade and remittances; and the political dimension has been widely influenced by the presence of a large expatriate community and religious affinities in the region. This has, in turn, provided an assurance that India is a long-term partner for the Gulf. Recently, there has been an increase in infrastructural investment by the Arab Gulf countries in India, and greater defence and security associations including regional and global initiatives on anti-extremism and counterterrorism, and other multi-lateral development projects.

India's connection with the Middle East dates to the third millennium B.C., when trade and travel flourished between the civilisations of India and the Arab world. The basic structure of exchange in the Arabian Seas from the 13th to 17th century consisted of India delivering textiles, pepper and rice to the Middle East; mainly exchanged for silver, gold and almonds from Arabia (Barendse, 2000). The extensive trade and cultural contacts via the Indian Ocean maritime route and Silk Route over land gradually led to semi-permanent Arab settlements on the western and southern coasts of India, with the Arabs first attempting to study the history of India and drawing maps (Ahmad, 1969). The UAE was also part of international trade, where Indian merchants brought spices and timber and UAE merchants traded copper and pottery (Harn, 2017).

With the unification of regions to form national boundaries, India (then British India) expanded relations with what is now Saudi Arabia and other Gulf states, promoted with the protectionism of the East India Company over the Indian Ocean. During the Kuwait-Najd trade blockade in the 1920s–1930s, the Government of India funded Najd through financial subsidies, as the region was a major supply route for India (Kostiner, 1993). The UAE was part of the Trucial States, which were a British protectorate from 1820 to 1971, where the nominally independent Sheikhdoms were administered from British India. This helped the UAE establish political and economic ties with India (then British India). It is interesting to note that the trade and banking aspects in the protectorates were administered

184　*Rhea Abraham*

by the Khoja and Kutchi communities of India (Tesorero, 2017). The currency used in this region was also the Indian rupee and Indian stamps were used for correspondence, till the countries became independent states. Trade between the two countries was dominated by traditional items such as pearls and dates; however, it underwent a drastic change with the discovery of oil in the UAE and oil exports from Abu Dhabi in 1962.

In the 1970s and 1980s, large numbers of people from India migrated to the Gulf in their quest for wealth and prosperity; both communities went ahead to invest economically and culturally in these regions. Although Indians formed a large part of the clerical and technical positions, in the oil companies of the Gulf during the oil boom in the 1930s, the overall number of Indians remained considerably small and mainly concentrated in unskilled and semi-skilled work in the construction and household sectors (Lal, 2006). Following the 1973 increase in oil prices and the beginning of large-scale developmental activities in the Gulf, there began an upsurge of workers and labourers from India, mainly owing to the insufficiency of the labour force from neighbouring West Asian countries like Egypt, which were facing crises at that time. The initial years of the 1970s required large-scale human resources in developmental activities involving industry, agriculture, communication, transport and infrastructure. India and the UAE established formal diplomatic relations in 1972 and 1973 with the setting up of embassies in Abu Dhabi and New Delhi, respectively. In 1975, Sheikh Zayed visited India and signed a cultural-cooperation agreement. He also visited India in 1992 to sign a double-taxation-avoidance agreement after signing a civil-aviation agreement in 1989. A few other agreements were also signed between the UAE and India during this period. From 1990 onwards, India's liberalisation policies opened the country to newer ventures and trading partners in the Middle East, mainly the UAE, which had established itself as a regional trading hub, and which remains one of India's largest trading partners even today. In the 2000s, India and the UAE entered several security-cooperation agreements. Post the Iraq War of 2003, there was an intensification of Saudi-Iran rivalry (sectarian divisions), and a fundamental shift in balance of power dynamics to the non-Arab states mainly Iran becoming a dominant player in the Arab system (Grabowski, 2020). During this time, India opposed the military action in Iraq and later restored diplomatic relations with the newly elected government of Iraq in 2005.

Reinforcing the strategic partnership

Understanding leadership and foreign policy

Foreign policy is created through several decision-making processes and its analysis is based on various factors at the individual, state and systemic levels. The individual level of foreign-policy decision making revolves around the individual human being who can make decisions and is influenced

India and the United Arab Emirates   185

through certain mechanisms that contribute to policymaking, such as emotional, psychological and cognitive factors and perceptions. It can be approached from three different perspectives: one is to examine fundamental human nature; to study how people act in organisations; and to examine the motivations and actions of specific persons (Rourke, 2007). State-level decision making emphasises the role of states in policymaking. The type of political system, the type of environment, the type of issue and the internal factors involved impact the decision-making process of the state (Chandra, 2003). The system level of foreign-policy decision making focuses on the external restraints on foreign policy. This is an approach to world politics that examines the social, economic and political-geographic characteristics of the system and how they influence the actions of countries and actors. Countries must make policy choices within the context of the realities of the international system to be effective and must deal with the structural realities of organisations (Sekhri, 2009). This level involves the power relations of actors and their structure involved in the overall policymaking system in the international environment and includes economic realities, norms and diplomatic reciprocity (Jayapalan, 2001). As mentioned above, a sudden boost to India-UAE relations and foreign-policy changes have been mainly attributed to the changes in the international security environment, popular unrest, protests in the Middle East (including in the Gulf), the possible withdrawal of the US, and uncertainty over major-power interventions and the future of strategic re-alignments in the region.

The foreign policy of a country also reflects its political culture, which is its society's widely held traditions and values, sometimes taking the form of ideology (Crabb Jr, 1972); and the policies formed by leaders tend to be compatible with these cultures. The foreign policies of states may change slightly with a given leader, but ultimately, the polarity and stability of the international system will dictate how they will behave (Murray, 2012). Scholarship on foreign policy stresses the importance of external shocks as key enablers for leaders to alter foreign-policy agendas or redirect their vision of foreign policy. The leaders' cognitive or ideological predisposition is also an intervening factor for their change in foreign policy. In this context, any change in personal belief or leadership can lead to alternative foreign-policy action (Blarel, 2021).

MBZ and regional aspirations

The UAE occupies a strategically important geographic location in the Persian Gulf, adjacent to the Strait of Hormoz, a potential chokepoint in the Arabian Sea. It is an important trade route and a key player in the maritime security of the region. The oil-wealth resources have provided an impetus for the UAE to develop its infrastructure considerably and conduct strategic relations with countries around the world. From the 1990s onwards, the UAE has been consolidating its economic sovereignty and expanding

186 *Rhea Abraham*

its role as a security and military power in the region. This has allowed it to expand its strategic vision to look beyond the Gulf, which has been further encouraged by the Abu Dhabi ruler, Mohammed bin Zayed Al-Nahyan (MBZ). The UAE strongman has been aiming to develop the federation as a regional and global power commensurate with its economic transformation (Miller and Verhoeven, 2020).

The UAE now plans to become a soft regional power by focusing on cultural and social issues and capitalising on global events through cultural diplomacy in the field of art and science. The power status achieved is a productive step towards achieving global leadership, through the role and identity of its leader and the strengthening of the domestic polity (Waever, 2017). Another aspect of Sheikh Mohammed Bin Zayed's policy has been his articulation of zero tolerance towards radical Islamists. He has banned Muslim Brotherhood affiliates and taken a proactive stand to promote interfaith harmony in the country. Sheikh Nahyan was appointed as the minister for tolerance, while the UAE hosted Pope Francis and the Grand Imam of Al Azhar to sign the historic Document of Human Fraternity. The opening of the Louvre in 2019, a major Hindu temple to be developed in Abu Dhabi, and an Abrahamic family house in the same complex hosting a mosque, church and synagogue together, are only some examples (Suri, 2020).

Modi's pragmatic look west policy

Prime Minister Manmohan Singh laid the foundation for India's successful outreach to the Middle East by inviting the King of Saudi Arabia as the Chief Guest of the Republic Day Parade in 2006. This was followed by high-level visits between the two countries, setting the stage for wider strategic engagements with other states of the GCC. Since 2014, India's Middle East policy has been intensified by Prime Minister Narendra Modi with India's economic strength providing a stronger standing in regional politics. In Modi's initial foreign-policy objectives, the Middle East was a peripheral region with standard interests. However, India's rising economic and military capabilities and India-US relations have brought a renewed interest of the big players, the UAE and Saudi Arabia in India's Look West policy. Just as former Prime Minister of India Narasimha Rao gets credit for the crafting of the "Look East Policy" focusing on East Asian countries, Modi's realistic approach to the "Look West Policy" has led India to attain a unique position in the Middle East, among regional powers such as Iran, Saudi Arabia and the UAE. The government has been vocal about its "Think West" initiative labelled as "Act West" or "Link West" to match the institutionalised engagement with the Southeast Asian countries (Blarel, 2021).

During his leadership, the Prime Minister publicly acknowledged the importance of the Middle East by visiting the Gulf countries, Turkey, Israel, Palestine and Iran, giving a profound boost to India's interests in the region. India's Prime Minister received the *"Order of Zayed,"* the highest

India and the United Arab Emirates 187

civilian order of the UAE and the *"King Hamad Order of the Renaissance,"* the third-highest civilian order of Bahrain in 2019 (Pulipaka, and Musaddi, 2020). There has been a high degree of security cooperation between India and the countries of the Middle East, including on joint military exercises, intelligence sharing and counterterrorism initiatives. India's new Look West Policy has taken inspiration from India's existing non-aligned policy in the Middle East but has forged pragmatic and proactive policies based on mutual interests. It has refrained from interfering in the political affairs or decisions of the Arabs and supported their efforts to reconcile with Israel. India has also made an effort to support Arab economic integration, political reconciliation and the strengthening of regional institutions (Mohan, 2020). The Indian government has de-hyphenated India's policy towards Israel and Palestine and signalled that it is necessary to dissociate the two by pursuing security cooperation with Israel and economic development support to the Palestinians.

The Look West Policy aims to leverage India's economic growth with its political relations and position India as a leading player in the international security environment. The main foci of Modi's new policy are the proper treatment of Indian migrants, the humanitarian evacuation of Indian nationals during crisis situations such as *"Operation Raahat,"*[2] large-scale investment and maritime security (Chauduri, 2017). The Abraham Accords that were recently signed between the UAE, Bahrain and Israel have opened opportunities for India to collaborate on joint defence production, and research and development between the various countries. This opens the way for multi-lateral partnerships in several fields that help India to synergise its resources and strengths with the Middle East.

India-UAE relations

India's relationship with the UAE is at the core of the new Look West Policy, which is assertive and pragmatic, mutually reinforcing compatible geopolitical and economic visions, and aiming at a more promising partnership between the regional players. India's need to unleash its economic potential has coincided with the UAE's plan to develop a diversified knowledge economy and has promoted economic engagement between them. The common security concerns of the Gulf and the Indian Ocean form the basis for a defence dialogue and cooperation in counterterrorism and maritime initiatives (Khushnam, 2021).

Politics

The leadership of India and the UAE has exchanged several bilateral visits since 1975. However, the pace of high-level visits and meetings has increased since 2010 and has further accelerated post-2014. Sheikh Mohammed bin Zayed Al Nahyan visited India in February 2016 and again in 2017 as the chief guest at India's Republic Day celebrations. The visits signified India's growing engagement with the UAE and set the momentum for enhancing bilateral relations. During the visit in 2017, bilateral relations were upgraded to a comprehensive strategic partnership (Government of India, Ministry of External Affairs, 2020). Thirteen Memorandums of Understanding were signed under this agreement in 2017 (Singh and Muddassir Quamar, 2017). The Joint Statement on the Comprehensive Strategic Partnership Agreement is an important shift in the Arab world's view of India. The comprehensive statement draws on the historically unique ties between the UAE and India and outlines close government-to-government and people-to-people relations. It is an assertion of a shared past, continuing relations and common challenges to be addressed in the future. Under the agreement, ministerial strategic dialogues were conducted to monitor the progress of various engagements, including institutional cooperation. A major aspect of the agreement was the importance of cooperation on regional and global issues and the strengthening of ties at multi-lateral forums, such as South-South cooperation, peace and development, aid and combating terrorism, including joint projects in Afghanistan (Government of India, Ministry of External Affairs, 2018). Modi visited the UAE in February 2018 for the *World Government Summit* as the guest of honour. He visited the UAE again to receive *"the Order of Zayed"* conferred on him by the UAE President in April 2019. The constant high-level exchanges between the leaders have ensured an empathetic outcome and they continued even during the pandemic to discuss the impacts on healthcare and the economy and to regularly review the comprehensive strategic partnership (Sen Gupta, 2021).

In the current context, the UAE, with its endorsement of multi-culturalism and pluralism, appreciates India's stance on the same, and hence, the joint statement suggests that the UAE values India's approach and its principle of religious and cultural tolerance (Baru, 2015). India's rise is seen by the pragmatic UAE as a convergence of their shared interest against religious extremism and terrorism.

Economics

The economic and commercial relations between India and the UAE have contributed to the stability and strength of their deepening bilateral relationship. The growing engagements between India and the UAE should be seen within the broader contexts of the UAE's policy of engaging with Asia to improve economic prospects and India's search for foreign investments to expedite economic growth and address the threat of extremism and terrorism. India-UAE trade has grown considerably over the years, particularly in the non-oil sector, amounting to a total of 59 billion US dollars. This has made the UAE India's third-largest trading partner for 2020 after China and the US. The UAE is India's second-largest export market accounting for US$29 billion per annum, marking India as the second-largest trading partner of the UAE. India's major exports to the UAE include petroleum products, food items, textiles, engineering products and chemicals. India's major imports from the UAE include crude oil, petroleum, chemicals, wood and minerals. The Gulf countries remain the largest trading partners of India and have pledged investments in food security, mining and manufacturing, and recently in India's start-up and technology sectors. India is also playing a key role in transportation and logistics projects in the Middle East (Swami, 2020). India and the UAE have been discussing cooperation in the management of logistics, warehousing and the need to operationalise the food corridor in the region. This will ensure food security, enhance trade in agricultural products and create opportunities for research and development in the agricultural sector (*Gulf News*, 2019).

In the form of direct investment and portfolio investment, UAE is India's ninth biggest investor in terms of FDI. These investments are mainly concentrated in the services, construction, power and transport sector. These investments have also expanded to include development projects and are widely managed by the UAE-India Infrastructure Investment Fund. Offices of both investment houses of India and the UAE will open in Dubai and Mumbai, respectively to support business at both ends. The Abu Dhabi Investment Agency has invested in India's National Infrastructure Investment Fund as an anchor investor and welcomes Dubai Ports World's agreement to create a joint investment with National Investment and Infrastructure Fund, India in transportation and logistics businesses in the country (Government of India, Ministry of External Affairs, 2018). India has also expanded its investment culture in the region by taking advantage of the UAE-Israel bonhomie. The International Federation of the Indo-Israel Chambers of Commerce (IFIICC) has been launched in the UAE to broaden the relationship between the Indian diaspora and Israel (India, UAE witness soaring relations in 2020, 2020).

In the last few years, India-UAE ties have been on the upswing, and have been further developed in the post-Covid era, especially on the economic front. Despite the small size of India's oil and gas firms, *Adnoc* (UAE) in a joint venture with *Aramco* (Saudi Arabia) has been working on a refinery and chemical complex, and a renewable-powered green petrochemicals plant in India (Gnana, 2020). India is also part of the Gulf diversification strategy, and *Masdar* of the UAE has invested in India's Hero Future Energies to develop renewable-energy projects (Mills, 2020). India offers opportunities for foreign investors to invest in sectors such as infrastructure, medical tourism, education and information technology. The success of health diplomacy and the timely dispatch of medical-response teams to the UAE have placed India at the forefront of health diplomacy in the region (Taneja, 2020). India has also invited further investments from the UAE in key sectors of the Indian economy, such as infrastructure, including logistics, food parks, highways, ports, airports, renewable energy and defence. Along with exploring the possibility of renewable-energy cooperation, both countries have also tried to

190   *Rhea Abraham*

institutionalise cooperation with the Emirates Nuclear Energy Corporation and Federal Authority for Nuclear Regulation. Another area of cooperation has been in the areas of green energy and climate change under the United Nations Framework Convention for Climate Change, including Masdar's intention to invest in India's solar-energy projects.

Security

In May 2016, Manohar Parrikar became the first Indian Defence Minister to visit the UAE to engage with his UAE counterpart and discuss the possibility of enhancing defence relations. A recent visit by India's Chief of Army Staff to the UAE was also historic, as it was the first ever by the head of the Indian Army to the country to discuss issues of "mutual cooperation" in defence (India, UAE witness soaring relations in 2020, 2020).

In 2017, India and the UAE upgraded their relationship to a "Comprehensive Strategic Partnership" and conducted bilateral defence exercises in India's mega-multi-lateral *Milan* exercise under Joint Defence Cooperation. India is active in its participation in the Indian Ocean Rim Association (IORA) and, for the first time, the UAE Navy confirmed that it would join the *Varuna* naval exercise in the Gulf of Oman (Gupta, 2021). India's naval chief held talks with the UAE's navy to explore ways to strengthen the partnership between the two Navies and they conducted their first bilateral exercise, the Gulf Star I (Singh, 2020). A memorandum of understanding was signed between the Indian Space Research Organisation and the UAE Space Agency for the exploration and use of outer space for peaceful purposes. The cooperation also includes remote sensing and academic interactions. In February 2017, ISRO launched the Emirati satellite Nayif-I (Ningthoujam, 2020). The two countries also hosted a Joint Task Force on the prevention and combating of human trafficking, and cooperate in the fields of money laundering, cyber-crime and terrorist financing.

Soft power

The UAE has been investing heavily in promoting pluralism and tolerance in a cultural and religious sense and fostering cultural diversity in the region. India has been the UAE's partner in synergising its experiences and efforts to promote religious tolerance and integrity (Bhaduri, 2020). The multi-cultural and inter-religious Indian expatriate community present in the UAE is approximately 3.3-million strong and is the largest ethnic community in the region. It constitutes roughly 30 per cent of the UAE's total population. Understanding the role of the diaspora and soft power in bilateral relations, the cultural agreement signed in 1975 provides the basic framework for cultural cooperation between India and the UAE. Prime Minister Modi and Sheikh Mohammed bin Zayed Al Nahyan, both have been instrumental in promoting cultural interaction and intensifying relations since 2015. The executive programme

India and the United Arab Emirates 191

for cultural cooperation was signed in 2016 between the two countries and provides for cultural exchanges between the two countries. India was also the guest of honour at the Abu Dhabi Festival of 2018 and the Abu Dhabi International Book Fair in 2019. Indian films, books, TV shows and yoga are areas of cooperation between India and the UAE. Indians in the UAE, mainly businessmen, have been honoured both in the UAE and in India for being instrumental in promoting India-UAE relations.

India and the UAE signed an MoU for cooperation in the field of manpower to streamline the process of sourcing manpower and information, from India to the UAE. Skill development and educational cooperation were other areas discussed under the Joint Declaration. The UAE recently commissioned an exhibition of India-UAE relations to underline the overlapping aspects of the two cultures at a cultural exhibition in the southern Indian state of Kerala (Ardemagni, 2019).

However, during the pandemic, India was initially reluctant to repatriate migrants from the Gulf due to the risk of a spike in cases in India. However, the UAE threatened to enforce strict restrictions on countries reluctant to take back migrants and threatened to restructure or suspend its MoUs on labour with these countries. This included imposing restrictions on the recruitment of workers from these countries and enforcing a quota system in recruitment operations (Nasrallah, 2020). Amidst mounting concerns, the central government initiated the *Vande Bharat* mission, the largest commercial-evacuation plan for Indian expatriates around the world, coordinated by the Ministry of External Affairs and the Ministry of Civil Aviation, to be conducted in a phased manner. Simultaneously, the Indian government also sent medical teams consisting of doctors, healthcare professionals and nurses to the UAE to provide medical assistance as well as training for responding to COVID-19. In May and June, nearly 500,000 overseas citizens returned to India, with Kerala receiving the largest number—135,000 people—mostly from the UAE (Srivastava, 2020). However, there were also reports of Indian migrant workers staying on throughout the crisis, accepting significantly reduced pay or even no pay to have the opportunity to retain their jobs once the economy improved. The fear of unemployment in India has forced low-skilled migrants to compete for the limited employment opportunities in the UAE, which may push up the migration costs of recruiting agencies.

Regional security as a common goal

India and the UAE have taken their relationship forward to explore cooperation in regional and global forums. Both the leaders of India and the UAE have expended considerable effort to explore the possibility of converting the strategic bilateral relationship into a multi-lateral partnership. This provides an opportunity for the Middle East regional security complex to cooperate with the South Asian regional security complex on multiple issues.

192   Rhea Abraham

Terrorism and anti-piracy cooperation

As India embarks on fostering bilateral relations, multi-lateralism has been an area of individual interest or joint concern for both countries. To this end, India and the UAE have been engaging in separate multi-lateral partnerships with various countries and are engaged in several multi-lateral forums to promote common interests in the region. Both India and the UAE have adopted measures to control international terrorism through multi-lateral partnerships. They have also focused on collaborating in regional organisations to promote multi-lateral engagement, such as the IORA for promoting the economic and security interests of countries in the region, promoting economic development, intensifying defence cooperation and safeguarding shipping lanes from piracy. The UAE is currently the chair of IORA and India has sought deeper maritime relations in the region. The shared interests for both the countries in the Indian Ocean include preserving freedom for commercial shipping navigation; the sustainable use of natural resources; search and rescue operations; countering piracy and smuggling; and managing any competition in the region (Jaishankar, 2016). Similarly, the *Indian Ocean Naval Symposium*, of which both India and the UAE are members, seeks to enhance maritime cooperation among the navies of the littoral states of the Indian Ocean. The main areas of focus include information sharing, maritime security, human-disaster management and interoperability. These regional forums promote a sustainable economy and security complex aligning with each country's perspective on ocean-based security.

Air power

Recently, India had sent its air force to participate in a multi-lateral drill in the Gulf region. The Indian Air Force also participated with the UAE Air Force in bilateral exercises and on humanitarian assistance and disaster relief in 2018. In 2019, an Indian Pavilion was present at the Dubai Air Show in collaboration with the Defence Research Development Organisation (DRDO). Recent reports show the participation of the Indian Air Force in the annual multi-national exercise, "Desert Flag," hosted by the UAE, along with the forces of the US, Saudi Arabia, South Korea, France and Bahrain at the Al Dhafra airbase (Rej, 2021a). Recently, India and the UAE collaborated on negotiating with France to purchase Rafale fighter jets. The UAE's Air Force Airbus transport tankers will provide air-to-air refuelling to these jets on their way to India (*News18*, 2021).

Pakistan

In 2019, India was invited to the Organisation of Islamic Conference summit as a special guest, and the revocation of *Article 370* of the Indian Constitution ending legal autonomy to Kashmir was backed by both Saudi Arabia and the UAE. The UAE, deviating from its usual stance on the

Kashmir issue, conveyed its support and non-interference in the internal matters of India. Pakistan, a traditional ally of the UAE, has been seeing a downwards spiral due to the changing geopolitical dynamics. The decline in bilateral ties and changing attitudes are factors of the newfound relationship of the GCC with Israel and Pakistan's refusal to accept the bonhomie or join the Yemen War in 2015 (Maini, 2020). Pakistan announced that the Muslim countries in the Middle East were not vocal enough in speaking out against the revocation of Kashmir's special status by the Modi government.

Recently, reports were also published suggesting that the UAE had brokered a ceasefire between India and Pakistan (Haidar, 2021). This was not the first time that the UAE had played an important role in securing peace in the region and containing any spillover into Afghanistan or the extended neighbourhood. Reports emerged in 2019 of a possible mediatory role by the UAE to help release an Indian pilot from Pakistani captivity after his plane was shot down by Pakistan (Rej, 2021b). This allows India to scale its regional initiatives on security and promote political moderation in the region (Mohan, 2020). This may even help India to leverage its position during its non-permanent membership and achieve support for a permanent seat at the UN Security Council through support from Arab and non-Arab players in the region. For the UAE, this diplomatic initiative is a soft-power win after the signing of the Abraham Accords, signifying the UAE as a strong regional partner capable of securing peace in South Asia in case of a US withdrawal from the Middle East (Karim, 2021).

Afghanistan

Afghanistan lies at the crossroads of the Middle Eastern and South Asian regional security complexes. Today, both India and the UAE are also involved in the stability and welfare of Afghanistan, cooperation on combating terrorism and providing developmental and infrastructural assistance to the Afghan people and government.

India has been playing a major role in Afghanistan for many years now, and especially with the withdrawal of the US, India's role in the region has only increased. India's Afghanistan policy has always been supportive of an Afghan-led, Afghan-controlled and Afghan-owned peace process. India has strengthened the Afghan army by providing defence equipment and has built roads and schools, as well as the Afghan parliament. India has provided developmental assistance in infrastructure, connectivity, capacity building and humanitarian affairs to Afghanistan. India is the largest non-OECD donor to Afghanistan. It has fostered commercial ties, provides training to the Afghan National Security Forces and provides scholarships to Afghan students. India is also committed to infrastructure projects in Afghanistan (Hanif, 2010). India has invested considerably in Afghanistan, such as in the extraction of minerals and providing connectivity through the Chabahar port and the North-South Transport Corridor (NSTC). The NSTC is a multi-modal

194 *Rhea Abraham*

transportation corridor that links the Persian Gulf to the Indian Ocean and the Caspian Sea. It is intended to ensure the unhindered flow of trade and commerce in the region. Recently, India called for its expansion by including Afghanistan as a member. The Modi government has reiterated its commitment to Afghanistan and may use it as a base for its "Look West" policy to connect with both the Middle East and Central Asia. At present, with the takeover of Taliban, India has continued to engage but is cautiously optimistic including the threat of security over its investments and people in the region.

On the other hand, the UAE and Afghanistan signed a strategic partnership in 2015 for cooperation in various fields of development. The UAE was the only Arab country contributing forces to the mission in Afghanistan, in Helmand province under the International Security Assistance Force. Afghanistan remains a loss in the UAE's list of foreign-policy achievements, as the inclusion of Afghan government representatives in the US-Taliban talks was declined and handed over to Qatar, instead of big players like Saudi Arabia and the UAE. Even in the aftermath of the American withdrawal from Afghanistan, Qatar has become the foreign interlocutor for the Taliban, which took power in September 2021. Similarly, the intra-Afghan dialogue was held in Turkey, another regional rival of the UAE, creating a loss of traditional influence that the UAE has enjoyed over Afghanistan. However, the UAE continues to pursue political and economic ambitions to influence long-term peace and stability in South Asia (Karim, 2021). The UAE had severed diplomatic ties with Afghanistan during the former Taliban regime. However, diplomatic relations were resumed with the opening of an Afghan embassy in the UAE in 2004 to manage consular relations with the Gulf region (Hoath, 2002). The UAE has continued to host the Afghan embassy even after the takeover of the Taliban regime in 2021 and has flown in humanitarian aid to Afghanistan and opened its airports to Afghan refugees (Fontenrose, 2021).

Therefore, both India and the UAE are committed to ending international terrorism coming from Afghanistan and supporting the stability and welfare of Afghanistan. The joint strategic agreement paves the way for this cooperation to ensure coordination in development assistance, infrastructure projects and the strengthening of the Afghan government.

Factors in a multi-lateral approach

The role of China

Chinese interest in the Middle East started to expand in the 1980s and 1990s, mainly to compete against the United States and the Soviet Union in the region and gain international recognition and economic dependence. Chinese think tanks have been conducting research on the Middle East due to the tremendous strategic importance of the region and its sizeable oil reserves and investment opportunities. China, like India, has been careful

India and the United Arab Emirates   195

not to meddle in the internal affairs of the countries of the Middle East, including the Israel-Palestine conflict, or to get involved with any non-state actors in the region. Instead, China has only focused on accessing natural resources, exploring markets for Chinese products and maintaining its power status through bilateral relations in the region. This has been achieved by targeting oil and natural gas commodities and pursuing opportunities for investment and infrastructure projects for Chinese firms in the region.

China's first policy paper on the Arab world, which was published in 2016, helps to coordinate Chinese interests with the OBOR (_"One Belt One Road"_) initiative, through the _1 + 2 + 3_ cooperation pattern, which refers to infrastructural developments and increasing trade ties focusing on aerospace, renewable energy, exploration of oil and gas fields and setting up institutions to encourage bilateral trade, including in the energy and agricultural sectors in the region (Cheraghlou, 2021). The OBOR initiative, inaugurated in 2013, is China's project to increase the economic activity of the Chinese government and strategically connect to Europe through Eurasia. The project is a roadway for China to entrench its naval presence in the Indian Ocean to advance its foreign-policy ambitions to other countries, including India's neighbours. OBOR has changed the traditional understanding of exclusive regional security complex and has allowed China to extend its national interests to the South Asian, Central Asian and Middle Eastern complexes (Tapan, 2021). Another aspect of China's Middle East policy is its objective of maintaining internal harmony and domestic stability within China's Muslim-majority Xinjiang Autonomous Region. This also provides a religious aspect to the otherwise authoritarian Chinese intentions. The Maghreb region has also been of interest to Chinese investors and businesspeople, with forums on China-Africa cooperation and China-Arab states cooperation created in 2000 and 2004, respectively. China has financed major projects and provided loans to governments in the Maghreb. In turn, both Morocco and Tunisia have supported the _"One China"_ policy; however, these North African countries are still dominated by European powers and have developed close relations with the US in recent years (Zoubir, 2020). Chinese engagement with Iran has come as a relief for the latter during US-led sanctions. Recently, both countries signed a 25-year cooperation agreement to boost bilateral trade and safeguard Iran's nuclear deal (_Iran and China sign 25-year cooperation agreement_, 2021). China has also exerted an influence in Turkey, Israel, Egypt and the Lebanese port of Tripoli (Dorsey, 2021).

The Gulf perceives China as a non-revisionist power with an interest-based agenda in the region (Kutty, 2020). China's OBOR initiative has placed the Middle East at the centre of its grand strategy; any development in China-Iran relations will impact China-Pakistan interests and stall India's relations with the region. The OBOR initiative places emphasis on certain South and Central Asian countries such as Myanmar, Pakistan and Kazakhstan and Iran in the Middle Eastern belt as these lie at natural waystations along either the overland or maritime paths and thereby provide

196   *Rhea Abraham*

a strategic dimension to China's interests in the region (Payne, 2016). However, recently trade between the UAE and China has increased considerably, and they are deepening their cooperation in the fields of health, science and technology and investments. The UAE has also collaborated with China in space exploration. The UAE hosts the largest Chinese community in the Middle East. China and the UAE signed a comprehensive strategic partnership in 2018, and the establishment of a Chinese vaccine production base in the UAE for combating the pandemic is an indicator of the strong relations between the two countries. Despite its confrontations with China over border incursions, India has been clear about its intention to continue to engage in a balancing act in multi-lateral engagements such as BRICS, the Shanghai Cooperation Organisation and the Quad, which have larger repercussions for its engagement in the Middle East (Krishnan and Haidar, 2021). China threatens to alter the existing power dynamics in the region in its favour, mainly through its prolonged economic presence, and this is a source of worry for India.

The role of Iran

Iran occupies a significant position in India's Middle East policy, and apart from historical ties, it remains important in terms of economic and geostrategic interests. India has maintained a balancing act regarding Iran, but it was further complicated by the nuclear dispute between the US and Iran and the sanctions imposed. The Joint Comprehensive Plan of Action (JCPOA) between the P5 countries + 1, the EU and Iran in July 2015, posed a challenge to India as it agreed to the verification arrangement. This was mainly to promote peaceful means for the international endorsement to prevent any military option in Iran and allow the resumption of India's energy cooperation with Iran. India had preferred to abstain from voting against Iran; however, India did not want to run afoul of the United States' non-proliferation policies in the Middle East. In 2014, India cut down its dependency on Iran in oil imports, leading to further ramifications for Indo-Iranian cooperation, with the Farzad B gas field slowly coming to a crawl, and the lagging of Iran's Chabahar port, which once promised to circumvent Pakistan and connect India to Afghanistan and Central Asia (Joshi, 2015). Indian companies such as Reliance were brought under the purview of sanctions and pressurised with the denial of a loan from the *United States Exim Bank* for the purchase of US arms equipment (Baghchi, 2009). Companies in India also stopped the export of refined gasoline to Iran, causing a 95 per cent reduction in Iran's refined fuel imports. In 2018, the US announced its withdrawal from the JCPOA with new sanctions on Iran and, in 2019, Iran retaliated by sabotaging tankers and conducting drone attacks on Saudi Arabia's Abqaiq processing facility (*Time to take out our swords'—Inside Iran's plot to attack Saudi Arabia,* 2019).

India and the United Arab Emirates 197

India called for diplomatic action to resolve the dispute. A waiver was granted to India to import 1,250,000 tons of oil per month until March 2019. This exemption was mainly allowed for the development of the Chabahar port, which could help revive Afghanistan's economic prospects. Chabahar can also give India a way to monitor Pakistan and China's naval developments in the Indian Ocean. Despite assurance from the US that it will not interfere with the Chabahar port, US sanctions targeted Iran's ports and shipping facilities, affected India-Iran trade considerably in terms of oil exports, and made it impossible for India to pay in dollars or euros for its imports from Iran (Verma, 2019). This has also been a major irritant in India's relations with the US (Pant, 2020). Earlier on, Iran was apprehensive of India's relations with the Gulf countries, particularly Saudi Arabia and the UAE. India has also maintained good relations with Israel, and this has put additional pressure on India's relationship with Iran.

The Iranian authorities recently criticised India for the revocation of Article 370 of the Indian Constitution, ending legal autonomy to Jammu and Kashmir, and have extended economic engagement with China. India has remained silent on US sanctions on Iran despite the drawbacks, while China and Pakistan have been pursuing competing interests in Iran by denouncing the sanctions. Iran has also not hesitated to leverage China in its policies regarding India, including the possible re-investment of China in the Chabahar port development. This new dynamics between Iran and China threatens to weaken India's leverage with Iran viz a vie the Gulf countries. Despite India's recent renewal of its vow to accelerate the Chabahar port development, India's silence on restarting the halted oil imports from Iran can exacerbate bilateral relations. Recently, considering the Taliban takeover of Afghanistan, Iran hosted a meeting to discuss establishing an inclusive government in Afghanistan. India was not invited to the meeting, while Pakistan, Tajikistan, Uzbekistan, Turkmenistan, China and Russia attended the same (Basu, 2021). India has struggled to implement and maintain a strategy of coherent connectivity (in terms of delayed project funding) in the region, including the Chabahar port. However, India still has time on its side to invest and accelerate its presence in the region and focus on better connectivity with initiatives such as Project Mausam, keeping its promise on the existing port facilities and reaching out to smaller nations in the Indian Ocean.

Bilateral relations

Despite strong bilateral relations, there are some irritants in India-UAE relations, which are marked by domestic constraints within India. These are mainly regarding economic and administration regulation, structural economic issues, lack of strategic planning and procedural issues when it comes to investing in India. The UAE has been insisting on the formalisation of the governance structure of funds in India for speeding up the

198 *Rhea Abraham*

process. Such challenges make China a more conducive partner in terms of economic investments and may be a major issue in bilateral relations between India and the UAE.

Conclusion

The quest to advance India-UAE relations in bilateral and regional initiatives has a newfound level of strategic depth and contributes to the enormous potential for collaboration on multi-lateral forums. There is a mutual recognition between the two countries to use the theory of regional security and multi-lateralism to advance economic interests, add value to south-south cooperation, enhance international partnerships, contribute to the fulfilment of the United Nations Sustainable Development Goals, and ultimately promote peace and security in the region. Although the regional efforts are still new and reaping benefits, the regional approach by India and the UAE focuses on mutual interests and regional stability through political, military and economic partnership (Janardhan, 2018).

Fortuitously for India, the Middle East countries' policies towards India have been delinked from Pakistan and Pakistan no longer dominates Indo-Arab engagements. The loss of Pakistan as a credible security player and uncertainty over the United States' withdrawal from or continuing commitment to the region have helped leverage India's position in the region. The Gulf countries are more focused on looking at India's strategic importance in terms of security and economic benefits. The Indian community has also been a key factor in the renewed relationship between India and the Gulf countries.

Future of regional cooperation

Several ventures are waiting for India-UAE cooperation, such as multi-lateral forums in Africa and Japan's Asia-Africa growth quarter. India-Japan joint ventures open opportunities for the UAE to engage in the recent quadrilateral summit of the US, Australia, India and Japan in the Indo-Pacific region, mainly as a counter to China's rise in the region. This partnership can also provide leverage to the UAE in its economic and strategic investments in Africa. India also conducts joint naval exercises with the US and Australia in the Asia-Pacific to focus on maritime security in the Indian Ocean. Recently, a quadrilateral forum was conducted between US, Israel, the UAE and India announced working groups on religious tolerance, water and energy and focused discussions mainly on economic aspirations and joint infrastructural projects in the Middle East (Alhasan, 2021).

India and the UAE have signed an MoU for development cooperation in Africa, also discussed in the Joint Comprehensive Statement. India's development projects in Africa have been applauded for its prioritisation of the needs of the locals and funding through a sustainable mechanism, and the UAE has been swift in collaborating with India. However, India and the UAE need to

India and the United Arab Emirates 199

combine their technical expertise in the African region and augment food security and quality of living.

The recent pandemic has brought home the sharp reality that security threats have become cross-national and have crossed borders, thereby requiring a regional solution to national problems. The intersection of these cross-border and cross-national challenges therefore requires a multi-lateral approach to empower international governance and institutions. In this regard, despite strengthening bilateral relations, both India and the UAE have taken responsibility to move forward in regional security initiatives and focus on the stage of multi-lateralism in projecting their foreign policy and promoting their image in the international security environment.

Notes

1 For India, the nomenclature 'Middle East' is a politically insensitive one as it connects to its European colonial legacy and geopolitical imagination. Officially, India has recognised the strategic region of the Middle East as West Asia (comprising the Persian Gulf, the Levant region and North Africa) in all documents and has been promoting the term enthusiastically. Unfortunately, the popularity of the term in the academic literature is limited to Asia and is unable to connect with the Western intelligentsia. However, Indian scholars are optimistic that in the coming years, a rising India in the Middle East may be able to influence academics and policymakers to shift to the geographical reality of the region.

2 Operation Raahat was the relief operation conducted by the Government of India to evacuate Indian nationals to India from Yemen during the Yemen Crisis in 2015.

References

Gulf News (2015). 'India, UAE set up joint business council', 4 September [Online]. Available at: https://gulfnews.com/business/india-uae-set-up-joint-business-council-1.1578273 (Accessed: 3 July 2021)

Gulf News (2019). 'The golden era of UAE-India relations', 26 January [Online]. Available at: https://gulfnews.com/uae/the-golden-era-of-uae-india-relations-1.1548240539461 (Accessed: 30 June 2021)

Reuters (2019). 'Time to take out our swords' - Inside Iran's plot to attack Saudi Arabia', 25 November [Online]. Available at: https://www.reuters.com/article/us-saudi-aramco-attacks-iran-special-rep-idUSKBN1XZ16H (Accessed: 26 June 2021)

The Economic Times (2020). 'India-UAE soaring relations in 2020', 26 December [Online]. Available at: https://economictimes.indiatimes.com/news/international/uae/india-uae-witness-soaring-relations-in-2020/articleshow/79965737.cms?utm_source=contentofinterest&utm_medium=text&utm_campaign=cppst (Accessed: 26 June 2021)

Business Standard (2021). 'In a first, Air Force to participate in Exercise Desert Flag VI in UAE', 2 March [Online]. Available at: https://www.business-standard.com/article/current-affairs/in-a-first-air-force-to-participate-in-exercise-desert-flag-vi-in-uae-121030201282_1.html (Accessed: 2 July 2021)

200 Rhea Abraham

Reuters (2021). 'Iran and China sign 25-year cooperation agreement', 27 March [Online]. Available at: https://www.reuters.com/article/us-iran-china-idUSKBN-2BJ0AD (Accessed: 2 July 2021)

News18 (2021). '3 more Rafale Jets to arrive in India from France today, UAE to provide mid-air refeling', 5 May [Online]. Available at: https://www.news18.com/news/india/3-more-rafale-jets-to-arrive-in-india-from-france-today-evening-uae-to-provide-mid-air-refuelling-3709778.html (Accessed: 2 July 2021)

Ahmad, Sayyid Maqbul. (1969). *India and the Arab World: Proceedings of the Seminar on India and the Arab World*, (New Delhi: Indian Council for Cultural Relations)

Alhasan, Hasan. (2021). *Is India abandoning Iran for a Middle Eastern Quad, or Merely Signaling China?* [Online]. Available at: https://agsiw.org/is-india-abandoning-iran-for-a-middle-eastern-quad-or-merely-signaling-china/ (Accessed: 6 November 2021)

Ammar, Radwa. (2020). 'Private Military and Security Companies and Regional Security Governance: An interpretive perspective of the United Arab Emirates policies', *Journal of Politics and Economics*, 7(6), 1–33 [Online]. Available at: https://jocu.journals.ekb.eg/article_128643.html (Accessed: 30 June 2021)

Ardemagni, Eleonora. (2019). *The Geopolitics of Tolerance: Inside the UAE's Cultural Rush* [Online]. Available at: https://www.ispionline.it/en/pubblicazione/geopolitics-tolerance-inside-uaes-cultural-rush-22155 (Accessed: 30 June 2021)

———. (2020). *The UAE's Military Training-Focused Foreign Policy* [Online]. Available at: https://carnegieendowment.org/sada/83033 (Accessed: 25 June 2021)

Baghchi, Indrani. (2009). 'US sanctions on Iran may hit RIL', *The Economic Times*, 29 April, [Online]. Available at: https://economictimes.indiatimes.com/industry/energy/oil-gas/us-sanctions-on-iran-may-hit-ril/articleshow/4461989.cms?from=mdr (Accessed: 30 June 2021)

Barendse, Rene Jan. (2000).'Trade and State in the Arabian Seas: A Survey from the Fifteenth to the Eighteenth Century', *Journal of World History*, 11 (2), 173–225 [Online]. Available at: https://www.jstor.org/stable/20078849 (Accessed: 30 June 2021)

Baru, Sanjaya. (2015). 'The sprouting of the "Look West" policy', *The Hindu*, 19 August [Online]. Available at: https://www.thehindu.com/opinion/lead/sanjaya-baru-writes-the-sprouting-of-the-look-west-policy/article7554403.ece (Accessed: 30 June 2021)

Basu, Nayanima. (2021). 'Iran expects 'friend' India to resume oil purchases soon, says envoy Chegeni', *The Print*, 1 November, [Online]. Available at: https://theprint.in/diplomacy/iran-expects-friend-india-to-resume-oil-purchases-soon-says-envoy-chegeni/759669/ (Accessed: 10 December 2021)

Bhaduri, Aditi. (2020). 'The UAE and India: Lessons to learn', *The Tribune*, 7 April [Online]. Available at: https://www.tribuneindia.com/news/comment/the-uae-and-india-lessons-to-learn-66936 (Accessed: 30 June 2021)

Blarel, Nicolas. (2021). 'Modi looks West? Assessing change and continuity in India's Middle East policy since 2014', *International Politics* [Online]. Available at: https://doi.org/10.1057/s41311-021-00314-3 (Accessed: 30 June 2021)

Brewster, David. (2013). *India: Regional Net Security Provider* [Online]. Available at: https://www.gatewayhouse.in/india-regional-net-security-provider/ (Accessed: 2 July 2021)

Chandra, Ramesh. (2003). 'Global Terrorism: Foreign Policy in the New Millennium', in Ramesh Chandra (ed.) *Global Terrorism: Foreign Policy in the Age of Terrorism*, (New Delhi: Kalpaz Publications)

India and the United Arab Emirates   201

Chaudhuri, Pramit Pal. (2017). *Think West to Go West: Origins and Implications of India's West Asia Policy Under Modi (Part II)* [Online]. Available at: https://www. mei.edu/publications/think-west-go-west-origins-and-implications-indias-west-asia-policy-under-modi-part-ii (Accessed: 5 November 2021)

Cheraghlou, Amin Mohseni. (2021). *MENA at the center of the West: China's opening up to the West Strategy* [Online]. Available at: https://www.mei.edu/publications/ mena-center-west-chinas-opening-west-strategy (Accessed: 5 November 2021)

Crabb Jr, Cecil V. (1972). *American Foreign Policy in the Nuclear Age*, (New York: Harper & Row)

Dorsey, James M. (2021). 'Looming large: The Middle East braces for fallout of US–China divide', *WION News,* 14 January [Online]. Available at: https://www. wionews.com/opinions-blogs/opinion-looming-large-the-middle-east-braces-for-fallout-of-us-china-divide-356710 (Accessed: 5 November 2021)

Fontenrose, Kirsten. (2021). *What the Arab Gulf Is Thinking after the Afghanistan Withdrawal Provider* [Online]. Available at: https://www.atlanticcouncil.org/ blogs/new-atlanticist/what-the-arab-gulf-is-thinking-after-the-afghanistan-withdrawal/ (Accessed: 5 November 2021)

Government of India, Ministry of External Affairs. (2018) *India-UAE Joint Statement during State Visit of the Prime Minister of India to UAE (February 10–11, 2018)* [Online]. Available at: https://mea.gov.in/bilateral-documents.htm?dtl/29476/ IndiaUAE+Joint+Statement+during+State+Visit+of+the+Prime+Minister+ of+India+to+UAE+February+1011+2018 (Accessed: 30 June 2021)

———. (2020). *India-UAE Bilateral Relations* [Online]. Available at: http://www. mea.gov.in/Portal/ForeignRelation/uae-august-2012.pdf (Accessed: 25 June 2021)

Gnana, Jennifer. (2020). 'No plans to scale back Adnoc-Aramco backed Indian refinery, minister says', *The National*, 13 October [Online]. Available at https:// www.thenationalnews.com/business/energy/no-plans-to-scale-back-adnoc-aramco-backed-indian-refinery-minister-says-1.1093156 (Accessed: 5 November 2021)

Grabowski, Wojciech. (2020). 'Application of the Regional Security Complex Theory for Security Analysis in the Persian Gulf', *Athenaeum Polskie Studia Politologiczne*, 68(4), 18–31 [Online]. Available at: https://czasopisma.marszalek. com.pl/images/pliki/apsp/68/apsp6802.pdf (Accessed: 30 June 2021)

Gupta, Shishir. (2021). 'Deepening India-UAE Defence cooperation enlarges India's footprint in West Asia', *Hindustan Times*, 15 March [Online]. Available at: https:// www.hindustantimes.com/analysis/deepening-india-uae-defence-cooperation-enlarges-india-s-footprint-in-west-asia-101615786054363.html (Accessed: 2 July 2021)

Haidar, Suhasini. (2021). 'India should make a move for peace, says Imran Khan', *The Hindu,* 17 March [Online]. Available at: https://www.thehindu.com/news/ international/peace-with-pakistan-will-give-india-direct-access-to-central-asia-says-imran-khan/article34091175.ece (Accessed: 2 July 2021)

Hanif, Melanie. (2010). 'Indian Involvement in Afghanistan in the Context of the South Asian Security System', *Journal of Strategic Security*, 3(2), 13–26 [Online]. Available at: http://dx.doi.org/10.5038/1944-0472.3.2.2 (Accessed: 30 June 2021)

Harn, Jessica. (2017). *An Introduction to the UAE's History with India* [Online]. Available at: https://theculturetrip.com/middle-east/united-arab-emirates/articles/ an-introduction-to-the-uaes-history-with-india/ (Accessed: 30 June 2021)

Hoath, Nissar. (2002). 'Afghanistan set to open embassy', *Gulf News*, 5 March [Online]. Available at: https://gulfnews.com/uae/afghanistan-set-to-open-embassy-1.380059 (Accessed: 2 July 2021)

202 *Rhea Abraham*

Jaishankar, Dhruva. (2016). *Indian Ocean region: A Pivot for India's Growth* [Online]. Available at: https://www.brookings.edu/opinions/indian-ocean-region-a-pivot-for-indias-growth/ (Accessed: 2 July 2021)

Janardhan, Narayanappa. (2018). 'How India and the UAE can benefit from a joint multilateral strategy', *The Diplomat* [Online]. Available at: https://thediplomat.com/2018/02/how-india-and-the-uae-can-benefit-from-a-joint-multilateral-strategy/ (Accessed: 2 July 2021)

Jarząbek, Jarosław. (2018). 'The Theory of Regional Security Complexes in the Middle Eastern Dimension', *Wschodnioznawstwo*, 12, 155–170 [Online]. Available at: http://cejsh.icm.edu.pl/cejsh/element/bwmeta1.element.desklight-04b92a93-42fd-439d-b10b-4f04b1c4ebe6 (Accessed: 30 June 2021)

Jayapalan, N. (2001). *The Foreign Policy of India*, (New Delhi: Atlantic Publishers and Distributors)

Joshi, Shashank. (2015), 'India and the Middle East', *Asian Affairs*, 46 (2), 251–269 [Online]. Available at: https://shashankjoshi.files.wordpress.com/2009/12/asian-affairs-india-and-the-middle-east.pdf (Accessed: 30 June 2021)

Karim, Umer. (2021). *The United Arab Emirates and A South Asian Peace Process* [Online]. Available at: https://agsiw.org/the-united-arab-emirates-and-a-south-asian-peace-process/ (Accessed: 2 July 2021)

Khushnam, P.N. (2021). *India-UAE Relations: Poised to Climb to New Heights* [Online]. Available at: https://www.mei.edu/publications/india-uae-relations-poised-climb-new-heights (Accessed: 25 June 2021)

Koch, Bettina, & Stivachtis, Yannis A. (2019). *Regional Security in the Middle East: Sectors, Variables and Issues* [Online]. Available at: https://www.e-ir.info/publication/regional-security-in-the-middle-east-sectors-variables-and-issues/ (Accessed: 30 June 2021)

Kostiner, Joseph. (1993). *The Making of Saudi Arabia 1916-1936: From Chieftaincy to Monarchical State*, (New York: Oxford University Press)

Krishnan, Ananth, & Haidar, Suhasini. (2021). 'New phase of U.S.-China ties comes with tests for India', *The Hindu*, 19 March [Online]. Available at: https://www.thehindu.com/news/international/new-phase-of-us-china-ties-comes-with-tests-for-india/article34111961.ece (Accessed: 2 July 2021)

Kutty, Sumitha Narayanan. (2020). *India's China crisis: Why the Gulf is silent* [Online]. Available at: https://www.orfonline.org/expert-speak/india-china-crisis-why-gulf-silent/ (Accessed: 2 July 2021)

Lal, Brij Vilash. (2006). *The Encyclopaedia of the Indian Diaspora*, (Honolulu: University of Hawaii Press)

Maini, Tridivesh Singh. (2020). *Shifting Sands: Pakistan and the Gulf Co-Operation Council* [Online]. Available at: https://www.futuredirections.org.au/publication/shifting-sands-pakistan-and-the-gulf-co-operation-council/ (Accessed: 2 July 2021)

Miller, Rory, & Verhoeven, Harry. (2020). 'Overcoming Smallness: Qatar, the United Arab Emirates and Strategic Realignment in the Gulf', *International Politics*, 57, 1–20 [Online]. Available at: https://doi.org/10.1057/s41311-019-00180-0 (Accessed: 2 July 2021)

Mills, Robin. (2020). 'How the Middle East can help balance India balance energy demand with sustainability', *The National*, 9 February [Online]. Available at: https://www.thenationalnews.com/business/comment/how-the-middle-east-can-help-india-balance-energy-demand-with-sustainability-1.975989 (Accessed: 25 June 2021)

Mohan, C. Raja. (2020). 'India's geopolitical interests are in close alignment with moderate Arab centre', *The Hindu* [Online]. Available at: https://indianexpress.com/article/opinion/columns/narendra-modi-arab-gulf-countries-middle-east-relations-c-raja-mohan-6558876/ (Accessed: 25 June 2021)

Murray, Robert W. (2012). *The Role of National Leaders in Foreign Policy* [Online]. Available at: https://www.e-ir.info/2012/11/07/the-role-of-national-leaders-in-foreign-policy/ (Accessed: 25 June 2021)

Nasrallah, Tawfiq. (2020). 'COVID-19: UAE considers imposing restrictions on these countries', *Gulf News* [Online]. Available at: https://gulfnews.com/uae/government/covid-19-uae-considers-imposing-restrictions-on-these-countries-1.1586688517978 (Accessed: 30 June 2021)

Ningthoujam, Alvite. (2020). 'Taking India-Gulf cooperation into space', *The Diplomat* [Online]. Available at: https://thediplomat.com/2020/07/taking-india-gulf-cooperation-into-space/ (Accessed: 30 June 2021)

Pant, Harsh V. (2020). *India's Middle East Conundrum* [Online]. Available at: https://www.orfonline.org/expert-speak/indias-middle-east-conundrum-60032/ (Accessed: 6 November 2021)

Payne, Jeffrey S. (2016). *The G.C.C. and China's One Belt, One Road: Risk or Opportunity?* [Online]. Available at: https://www.mei.edu/publications/gcc-and-chinas-one-belt-one-road-risk-or-opportunity (Accessed: 6 November 2021)

Pulipaka, Sanjay, & Musaddi, Mohit. (2020). 'Power shifts and re-calibrations: India and the Gulf', *The Economic Times* [Online]. Available at: https://economictimes.indiatimes.com/blogs/et-commentary/power-shifts-and-re-calibrations-india-and-the-gulf/ (Accessed: 25 June 2021)

Rej, Abhijnan. (2021a). 'Indian Air Force takes part in multination exercise hosted by UAE', *The Diplomat* [Online]. Available at: https://thediplomat.com/2021/03/indian-air-force-takes-part-in-multination-exercise-hosted-by-uae/ (Accessed: 30 June 2021)

———. (2021b). 'UAE brokered India-Pakistan Ceasefire: Report', *The Diplomat* [Online]. Available at: https://thediplomat.com/2021/03/uae-brokered-india-pakistan-ceasefire-report/ (Accessed: 2 July 2021)

Rourke, John T. (2007). *International Politics on the World Stage*, (New York: McGraw-Hill Publishers)

Saab, Bilal Y. (2021). *The Roadblocks to a Regional Security Dialogue in the Middle East* [Online]. Available at: https://www.mei.edu/sites/default/files/2021-04/The%20Roadblocks%20to%20a%20Regional%20Security%20Dialogue%20in%20the%20Middle%20East.pdf (Accessed: 30 June 2021)

Salisbury, Peter. (2020). *Risk Perception and Appetite in UAE Foreign and National Security Policy.* [Online]. Available at: https://doi.org/10.1515/sirius-2020-4015 (Accessed: 30 June 2021)

Sekhri, Sofiane. (2009). 'The Role Approach as a Theoretical Framework for the Analysis of Foreign Policy in Third World Countries', *African Journal of Political Science and International Relations*, 3 (10), 423–432. [Online]. Available at: https://academicjournals.org/journal/AJPSIR/article-full-text-pdf/FCD3D6340543 (Accessed: 30 June 2021)

Sen Gupta, Joydeep. (2021). 'UAE-India ties became stronger since Covid-19: Envoy', *The Khaleej Times* [Online]. Available at: https://www.khaleejtimes.com/news/uae-india-ties-became-stronger-since-covid-19-envoy (Accessed: 30 June 2021)

204 *Rhea Abraham*

Singh, Abhijit. (2020). *India's Evolving Maritime Posture in the Indian Ocean: Opportunities for the Gulf* [Online]. Available at: https://www.agda.ac.ae/docs/default-source/Publications/eda-insight-aug-2020-eng-abhijit.pdf?sfvrsn=4 (Accessed: 2 July 2021)

Singh, Meena, & Muddassir Quamar, Roy. (2017). 'India—UAE relations: New dimension to strategic partnership', *IDSA Issue Brief* [Online]. Available at: https://idsa.in/issuebrief/india-uae-relations_msroy_170217 (Accessed: 25 June 2021)

Srivastava, Roli. (2020). 'Milking their misery: Indian state makes returning migrants pay for quarantine', *Reuters,* 22 July [Online]. Available at: https://www.reuters.com/article/us-health-coronavirus-india-migrants-trf/milking-their-misery-indian-state-makes-returning-migrants-pay-for-quarantine-idUSKCN24N1QR (Accessed: 25 June 2021)

Suri, Navdeep. (2020). *Between Two IPLs, a Relationship Blossomed* [Online]. Available at: https://www.orfonline.org/research/between-two-ipls-a-relationship-blossomed/ (Accessed: 25 June 2021)

Swami, Praveen. (2020). 'India's shooting its new opportunities in West Asia through the back of the head', *CNBC,* 29 April [Online]. Available at: https://www.cnbctv18.com/views/indias-shooting-its-new-opportunities-in-west-asia-through-the-back-of-the-head-5794821.htm (Accessed: 25 June 2021)

Taneja, Kabir. (2020). 'Decoding India's latest diplomatic push in the West Asian theatre', *Hindustan Times,* 9 December [Online]. Available at: https://www.hindustantimes.com/analysis/decoding-india-s-latest-diplomatic-push-in-the-west-asian-theatre-opinion/story-RoTBWrjp3P7jdMvDfAxtIN.html (Accessed: 25 June 2021)

Taneja, Kabir. (2021). *What the UAE Hopes to Achieve in between India and Pakistan* [Online]. Available at: https://www.orfonline.org/expert-speak/what-the-uae-hopes-to-achieve-in-between-india-and-pakistan/ (Accessed: 25 June 2021)

Tapan, Oorja. (2021). 'How relevant is Barry Buzan's regional security complex theory in today's South Asia and beyond?', *The Kootneeti* [Online]. Available at: https://thekootneeti.in/2021/08/19/how-relevant-is-barry-buzans-regional-security-complex-theory-in-todays-south-asia-and-beyond/ (Accessed: 6 November 2021)

Tesorero, Angel. (2017). 'UAE-India: A partnership that dates back centuries', *Khaleej Times* [Online]. Available at: https://www.khaleejtimes.com/uae-india-ties/uae-india-a-partnership-that-dates-back-centuries (Accessed: 30 June 2021)

Vakil, Sanam, & Quilliam, Neil. (2021). *Steps to Enable a Middle East Regional Security Process* [Online]. Available at: https://www.chathamhouse.org/2021/04/steps-enable-middle-east-regional-security-process/05-engaging-multilaterally (Accessed: 30 June 2021)

Verma, Nidhi. (2019). 'Indian refiners pay for Iranian oil in rupees - UCO Bank executive', 8 January Available at: https://www.reuters.com/article/us-india-iran-payment-exclusive-idUSKCN1P21XF (Accessed: 30 June 2021)

Waever, Ole. (2017). 'International Leadership after the Demise of the Last Superpower: System Structure and Stewardship', *Chinese Political Science Review*, 2, 452–276 [Online]. Available at: https://doi.org/10.1007/s41111-017-0086-7 (Accessed: 3 November 2021)

Zoubir, Yahia H. (2020). *Expanding Sino-Maghreb Relations: Morocco and Tunisia* [Online]. Available at: https://www.chathamhouse.org/sites/default/files/CHHJ7839-SinoMaghreb-Relations-WEB.pdf (Accessed: 30 June 2021)

Index

Note: Folios followed by "n" refers notes and **bold** tables.

Abbasi, Shahid Khaqan 41, 52
Abdul Aziz (King) 73, 153–154, 158–159
Abdulaziz, Salman bin 119
Abdullah (Crown Prince) 156, 164
al-'Abidin, Zain 4
Abraham Peace Accords 11, 39, 40, 46, 54–56
Abu Dhabi National Oil Company (ADNOC) 189
Afghanistan 5, 8, 9, 10, 64, 65, 156, 158–159, 193–194
Afghanistan-Pakistan (Af-Pak) 47
Africa 4, 20, 115, 122, 182, 198–199
Ahamed, E. 26
Ahmad, T. 1, 17, 18
Ahmadinejad, Mahmoud 64, 69
air power 192
Alawi, Yusuf bin 138, 140
Ali, A. 108
All India Muslim League 153
Al-Qaeda 117
Analytical History of Terrorism (Shughart II) 115
Ansari, Mohammad Hamid 73
anti-Houthi coalition 50
Arab Gulf 8, 18, 22, 25, 29, 30
Arabian Peninsula 8, 9
Arab League 136–137
Arafat, Yasser 116
Aramco (Saudi Arabia) 189
Article 370 192
Asad, Muhammad 154
Ashrafi, Tahir 171
Asif, Khawaja 51
Azani, E. 117
Aziz, Bin Abdul 158–159
Aziz, Sartaj 53

Baghdad Pact in 1955 154
Bahmani, Ahmad 2
Bahmani, Ahmad II 2
Bahmani, Firuz 2
Al-Bahr, Naseem 166
Bahrain 4–5, 11, 12, 39, 41, 43–44, 86, 94
Bahria (Naval) Foundation 43
Bajwa, Qamar Javed 49, 52, 54, 161, 163, 169
Bandaranaike, S.W.R.D. 110
Bangladesh 8, 12, 82–97; bilateral relations with Gulf countries 95–97; and Gulf countries 88–95; regional security architecture in Gulf 86–87; security and complex interdependence in the 21st century 84–86; standard-bearer of South Asia 87–97
Bangladesh Armed Forces 95
Bangladesh War of Independence 145
Belt and Road Initiative (BRI) 65, 85
Berger, L. 118
Bharatiya Janata Party (BJP) 1, 16
Bhutan 4, 8
Bhutto, Zulfiqar Ali 155–156, 157–158
Biden, Joe 16, 119
Biden administration 23
bilateral defence relations 42
bilateral relations 13–14, 28, 44, 49, 90, 92, 138–139, 197–198
bilateral ties in crisis, Pakistan and Saudi Arabia 169–171
bin-Abdul-Aziz, Salman 73
Bishku, M. B. 108
Black September Organization 116
Blarel, N. 18
Bohingamuwa, W. 108

206 *Index*

Brahmins 4
buffer state 5
Burton, G. 17
Bushire Residency 5
Buzan, Barry 6–9, 18–21, 23, 32, 40, 105–109, 126n1, 181

Cameron, David 126n2
Central Asia 4, 64
Central Treaty Organization (CENTO) 63
Chabahar-Zahedan rail project 28
Chaudhuri, P. P. 17–18
Chebab, Zaki 126n2
China 1, 19, 20, 65, 67, 72, 73, 142, 147, 195–198
China-Pakistan Economic Corridor (CPEC) 9, 46, 65, 169
Chomsky, Noam 126n2
climate change in Sri Lanka 120–125, **123**
CO_2 emissions 124
collective security order 106
competitive interdependence 84
complex interdependence 12, 82–97
concert security order 107
Cook, Jonathan 126n2
coronavirus pandemic 20, 82

Deccani Muslims 2–3
Deccan Plateau 2–3
defence cooperation, Pakistan and Saudi Arabia 165–167
Defence Research Development Organisation (DRDO) 192
Defence Services Command & Staff College (DSCSC) 95
Delhi 2, 11, 18, 20, 63–64, 74–77
Delhi Declaration 73
Deva Raya II (King) 3
de Wilde, Jaap 105

East India Company 4–5
Eaton, R. M. 1
economic cooperation, Pakistan and Saudi Arabia 167–168
Economic Cooperation Organization (ECO) 71
economics, India and United Arab Emirates 188–190
Erdogan, Tayyip 170
European Coal and Steel Community (ECSC) 84

Exclusive Agreements 5–6
expatriates, Oman 132–135, 141

Fahd (Crown Prince) 155–156, 159
Faisal (King) 41, 155, 157, 165
Al-Faisal, Turki 158
Faisal Mosque 168
Fauji (Army) Foundation 43
Federally Administered Tribal Areas (FATA) 70
foreign direct investments (FDI) 91–92, 131, 189
Foreign Office Consultation (FOC) 94
foreign policy: balanced 53; Bangladesh 92; India 17–21; India and United Arab Emirates 184–187; Iran 66; Oman 143–147; Pakistan 75
France 5, 6, 84, 192
Frazier, D. 106
Free and Open Indo-Pacific (FOIP) 85
Free-Trade Agreement 43
fundamental complementarities 26
Future Investment Initiative (FII) 169

Gandhi, Indira 135
Gandhi, Rajiv 132
Ganguly, S. 18
Ganji, Sadegh 69
Ganor, B. 117
Gargash, Anwar Mohammed 49, 51
Gawan, Mahmud 2
General Trade Agreement 92
Germany 5, 84
Ghani, Ashraf 9
gharbian (Westerners) 2
Gignoux, S. 121
great powers 7, 11, 17–27, 31, 32, 95
greenhouse gas emissions 122, 124, 125
gross domestic product (GDP) 90, 107, 120, 144
Gulf, Iran and Israel (GII) 12; in Sri Lanka 107–109
Gulf, relations with India 23–30
Gulf Cooperation Council (GCC) 1, 39–41, 45–49, 50–54, 141, 193
Gulf Information Technology Exhibition (GITEX) 92
Gulf War 13, 86, 93, 95, 96, 158–159

Hadi, Abdrabbuh Mansur 50
Haji-Yousefi, A. Mohammad 67
Al-Hajri, Abdul Hadi Mana 52
Hamadani, 'Ali 3

Index 207

Hamadani, Saiyid Muhammad 3
Hameed, A.C.S 111
hegemonic security order 106, 107
Hindu Vaishnava 1
Honardoost, Mehdi 67
housemaid migration 113, 114
Humaid, Saleh Bin 41
Hussain, Saddam 52
Hussain, Z. 17–18, 22

Ibn Batuta 2
Imam-e-Kaaba 41
India 1, 8–9, 16–33, 199n1; diplomacy
    between Arab Gulf 30; economy of
    26; foreign policy 17–21; and Iran
    162–165; Iran and 63–67; and Oman
    131–132, 145–146; paradigm shift
    21–23; regional security in Gulf and
    181–182; relations with Gulf 23–30;
    relations with Pakistan 48–50
India and United Arab Emirates
    180–199; Afghanistan 193–194;
    air power 192; bilateral relations
    197–198; China 194–196; econom-
    ics 188–190; historical ties 183–184;
    Iran 196–197; leadership and
    foreign policy 184–187; multi-lateral
    approach 194–198; Pakistan 192–193;
    politics 187–188; regional cooper-
    ation 198–199; regional security
    180–183, 191–194; security 190; soft
    power 190–191; strategic partnership
    184–191; terrorism and anti-piracy
    cooperation 192
Indian Air Force 192
Indian Empire 5–6
Indian Ministry of External Affairs
    (MEA) 23–24
Indian Ocean Rim Association
    (IORA) 190
India-Saudi ties 164–165
India-UAE: relations 13–14, 30, 185,
    187–191; strategic partnership 18
India-US nuclear deal 25–26
Indo-Pacific Strategy (IPS) 85
instinctively multipolar 26
International Atomic Energy
    Agency 25
International Federation of the
    Indo-Israel Chambers of Commerce
    (IFIICC) 189
International Islamic University (IIU)
    167–168

international relations (IR) 82, 84–86
interpersonal relations, Pakistan and
    Saudi Arabia 153–157
Inter-Services Intelligence (ISI) 158
Inter-Services Public Relations (ISPR)
    147
Iran 2, 3, 4, 24, 62–77, 196–197; and
    India 162–165; India and 63–67;
    nuclear programme 25; Pakistan
    and 68–71; Pakistan relations with
    19, 46–48; Persian Gulf and 71–76;
    relations with Pakistan 46–48
Iranian Revolution of 1979 63, 116
Iran-Pakistan relations 162–163
Iraq 2, 5, 7, 40, 42, 63, 89, 108, 110,
    118, 121
ISIS 115, 117–120, 125
Islamabad 39, 63
Islamic Military Alliance to Fight
    Terrorism (IMAFT) 11, 42
Islamic Military Counter Terrorism
    Coalition (IMCTC) 160
Islamic Revolution of Iran 158
Islamic State in Iraq and Syria (ISIS)
    115, 117–120, 125
Israel 22, 107–111, 116–117, 119, 120,
    122, 124, 126n1

Jagran-IV Hydropower Project 167
Jammu and Kashmir (J&K) 18, 40, 45,
    47, 49, 56, 169, 197
Jarząbek, Jarosław 119
Jasim, Hamad Bin 161
Jayewardena, J. R. 111
Jinnah, Quaid-e-Azam Muhammad
    Ali 153
Joint Comprehensive Plan of Action
    (JCPOA) 16, 27–28, 31–32, 46, 196
Joint Military Cooperation Committee
    (JMCC) 167
Joint Ministerial Commission
    (JMC) 168
Al-Jubeir, Adel 73, 165

Kashmir 8
Khalid (King) 155
Khalifa, Hamad Bin Isa Al 43
Al-Khalifa, Salman bin Hamad 43
al-Khalili, Ahmad bin Hamad 146
Khalilzad, Zalmay 161
Khan, Abdul Qadeer 66
Khan, Ali Muhammad 55
Khan, Ayub 157

208 *Index*

Khan, Imran 48, 52, 55, 56, 57n1, 70, 75, 161, 163, 165, 168–170
Khan, Isma'il 3
Khan, Khizr 2
Khan, Sahibzada Yaqub 156
Khan, Yusuf 'Adil 2–3
Khashoggi, Jamal 169
Khatami, Mohammad 23, 24
Khomeini, Ayatollah 75
Khurshid, S. 25–27
Kindt, M. T. 116
King Salman Humanitarian Aid and Relief Center (KSrelief) 96
Kiribamune, S. 108
Krampe, F. 121
kulah 3
kullayi 3
Kumar, Mridul 29
Kuwait 4, 5, 18, 93–96; Pakistan relations with 44–45
Kuwait Foreign Petroleum Exploration Company (KUFPEC) 45

Laden, Osama Bin 117–118
Lake, D. 106
Lashkar-e-Jhangvi 69
leaderships: India and United Arab Emirates 184–187; Pakistan and Saudi Arabia 153–157
Liberation Tigers of Tamil Eelam (LTTE) 114
liquid natural gas (LNG) 44, 93, 161
Lower Gulf Agency 5

Madhava 1
Mahabharata 3
Mahajan, S. 1, 5
Malayali 4
malik al-tujjar (prince of merchants) 2
Maoists 27
MBZ and regional aspirations 185–186
Memorandum of Understanding (MoU) 95, 135, 140, 145, 147, 167, 191, 198
merger 19
migration, Sri Lanka 112–114, **112**
Modi, Narendra 10, 13, 16–18, 20, 22, 29, 31, 49, 64, 145, 181, 190; pragmatic look west policy 186–187; trip to UAE 30
Modi administration 22, 23
Modi government 28, 29
Mohammadally, Safia 68
Mohan, C. R. 17, 18, 22
Morgan, P. 106

Muhammad, Ghulam 154
Mukherjee, Pranab 26
Musharraf, Pervez 42, 49, 165
Muslim Brotherhood 117
Myanmar 8, 141–142, 195

Nahyan, Mohammed Bin Zayed Al 14, 181, 187, 190
Narasimha, Rao 67
Naravane, N. M. 164
Narouei, Hadi 67
Nehru, Jawaharlal 26, 63, 154, 157
Nepal 4–5, 8, 27
Netanyahu, Benjamin 119
New Delhi 62, 63
Nimbarka 1
al-Nimr, Nimr 48
Non-Aligned Movement (NAM) 89
Noon, Malik Feroz Khan 153, 154
normal politics 105
North Atlantic Treaty Organization (NATO) 84
Nuclear Non-Proliferation Treaty (NPT) 66, 87
nuclear programme 9, 25, 31, 64, 66
Nujum al-'Ulum (Stars of the Sciences) (Shah) 3

Oman 130–148; expatriates 132–135, 141; external affairs 5; foreign policy 143–147; growing ties 138–141; and India 12, 131–132, 145–146; and Pakistan 12, 45–46, 136–141, 146–147; political and military ties 134–135; relations with South Asian Security Complex (SASC) 141–143
Omanibalancing 143
One Belt One Road (OBOR) 195
One China policy 195
ONGC Videsh Ltd 28
Onley, J. 1, 5–6
open-air prison 121, 127n2
Operation Raahat 187, 199n2
Operation Reconstruction Kuwait (ORK) 96
Operation Sankalp 74
Organisation of Islamic Cooperation 29, 89, 152
Organization of Islamic Conference (OIC) 165
Organization of Islamic Countries 66
Ottoman Empire 5
overseas development assistance (ODA) 90

Index 209

P5+1 Nuclear Agreement 119
Pahlavi, Mohammad Reza 68
Pakistan 1, 7–9, 39–57, 192–193; defense minister 173n5; disturbances in 50–56; India relations with 48–50; Iran and 68–71; and Oman 45–46, 136–141, 146–147; relations with Bahrain 43–44; relations with Gulf States 40–46; relations with Iran 19, 46–48; relations with Kuwait 44–45; relations with Oman 45–46; relations with Qatar 44; relations with Saudi Arabia 19, 41–43; relations with UAE 43; security forces 172n2; security policy 172n1
Pakistan Aeronautical Complex/ Chengdu Aerospace Corporation (PAC/CAC) 45
Pakistan and Saudi Arabia 152–173; bilateral ties in crisis 169–171; current trends 168–171; defence cooperation 165–167; economic cooperation 167–168; history 153–157; interpersonal ties among leaderships 153–157; rapprochement 171; strategic relationship 157–165
Pakistan Armed Forces 88
Pakistani Balochistan 45
Pakistan Muslim League–Nawaz (PML-N) 43
Pakistan Peoples Party (PPP) 43
Pakistan Tehreek-e-Insaf (PTI) 159
Palestine Liberation Organization (PLO) 115, 116
Palestinian Mandate 115
Panamagate 44, 53, 57n1
paradigm shift, India 21–23
Pardesi, M. S. 20, 21, 32
pardesis (foreigners) 4, 131, 182
Parrikar, Manohar 190
Persia Agency 5
Persian Gulf 1, 17, 19, 22, 23; historical connections with South Asia 1–6; Iran and 71–76; security linkages 7–10
Persians 2, 108
Peterson, John E. 137
politics, India and United Arab Emirates 187–188
power restraining power 107
Pradhan, Dharmendra 17, 18, 73
Pradhan, Samir 133
Premadasa, Ranasinghe 114
Pröbsting, M. 20, 21

Prophet Muhammad (PBUH) 1, 16, 18
Protocol Agreement 42
Ptolemy 107
Punjab 2

Qaboos (Sultan) 132, 134–135, 138–139
Qatar 4, 92–93, 194; diplomatic crisis 49; goods and services 53; Pakistan relations with 44; Qatar-Gulf crisis 52–54
Qatar-Gulf crisis 52–54
Quli (Sultan) 3
Qureshi, Shah Mahmood 49, 55, 170
Qutb al-Mulk 3

Al-Rahbi, Saif bin Nasser bin Mohsen 146
Rahman, Mujibur 88
Ramanuja 1
Rao, Nirupama 26
rapprochement, Pakistan and Saudi Arabia 171
Raya, Krishna (King) 3
Raya, Rama (King) 3
al-Razzaq, 'Abd 3
readymade garments (RMG) 92
regional cooperation 198–199
Regional Cooperation for Development (RCD) 71
regional security complexes (RSCs) 6–7, 10, 16, 18–20, 32, 39; Sri Lanka 105–107
remittances 182–183; foreign 90, 92; for Pakistan 41–42; Sri Lanka **112**
Research and Analysis Wing (RAW) 163
Riyadh Declaration of 2010 18, 26, 29
Rizvi, G. 7
Rohingya refugee 12
Rouhani, Hassan 28, 47
Rukh, Shah 2, 3
Russia 2, 5, 9, 95, 182

Sa'id, Ahmad Abu 134, 136
Saiyid dynasty 2
Salman, Mohammed bin 29, 41, 157, 161, 164, 165, 170
Saud, Saud bin Abdulaziz Al 41
Al-Saud, Abdul Aziz 153
Saudi Arabia 8, 9, 17, 24, 26, 29, 71–76; Pakistan relations with 19, 41–43
Saudi Development Fund 167
Saudi Fund for Development (SFD) 91

210 *Index*

Saudi Public Assistance for Pakistan Earthquake Victims (SPAPEV) 167
Sayf, Sultan bin 137
Schuman, Robert 84
Schwartzstein, P. 121
Second World War 68, 86, 115
securitisation, Sri Lanka 105–107
security, India and United Arab Emirates 190
security linkages 7–10
Senanayake, Dudley 110–111
Sepah-e-Sahaba 69
Shah, 'Ali 'Adil 3
Shahid, K. K. 53
Shariah law 138
Sharif, Nawaz 44, 52, 156, 157, 161, 169
Sharif, Raheel 42, 160
Shaw, J. 113
Shi'ism, Ithna 'Ashari 3
Shi'ite Hazara 9
Shughart II, W.F. 115
Sikandar (Sultan) 2
Singh, Karambir 146
Singh, K. R. 22, 23, 25
Singh, Manmohan 18, 164
Singh, S. 20, 21, 30
Sinha, A. 29
Sinha, Y. 24
Sinhala Only Act of 1956 114
Siyech, M. S. 17, 18, 22
soft power, India and United Arab Emirates 190–191
Sonar Bangla 88
South Asia 1, 10, 27; historical connections with Persian Gulf 1–6; security linkages 7–10
South Asian Security Complex (SASC) 8; Oman relations with 141–143
Soviet Union 84, 88
special economic zones (SEZs) 93
Special Services Group (SSG) 166
Sri Lanka 8, 27, 105–126; climate change 120–125, **123**; Gulf, Iran and Israel (GII) and 107–109; migration in 112–114, **112**; regional security complex theory 105–107; securitisation in 105–107; terrorism in 114–120; trade in 109–112; trade relations with GII **109**
Sri Lanka Freedom Party 111
Stewart-Ingersoll, R. 106
strategic relationship, Pakistan and Saudi Arabia 157–165
Subramanian, A. 20

Sufism 1
Sultan of Oman 132
supercomplex 6, 11–12, 17, 19, 32–33, 108
superpowers 8, 17–18, 20, 23
Suri, Navtej 30
Swaraj, Sushma 29

Talal, Waleed Bin 157
Tata Consultancy Services 29
Taymur, Sayyid Fahar bin 135
Tehran 26, 63
Tehreek-e-Taliban Pakistan (TTP) 160
terrorism: and anti-piracy cooperation 192; in Sri Lanka 114–120
Thani, Sheikh Khalifa bin Hamad Al 44
Al-Thani, Hamad Bin Jassim bin Jaber 52
al-Thani, Mohammed bin Abdulrahman 52
Timurid Empire 2
trade in Sri Lanka 109–112
Trofimov, Yaroslav 158
Trump, Donald 16, 65, 72
Trump administration 22, 85
Turki, Taimur bin Faisal bin 143

Umrah pilgrims 41
unintended interdependence 84
United Arab Emirates (UAE) 4–5, 17, 73; Pakistan relations with 43; *see also* India and United Arab Emirates
United National Party (UNP) 110
United Nations (UN) 14, 25, 28, 50, 86, 153
United Nations Security Council (UNSC) 25
United Nations Sustainable Development Goals 198
United States (US) 17, 19, 77, 84, 158, 198; Arab Gulf and 26; Iran and 25; Islamabad's military cooperation 70; nuclear deal 31; Western bloc 68
unstructured security order 107

Vajpayee, Atal Bihari 10, 23
Vishnuswami 1

Waever, Ole 6, 9, 18–19, 32, 40, 105–109, 126n1, 181
al-Wahhab, Muhammad Abd 116
Wani, Burhan 49
War of Liberation 88

Wickramage, K. 113
Worrall, James 144

Xi Jingpin 85

Yayati Caritramu 3
Yemen 172–173n4; and Qatar crises
159–162

Yemeni Civil War 50
Yemen War 11

Zardari, Asif Ali 157
Zayed, Muhammad
Bin 49
Zia-ul-Haq, Muhammad 44, 68, 76,
138, 155–156, 165